NAACP

A History of the National Association for the Advancement of Colored People

Volume I 1909-1920

by Charles Flint Kellogg

The Johns Hopkins Press, Baltimore

05391

To Mary-Margaret

Contents

Preface

The organization of the NAACP and the names of its founders have been familiar to me since boyhood. I heard my father speak frequently of William Edward Burghardt Du Bois, probably the most distinguished citizen Great Barrington, Massachusetts, has ever produced. Both men spent their boyhood near the Green River, less than a quarter of a mile from each other.

It was on the same stream in the adjoining village of Alford that Mary White Ovington converted an old barn into a delightful summer home—"Riverbank"— in 1920. She spent a portion of her summers there for the next twenty years. "Riverbank" also provided a refuge from the city heat for the young Negro students Miss Ovington assisted financially through Smith College, as well as for the office workers and staff members of the NAACP. Among those who visited her were the Walter Whites, the Herbert Seligmanns, the Robert Bagnalls, the James Weldon Johnsons, and Richetta Randolph. The Spingarns and Du Bois were also frequent visitors. (Du Bois later began restoration of his birthplace there but the work was never completed.) Far from being ostracized by the old New England families because of her activities, Miss Ovington was welcomed into the life of the community, and for a time served as president of the Alford Garden Club.

In 1926 the James Weldon Johnsons purchased and developed an old property in the township of Great Barrington and called it "Five Acres." Johnson did most of his writing there in his study with a magnificent view of Mt. Washington in the Berkshires. Mrs. Johnson's brother, John E. Nail, who was an officer of the New York branch of the NAACP, developed the adjoining property as a summer home. The Johnsons and the Nails were lionized as the result of Johnson's reputation as an author and poet, and Mrs. Johnson and Mrs. Nail were invited to attend the Thursday Morning Club, the most select group of women in Great Barrington.

I was born the year the NAACP was founded. It was during this period that the status of the Negro deteriorated into a "new slavery." Negroes were disfranchised, their educational opportunities were restricted, and their freedom of association, work, travel, and recreation were circumscribed by law and by custom. They were the victims of savage lynchings and race riots in the South. But it was the outbreak of mob violence against Negroes in the North which led to the founding of the NAACP. The aim of the "new abolitionists" was to fight the "new slavery" by means which were then considered radical—non-violent agitation, well-publicized protest, propaganda, and legal action. It is the object of this study to trace the history of the NAACP during its formative years until a Negro became Executive Secretary, and the Association was accepted by Negro intellectuals as the most effective organization dedicated to their struggle to achieve full equality and first-class citizenship.

My greatest debt is to Professor C. Vann Woodward of Yale University, who read the manuscript and made many suggestions as to style, emphasis, and structure. I am also grateful to Professor Charles A. Barker of The Johns Hopkins University who read the manuscript and recommended improvements. Professor John Hope Franklin of the University of Chicago made valuable suggestions as to sources, and did much to clarify various aspects of Negro history. I am also indebted to Professor Elliot M. Rudwick of Southern Illinois University and Professor August Meier of Roosevelt University for direction in the use of the massive Booker T. Washington collection in the Library of Congress. I am under obligation to the late Dr. W. E. B. Du Bois for giving me access to his personal papers. Dr. Herbert Aptheker, Dr. Hugh H. Smythe, and especially Dr. Francis L. Broderick of Lawrence University provided guidance in the use of the Du Bois papers. Roy Wilkins and the late Walter White permitted me to use the files and Board Minutes of the National Association for the Advancement of Colored People. I am particularly indebted to James W. Ivy, Madison S. Jones, Gloster B. Current, Henry Lee Moon, Herbert Hill, and John A. Morsell, staff members at the national office of the NAACP, who provided me with valuable insights into the functioning of the Association. Miss Bobbie Branche, office manager of the NAACP, took unlimited pains to make me comfortable and to provide me with office space and with access to the files of the Association. Arthur B. Spingarn, who was president of the NAACP at that time, placed his office and personal papers at my disposal. He also introduced me to Mrs. Joel E. Spingarn, who permitted me to use her husband's papers at "Troutbeck," Amenia, New York. Charles Storey of Boston made his father's correspondence available to me. Mrs. James Weldon Johnson and Mrs. Poppy Cannon White consented to my use of the personal papers of their husbands. I am grateful for the help and consideration of the custodians of the James Weldon Johnson Collection at the Sterling Memorial Library at Yale University, the Schomburg Collection at the New York Public Library, the Houghton Library of Harvard University, and the Manuscript Division of the Library of Congress. I am especially indebted to Mrs. Dorothy Porter, curator of the Moorland Foundation of Howard University, for her cooperation and many helpful suggestions. Most of the pictures used in this volume are from *The Crisis* and the files of the NAACP. Pictures were also made available by the Schomburg Collection of the New York Public Library, Mrs. Joel Spingarn, and *The Christian Advocate*. I am indebted to the University of Chicago Press for permission to reproduce the photographs of the Chicago riot. I gratefully acknowledge a grant from the Fund for the Republic which assisted me in undertaking the research for this study. I also wish to express my appreciation for a grant-in-aid from the Dickinson College Faculty Research Fund for the final typing of the manuscript. My deep appreciation also goes to my wife who helped me in innumerable ways.

NAACP

A History of the National Association for the Advancement of Colored People

Introduction

In the first decade of the twentieth century few voices were raised in defense of the Negro and his rights as a citizen of the United States. In 1877 the North had abandoned Reconstruction, acquiescing in Southern assurances that the constitutional rights of Negroes would be protected. Reactionary attitudes toward race had been strengthened with the triumph of imperialism in the war of 1898. By 1909, the civil rights the Negro had gained during Reconstruction had been severely limited. The prevailing attitudes toward the Negro were reflected in the sensational press, in the hate literature, in the periodicals of the middle class and the intellectuals, in court decisions reinterpreting the Fourteenth and Fifteenth Amendments, and in legislation providing for Negro disfranchisement and segregation in the South. Anthropologists, sociologists, historians, and political theorists had put their stamp of approval on the popular belief in the Negro's inferiority, which had been used to justify racist policies on national and local levels.

Voices that had once been raised in defense of the Negro and his rights now uttered words of reaction. After a trip to Africa, Charles Francis Adams, Jr., repudiated what he termed the self-sufficient ignorance of the philanthropists and theorists of New England, those successors of the abolitionists and humanitarians of the antebellum period who still claimed that the Negro had never been given an opportunity—a conception which had been one of the foundation stones of Reconstruction but which Adams now called the sheerest of delusions.[1] Thomas Wentworth Higginson, the abolitionist who had commanded the first Negro regiment during the Civil War and had later founded a school for Negroes at

[1] Charles Francis Adams, "Reflex Light from Africa," *Century Magazine*, LXXII (May, 1906), 101–111.

Calhoun, Alabama, now believed that giving the suffrage to all Negroes as a class was a mistake and that no white community would ever consent to the political supremacy of any of the colored races.[2] President Charles W. Eliot of Harvard openly deplored miscegenation, denounced any admixture of racial stocks, and endorsed the absolute separation of races on which the South insisted.[3]

Public opinion in the North, lulled by the success of the new economic order evolving out of the Civil War and Reconstruction, was apathetic and indifferent to the problems of the Negro. The North was willing to leave the solution of these problems to the South, and the South had entrenched itself behind legislation that assured the dominance of the Anglo-Saxon in Southern society, with the Negro firmly fixed "in his place"—at the bottom.

When Booker T. Washington, head of the industrial school for Negroes at Tuskegee, Alabama, gave his celebrated address at Atlanta in 1895, rejecting social equality and (at least temporarily) renouncing civil rights and political aspirations for Negroes, the acquiescence of the Negro to this state of affairs seemed assured. In return for the friendship and cooperation of Southern whites, Booker T. Washington, by emphasizing practical education that would fit the Negro to earn a living, virtually promised a docile labor force to the new industrial South. His speech won national acclaim, and Washington himself was hailed as the leader of his race.

In spite of Booker T. Washington's compromise with the white South, race relations continued to deteriorate. One answer to any challenge the Negro might raise against white supremacy in the South was lynching. Fear and tension, exaggerated by demagogues like Hoke Smith and fanned into flames by the sensational press, broke out in mob violence, culminating in the Atlanta riots of 1906 and in racial disturbances in the North as well.

The response of Northern philanthropy was based on the belief that education was the cure for all Southern problems. Northern money poured into the South in the endeavor to raise the literacy levels of whites and blacks, but always the Negro slipped into the lowest rank, the vocational training that had been approved by Booker T. Washington. Few funds were provided for the higher education of intelligent Negroes.

This trend did not go unnoticed by a young Negro scholar, William Edward Burghardt Du Bois, a professor at Atlanta University. Within half a dozen years of Booker T. Washington's Atlanta speech, Du Bois was pointing out the weaknesses of Washington's philosophy. According to Du Bois, a large and impor-

[2] *New York Sun*, May 30, 1909. See also *Boston Evening Transcript*, June 1, 1909.
[3] Francis Jackson Garrison to Oswald Garrison Villard, March 9, 1909; March 12, 1909, in Oswald Garrison Villard Papers (Houghton Library, Harvard University). See also *Boston Evening Transcript*, editorial, "The Anglo-Saxon Solvent," March 9, 1909; *Boston Globe*, cartoon, March 10, 1909.

tant group of Negro intellectuals, who refused to accept Washington as a popular leader, was seeking "that self-development and self-realization in all lines of human endeavor which they believe will eventually place the Negro beside other races."[4]

Among those who sympathized with Booker T. Washington and his work, but were nevertheless becoming increasingly aware of Du Bois's writings, were the Garrison family of Boston. They objected to the spirit of reaction in the North and were shocked and pessimistic at the retreat from New England enlightenment. Fanny Garrison Villard, daughter of the abolitionist William Lloyd Garrison, was stunned by the "wave of passion and hatred towards the race to whom opportunity has been denied." She was moved to remark after reading Du Bois's *The Souls of Black Folk,* published in 1903, that there were no champions like those of antislavery days.[5] Her brother, the second William Lloyd Garrison, was sure that there had never been an affirmative majority for the abolition of slavery in the North except for a brief period at the Emancipation climax. He saw no marked change of feeling in the North regarding the Negro. The North as well as the South intended to keep Negroes in the lowest industrial levels, he observed, but the Northern intention was expressed "more by subtle action, and less by war cries."[6]

The third generation of the Garrison family continued to fight for fair treatment of the dark race. Oswald Garrison Villard, grandson of the abolitionist, son of Fanny Garrison Villard, and nephew of William Lloyd Garrison, Jr., prided himself on his abolitionist ancestry. His first opportunity to say a word in public in behalf of the colored man came in 1903, although he had dared to remark in an earlier address to an educational conference at the governor's mansion in Richmond that changed conditions made it possible for him "to speak where [his] grandfather would so cheerfully and happily have been hanged."[7]

Villard was also opposed to the prevailing spirit of imperialism. He had been "utterly miserable mentally" when the United States declared war in 1898 and he had cried out against the injustice of what he called the iniquitous war with Spain. He was thankful that the *New York Evening Post,* which was eventually to come under his management, had steered so straight a course during the war, and he looked forward to the day when he would have complete control of the paper and could make it a worthy successor to his grandfather's *The Liberator.*[8]

[4] William E. B. Du Bois, "The Evolution of Negro Leadership," *Dial,* XXXI (July 16, 1901), 53–55.
[5] Fanny Garrison Villard to Oswald Garrison Villard [March 10, 1903]; May 18, 1904, Villard Papers; Du Bois, *The Souls of Black Folk: Essays and Sketches* (Chicago, 1903).
[6] William Lloyd Garrison to Oswald Garrison Villard, July 30, 1907, Villard Papers.
[7] Oswald Garrison Villard to Fanny G. Villard, July 31, 1903, Villard Papers; Oswald Garrison Villard, *Fighting Years: Memoirs of a Liberal Editor* (New York, 1939), p. 173.
[8] Oswald Garrison Villard to Francis J. Garrison, April 28, 1898, Villard Papers.

The *Evening Post* was one of the few papers that reported the activities of Negroes sympathetically. In 1926 Mary White Ovington was to write: "Long before there was a N.A.A.C.P., there was a Garrison in New York setting forth in his larger *Liberator* the wrongs of the Negro Race." Miss Ovington was a social worker who was associated with Villard in the turbulent early years of the NAACP. She knew from experience how seldom the Negro was given fair play in the press. Even the muckraking *McClure's Magazine* had turned down an article of hers in which the Negro was shown in a self-respecting light.[9]

Another Bostonian, Moorfield Storey, whose views on race had been influenced by his early association with the abolitionist Charles Sumner, was convinced that the condition of the colored race could be improved only if the solid South could be broken up and the Fifteenth Amendment enforced. Rather than leave the solution of the race problem to the South, he insisted that the rights of the colored people should be protected by public opinion from other parts of the country.[10] Storey was president of the Anti-Imperialist League. When W. E. B. Du Bois congratulated Storey on his illuminating pamphlet on United States policy in the Philippines and the atrocities perpetrated by American soldiers, he learned that Storey was familiar with his own writings and anxious to meet him because of their mutual concern over imperialism and the race question.[11]

Du Bois had attended the first Pan-African Congress in London in 1900, where he had been chosen vice-president of what was intended to be a permanent organization protesting imperialism and working for the granting of self-government to subject peoples.[12] The theme that ran through all his writings was that "the problem of the twentieth century is the problem of the color line; the relation of the darker to the lighter races of men in Asia and Africa, in America and the islands of the sea."[13]

[9] Mary White Ovington, "Beginnings of the N.A.A.C.P.," *Crisis*, XXXII (June, 1926), 76.
[10] Moorfield Storey to William Monroe Trotter, March 11, 1909, Moorfield Storey Papers (in the possession of Mr. Charles Storey, Boston, Massachusetts).
[11] Du Bois to Storey, October 21, 1907; Storey to Du Bois, October 24, 1907, in W. E. B. Du Bois Papers (now in the possession of Mrs. W. E. B. Du Bois, New York City). These papers were made available to the writer during the summer of 1949. After this, Dr. Du Bois closed his papers to all persons engaged in research. Francis L. Broderick, author of *W. E. B. Du Bois: Negro Leader in a Time of Crisis* (Stanford, 1959), has deposited his notes on the Du Bois Papers in the Schomburg Collection (New York Public Library, New York).
[12] Alexander Walters, "The Pan-African Conference," *A. M. E. Zion Quarterly Review*, XI (1901), 164–65; Walters, *My Life and Work* (New York, 1917), pp. 253–62.
[13] Du Bois, *The Souls of Black Folk*, Premier Americana ed. (Greenwich, Connecticut, 1961), p. 23; Du Bois, "The Reconstruction Period: The Freedmen's Bureau," *Atlantic Monthly*, LXXXVII (March, 1901), 354. In writing the "Address to the Nations of the World" of the Pan-African Congress of 1900, Du Bois had used much the same phraseology. *Crisis*, XXI (March, 1921), 198.

Before the first decade of the twentieth century was over, these three men—
Oswald Garrison Villard, Moorfield Storey, and W. E. B. Du Bois—were to become united in an organization dedicated to securing for Negro Americans first-
class citizenship in the United States and to the abolition of the "new slavery."
The train of events that was to bring them together was set off by two days of
bloody rioting, not in the South, but in Abraham Lincoln's own city, Springfield, Illinois.

CHAPTER I

The Founding of the NAACP

On the fourteenth of August, 1908, race riots broke out in Springfield, Illinois. White mobs raged through the Negro district, burning homes and interfering with the work of firemen. It was two days before 4,200 militiamen brought the riots under control. By that time two persons had been lynched, six had been killed, and over fifty wounded. More than 2,000 Negroes fled the city, and hundreds took shelter in the camps of the militia.[1]

Lynchings and anti-Negro riots in the city where Lincoln had lived and was buried were too much for Oswald Garrison Villard, who, as the grandson of William Lloyd Garrison, had been reared in the abolitionist tradition.[2] In the *New York Evening Post*, of which he was president, Villard spoke out indignantly against the outbreak in Springfield, calling it the climax of a wave of crime and lawlessness that was flooding the country.[3]

The liberal periodical *The Independent* was also shocked that such violence against Negroes could occur in the North. "Springfield," wrote the editor, "will have to carry a heavier burden of shame than does Atlanta, for Illinois was never a slave state." Horrified at the thought that rioting might break out in other cities, *The Independent* urged Negroes, when attacked, first to seek protection from the proper authorities; if that failed, they should defend themselves and resist to the utmost of human power so that invaders of the home would be

[1] *Independent*, XLV (August 20, 1908), 339–400. For a study of the Springfield riot, see James L. Crouthamel, "The Springfield Race Riot of 1908," *Journal of Negro History*, XLV (July, 1960), 164–81.
[2] Oswald Garrison Villard to Fanny Garrison Villard, August 17, 1908, Oswald Garrison Villard Papers in the Houghton Library, Harvard University. (Hereafter Villard refers to Oswald Garrison Villard unless otherwise indicated.)
[3] *New York Evening Post*, August 17, 1908.

sorry that they came and be slow to come again.[4] Booker T. Washington, the most prominent Negro of the day, issued a statement which was sharply critical of lynching, although it did not mention the Springfield affair. *The Horizon*, a Negro periodical usually critical of Washington, called his statement the clearest, strongest and most courageous he had uttered.[5] On the whole, Northern newspapers had responded satisfactorily, Villard felt, but he was concerned with the spreading of what he called the Southern attitude in the press.[6]

Neither Villard's indignation at the prevailing lawlessness of the time nor Washington's indictment of lynching resulted in any definite action to combat the rising tide of racism. This stimulus was provided by William English Walling in his article "The Race War in the North," which appeared the following month in *The Independent*.[7]

Walling was a wealthy Southerner from a former slave-owning Kentucky family.[8] He was a writer, settlement house worker, and a socialist. Beginning as a factory inspector in Illinois, he had devoted his life to the labor movement. In 1903, he joined Jane Addams, Lillian Wald, and others in founding the National Women's Trade Union League. He had married Anna Strunsky, a Jew who, in youth, had been imprisoned in her native Russia for revolutionary activities.[9] The Wallings went to Springfield to investigate the riots. Inquiry convinced them that America's treatment of the Negro was even worse than Russia's treatment of its Jewish minority.[10]

In his article on the Springfield riots, Walling blamed the local press for inflaming public opinion against Negroes prior to the outbreak, and showed how one newspaper subtly linked crime with the race problem, at the same time suggesting to its readers that the South knew how to deal promptly and effectively with such situations. Walling held that the public had shut its eyes to the initiation of a permanent warfare against Negroes, modeled in all respects on that in the South. The small Negro population in Springfield was of no possible

[4] *Independent*, LXV (August 20, 1908), 442–43.
[5] *Horizon*, IV (August, 1908), 13–15.
[6] Villard to Francis Jackson Garrison, August 25, 1908, Villard Papers.
[7] William English Walling, "The Race War in the North," *Independent*, LXV (September 3, 1908), 529–34.
[8] Mrs. William English Walling to writer, August 14, 1963.
[9] Villard, *Fighting Years: Memoirs of a Liberal Editor* (New York, 1939), pp. 191–92. Interview with Mrs. Charles Edward Russell, Washington, D.C., July, 1957. See also David A. Shannon, "William English Walling," in Robert Livingston Schuyler and Edward T. James (eds.), *Dictionary of American Biography: Supplement Two* (New York, 1958), XXII, 689–90.
[10] Mary White Ovington, *The Walls Came Tumbling Down* (New York, 1947), p. 102. For brief accounts of the founding of the NAACP, see Jack Abramowitz, "Origins of the NAACP," *Social Education*, XV (January, 1951), 21–23; Gunnar Myrdal, *An American Dilemma: The Negro Problem and Modern Democracy* (New York, 1944), pp. 819–36.

threat to white supremacy, and Walling deplored the belief held in the North that there were mitigating circumstances, not for mob violence but for race hatred. No less shocking was Springfield's lack of shame. The common people approved the action of the mob and hoped all Negroes would leave. Prevailing opinion in Springfield, Walling wrote, was expressed by the *Illinois State Journal*, which called the outbreak inevitable and blamed not the white's hatred of the Negro, but the Negro's "misconduct, general inferiority, or unfitness for free institutions."[11]

Walling reported that after the riot there was a political and business boycott to drive out of Springfield those Negroes who had not already fled, an effort which the local press failed to oppose. He considered this a far more serious attack upon Negroes than the riot. If this kind of attack were allowed to continue, whites would take over the Negroes' property, jobs, and businesses, thus conferring automatic rewards on the rioters. Race baiters would dominate Springfield, and other Northern towns would be tempted to follow the example. Political democracy would die, warned Walling, and American civilization would degenerate if these methods should become general in the North.

"Who realizes the seriousness of the situation?" he asked. "What large and powerful body of citizens is ready to come to [the Negro's] aid?"[12]

One of the readers of Walling's article in *The Independent* was Mary White Ovington, a Unitarian, a socialist, the descendant of an abolitionist, and a social worker of independent means. Her life was already dedicated to the cause of the Negro. She had spent nearly four years gathering material for a study of the Negro in New York, and at the time Walling's article appeared she was living in a Negro tenement. Walling's appeal so moved her that she wrote an answer to his plea within the hour.[13]

Walling had conceived the idea of a national biracial organization of "fair-minded whites and intelligent blacks" to help right the wrongs of the Negro. On returning from Springfield he outlined his plan to his close friend, Charles Edward Russell, and to other sympathetic members of the Liberal Club in New York.[14] There was much enthusiasm at that time in the Liberal Club and in other radical organizations regarding the Negro, but there was little concrete knowledge on which to base a course of action.[15] Then several weeks later Mary

---

[11] Quoted in Walling, "Race War in the North," 531–33.
[12] Walling, "Race War in the North," 532–33.
[13] Ovington, "The National Association for the Advancement of Colored People," *Journal of Negro History*, IX (April, 1924), 109; Villard, *Fighting Years*, p. 192; Ovington, *The Walls Came Tumbling Down*, pp. 4–6, 13, 34, 39, 102–3. Miss Ovington's study was published under the title *Half a Man: The Status of the Negro in New York* (New York, 1911).
[14] Charles Edward Russell, *Bare Hands and Stone Walls* (New York, 1933), p. 224.
[15] Ovington, "Beginnings of the N.A.A.C.P.," *Crisis*, XXXII (June, 1926), 77.

White Ovington attended a lecture on Russia given by Walling at Cooper Union, in the course of which Walling stated that the race situation in America was worse, in some respects, than anything in Russia under czarism. After the lecture, Miss Ovington proposed to Walling that they undertake at once to form an organization like the one he had in mind.[16] It was not until she had written him again, however, that he arranged a meeting at his New York apartment for the first week of the year 1909.[17]

The meeting was to have included Walling's friend Russell, a writer and fellow-socialist, whose father had been an abolitionist editor of a small newspaper in Iowa,[18] but Russell was unable to be present, and Dr. Henry Moskowitz, a social worker among New York immigrants, took his place.[19] These three, Miss Ovington, Moskowitz, and Walling, whose immediate interests were so closely knit, were from widely varied backgrounds—Miss Ovington later reminisced that "one was a descendant of an old-time abolitionist, the second a Jew, and the third a Southerner."[20]

Two steps were taken at this informal gathering at Walling's apartment in January, 1909. It was decided that Lincoln's birthday should mark the opening of a campaign to secure the support of a large and powerful body of citizens, and it was agreed that Oswald Garrison Villard should be invited to become the fifth member of the group. Looking back on this event thirty years later, Villard wrote with feeling: "No greater compliment has ever been paid to me."[21]

THE "CALL"

Shortly after that first decisive meeting, the group was further expanded on the initiative of Miss Ovington and made biracial by including two prominent colored clergymen, Bishop Alexander Walters of the African Methodist Episcopal Zion Church and the Reverend William Henry Brooks, minister of St. Mark's Methodist Episcopal Church of New York. Walling enlisted Lillian Wald and Florence Kelley,[22] who were to take an active part in the NAACP for many years. Florence Kelley, one of the first women graduates of Cornell University,

[16] Walling, "The Founding of the N.A.A.C.P.," *Crisis*, XXXVI (July, 1929), 226.
[17] Ovington, *The Walls Came Tumbling Down*, p. 103; Ovington, *How the National Association for the Advancement of Colored People Began*, pamphlet (New York, 1914), p. 1.
[18] Russell, *A Pioneer Editor in Early Iowa: A Sketch of the Life of Edward Russell* (Washington, 1941); Russell, *Bare Hands and Stone Walls*, p. 224.
[19] Ovington, *The Walls Came Tumbling Down*, p. 103; Ovington, *How the National Association for the Advancement of Colored People Began*, p. 1.
[20] Ovington, "William English Walling," *Crisis*, XLIII (November, 1936), 335.
[21] Villard, *Fighting Years*, p. 192; O. G. Villard, "The Negro Militant," *Progressive*, XI (January 20, 1947), 5–8.
[22] Walling, "Founding of the N.A.A.C.P.," 226.

had done graduate study in Switzerland in social problems, and had graduated in law from Northwestern University. As a member of the staff at Hull House in Chicago, she had become a close friend of Jane Addams and Julia Lathrop. She was instrumental in securing the passage of a factory inspection law in Illinois and was appointed chief inspector for that state in 1893. It was probably here that she met Walling. When she became general secretary of the National Consumers' League, she took up residence at Lillian Wald's Nurses' Settlement on Henry Street in New York City.[23]

Villard accepted with enthusiasm the invitation to join this group in a call for a conference on the Negro problem. He had already come to the conclusion that an organization should be formed to advance the welfare of the Negro. In reply to a letter from Booker T. Washington, suggesting that there should be a test case against peonage in Alabama, Villard had answered, "This is precisely the kind of case for which I want my endowed 'Committee for the Advancement of the Negro Race.' With such a body we could instantly handle any similar discrimination against the negro, and carry the case, if necessary, to the higher court. Sooner or later we must get that committee going."[24]

Here was the opportunity for Villard to carry out his idea of a defense committee. The members of the newly formed group were earnest workers in Villard's opinion, but "not very strong before the public," and he plunged into rewriting their rough draft of the call for a conference.[25] He asked his uncle, William Lloyd Garrison, Jr., of Boston, to endorse it, assuring him there was nothing in it that a Garrison should hesitate to sign.[26]

The abolitionist tradition was strong in Oswald Villard. His uncles and his mother had fostered his pride from boyhood in his famous grandfather, William Lloyd Garrison. His closest tie was with his uncle, Francis Jackson Garrison, who had helped him to hold fast to the Garrison ideals and to most of "dear Grandpapa's principles." His uncle had written: "I feel that you are my natural successor to the custodianship of the anti-slavery books and documents, the Liberator among them." Booker T. Washington, too, had asked Villard to be the link between the abolitionists and the modern Negro movement.[27]

---

[23] Sophonisba P. Breckinridge, "Florence Kelley," in Harris E. Starr (ed.), *Dictionary of American Biography: Supplement One* (New York, 1944), XXI, 462–63. See also Josephine Goldmark, *Impatient Crusader: Florence Kelley's Life Story* (Urbana, 1953), p. 143; Beryl Williams Epstein, *Lillian Wald: Angel of Henry Street* (New York, 1948).

[24] Booker T. Washington to Villard, September 7, 1908; Villard to Washington, September 10, 1908, Villard Papers.

[25] Villard to F. J. Garrison, February 3, 1909, Villard Papers.

[26] Villard to William Lloyd Garrison, Jr., February 10, 1909, Villard Papers.

[27] Villard to F. J. Garrison, April 28, 1898; March 18, 1902; F. J. Garrison to Villard, January 4, 1905; Villard to F. J. Garrison, February 8, 1906, Villard Papers.

Villard had been interested in the industrial schools for Negroes in the South since 1902, when Robert C. Ogden, president of the Southern Education Board, and a trustee of Tuskegee Institute, invited him to become a member of his party traveling by special train to the annual Conference on Education in the South. This trip had a profound influence on Villard. Not only did he meet the young Southern woman from Covington, Kentucky, who was to become his wife, but also he gained new insights into living conditions of Negroes in the South.[28] "I feel as if I had emerged from darkest America and the sense of the wrongs of the people of color is strong upon me," he wrote his mother after visiting a small Negro school in Alabama. The conviction that he must take an active part in the cause of Negro education led him to become President of the Board of Directors of the Manassas Industrial School in Virginia,[29] and to support the work at Tuskegee Institute in Alabama under the direction of Booker T. Washington.[30] As publisher of the *New York Evening Post* and writer for *The Nation* (at that time the literary supplement to the *Evening Post*), he frequently spoke out for the cause of the Negro.

Years later, Villard wrote that from the beginning his conception of the new organization formed in 1909 was that it should be aggressive, a watchdog of Negro liberties, and should allow no wrong to take place without a protest and a bringing to bear of all the pressure that it could muster.[31] This determination was reflected in the "Call" (for a conference) which was issued by the group on Lincoln's Birthday, and which Villard sometimes called his manifesto. Signed by some sixty prominent Negroes and whites, it directed attention to the disfranchisement of the Negro and stated that the Supreme Court had side-stepped several opportunities to pass squarely upon this disfranchisement; that taxation without representation was the fate of millions of Americans; that the Supreme Court in the Berea College case had upheld the right of a state to make it a crime for whites and blacks to assemble together for any purpose; that Jim Crow was being practiced in regard to public transportation and places of amusement; that many states were failing to do their elementary duty in educating the Negro; and, finally, that the wave of brutal attacks upon the Negro in all sections of the country—even in the Springfield made famous by Lincoln—could not be allowed to continue. It closed with an appeal to all believers in democracy to cast off silence, which was equivalent to tacit approval; to dispel the indifference of the North, which had played a large part in bringing about these attacks upon the principles of democracy; to end discrimination which, once permitted,

[28] Villard, *Fighting Years*, pp. 173–75.
[29] Villard to Fanny G. Villard [April, 1902]; Fanny G. Villard to Villard, April 21, 1904, Villard Papers.
[30] *New York Age*, April 12, 1906.
[31] Villard, *Fighting Years*, p. 194.

could not be bridled; and to join in a national conference for the discussion of present evils, the voicing of protests, and the renewal of the struggle for civil and political rights.[32]

The emphasis in the "Call" on civil and political rights of Negroes to the exclusion of their economic problems was to set the tone of the new organization for many years to come.[33]

In spite of strenuous efforts to obtain publicity for his "manifesto," Villard was disappointed by the reaction of the New York press. This lack of response chilled his ardor, and he hesitated, though not for long, over the next step, the calling of the conference, because he felt he would have the major responsibility for it.[34] The Negro press, as represented by the *New York Age*, gave scant attention to the appeal. A brief news item appeared in the issue of February 18, stating that a call had been issued for a conference "for discussion of the present state of the Negro."[35]

In the meantime, however, the founders of what was eventually to become known as "The National Association for the Advancement of Colored People" continued to hold their meetings at Walling's apartment, because its central location made possible the frequent attendance of some very busy people.[36] The number varied. One afternoon in March five persons assembled. At other times there were as many as eight. Rabbi Stephen S. Wise of the Free Synagogue and Miss Leonore O'Reilly, a teacher in the Manhattan Trade School for Girls, were among those who attended these early meetings.[37]

The group continued to expand. Soon Walling's apartment was too small to accommodate all the members, and the first meeting for which minutes are extant was held in the Liberal Club at 103 East 19th Street. The exact date was not recorded, but presumably it was about the middle of March. Fifteen were

[32] The "Call," in Villard Papers in uncatalogued box of NAACP Papers with typed note attached by Konrad C. Mueller, who arranged Villard's papers prior to their deposit at Harvard. The note reads: "The attached are a copy of the original Call for the Lincoln Emancipation Conference in 1909, together with a first list of the signers. The Call was written by Oswald Garrison Villard. The proof also enclosed is from Mr. Villard's address in September, 1909, proposing the National Association for the Advancement of Colored People." The phrasing of this copy of the "Call" varies slightly from that given by Miss Ovington in *How the National Association for the Advancement of Colored People Began*. Also Miss Ovington lists fifty-three signers, whereas Villard's "Call" has sixty names. See Appendix A for a complete copy of the "Call."

[33] Ralph J. Bunche, "The Programs, Ideologies, Tactics and Achievements of Negro Betterment and Interracial Organizations," unpublished memoranda for the Myrdal Study, 1940, p. 28, in Schomburg Collection (New York Public Library, New York).

[34] Villard to F. J. Garrison, February 17, 1909, Villard Papers.

[35] *New York Age*, February 18, 1909.

[36] Walling, "Founding of the N.A.A.C.P.," 226.

[37] Russell, *Bare Hands and Stone Walls*, p. 225; Robert Luther Duffus, *Lillian Wald: Neighbor and Crusader* (New York, 1938), pp. 67–68.

present and it was spoken of as "the first meeting of all the members of the Committee on the Negro." At this time plans were being made for the conference, which had been called for May 31 and June 1 at the Charity Organization Hall.[38]

Three meetings were held before the conference. At one meeting Walling was in the chair, at another, Russell. Miss Ovington was recording secretary, and Walling treasurer. Walling was also to be in charge of the conference with the title of Secretary. The members groped for leadership; they fumbled for a name—a problem that was to plague them for a long time. At first, they were the "Committee on the Negro," then the "Committee on the Status of the Negro." Villard, however, made constant references to the "advancement" of the race, a term that was to stick.[39]

Another unresolved problem was that of merging with the Executive Board of the Constitution League, an idea proposed and urged by the League's president, John E. Milholland. He was a wealthy New Yorker, an anti-imperialist, and a former newspaper man, who was active in Republican Party politics. He founded the Republican State Club of New York, promoted primary election reform, and took part in many of the reform movements of the day, prison reform, pacifism, labor reform, woman suffrage, and federal aid to education.[40] He had founded the Constitution League[41] in 1903, with the conviction that establishing the constitutional rights of Negroes could best be accomplished by means of legal test cases. In spite of the similarity of aims, however, a decision on the merger was put off until the following year.[42]

Plans moved forward for the holding of the conference. One thousand invitations to "A Conference on the Status of the Negro" were sent out, and about

[38] Minutes, The Committee on the Negro, March, 1909 (pencil notation), in "Minute Book of the Board of Directors of the National Association for the Advancement of Colored People" (formerly in NAACP offices, New York; now in the Manuscript Division, Library of Congress; hereafter referred to as Board Minutes, NAACP). Those present were Ray Stannard Baker, Dr. William L. Bulkley, Miss Madeline Z. Doty, the Reverend John Haynes Holmes, Mr. Alexander Irving, Miss Helen Marot, Miss Mary White Ovington, Mrs. Anna Garlin Spencer, Mr. J. G. Phelps-Stokes, Miss Helen Stokes, Miss Lillian D. Wald, Dr. Owen M. Waller, Dr. Stephen S. Wise, Mr. Gaylord S. White, Mr. William English Walling, and Mr. Charles Edward Russell, presiding.
[39] Minutes, Committee on the Negro, March, 1909; Minutes, Committee on the Status of the Negro, April 27, 1909; May 4, 1909; all in Board Minutes, NAACP.
[40] New York Times, July 1, 1925; Russell, Bare Hands and Stone Walls, pp. 231–35.
[41] The organization was commonly referred to by its members and others as "Constitution League" though the official letterhead carried the name "Constitutional League of the United States." Andrew B. Humphrey to Booker T. Washington, May 4, 1904, in Booker T. Washington Papers (Manuscript Division, Library of Congress).
[42] Minutes, Committee on the Negro, May 4, 1909, in Board Minutes, NAACP.

150 persons agreed to act as sponsors.[43] One of these was Moorfield Storey of Boston, constitutional lawyer, anti-imperialist, and one-time secretary to Senator Charles Sumner of Massachusetts.[44] Storey could not attend the conference, but he was to play an important role in the development of the organization.

To link the old abolition movement with the new, Villard asked his uncle, William Lloyd Garrison, Jr., to act as presiding officer. Garrison (who died a short time later) was too ill to attend, but he wrote a message for the conference, urging that the rising tide of race prejudice and caste be met unflinchingly. The greatest danger, he thought, was that reformers had lost interest in problems of the Negro. Men who were interested in social problems, while arrogating to themselves the position of advisers to the Negro, had acquiesced in the abrogation of the Fifteenth Amendment, and approved of separate schools.[45] Villard attached great importance to this "last bugle blast" of his uncle, an echo of the elder Garrison.[46]

The task of raising money and arousing the interest of Bostonians fell to William's younger brother, Francis Jackson Garrison. He enlisted the aid of Butler Wilson, a prominent Negro attorney who sometimes assisted Moorfield Storey with his legal work. Since Storey was one of the sponsors, the fact that he was out of the country at the time made the project difficult,[47] and Garrison was not optimistic. Because of the dullness of his hearing, Garrison himself begged off from attending the conference, although he admitted that his conscience was pricked. Only Villard and his mother, Fanny Garrison Villard, were left to represent the family.[48]

Villard was influential in bringing to the conference Judge Wendell Phillips Stafford of the Supreme Court of the District of Columbia, member of an abolitionist family. To represent the liberal Southern point of view he called on

[43] Minutes, Committee on the Status of the Negro, April 27, 1909; Minutes, Committee on the Negro, May 4, 1909; in Board Minutes, NAACP.
[44] Mark A. DeWolfe Howe, *Portrait of an Independent: Moorfield Storey, 1845–1929* (Boston, 1932), pp. 38–39, 196–98.
[45] Letter from William Lloyd Garrison to [The National Negro Conference], n.d., in *Proceedings of the National Negro Conference 1909: New York May 31 and June 1* (n.p., n.d.), pp. 226–27. This same letter addressed to "William English Walling, Sec'y, May 29, 1909," appears in *Horizon*, V (February, 1910), 11.
[46] Villard to F. J. Garrison, October 12, 1909; F. J. Garrison to Villard, November 14, 1909, Villard Papers.
[47] F. J. Garrison to Villard, May 5, 1909; May 6, 1909, Villard Papers; Ovington, *The Walls Came Tumbling Down*, p. 23.
[48] A year later, at the second conference, Clarence Darrow asked, "Where are the Garrisons of the present generation?" Since Villard and his mother were sitting on the platform beside Darrow, who seemed to ignore Villard's claim to rank as one of the founders of this movement, Villard was understandably annoyed. F. J. Garrison to Villard, May 16, 1909; Villard to F. J. Garrison, May 17, 1910, Villard Papers.

John Spencer Bassett, professor of history at Smith College, who had left the South because of his advanced views. Villard was enthusiastic about the approaching conference, confident that its success would be due mostly to his own efforts. "I wish I could give more time to it," he wrote. "The people who have it in charge are well-meaning but they are inexperienced and impractical. . . . It all ought to be the beginning of something big."[49]

Meanwhile, a rift was developing between Villard and Booker T. Washington. The editor was sharply critical of his old friend. In describing a fund-raising meeting for Hampton Institute, at which President Taft appeared with Washington, Villard wrote to his uncle: "I grow very weary of hearing it said that Hampton and Tuskegee provide the absolute solution [to the Negro problem]. It is always the same thing, platitudes, stories, high praise for the Southern white man who is helping the negro up. . . . Last night he bellowed like a hoarse bull-frog."[50]

A few weeks before the conference, Villard visited Tuskegee to talk to the students. He felt that he was much too radical and outspoken for Washington's comfort and that Washington disapproved of what he said. He was critical of the school. He complained of its lack of coordination and of the need for expert educational supervision and deplored the "essentially commercial" tone. On the other hand, he was delighted and charmed with what he found at Calhoun, an industrial school near Montgomery, Alabama, where white and colored teachers dined together.[51]

Although Villard never broke with Washington completely, his growing relationship with the more "radical" group contributed to his disillusionment. He realized that Washington could have little influence with a gathering of men and women such as were behind the coming conference, and that Washington would be "simply disregarded as a man who is lost for the righting of any of the spiritual, or civil, or legal wrongs of his people."[52] Aware as he was of the presence of two factions in the Negro world—one headed by Booker T. Washington, the other by Atlanta University Professor William E. B. Du Bois—Villard was nevertheless determined not to let this controversy interfere with the conference nor with the formation of a permanent organization.

[49] Villard to F. J. Garrison, May 4, 1909; Villard to Wendell Phillips Stafford, April 22, 1909, Villard Papers; Harvey Wish, The American Historian (New York, 1960), p. 238.
[50] Villard to W. L. Garrison, February 24, 1909, Villard Papers.
[51] Villard to F. J. Garrison, April 15, 1909, Villard Papers. Villard's observations were substantially correct; the following month Seth Low, chairman of the Board of Trustees of Tuskegee, wrote Washington asking him to make statistical information available so that a study could be made in the direction of decreasing the enrollment and increasing the efficiency and standards of Tuskegee. Seth Low to Washington, May 24, 1909, Washington Papers.
[52] Villard to W. L. Garrison, February 24, 1909, Villard Papers.

It was in this spirit that he wrote a frank but cordial letter to Washington, inviting him to attend the conference, but tactfully making it possible for him to decline. It was not to be a Washington movement or a Du Bois movement, he explained. It was to be an aggressive organization, ready to strike hard blows for the rights of the colored people. Because of Washington's educational affiliations, Villard understood the delicacy of his position. Washington would be welcome at the conference, but his absence would not be misinterpreted.[53] In turning down the invitation, Washington showed insight not borne out by his subsequent actions. "I fear that my presence might restrict freedom of discussion and might, also, tend to make the conference go in directions which it would not like to go."[54]

Four days before the conference convened, Villard's uncle prophesied the passing of Washington's influence but expressed relief at his absence. "It seems strange to have a Negro Conference without B.T.W.," he wrote to his nephew, "but I fear he would be much too politic in his utterance."[55]

THE CONFERENCE

The National Negro Conference was held in the Charity Organization Hall in New York City on Monday and Tuesday, May 31 and June 1, 1909. The evening mass meetings were held at Cooper Union. The opening meeting on Monday morning was attended by some 300 men and women of both races. William Hayes Ward, editor of *The Independent*, gave the keynote address. "The purpose of this conference," said Ward, "is to re-emphasize in word, and so far as possible, in act, the principle that equal justice should be done to man as man, and particularly to the Negro, without regard to race, color or previous condition of servitude." He observed that after abolition and the legal and nominal granting of suffrage and equal rights, interest in the Negro had waned. The fervor of the abolitionists had been followed by a "cooling sympathy." In the meantime, the ruling majority in the South was holding the Negro in serfdom, basing this practice on the widely held belief that the Negro was essentially inferior, less than fully human, half a brute, and incapable of attaining civilized standards. The theme of the conference, then, was to be refutation of arguments that had been in vogue since pre-Civil War days—that the Negro was physically and mentally inferior.[56]

[53] Villard to Washington, May 26, 1909, Villard Papers.
[54] Washington to Villard, May 28, 1909, Washington Papers.
[55] F. J. Garrison to Villard, May 27, 1909, Villard Papers.
[56] *Boston Evening Transcript*, June 1, 1909; *Proceedings of the National Negro Conference 1909*, pp. 9–10.

Leading scientists of the day appeared at the conference. Anthropologist Livingston Farrand of Columbia University and neurologist and zoologist Burt G. Wilder of Cornell University presented detailed scientific evidence exploding theories that the Negro is inherently inferior because of differences in brain structure. They cited studies showing significant differences between the brains of humans and apes, but not between those of Negroes and whites. They described "race" as an indeterminate term used loosely to designate physical differences in groups.[57] Another Columbia professor, Edwin R. A. Seligman, applied his economic theory of history[58] to the development of the Negro, indicating that the economic environment had prevented his advancement rather than any innate inherited inferiority. John Dewey, the philosopher, declared that with a full, fair and free social opportunity each individual regardless of color would be able to make his potential contribution to society. Celia Parker Wooley of the Frederick Douglass Center in Chicago linked the Negro problem with other social problems of the day, such as women's rights and the rights of labor.

To William E. B. Du Bois, the basis of the problem was political as well as economic. Elimination of the Negro as a voter also eliminated him as a competitor in industry. There would be no solution of the Negro problem until the Negro in the South could cast a free and intelligent vote. Disfranchisement, limitation to vocational education, curtailment of civil freedoms—all these were part of a systematic effort to instill in others contempt for the Negro, to kill the Negro's self-respect, and to force him into a "new slavery."[59] Other speakers proposed positive methods for solving these problems: build favorable public opinion toward the Negro; work for federal legislation to control lynching; work for reduction of representation in Southern states where Negroes were disfranchised; work for federal aid to education; and build an organization to carry out these proposals.

All were agreed on the need for a permanent organization. Villard outlined his conception of such an organization and how it should work. He favored an association national in scope, incorporated, and able to raise large amounts of money. He believed that Negroes would contribute toward the organization's support as soon as they were convinced of its sincerity and unselfishness, its independence of factions within the race, its efficiency, and its belief in all forms of education for Negroes.

One of its chief functions, Villard said, should be a campaign of education to make known the truth about the achievements of Negroes. A publicity bureau with a press section guided by a competent newspaper man should investigate

[57] *Ibid.,* pp. 67–70.
[58] Wish, *American Historian,* p. 266.
[59] *Proceedings of the National Negro Conference 1909,* pp. 71–88, 144.

lynchings and other injustices to the Negro and give wide publicity to its findings. In addition, the Negro needed a strong central legal bureau with the ablest
counsel possible to prosecute men "who kill and call it law." A political and civil
rights bureau should work to bring about the enforcement of the Fourteenth
and Fifteenth Amendments and to obtain court decisions on disfranchising laws
and other discriminatory legislation.

Villard envisaged the education department of such an organization as serving
in an advisory capacity to Negro institutions to aid them in raising standards, in
coordinating fund-raising campaigns, and in devising more efficient methods of
business administration; if resources permitted, they would make grants to
various types of educational institutions. There would be an industrial bureau
to deal with the relationship of the Negro to labor, the problem of housing and
land-owning, and the migration of Negroes from one section of the country to
another. If necessary, the organization should be empowered to purchase land
in large quantities for resale to Negroes. And lastly, Villard felt that an important function of the association's "board" would be its ability to educate and
train the exceptional Negro and to place him where he could be of the greatest
possible service to his people. He reported that two of the most useful of the
political organizations fighting for Negroes' rights, the Niagara Movement and
the Constitution League, were ready to cooperate with or coalesce with the
proposed board.[60]

The final session of the two-day conference was a stormy meeting which lasted
until midnight, but by the time the conference adjourned, it had chosen a Committee of Forty on Permanent Organization, had ordered the incorporation of a
national Committee for the Advancement of the Negro Race, and had passed a
series of resolutions demanding equal civil and educational rights for the Negro,
the right to work, and protection against violence, murder, and intimidation, and
criticizing President Taft for his position on the enforcement of the Fifteenth
Amendment.[61]

Annoyed that his good friend Walling had failed to do a satisfactory job on
the resolutions, Villard used his editorial experience to pound the resolutions
into some kind of shape. Getting them adopted by the assembly was another
hurdle. William Monroe Trotter and the Reverend J. Milton Waldron took issue
with the language of nearly every resolution. Trotter was editor of the *Boston
Guardian*, president of the National Independent Political League, and a Harvard
graduate. Waldron was president of the National Negro Political League of
Washington, D.C.[62] The suspicion and hostility reached such proportions that at

---

[60] *Ibid.*, pp. 197–206.
[61] *Ibid.*, pp. 222–25. See Appendixes B and C.
[62] *Proceedings of the National Negro Conference 1909*, p. 159.

one point Villard and Walling seriously considered withdrawing the whole scheme of a national committee and continuing the work as they saw fit.[63]

The committee on nominations for the Committee of Forty on Permanent Organization ran into even more difficulty. They feared that without Booker T. Washington's name the organization would have difficulty getting funds from white philanthropists, and it was impossible to get Washington followers into a meeting of this kind unless Washington publicly set his seal of approval upon it. "The whole colored crowd was bitterly anti-Washington," wrote Villard, to his uncle.[64]

The nominating committee took a middle course which suited nobody. In an attempt at compromise they not only omitted Washington's name and those of his supporters but also omitted such severe critics of his policies as Trotter and Mrs. Ida Wells-Barnett, crusader against lynching and founder of the Negro Fellowship League in Chicago. Both were incensed at being left out. J. Milton Waldron, too, was bitterly angered at not being appointed. When Mrs. Wells-Barnett complained to Russell after the meeting, he illegally (but wisely according to Miss Ovington) put her on the committee.[65]

An attempt was made from the floor to have the Committee of Forty chosen by the conference without regard to the report of the nominating committee. Villard's defense of the slate of the nominating committee was warmly received. In the ensuing discussions he again felt elements of doubt and suspicion, but his conscience overcame his irritation. "I suppose we ought really not to blame these poor people who have been tricked so often by white men, for being suspicious," he wrote Garrison, "but the exhibition was none the less trying."[66]

Villard was pleased with the stories in the New York daily newspapers about the conference, and with the favorable comment in the *Boston Evening Transcript*. He considered that the papers had treated the conference liberally from the standpoint of space, and with as much seriousness as they would have treated any similar gathering of white men.[67] All were agreed on the skill with which Russell handled the meeting as presiding officer. A "resourceful chairman," said

[63] Villard's letters to his uncle reveal his estimates of his colleagues on the committee and give a glimpse of his own role behind the scenes. Walling, though an "able" fellow, was no writer. Du Bois was "most useful," and his attitude and bearing all through the committee sessions was impressive. Trotter and Waldron, on the other hand, made trivial changes in the resolutions "always with a nasty spirit," spoke "incessantly," and conducted themselves "very badly." At the close of the meeting, Villard "took great pleasure" in telling Trotter that the wrangling had been "unbearable." Villard to Garrison, June 4, 1909. Villard Papers. (Hereafter Garrison refers to Francis Jackson Garrison unless otherwise indicated.)
[64] Villard to Garrison, June 4, 1909, Villard Papers.
[65] Villard to Garrison, June 4, 1909, Villard Papers; Ovington, *The Walls Came Tumbling Down*, p. 106.
[66] Villard to Garrison, June 4, 1909, Villard Papers.
[67] *Ibid.*

the *New York Evening Post*, confronted by "such aggressive parliamentary practice" had to "take recourse at times to arbitrary methods in order to expedite
business."[68] Mary White Ovington commented that, although the resolutions had
to be adopted almost word by word, the chairman was undaunted by amendments to amendments and at no time showed impatience.[69]

The *New York Age*, a Negro weekly dominated and controlled by Booker T.
Washington, was critical of the conference, however. White participants were
characterized as able, distinguished, earnest friends of the Negro, but the *Age*
had nothing but scorn and ridicule for the Negroes present. Other protest organizations patronized by the same people had failed in the past, and the weekly
predicted failure for this new attempt. In Chicago, the Equal Opportunity
League had fallen apart because of internal dissensions. The Niagara Movement, which, according to the *Age*, combined all the elements and included all
the individuals which were represented in the recent New York conference, had
been wrecked by discord. The Constitution League and Trotter's National Political League were both disintegrating. The Negro must solve his own problems
by work and thrift, said the *Age*, and by hanging together—as doers, not as
talkers.[70]

Though acid in its presentation, the *New York Age* was correct in its assess-
ment of other organizations devoted to betterment of the Negro's role. The Equal
Opportunity League and the National Political League were limited in their
influence. The Constitution League had been founded and was almost wholly
supported and financed by John Milholland. The Niagara Movement was an
earlier attempt to counteract the curtailment of political and civil rights. Called
together in 1905 by Du Bois, it was composed of those Negroes whom he considered the "talented tenth"—with sufficient ability and education to assume
leadership among Negroes.[71] Through publicized agitation this group attempted
to rouse the Negro population to protest, and to engage the attention of whites.[72]
The platform called for manhood suffrage and listed a series of complaints
against loss of civil rights, against denial of equal opportunities in economic
life, against the Jim Crow car, the treatment of colored soldiers, and the "recent

[68] *New York Evening Post*, June 2, 1909.
[69] Ovington, "Beginnings of the N.A.A.C.P.," p. 77.
[70] *New York Age*, June 10, 1909.
[71] Though the Niagara Movement was composed of Negroes, in 1907, Du Bois invited Mary
White Ovington to join and she indicated she would do so "if the members really want me."
Ovington to Du Bois, April 20, 1907, Du Bois Papers (now in the possession of Mrs. W. E.
B. Du Bois, New York City).
[72] Francis L. Broderick, *W. E. B. Du Bois: Negro Leader in a Time of Crisis* (Stanford,
1959), p. 76; Elliott M. Rudwick, "The Niagara Movement," *Journal of Negro History*,
XLIII (July, 1957), 177–200.

attitude of the church." The theme was that persistent manly agitation was the way to liberty.[73]

The *New York Age* also pointed out that the two Negro periodicals, *The Moon* and *The Horizon*, edited and published by Du Bois, had likewise been unsuccessful.[74] From 1907 to 1910 Du Bois, together with F. H. M. Murray, and L. M. Hershaw, published *The Horizon*, a small periodical which served as an organ for the Niagara Movement.[75] But the Niagara Movement did not gain momentum, and by 1909 *The Horizon*, as well as the Niagara Movement, was in serious financial straits.[76] What confidence, therefore, could Negro readers of the *New York Age* have in the success of another movement?

That the conference nevertheless kindled excitement and optimism was reflected in the article Du Bois wrote for *The Survey*. He stated that the conference was the result of long thinking and brooding over serious social problems. Some sympathizers had been afraid that it would prove too radical and would unleash a flood of passion and bitterness, but Du Bois thought the white leaders inspired confidence and gave a sense of stability to the group. He saw the heart of the race problem as a question: "From the standpoint of modern science, are Negroes men?" Professors Wilder and Farrand had answered this question, leaving no doubt that the stereotypes of popular opinion as to the inferiority of the Negro were without scientific basis.

To Du Bois the last session was a night of great interest and burning earnestness, as the "black mass moved forward . . . to take charge."[77] A passionate desire to get the problem before the public without compromise and quibbling, uncertainty as to what practical steps were needed and suspicion of the white hands stretched out in brotherhood dominated the meeting. Despite this suspicion, however, Du Bois observed that the Negroes present had confidence in the grandson of William Lloyd Garrison and voted for the plan of national organization which he placed before them. Writing in *The Horizon* five months later, Du Bois called the conference the most significant event of 1909.

[73] "The Niagara Movement: Address to the Country," broadside (n.p., n.d.), Moorland Foundation, Howard University.
[74] *New York Age*, June 10, 1909.
[75] *Horizon*, I–V (1907–10). *The Moon*, *The Horizon*'s predecessor, was published at Memphis with the help of two former students of Du Bois, Edward L. Simon, a printer, and Harry H. Pace, a banker and insurance man. It was "not financially successful" and lasted less than a year, ceasing publication in 1906. One copy remains in the Moorland Collection: *The Moon: Illustrated Weekly*, I (March 2, 1906). Du Bois to Mrs. Dorothy Porter, June 11, 1957, Moorland Collection.
[76] Du Bois to "Dear Colleague" [February, 1909], Moorland Collection. In the four years since its inception, the Niagara Movement had taken in $1,653.70 in receipts, and in January, 1909, had $75.10, cash on hand, and bills outstanding of $150.00.
[77] Du Bois, "National Committee on the Negro," *Survey: A Journal of Constructive Philanthropy*, XXII (June 12, 1909), 407–9.

In *The Horizon* article, Du Bois put his finger upon a serious situation—the separation of the Negro problem from the other humanitarian movements of the time, and its consequent neglect. The Negro problem was not and could not be kept distinct from other reform movements—women's rights, consumer's leagues, prison reform, social settlements, universal peace. White reformers seemed to be unaware of the Negro problem or refused to admit its existence. On the other hand, Negroes had considered their own situation distinct from other social problems, subject to its own particular remedies. The New York Conference on the Negro had marked an "awakening" from this mistaken thinking. The social workers who called the conference realized that all human problems of advance and uplift in some way involved the Negro and his condition, and Negroes who responded to the call became aware that the Negro problem was a universal problem of poverty, ignorance, suffrage, women's rights, distribution of wealth, and law and order among both blacks and whites. The attack on any of these evils demanded close cooperation. To Du Bois it was not simply a matter of "millionaires and almsgiving." It was a "human problem" demanding "human methods."[78]

The separation of the Negro problem from the other humanitarian movements of the time was a post-Civil War phenomenon. In antebellum days the movement for the emancipation of women had become closely tied in with other reform activities, especially the temperance movement and the agitation for the abolition of slavery. This was natural as the status of women in many ways was not unlike that of the Negro. Women were held to be inferior to men in most respects, and arguments used to prove that point bore a striking resemblance to those used to argue the inferiority of Negroes. Both had a place in society; both were thought to be content with a subordinate position. By keeping women and Negroes in their "place," white men believed they were acting in the best interest of these "inferior" groups.[79]

The abolition and temperance movements had served as training grounds for leaders of the feminist movement, who were generally supported in their aims by such abolitionists as William Lloyd Garrison and Wendell Phillips. The Civil War and the passage of the Fourteenth and Fifteenth Amendments (which were relevant only to males) ended the alliance between the feminist movement and the Negro movement. By 1903, the two movements were so far apart that only a few liberals, Negro and white, supported both causes.[80] Villard championed both causes as had his father and grandfather before him. His mother, Fanny Garrison Villard, was active in the suffrage movement and in the battle for

---

[78] Du Bois, "National Negro Conference," *Horizon*, V (November, 1909), 1.
[79] Myrdal, *An American Dilemma*, Appendix 5, "A Parallel to the Negro Problem," pp. 1073–76, 1097.
[80] *Ibid.*, pp. 1073–75.

Negro rights. In his memoirs, Villard mentioned that his first public speech given in Boston, while he was still an assistant to historian Albert Bushnell Hart at Harvard, was in the cause of the suffragettes. The lifelong friendship between Hart and Villard was in a large measure due to their common interest in these two causes.[81]

Along with his plans for the Committee for the Advancement of the Negro, Villard had for some time dreamed of a men's club to champion the cause of woman suffrage. He thought of a "paper organization for use on special occasions." By the end of 1909, his "Men's League for Woman Suffrage" had had an auspicious launching, and in 1911 he was one of eighty-four men that were booed and hissed, as they took part in a suffragist parade down Fifth Avenue. He looked upon this as a very thrilling and inspiring experience.[82]

The suffragists, however, continued to be hostile to the cause of the Negro. A bitter flare-up took place as late as 1916, at the funeral of Mrs. Inez Milholland Boissevain, daughter of John E. Milholland, attorney, suffragist leader, and champion of Negro rights. Here the suffragists snubbed Negro women delegates and attempted to prevent them from speaking at the service.[83] In spite of Du Bois's prophecy that the 1909 Conference on the Negro marked a turning point, an awakening to the realization that the Negro problem was not a separate question but was intimately connected with other areas of humanitarian concern, many years passed without an alliance or a working agreement between the feminists and the new abolition movement.

It is interesting to note, nevertheless, that women played a conspicuous part in the founding of the NAACP.[84] Approximately one-third of the signers of the "Call" were women, including two Negroes, Mrs. Mary Church Terrell, Oberlin graduate, writer, and lecturer, and Mrs. Ida Wells-Barnett, who attended Rusk College and Fisk University. Both women were appointed to the Committee of Forty set up by the 1909 Conference.

THE OPPOSITION

Among those who neither responded to the "Call" nor participated in the first conference was Charles Waddell Chesnutt, prominent in the Negro world as an author and lecturer and one of the Negro intellectuals of the day. He declined

---

[81] A. B. Hart to Villard, July 12, 1894, Villard Papers. Villard worked for two years with Hart at Harvard. Villard, *Fighting Years*, pp. 4–5, 104–5.
[82] Villard to Garrison, January 15, 1908; December 7, 1909; May 8, 1911, Villard Papers; Villard, *Fighting Years*, pp. 199–200.
[83] *Crisis*, XXVIII (October, 1924), 268; XI (February, 1916), 169.
[84] Wilson Record, "Negro Intellectual Leadership and the NAACP," *Phylon*, XVII (1956), 380. See Appendixes A and B.

to speak at the Cooper Union mass meeting, but privately gave approval to the principles which were enunciated there. He avoided, however, a public statement and neither endorsed nor disapproved the resolutions of condemnation and protest and the proposal to form a permanent national organization. Chesnutt remained on good terms with Booker T. Washington though he disagreed with much of Washington's philosophy, notably his subordination of civil and political growth and his failure to comprehend or acknowledge the proper role that higher education should play in the advancement of the Negro. In like manner he made it clear to the radicals, Monroe Trotter and Du Bois, that he could not adopt their point of view regarding Washington. He stated his position to Trotter as early as 1901, refusing to be drawn into the acrimonious personal quarrels projected by Trotter in the *Guardian*.[85]

Other Negro intellectuals whose absence was noted were Professor Kelly Miller of Howard University, and the Reverend Francis J. Grimke.[86] Judge Robert H. Terrell, a Republican appointee to the District of Columbia municipal court and a loyal supporter of Booker T. Washington, did not attend the conference, but his wife, Mary Church Terrell, did, and was appointed to the Committee of Forty. Mrs. Terrell was concerned about the resolution denouncing President Taft and was afraid it would harm the cause. But, she wrote to her husband, she would not allow this to deter her "from doing something to help remove the awful conditions which injure you and me—all the rest of us." She felt it was a mistake to stay out of organizations simply because of the political and personal attitudes of a few members.[87]

The opinions of Mrs. Terrell and Charles W. Chesnutt were representative of the thinking of some of the small group of Negro intellectuals whose influence was limited in scope. But the big question remained: What attitude would Booker T. Washington take toward the new movement? If Villard could not persuade Washington to support the new movement, he would do all he could to prevent Washington's open hostility. Accordingly, two days after the close of the conference, he wrote the Tuskegean, thanking him for his "friendly spirit" and sending copies of his own address, the resolutions, and the names of those appointed to the Committee of Forty. He was confident that Washington would approve the work of the organization as it unfolded.[88]

[85] Charles W. Chesnutt to Judge Wendell P. Stafford, June 25, 1909; Chesnutt to Du Bois, November 21, 1910; Chesnutt to Trotter, December 28, 1901, quoted in Helen M. Chesnutt, *Charles Waddell Chesnutt: Pioneer of the Color Line* (Chapel Hill, 1952), pp. 191–207, 231–32, 240–44; Chesnutt to Washington, August 11, 1903, Washington Papers.
[86] Garrison to Villard, June 8, 1909, Villard Papers.
[87] Washington Papers, *passim*; Terrell Family Papers (Manuscript Division, Library of Congress), *passim*; Mary Church Terrell to Judge Robert Terrell, June 14, 1909, in Mary Church Terrell Papers (Manuscript Division, Library of Congress).
[88] Villard to Washington, June 4, 1909, Villard Papers.

If it was the intent of Villard to turn away wrath with soft words, he soon learned that he had failed. Less than a week later he heard from his uncle, Francis Garrison, that Washington in a public address had gratuitously slurred and reflected on the work and purpose of the conference by minimizing the importance of the vote and magnifying the value of money-getting and hoarding. Garrison was worried lest Washington "chill and prevent the interest of a good many people who ought to be with us."[89]

William E. Walling, instead of trying to conciliate Washington, attacked his policies in a national periodical, *The Independent*, two weeks after the conference. The exclusive endorsement of these policies which were universal in the North, he wrote, was causing a general postponement of the Negroes' claim for political and social equality, universally denied by the Southern whites.[90]

T. Thomas Fortune, editor of the *New York Age*, answered this with a counterattack. He damned Walling, the chief moving spirit behind the conference, as a Southerner with the usual Southern prejudices. Walling had confused social privileges and civil rights, a common practice among Southern whites, "with whom the madness is method designed." Fortune further discredited Walling by calling him a socialist, "whatever that may be."[91] These recriminations marked one phase of a long period of growing hostility between the forces of Washington and the new movement, which will be discussed in a later chapter.

Reactions to the conference of some so-called liberal whites who were sympathetic to the cause of the Negro were not without hostility. Edgar Gardner Murphy, an Episcopal clergyman of Montgomery, Alabama, writer and, until 1908, executive secretary of the Southern Education Board, supported Washington in his boycott of the conference and referred to the Negroes who attended as the silly element of the race.[92] George McAneny, president of the Civic Association of America, thought it was a mistake to launch the project at a time when "the new South was rallying so splendidly."[93]

Another adverse comment came from Albert Shaw, editor of *Review of Reviews*. At a reception given by Villard's mother on the Saturday following the conference, Villard noted that Shaw took the opportunity in a conversation with Florence Kelley and Lillian Wald to express his surprise that they should lend

[89] Garrison to Villard, June 8, 1909, Villard Papers.
[90] Walling, "Science and Human Brotherhood," *Independent*, LXVI (June 17, 1909), 1318.
[91] *New York Age*, June 24, 1909.
[92] "Edgar Gardner Murphy," in *Who Was Who in America* (Chicago, 1942), I, 882; Edgar Gardner Murphy to Washington, June 4, 1909, Washington Papers.
[93] Basil Mathews, *Booker T. Washington: Educator and Interracial Interpreter* (London, 1949), p. 217; Villard to Garrison, June 7, 1909, Villard Papers. McAneny was at this time fusion candidate for the presidency of the Borough of Manhattan and was warmly supported by Washington's paper, the *New York Age*, which greatly rejoiced in his election. *New York Age*, October 28, 1909; November 18, 1909.

their support to the movement. Villard's pique at the criticism of "his" conference may have colored his judgment of the character of the rival editor,
when he wrote of Shaw's "mental shiftiness and devotion to compromise and
expediency."[94]

THE COMMITTEE OF FORTY

In spite of skepticism and criticism, Villard was not deterred from perfecting
his plans for the new organization. By publishing the proceedings of the conference in a pamphlet he hoped to enlist the sympathy of philanthropists like
Henry C. Phipps and Andrew Carnegie. He optimistically visualized an endowment of a million dollars with which to launch the work of the organization.[95]

Meanwhile, there were maneuvers to make the Committee of Forty more representative of contrasting opinions. Miss Ovington, who had left New York immediately after the conference, received letters from Russell and Walling asking her
advice "as to what to do with the howling residue that hadn't received office."[96]
Writing to Du Bois a week afterward, Walling said it was fortunate there were
four vacancies on the committee. In addition to Mrs. Wells-Barnett, Russell had
added Dr. William A. Sinclair, a physician, member of the Constitution League,
and leader of Philadelphia Negroes. Russell had demurred at including Kelly
Miller, even though Mrs. Wooley of Chicago and a number of Niagara Movement men had urged his appointment. Russell had favored Waldron's appointment, wrote Walling, until he talked with Villard, who was opposed to it. However, as Walling had obtained the consent of Sinclair, Brooks, Dr. William L.
Bulkley, Dr. Owen M. Waller, Mrs. Wooley, and Miss Ovington, he wrote
Waldron and Trotter that he expected Russell to make the appointment. If this
were not done, he himself would name Waldron to the next vacancy. He suggested that Du Bois telegraph Russell, urging Waldron's appointment.[97]

Walling had not attended the meeting of the subcommittee, which considered
the thirty names that Villard had so carefully drawn up, as he was confident
that no important changes would be made other than the adding of several
colored members, but he was "shocked to learn that where three or four had
been added six or seven had been taken off." Both Milholland and Walling considered this to be a stupendous error, which the appointment of Mrs. Wells-
Barnett and Dr. Sinclair had only partially corrected. Even so, Walling was not
satisfied with the committee as it was reorganized. He considered that the appointment of Waldron and Kelly Miller would represent the very minimum

[94] Villard to Garrison, June 7, 1909, Villard Papers.
[95] Ibid.
[96] Ovington, "Beginnings of the N.A.A.C.P.," 77.
[97] Walling to Du Bois, June 8, 1909, Du Bois Papers.

correction that could be made, whereupon he would resign quietly and leave the Committee entirely in the hands of Russell and Villard. If these appointments were not made, he would continue as chairman with the intention of appointing these men to the first vacancies, in order to keep the committee from becoming the mere tool of any faction.

Walling wanted these "strong and energetic personalities" included so as to correct the impression already afloat that the various cliques were not fully represented. "It is impossible," he wrote to Du Bois, "that twelve colored members could thoroughly represent all the ideas, sentiments, standpoints, and organizations which ought to receive a constant hearing inside of our Committee."[98]

Du Bois made an effort to comply with Walling's request. He wrote to Villard, suggesting the committee be enlarged, but Villard was under the influence of his uncle who considered a committee of fifty preposterous. He suggested reducing the entire committee to twelve.[99]

But the founding group, as Walling later recalled, was determined to choose the personnel of the committee on the broadest possible lines and not to become a little sect. It was for this reason that the so-called radicals had held themselves in the background and given prominence to Villard, whom Walling called the conservative editor of the conservative *New York Evening Post*. Nor was any colored citizen of prominence barred because of his critics, even though the conservative minority wanted to adopt standards "so high, as they thought—or so narrow, as it appeared to us" (wrote Walling) that many of those who eventually became leaders would have been excluded from the ruling circles had these ideas prevailed.[100]

In the end, the comprehensive organization as conceived by Walling and his supporters, including all shades of opinion, predominated over the concept of the small, select group envisaged by Francis Garrison and became a fundamental policy of the Association.

[98] Walling to Du Bois, June 8, 1909, Du Bois Papers.
[99] Garrison to Villard, June 24, 1909, Villard Papers.
[100] Walling, "The Founding of the N.A.A.C.P.," 226.

CHAPTER II

A Permanent Organization Is Formed

By the autumn of 1909, Villard had arranged for a Garrison memorial meeting to be held in Boston to bring together persons in that area whose interest could be counted on.[1] Out of this meeting came the Boston Committee to Advance the Cause of the Negro, which expanded and became, in 1911, a branch of the NAACP. Among the early members were the Garrisons, Boston lawyers Storey, Butler Wilson, and Albert E. Pillsbury, and Dr. Horace Bumstead, president of Atlanta University.[2]

Meanwhile, some of the "New York members" were busy planning for the next annual meeting and drawing up a tentative outline for a permanent organization to be submitted to the 1910 conference, which they hoped to hold in Washington, D.C., in spite of the city's predominantly Southern point of view. There were many people in the capital who were in sympathy with the movement and could be counted on to cooperate, including political figures whose positions on the Negro was known to be favorable. Villard therefore asked Judge Stafford to suggest the names of white people who would be willing to serve on a District of Columbia committee.

From the beginning the leaders had hoped to acquaint the executive and legislative branches of the government with the association's aims and objectives so that it might be possible to exert political influence on behalf of the Negro. By holding some of the meetings in white churches and issuing tickets, Northern congressmen and their wives might be attracted. Moreover, it was hoped that President Taft might be persuaded to address the conference, although little was

---

[1] Oswald Garrison Villard to Francis Jackson Garrison, September 30, 1909, in the Oswald Garrison Villard Papers (Houghton Library, Harvard University). (Hereafter Garrison refers to Francis Jackson Garrison unless otherwise specified.)

[2] Moorfield Storey to William Lloyd Garrison, Jr., November 12, 1909, Moorfield Storey Papers (in the possession of Mr. Charles Storey, Boston, Massachusetts).

31

expected of Taft other than that he attract nationwide attention to the conference.[3]

Tuskegee was soon apprised of the plans for the conference. James A. Cobb of the Office of the United States Attorney for the District of Columbia reported that Oswald Garrison Villard had sought his aid in drawing up a list of names of both races to be invited. In asking Booker T. Washington for guidance, Cobb referred to Villard as president of the Constitution League, confusing the League with the new organization.[4] The National Negro Conference had as yet made little impact on the Negro world.

Early in November, 1909, the Committee of Forty met at the Liberal Club in New York City with Walling in the chair to discuss plans for the Washington conference. Yielding to the capital's pattern of segregation, they at first considered holding separate meetings in white and colored churches to be addressed by the same speakers. But after lengthy discussion the decision was reached that unless certain congressmen and jurists could be secured as speakers, the meeting should be held in some other city.[5]

Before the meeting adjourned, two important pieces of business had been transacted. First, a committee of three, composed of Villard, Miss Ovington, and Dr. William L. Bulkley, Negro principal of a New York white public school,[6] was authorized to select an executive secretary for the Committee of Forty. Secondly, a temporary chairman was chosen to head the Committee of Forty, since Walling had informed the meeting that ill health prevented his continuing as chairman, although he fully intended to be present at the meetings.[7] Walling's resignation may have been the result of friction engendered by his attempt to appoint additional colored people to the Committee of Forty, or it may be that the disgrace of a pending breach of promise suit, which had been publicized to the Negro world by the *New York Age*,[8] had something to do with his withdrawal from active leadership. Nevertheless, at the time of the conference in May, 1910, he accepted chairmanship of the Executive Committee in the perma-

[3] Villard to Wendell Phillips Stafford, October 19, 1909, Villard Papers.
[4] James A. Cobb to Emmett J. Scott, November 22, 1909, Booker T. Washington Papers (Manuscript Division, Library of Congress).
[5] Minutes, National Negro Conference [Committee of Forty], November 8, 1909, held at the Liberal Club, 19 East 26th Street, New York City, in "Minute Book of the Board of Directors of the National Association for the Advancement of Colored People" (now in the Manuscript Division, Library of Congress; hereafter referred to as Board Minutes, NAACP). There are no minutes for the earlier meeting referred to in Villard to Stafford, October 19, 1909.
[6] Mary White Ovington, *The Walls Came Tumbling Down* (New York, 1947), p. 103.
[7] Minutes, National Negro Conference, November 8, 1909, in Board Minutes, NAACP.
[8] *New York Age*, August 5, 1909. The *Age* announced with evident satisfaction: "William English Walling, the Socialist, who started out to settle the troubles of the Negro, seems now to have troubles of his own. He is being sued by a young French woman for $100,000 for a breach of promise. Mr. Walling is at the head of the Committee of Forty."

nent organization.[9] Walling held this post until January, 1911,[10] when the breach of promise suit was in process of being tried. It is possible that he accepted the job in the belief that public clamor had quieted down, or that the suit could be settled out of court and thus avert a scandal which would seriously reflect on the character of the white leadership of the new organization for the advancement of the Negro.

The committee wished to elect as chairman Charles Edward Russell, who had been acting chairman in Walling's absence, but prior commitments necessitated Russell's absence from the city for several months, so Villard was made temporary chairman during Russell's absence.[11]

Villard was discouraged with what he called Walling's erratic nature and was not at all in sympathy with his methods. He and Miss Ovington, whom he called a trump, assumed the bulk of the work. That there was confusion and lack of system is evident in the failure to notify Moorfield Storey of his election to the Committee of Forty prior to the announcement of the November meeting of the Committee in New York.[12]

The organization was immediately threatened by the development of a serious personal conflict between Villard, the temporary chairman, and Du Bois. Unfortunately, it had fallen to Villard to write a review of Du Bois's biography of John Brown in the pages of *The Nation*.[13] One cannot help feeling that it was extremely tactless for Villard to have accepted this assignment since he himself was the author of a book on John Brown which was shortly to appear in print. In any event, Du Bois's reaction was violent and abusive. He regarded Villard's review as a peculiarly wanton assault and complained when *The Nation* refused to print his rebuttal. He would not seat himself at the feet of Mr. Villard for instruction either in history or English. Villard, he said, had savagely picked numberless immaterial flaws in absolute accuracy and had emphasized them beyond reason.[14] Villard, seeing in Du Bois's reaction proof of his temper and

[9] Minutes, National Negro Committee, May 12, 1910, in Board Minutes, NAACP; Ovington, *How the National Association for the Advancement of Colored People Began*, pamphlet (New York, 1914), p. 4. After incorporation of the NAACP on June 19, 1911, a Board of Directors replaced the Executive Committee as the governing body.
[10] Minutes, Executive Committee, NAACP, January 3, 1911, in Board Minutes, NAACP.
[11] Minutes, National Negro Conference, November 8, 1909, in Board Minutes, NAACP.
[12] Villard to Garrison, December 7, 1909, Villard Papers; Storey to Charles Edward Russell, October 29, 1909, Storey Papers.
[13] Villard's father, Henry Villard, bought the *New York Evening Post* in 1881, together with *The Nation*, which served as the paper's weekly literary supplement. In 1897, Oswald Garrison Villard took over the *Evening Post* as president and editorial writer. He sold the property in 1918, becoming editor and owner of *The Nation*, 1918 to 1932, and publisher and contributing editor from 1932 to 1935. "Oswald Garrison Villard," in Maxine Block (ed.), *Current Biography Who's News and Why: 1940* (New York, 1940), pp. 830–32.
[14] Du Bois to Paul Elmer More, November 15, 1909, Villard Papers.

spirit, was convinced that it would be difficult to work with him in the National Negro Committee.[15]

Francis Jackson Garrison, siding with his nephew, wrote that Du Bois, as a statistician and exact writer, ought to be chagrined at his carelessness in accepting without challenge or investigation the "sloppy" work of his research assistants. He put his finger on what he thought was the source of Du Bois's violent reaction to criticism: "We must not wonder at the super-sensitiveness of one whose color constantly subjects him to insult and contempt." The sharp exchange between Du Bois and Villard continued throughout November. It was not until the following May when they met at the conference that they "shook hands across the chasm."[16]

THE CHOICE OF A THEME

Throughout the winter of 1909–10, the National Negro Committee, or Committee of Forty, struggled to survive. Attendance at the December, 1909, meeting was limited to seven because of a severe storm. Villard led the discussion of the program for the coming conference. Though the program committee had in November suggested a session on the Negro and trade unions, Walling now advised that, although the matter was of vital importance, it should be omitted from the conference program.[17]

With the rise of national trade unions in number and influence Negroes had been for the most part left out. The policy of the American Federation of Labor to look with disfavor upon the exclusion of persons on account of race or color[18] had given way to a practice of allowing a union to affiliate if its constitution did not specifically exclude Negroes. Thus, unwritten policies and rituals became the means of effecting discrimination. In some cases separate Negro locals were organized where there was no opposition on the part of white workers. Other national labor unions had no provision against discrimination. In 1910 the number of Negro workers in unions was negligible, except in the South in undesirable job areas such as timber working and mining. During wage conflicts even these organizations fell victim to racism and tended to disintegrate. In the field of transportation the Railway Brotherhoods drew the color line in a variety of ways. Locomotive engineers and railway conductors limited their membership to whites. Firemen and trainmen, although excluding Negroes from

[15] Villard to Garrison, November 17, 1909, Villard Papers.
[16] Garrison to Villard, November 18, 1909; November 23, 1909; May 18, 1910, Villard Papers.
[17] Minutes, National Negro Conference, December 13, 1909, in Board Minutes, NAACP. Present were Villard (presiding), Leslie Pinckney Hill, Moskowitz, O. M. Waller, Walling, Miss Ovington, Mrs. Mary Dunlop Maclean.
[18] As quoted in Rayford W. Logan, *The Negro in American Life and Thought: The Nadir 1877–1901* (New York, 1954), p. 147.

their organizations, could not keep them from being hired, especially in the South. Here management used the Negro to fight unionism by depressing wages through lower pay for equal work, with the consequent threat to job security.[19]

The early manifestation of concern for the Negro in his relation to the American labor movement by the founders of the NAACP is of particular interest in view of charges made in the 1930's by some Negro intellectuals that the Association was too much oriented toward securing legal redress and the ballot. Throughout its existence the Association made repeated attempts, in spite of the hostile climate of public opinion, to secure admission of Negroes to unions on a basis of equality with white workers, but without much success.[20]

Walling was realistic in advising that it would be useless to attempt to deal with the problem at the 1910 conference in light of the attitude of labor leaders toward the Negro, to say nothing of the attitude of rank-and-file workers. Walling was in a position to know—the labor movement had been his chief interest since his early twenties. In addition to founding the National Women's Trade Union League, he had helped to establish the Intercollegiate Socialist Society, which later became the League for Industrial Democracy. Although he was a socialist, he collaborated with Samuel Gompers and gave a large portion of his time to the advancement of the American Federation of Labor.[21]

Having decided not to hold a session on labor unions, the group now planned to organize the entire conference around a central theme. The topic chosen was disfranchisement.

At the first conference, in 1909, Du Bois had named disfranchisement in the South as a major barrier to Negro advancement. Disfranchisement of the Negro was in large measure brought about as a result of conflict between the conservative Democratic leadership of the South and the Populists, who represented the resurgent farmers.[22] The Populists attempted to convince the white and Negro masses that they were bound together by common economic and political problems, and sought Negro cooperation and support at the polls. To fight the Populist movement, which threatened the weakened conservative supremacy, conservatives resorted to trickery, fraud, and violence. Both sides competed for Negro support. Conservatives finally broke up the Populist attempt at interracial cooperation by appealing to racism and to the argument that once the

[19] Sterling D. Spero and Abram L. Harris, *The Black Worker: The Negro and the Labor Movement* (New York, 1931), pp. 284–86, 330–32.
[20] Board Minutes, NAACP, *passim*.
[21] David A. Shannon, "William English Walling," in Robert Livingston Schuyler and Edward T. James (eds.), *Dictionary of American Biography: Supplement Two* (New York, 1958), XXII, 689–90.
[22] C. Vann Woodward, *Origins of the New South 1877–1913*, Vol. IX of *A History of the South*, ed. Wendell Holmes Stephenson and E. Merton Coulter (Baton Rouge, 1951), pp. 264–70; Woodward, *The Strange Career of Jim Crow* (rev. ed.; New York, 1957), pp. 56–62.

Negro was disfranchised, politics could be purified, and an effective two-party system would become possible in the South.[23]

To avoid extralegal methods of disfranchisement, such as violence, intimidation, and the manipulation of the technical requirements of registration, the conservatives decided to amend state constitutions to accomplish Negro disfranchisement. It was first necessary to overcome the opposition of many upland whites, who feared they would also be disfranchised in the process. Therefore, in addition to poll taxes, residence requirements, property qualifications, and literacy tests, all of which could be used to disqualify lower-class whites as well as Negroes, certain loopholes were provided, such as the ability to read or give a reasonable interpretation of the federal or state constitution. The most widely used device was the "grandfather clause," which gave the vote to persons who had done military service in wartime, or to those who had voted before 1867 and to their descendants. This technique allowed whites who could not meet educational or other qualifications to be admitted to the suffrage. At the same time it systematically deprived Negroes of the vote. By 1910, with the rapid spread of the white primary in the South, which excluded Negroes on the legal theory that the Democratic Party was a private organization and could formulate and enforce its own rules of admission, Negro disfranchisement was virtually complete.[24]

Another factor in the selection of this subject for the second conference was that in 1910 a national census would be taken, and 1910 seemed a fitting time to make a survey of educational and legal conditions resulting from disfranchisement.

At the December, 1910, meeting, the committee also decided to give up the idea of holding the conference in Washington because of the pattern of segregation in that city. They chose New York instead. Keeping in mind the stormy sessions at the first conference, they agreed that admission this time would be by invitation only, and a committee on membership and credentials was set up, in addition to a committee on general arrangements.

They next turned to some of the problems of permanent organization and authorized Dr. Henry Moskowitz and Rabbi Stephen S. Wise to appoint a treasurer. A paid worker was to be engaged, beginning January 1, 1910. By "paid worker" was doubtless meant the secretary authorized at the November meeting.[25]

[23] Woodward, *Origins of the New South*, pp. 322–27, 337, 347–48; Woodward, *The Strange Career of Jim Crow*, pp. 63–65.
[24] Woodward, *Origins of the New South*, pp. 330–31, 372–73; V. O. Key, Jr., *Southern Politics in State and Nation* (New York, 1950), pp. 619–20.
[25] Minutes, National Negro Conference, December 13, 1909, in Board Minutes, NAACP. The committee on membership and credentials was made up of O. M. Waller, Hill, Sinclair, Archibald Grimke, Holmes, Walling, Mrs. Terrell, and Miss Ovington. The committee on general arrangements was composed of Moskowitz, Bishop Walters, and Miss Eaton.

PLANNING THE CONFERENCE

No meeting was held in January. In February, the five committee members present proceeded in desperation to call on Mrs. Mary Dunlop Maclean, a staff writer on the *New York Times*, Paul Kennaday, social worker and journalist, and Professor Seligman[26] to expand the executive group. Mrs. Maclean and Kennaday were competent volunteer workers, and the latter replaced Dr. Moskowitz as chairman of the committee on arrangements.[27]

Financial problems also pressed upon the group. Dr. Moskowitz and Rabbi Wise had been unable to find a treasurer and Dr. Bulkley was asked to enlist Jacob W. Mack, a woolen manufacturer, who was interested in Bulkley's work in the evening trade schools.[28] Funds for the conference were lacking. Members of the Committee of Forty agreed to raise money, "each according to his means in sums from a minimum of five dollars," and to subscribe to the "Proceedings" of the first conference.

The minutes for February 14, 1910, and the following meetings carry the typed signature of "Frances Blascoer, Secy," the committee's first salaried worker. Miss Blascoer attended in the role of recorder and not as a member of the Committee of Forty.[29]

Although Walling, Seligman, and Kennaday, together with Miss Blascoer, met as a subcommittee to discuss arrangements and problems connected with the annual meeting, Villard returned from a vacation at the end of February, 1910, to find "his" project near disintegration.[30] The tone of the minutes of the March meeting confirms his estimate of the situation. Those present were Villard, Russell, Kennaday, the secretary, and Dr. Owen M. Waller, Brooklyn physician and a member of the Niagara Movement. An important member of the committee, Samuel Bowles, editor of the *Springfield Republican*, had resigned. The

[26] E. R. A. Seligman was the Columbia University economics professor who had spoken at the 1909 Conference. (His father founded the banking firm of J. W. Seligman & Co.). He was interested in all movements for social and economic reform and was president of the Society for Ethical Culture, 1908–21, chairman of the National League on Urban Conditions Among Negroes, 1911–14, and aided in founding Greenwich Settlement House. Joseph Dorfman, "Edwin Robert Anderson Seligman," in Schuyler and James (eds.), *Dictionary of American Biography: Supplement Two*, XXII (New York, 1958), 606–9.
[27] Minutes, National Negro Conference, February 14, 1910, in Board Minutes, NAACP. Those present were: Walling, Villard, Brooks, Bulkley, and Miss Ovington.
[28] *New York Age*, April 18, 1912.
[29] *Ibid.* Frances Blascoer was described by Arthur B. Spingarn as "a friend of mine and a colleague in a social settlement *ca.* 1902. . . . She was a very attractive and intelligent woman . . . author of a monograph on Negro children in the New York Schools." A. B. Spingarn to the writer, September 5, 1958. The book was Frances Blascoer, *Colored School Children in New York* (New York, 1915).
[30] Minutes, subcommittee meeting, National Negro Conference, February 23, 1910, in Board Minutes, NAACP; Villard to Garrison, March 9, 1910, Villard Papers.

organization was still without a treasurer. Funds were desperately low with a balance on hand of $67.35. Villard had provided $150 for Miss Blascoer's salary for six weeks and his mother was contributing to the general expenses.[31] There were no speakers for the conference, now only two months away. Many names were mentioned, but nothing could be resolved. Moreover, no progress had been made toward formal organization.

Villard at once set up a Preliminary Committee on Permanent Organization with himself as chairman, consisting of Seligman, Du Bois, Walling, Milholland, and Russell. As a guide to the formulation of organizational plans they were to prepare a questionnaire to be sent to all members of the national committee. Villard called for a special meeting within ten days to expedite the resolution of financial, organizational, and conference problems.[32]

The crisis was passed. Villard's administrative ability and vigor aroused new interest and enthusiasm. When the special meeting convened on March 24, nine members were present, the financial situation had been somewhat eased, the main outline of the conference was at last agreed on, and the date set for May 12–14. A plan of organization submitted by Du Bois was referred to the Preliminary Committee on Permanent Organization, together with Milholland's proposal that the National Negro Committee be taken over by the Constitution League.[33]

Contributions had begun to flow in, and there was a balance of $265. Jacob Schiff of the banking firm of Kuhn, Loeb and Company[34] wrote of his sympathy with the work of the committee and contributed $100. Schiff's interest was a boost to the committee's morals. It was due to the influence of Lillian Wald, for whose Nurses' Settlement Schiff had provided most of the money. Schiff, an admirer of Booker T. Washington, had also contributed to Tuskegee. In addition, 123 copies of the Proceedings of the 1909 conference had been sold, more

[31] Minutes, National Negro Conference, March 14, 1910, in Board Minutes, NAACP. "Financial Statement to date," March 14, 1910, and "Cash Statement February 1 to March 14, inclusive," unsigned financial statements following the minutes. The minutes of the special meeting, National Negro Committee, April—[March 24], 1910, confirm the fact that Villard was contributing the secretary's salary, and that his mother had given $50 for general expenses of the group. Three months later, Miss Blascoer wrote Du Bois that Villard's mother had "provided" her salary. Frances Blascoer to Du Bois, June 15, 1910, W. E. B. Du Bois Papers (now in possession of Mrs. W. E. B. Du Bois, New York City).
[32] Minutes, National Negro Conference, March 14, 1910, in Board Minutes, NAACP.
[33] Minutes, Special Meeting, National Negro Committee, April—[March 24], 1910. Beginning with this meeting the minutes of the "National Negro Conference," (Committee of Forty) are labeled "National Negro Committee." The date is in pencil in Miss Ovington's handwriting, and was added to the typed minutes. There is evidence in the minutes themselves that this special meeting was held on the Thursday prior to the convening of the Preliminary Committee on Permanent Organization held on Wednesday, March 30. Hence the date of these minutes must be March 24, 1910.
[34] "Jacob Henry Schiff," in *Who Was Who in America* (Chicago, 1942), p. 1087.

than had been subscribed to, and 1,000 copies had been ordered from the Nation Press. Nevertheless, it was estimated that the expenses of the conference would amount to between $1,500 and $2,000, and Villard appointed a committee to solicit additional funds.[35]

In the meantime, Booker T. Washington's friends were keeping him well informed as to the plans and progress of the National Negro Committee. The day after the special meeting, Fred R. Moore, editor of the *New York Age*, wrote the Tuskegeean, giving the time and place of the conference, its theme, and the names of some of the speakers. When amalgamation with the Constitution League was being considered, Gilchrist Stewart, a New York attorney, passed the relevant information on to Charles W. Anderson, Washington's chief political henchman.[36] Stewart, a former Tuskegee student, had been an investigator for the Constitution League[37] and worked with Milholland. According to the reports conveyed to Washington, Du Bois was to be given an office in New York as secretary of the organization at a salary of $4,000 a year. Stewart wanted the job for himself but felt sure Du Bois would get it.

Relations between Villard and Washington began to deteriorate with the publication on April 1, 1910, in the *Evening Post* of an editorial by Villard entitled, "Mr. Washington in Politics." He compared Du Bois's philosophy with that of Washington, and described the cleavage between their followers. Villard supported Du Bois's belief that agitation and protest were necessary, not only to recover lost ground but to prevent the loss of more. He deplored Washington's subordination of political rights to the industrial and economic betterment of the Negro. If he continued his work at Tuskegee in silence, said Villard, no one would object, but to assume the role of "political boss of his race" was hopelessly inconsistent with his often-stated philosophy.

Villard quoted Du Bois who had attacked Washington on much the same ground, asserting that only those Negroes were given political office who agreed with Washington's policy of nonresistance, who relinquished agitation, and acquiesced to semiserfdom.[38] To reinforce his argument, Villard recalled that Carl Schurz, a friend of the Garrison and Villard families, had warned Washington that his influence would wane if he went into politics. Villard urged Washington to exchange his political dictatorship for the regard of the most intellectual portion of the colored people.[39]

[35] Minutes, Special Meeting, National Negro Committee, April—[March 24], 1910. The fundraising committee was composed of Walling, Russell, Wise, Moskowitz, and Kennaday.
[36] Fred R. Moore to Washington, March 25, 1910; Charles W. Anderson to Washington, April 19, 1910, Washington Papers.
[37] *Crisis*, II (August, 1911), 147.
[38] Du Bois to the *Boston Transcript*, quoted in Villard, "Mr. Washington in Politics," *New York Evening Post*, April 1, 1910.
[39] *New York Evening Post*, April 1, 1910.

Thus, six weeks before the Second Annual Conference, Villard publicly took Washington to task and openly aligned himself with Du Bois and the radicals. In effect, he served notice that the National Negro Committee would take a forthright stand in opposition to the policies and program of the Tuskegeean, and that the scheduled conference would sound a call for radical action.

Villard's espousal of the radical cause brought immediate reaction from Charles Anderson, who wrote to Washington's secretary, Emmett J. Scott, denying that he had ever regarded Villard as sympathetic to Washington's program, and voicing his fears that "certain white men" were attempting to "lessen the Doctor's influence."[40]

The Tuskegeeans, far from eschewing politics, were privately mourning their waning political power and prestige, and were taking counsel how best to meet a deteriorating situation in regard to the Republican Party and political patronage. Robert R. Moton, a good friend of Washington's, and head of the cadet corps at Hampton Normal and Agricultural Institute, urged Washington to try to influence Taft, who was making sweeping changes by replacing deserving Negroes with lily-white Republicans. "The actions of the President of the United States," wrote Moton, "may go a long ways to dishearten a people."[41]

Washington attempted to keep on good terms with Villard and invited him to speak at a meeting of the National Negro Business League. Villard replied that he was honored, but that he had become more radical and questioned Washington: "Are you really sure . . . you want me?"[42]

Villard was immersed in problems of permanent organization, which went hand in hand with plans for the National Negro Committee's annual conference. During the special meeting on April 7, at which the report of the Preliminary Committee was read,[43] the discussion centered on Milholland's proposal to merge with the Constitution League. His idea was to combine the two organizations in such a way as to preserve the name of The Constitution League of the United States. If the consolidated organization secured a federal charter combining both names, it would be easy for the League to turn over or merge its various state and other organizations. It was decided to submit Milholland's resolution to members of the whole Committee of Forty for a vote, recommending consolidation of the two organizations. Each was to retain its separate identity, and

[40] Anderson to Emmett J. Scott, April 11, 1910; April 19, 1910, Washington Papers.
[41] Robert Russa Moton to Washington, April 13, 1910, Washington Papers.
[42] Villard to Washington, May 11, 1910, Villard Papers.
[43] This report is not extant, but part of Du Bois's plan for organization submitted to the National Negro Committee on March 24, 1910, remains. Memorandum to [Walling], n.d., Du Bois Papers.

there would be an Executive Committee which would "organize other activities for the advancement of the colored people."[44]

Another special meeting was held on April 21, but the matter of consolidation with the Constitution League was not resolved. At the May 5 meeting, when the report of the Preliminary Committee was adopted for recommendation to the business session of the conference, the only reference to Milholland's organization was a recommendation to the effect that the work of the Constitution League be endorsed as filling the need for the proposed Legal Aid Bureau.[45] Thus, what was to become the most important phase of the Association's work was at this point relegated to another organization. The temporary arrangement did not, however, lead to a merger of the two groups. Milholland seems to have been the only one in favor of the merger, though opinions of other committee members are not recorded in the minutes. Mary White Ovington was on the Board of Directors of the Constitution League; Du Bois had been on the Board since 1907, but he was in Atlanta and unable to attend the meetings of the Committee of Forty.[46] When the NAACP was incorporated in June, 1911, all connections between the two organizations were severed.[47]

The Preliminary Committee's report recommended that the new organization be known as "The National Association for the Advancement of Colored People; its object to be equal rights and opportunities for all."[48] It was to be composed of a National Committee of 100 members, with an Executive Committee of 30 members elected from the National Committee. Of these, half were to be resident in New York City.[49]

[44] Minutes, Special Meeting, National Negro Committee, April 7, 1910, in Board Minutes, NAACP.

[45] Minutes, Special Meeting, National Negro Committee, April 21, 1910; May 5, 1910, in Board Minutes, NAACP.

[46] Ovington, "Beginnings of the N.A.A.C.P.," *Crisis*, XXXII (June, 1926), 76; Du Bois to A. B. Humphrey, Secretary of the Constitution League of the United States, May 2, 1907, Du Bois Papers.

[47] Villard to Washington, January 19, 1911, Villard Papers.

[48] It is possible that the idea for the name of the Association originated with Villard. He had used the term "Committee for the Advancement of the Negro Race" as early as September, 1908. He worked closely with the Garrisons in the formation of the Boston group known as the "Committee to Advance the Cause of the Negro." He was chairman of the Preliminary Committee on Permanent Organization that suggested the name, National Association for the Advancement of Colored People.

[49] Report of the Preliminary Committee on Permanent Organization, in Minutes, Special Meeting, National Negro Committee, May 5, 1910, in Board Minutes, NAACP. A suggestion made by Dr. Milton Waldron to move headquarters to Washington, D.C., in the hope of receiving more favorable publicity from that city was tabled, no doubt for the same reason that had prevented the conference from being held there. Minutes, Executive Session, May 14, 1910, in Board Minutes, NAACP.

The three major activities of the new organization (aside from legal aid) were to be mass meetings, investigation, and publicity. Public meetings were to be held in various cities for the purpose of discussing such subjects as peonage, public education, lynching, and injustice in the courts. Reports of these meetings were to be published and distributed by the Association as part of the publicity program. It was recommended that a full-time Department of Investigation be set up as soon as possible. Until funds became available, it was suggested that the organization rely on voluntary help for gathering data and for publicity, in the hope that volunteer workers would be somewhat compensated through the sale of articles based on the "novel and interesting" materials compiled for the Association. A member of the committee was to supervise this work, and articles were to be approved by a press committee before publication.

The Association was to expand its membership and to seek funds wherever a foothold had been established—in Boston, Philadelphia, Chicago, and Washington. Meetings could be held in those cities before the third annual conference and money secured for the services of a secretary and maintenance of a permanent headquarters. The special meeting, having adopted the report of the Preliminary Committee, adjourned, to reconvene on the first day of the conference, May 12, 1910.[50]

There were some encouraging signs that predicted success for the second annual conference. Walling was confident that widespread attention would be attracted because of the committee's association with the Pink Franklin case involving peonage.[51] Charles Chesnutt, who had declined an invitation to speak at the first conference, agreed to talk on the "Effect of Disfranchisement in the Courts,"[52] and Professor Hart of Harvard promised Villard that he would speak at the closing meeting.[53]

On the other hand, Albert E. Pillsbury, who was to be chairman of the sessions on Disfranchisement, sent a letter to Villard two days before the opening meeting, expressing the view that it was impossible to bring about the enfranchisement of the Negro, and that the group might as well abandon plans for work along this line. Villard was appalled. The letter seemed to represent a complete and absolute collapse on the part of Pillsbury. Villard's uncle, too, was completely astonished at what he called Pillsbury's "surrender."[54]

[50] Report of the Preliminary Committee on Permanent Organization, in Minutes, Special Meeting, National Negro Committee, May 5, 1910, in Board Minutes, NAACP.
[51] Walling to Mary Church Terrell, April 7, 1910, Mary Church Terrell Papers (Manuscript Division, Library of Congress). The Pink Franklin case and the Association's involvement in the case are described in the next chapter.
[52] Charles W. Chesnutt to William E. Walling, April 18, 1910, quoted in Helen M. Chesnutt, *Charles Waddell Chesnutt: Pioneer of the Color Line* (Chapel Hill, 1952), p. 235.
[53] Villard to Hart, May 3, 1910; Hart to Villard, May 16, 1910, Villard Papers.
[54] Villard to Garrison, May 10, 1910; Garrison to Villard, May 11, 1910, Villard Papers.

THE SECOND CONFERENCE

The Second Annual Conference opened on Thursday, May 12, 1910, at three
o'clock in the Charity Organization Hall in New York, with the resumption of
the meeting of the National Negro Committee, which had been adjourned on
May 5. At this time the final report of the Preliminary Committee on Permanent
Organization, with its recommendations as to name, objectives, composition, and
organization, was adopted. The permanent organization provided for a National
Committee to raise funds and give prestige to the organization. Moorfield Storey
was named president. It also provided for an Executive (or Working) Com-
mittee, consisting largely of the former Committee of Forty, or National Negro
Committee.[55] After adoption of the report, the Executive Committee selected
officers: Walling, Chairman; Milholland, Treasurer; and Villard, Assistant
Treasurer, or, as he was later called, Disbursing Treasurer.[56] The National
Association for the Advancement of Colored People was officially launched.

On Saturday morning May 14, William English Walling called to order an
executive session of the Association. The purpose of this meeting was to make
recommendations to the Executive Committee for study and action, since there
would not be another general meeting until the following year. Charles Edward
Russell, who had shown such skill in handling the stormy business session at
the close of the first conference, was chosen to preside.

The meeting recommended that there be a Secretary, Executive Secretary, and
Chairman of the Executive Committee, and that the Chairman of the Executive
Committee should be a salaried position, while the positions of Secretary and
Executive Secretary should be appointive.[57] This seemingly innocuous action
was in fact a complete change in emphasis and implementation of the program
that had been adopted two days before. At that time it had been recommended
that "first efforts be directed to securing funds . . . and as many members as
possible," that is, to consolidate and build up the organization, while the
publicity and investigation programs were carried on by volunteer workers.

Now, however, it was decided to concentrate on an aggressive campaign of publicity and investigation. This was not surprising considering that people like Wal-
ing, Russell, and Miss Ovington were activists by temperament and would naturally

---

[55] Minutes, National Negro Committee, May 12, 1910, in Board Minutes, NAACP. Though
the provisions called for an Executive Committee of 30 out of the General Committee of 100,
in December, 1910, when the names of the committees were printed on the cover of *The
Crisis*, there were only 66 on the "General Committee," and of these an Executive Committee
totaled 21. *Crisis*, I (December, 1910).
[56] See Appendix D for a list of the General (National) Committee, Executive Committee,
and Officers. See also Du Bois, "The National Association for the Advancement of Colored
People," *Horizon*, VI (July, 1910), 1.
[57] Minutes, Executive Session, May 14, 1910, in Board Minutes, NAACP.

43

be more interested in a program of action than in building the traditional type of organization. That Du Bois was their candidate for salaried Chairman of the Executive Committee is evident from Walling's statement, made many years later, that they had been able to do little until they had secured "the permanent interest of a colored leader of nationwide prominence, Dr. Du Bois." The avowed purpose of this maneuver, according to Walling, was that the organization itself must provide an example of successful interracial cooperation.[58]

On Walling's initiative Du Bois was engaged.[59] This marked the culmination of a tug-of-war that had been going on during the first year between the conservatives and radicals within the organization. With the coming of Du Bois, wrote Miss Ovington, "we nailed our banner to the mast. . . . From that time onward no one doubted where we stood."[60]

Miss Blascoer opposed this change of policy. She favored having the publicity and research done by volunteers until the organization was perfected and funds raised. She had been hired for this purpose and thought it would take at least a year to accomplish. At the Saturday morning meeting she had tried to prevent the reversal, but had been afraid that her attitude would be misinterpreted as concern for her own job and prestige. As a matter of fact, her determination to undertake nothing but organization work and her refusal to do publicity and research was interpreted as a refusal to work with Du Bois, an interpretation which she subsequently refuted in a lengthy letter to Du Bois.[61]

Other matters were called to the attention of the Executive Committee. It was recommended that membership in the Association be composed of the following classes: Life Members, $500; Donors, $100; Contributors, $2.00; Associates, $1.00. Membership was also to be open to groups such as clubs, lodges, and churches that might desire to join in a body.[62] Because of the pressing financial needs of the Association, it was also recommended that each member of the "National Committee of One Hundred" be pledged to raise $100 for the organization.

From the very beginning, the Association aligned itself with other oppressed minority groups, a policy which has continued down to the present. The so-called Russian Resolution of the 1910 conference protested and condemned the expulsion of Jews from Kiev.

[58] Walling, "The Founding of the N.A.A.C.P.," *Crisis*, XXXVI (July, 1929), 226.
[59] Ovington, "William English Walling," *Crisis*, XLIII (November, 1936), 335.
[60] Ovington, "Beginnings of the N.A.A.C.P.," 77.
[61] Blascoer to Du Bois, June 15, 1910, Du Bois Papers. Du Bois was not convinced of Miss Blascoer's sincerity (see Chapter III).
[62] Minutes, Executive Session, May 14, 1910, in Board Minutes, NAACP. The idea of life membership was introduced here, but not until much later was any effort made to enroll life members. The report of the Committee on Preliminary Organization had also provided for three classes of "Auxiliary Memberships," at $100, $10, and $2. Minutes, Special Meeting, National Negro Committee, May 5, 1910, in Board Minutes, NAACP.

After reaffirming the platform of the 1909 conference demanding equal civil, educational, and voting rights for Negroes in all parts of the United States, the executive session adjourned until the following year.[63]

There was detailed coverage of the conference in Villard's *New York Evening Post* and an editorial regarding it in *The Nation*. The other papers were silent on the subject, a fact which Villard attributed to Booker T. Washington, who was in New York at the time. The *Sun* had sent reporters to the conference and had accepted prepared copy but had printed instead an interview with Washington. In Boston, on the same page with the story of the conference, the *Transcript* printed an optimistic report on conditions in the South written by Washington.[64]

In contrast to the vitriolic and distorted account which it had printed about the 1909 conference, the *New York Age* printed all the news of the 1910 conference from the *Washington Post* as well as Villard's *Evening Post* editorial. Editorially, however, the *Age* concentrated on the claim that Clarence Darrow and Professor Franz Boas, Columbia University anthropologist, had advocated intermarriage. The *Age* was certain that no good could come "in agitating such a question."[65] Villard, too, was privately critical of Darrow's "sweeping assertions," although he admitted his feelings were not shared by many of his socialist co-workers. The applause for Darrow, he reported to his uncle, was tumultuous.[66]

The first conference had concerned itself with scientific refutation of erroneous popular beliefs about the Negro. The theme of the second, Disfranchisement, had included: the use of the Negro vote for the candidate who would champion his cause, rather than blind devotion to one party; the need for vigorous efforts to reduce Southern representation in Congress to counteract violations of the Fourteenth and Fifteenth Amendments; the effect of disfranchisment on common school education in the South; and the relationship of disfranchisement to lynching.[67]

[63] Minutes, Executive Session, May 14, 1910, in Board Minutes, NAACP.
[64] *New York Evening Post*, May 13, 14, 16, 21, 1910; *Nation*, XC (May 19, 1910), 501–2; Villard to Garrison, May 17, 1910, Villard Papers; *Boston Evening Transcript*, May 14, 1910.
[65] *New York Age*, May 19, 1910.
[66] "The most ardent workers who are really accomplishing something, Miss Ovington, Miss Blascoer, Walling, Mrs. Maclean, etc., are all Socialists." Villard to Garrison, May 17, 1910, Villard Papers.
[67] Principal speakers were Clarence Darrow, New York Congressman William S. Bennet, Ray Stannard Baker, Reverdy Ransom, Mrs. Ida Wells-Barnett, Albert E. Pillsbury, John Haynes Holmes, W. E. B. Du Bois, Moorfield Storey, Charles Chesnutt, Jacob Schiff, John Dewey, Kelly Miller, Horace Bumstead, Professor Hart, Franz Boas, and Mrs. Mary Church Terrell. "Program, National Negro Committee, Second Annual Conference, New York, May 12–14, 1910," in Du Bois Papers. Texts of some of the speeches appeared in the *Boston Transcript*, May 13, and 14, 1910; the *New York Evening Post*, May 13, 14, 16, and 21, 1910; and the *New York Age*, May 19, 1910.

CHAPTER III

First Undertakings

On May 25, 1910, less than two weeks after the Second Annual Conference, the Executive Committee of the NAACP took steps to perfect the organization and implement recommendations made at the executive session of the conference. The minutes of the Executive Committee meeting indicate that it was Villard who provided direction and ideas. Nearly every action was initiated by him.

The committee first concerned itself with leadership of the organization. We have seen that a major change of policy took place at the executive session of the conference, emphasizing the propaganda program under Du Bois rather than fund raising and organizational work under the direction of Frances Blascoer. At the May 25 meeting, the Executive Committee took up a recommendation to appoint a paid national secretary, who should also be chairman of the Executive Committee, and a secretary to carry on the office routine. This varies from the recommendation recorded at the executive session of the conference calling for an appointed executive secretary and a salaried chairman of the Executive Committee. What had originally been two separate positions was now referred to as a single position (the national secretary would also be chairman of the Executive Committee). Whether this change of wording was the result of a stenographic error or represented a change in thinking is not clear. In any event, the first action at the May 25 meeting was another drastic alteration in the functions and titles of these positions. On Villard's motion, the title national secretary was changed to "director of publicity and research," as distinct from the chairman of the Executive Committee. The incumbent "secretary" (Miss Blascoer), or "executive secretary" as she was sometimes called, was to carry on all the organizational work until a "national secretary" could be appointed.[1]

[1] Minutes, Executive Committee, May 25, 1910, in "Minute Book of the Board of Directors of the National Association for the Advancement of Colored People" (now in the Manuscript

The object of this maneuver was clearly to create a position for Du Bois in which he could carry on his program of publicity and research and at the same time be relieved of his duties as chairman of the Executive Committee. The renting of two offices was authorized—one for the director of publicity and research, the other for the secretary. The latter was to be known as the "Executive Office of the Association."[2] Although the separate offices were set up on Villard's motion, Frances Blascoer's influence was obvious. She threatened to resign if she were expected to do other than organizational work.[3]

The next step was to guarantee a year's salary for Du Bois so that he could be brought to New York as soon as possible. Walling wrote to him the following month, "the whole effort and hope of our Committee is built almost exclusively on obtaining you as our director of its investigations."[4]

The committee undertook to raise money in several ways. Plans to approach philanthropists for large gifts were shelved until autumn; the wealthy citizens of New York and Boston had already left for the summer. The alternative was to secure immediate pledges from the Committee of One Hundred. A special committee, composed of Miss Ovington, the treasurer, and the secretary, was ordered to draw up a budget on the basis of which members of the Committee of One Hundred would be asked to raise money. Another source of funds was to be from memberships. A third device was the publication and sale of the speeches of the second conference in the form of pamphlets, which could also be used for promotional literature.[5]

A subcommittee was appointed to consider the names of colored people to fill vacancies on the Committee of One Hundred.[6] This was the primary concern of the next meeting, which took place in June. The subcommittee voted on the names individually, electing fourteen colored and two white members. Dr. C. E. Bentley, a Negro dentist of Chicago, was added to the Executive Committee. In line with Walling's intention of drawing more Negroes into active work in the Association, it was decided that no more white members should be chosen before fall.[7]

Division, Library of Congress; hereafter referred to as Board Minutes, NAACP). Present at this meeting were: Walling, Mrs. Wells-Barnett, Mrs. F. R. Keyser, Mrs. Maclean, Miss Ovington, Villard, Bulkley, Brooks, and O. M. Waller.
[2] *Ibid.* The Executive Office was to be in the *Evening Post* building at a rent of $260 per year.
[3] Frances Blascoer to W. E. B. Du Bois, June 15, 1910, W. E. B. Du Bois Papers (now in the possession of Mrs. W. E. B. Du Bois, New York City).
[4] William English Walling to Du Bois, June 9, 1910, Du Bois Papers.
[5] *Ibid.*; Minutes, Executive Committee, May 25, 1910, in Board Minutes, NAACP.
[6] Minutes, Executive Committee, May 25, 1910, in Board Minutes, NAACP. The subcommittee was composed of O. M. Waller, Mrs. Keyser, and Miss M. R. Lyons.
[7] Minutes, Executive Committee, June 7, 1910, in Board Minutes, NAACP. Present were: Walling, Holmes, Kennaday, Russell, Sinclair, Mossell, Villard, Mrs. Keyser, Mrs. Maclean,

The financial situation remained critical. It is an indication of the temper of the times that "among the descendants of the Boston abolitionists only one of means" (Mrs. W. H. Forbes of Milton, Massachusetts) displayed an interest in the cause.[8] Though Villard had earlier visualized a million-dollar endowment, he now proposed that they aim for $10,000 to ensure the proper functioning of the executive work as well as the work of the publicity and investigation department. Another meeting was set for the end of June in the hope that the Committee of One Hundred would supply enough contributions so that Du Bois could begin his work.[9]

Walling explained to Du Bois that his salary could not be guaranteed beyond the first year, but Du Bois indicated his willingness to accept any reasonable risk for the privilege of engaging in work of such paramount and critical importance.[10] It was a decisive moment in his career. In a way, no matter how uncertain the future of the new organization seemed, Du Bois was being rescued from a "series of recent failures."[11] At Atlanta University, where financial support came from philanthropists more inclined to agree with Booker T. Washington's accommodating attitude to the white South than with Du Bois's philosophy of agitation and protest, his position was becoming increasingly uncomfortable.[12] His efforts at "scientific" research had not been wholly acceptable to scholars. Although his articles had once been published in general periodicals, by 1910 only *The Independent* was receptive to his work. His attempt to organize an effective protest in the Niagara Movement had been far from successful, and his outspoken criticism of Booker T. Washington was costing him his Negro audience.[13] There was every reason therefore why Du Bois should accept Walling's offer. He began at once to make suggestions regarding the scope of his new work.[14]

---

and Miss Ovington. The fourteen elected were: James Wolf, Boston; Harry Smith, Editor of the *Cleveland Gazette;* E. Justin Carter, Harrisburg; George W. Crawford, New Haven lawyer; William H. Pickens, Alabama; George Wibecan, Brooklyn; Edward Everett Brown, Boston; Dr. Wheatland; Professor Moore, Howard University; Hon. William F. Powell, New Jersey; the Rev. John H. White, Augusta, Georgia; Mrs. J. S. Yates, Kansas City, Missouri; Mrs. W. H. Clifford, Ohio and Washington; and Mrs. Talbott, Buffalo. The two white people elected were: Col. N. P. Hallowell, Boston; President W. P. Thirkield, Howard University.
[8] Francis Jackson Garrison to Oswald Garrison Villard, June 2, 1910, Oswald Garrison Villard Papers (Houghton Library, Harvard University).
[9] Minutes, Executive Committee, June 7, 1910, in Board Minutes, NAACP.
[10] Walling to Du Bois, June 9, 1910; Du Bois to Walling, June 23, 1910, Du Bois Papers.
[11] Francis L. Broderick, *W. E. B. Du Bois: Negro Leader in a Time of Crisis* (Stanford 1959), p. 89.
[12] Du Bois, *Dusk of Dawn: An Essay Toward An Autobiography of a Race Concept* (New York, 1940), p. 93.
[13] Broderick, *W. E. B. Du Bois,* pp. 55–62.
[14] Du Bois to Walling, June 23, 1910; June 27, 1910, Du Bois Papers.

At the June 28 meeting the committee voted to engage Du Bois on October 1, and Mrs. Maclean wired him that there was great enthusiasm for his proposed program.[15] Miss Blascoer showed none of Mrs. Maclean's cordiality. She felt called upon to explain the position she had taken at the conference. Some committee members had misinterpreted her actions, believing that she opposed the engaging of Du Bois for fear of losing her own position or that she refused to work with him because of his color. Du Bois was not convinced. He later wrote: "The secretary then in charge was alarmed about her own job. . . . I placated [her] by disclaiming any design or desire for executive work."[16]

This misunderstanding between officials boded ill for the success of the Association. While Miss Blascoer tried to convince Du Bois that she wanted nothing to do with publicity and research, Du Bois claimed that he wanted nothing to do with executive work. But in some ways the two jobs overlapped. Miss Blascoer took trips to various cities to organize committees and increase membership. So did Du Bois—and it was Du Bois who formulated and spread the philosophy of the organization and became an inspiration to thousands of Negroes. The part that Villard played in the misunderstanding between Miss Blascoer and Du Bois is not clear. He wanted to amass funds and build a substantial membership first, and in this he appeared to support Miss Blascoer. At the same time he threw all his weight behind the launching of *The Crisis*, and in this he seemed to support Du Bois, in spite of previous friction between them.

THE CRISIS

Du Bois, as director of publicity and research, did not wait until October but took up his work about the middle of July. His first project was the publication of a magazine, which would be the official organ of the Association.[17] At the 1910 conference George Wibecan, a newspaper man and Negro leader of Brooklyn, had urged the establishment of such an organ.[18] Du Bois, who had edited first *The Moon* and then *The Horizon*, believed this means of propaganda vital to a successful protest movement.[19] A few years later, in her pamphlet on the origins of the NAACP, Miss Ovington told the story of the naming of the magazine. While "sitting around the conventional table that seems a necessary adjunct to every Board [and] having an informal talk regarding the new maga-

---

[15] Minutes, Executive Committee, June 28, 1910, in Board Minutes, NAACP; Mary Dunlop Maclean to Du Bois, telegram, June 28, 1910, Du Bois Papers.

[16] Blascoer to Du Bois, June 30, 1910, Du Bois Papers; Du Bois, *Dusk of Dawn*, p. 225.

[17] Du Bois to Dean Edward T. Ware, Atlanta University, August 1, 1910; Du Bois to Walling, August 16, 1910; August 24, 1910, Du Bois Papers; *Washington Bee*, July 16, 1910; *Horizon*, VI (July, 1910), 1–3.

[18] Minutes, Executive Session, May 14, 1910, in Board Minutes, NAACP.

[19] Du Bois, *Dusk of Dawn*, pp. 92–93.

zine," she happened to mention "The Present Crisis," a poem by James Russell Lowell. "There is the name for your magazine," said Walling—"*The Crisis.*"[20]

The informal talk described by Miss Ovington must have taken place some time between the middle of July and August 16, the date of Du Bois's first use of the title.[21] During the early years of the Association, business was transacted informally. Executive Committee members stopped in at the offices almost daily to give of their time and services. With a majority of the Committee living in New York it was easy to reach consensus by telephone or through the informal gatherings at headquarters. Consequently few records were kept of decisions made.[22]

On August 19, Du Bois wrote Walling, who was on vacation, that Villard was enthusiastic about his plans for a publication, but first he wanted approval of the Executive Committee. With Villard's assurance that his plan would be approved, Du Bois decided to wait for the next Executive Committee meeting. He was sure the Committee would be in perfect agreement with his plans.[23] A few days later, he was shocked to discover that the next regular meeting of the Executive Committee was not until October 11. This seemed too long a delay, and he again wrote Walling, asking him to urge Villard that they begin publication October 1.[24] He also asked Walling to write to Albert Pillsbury, who had a low opinion of periodicals. According to Pillsbury, newspapers were the sole effective means of dispensing propaganda. Periodicals were "pestilential . . . as flies in Egypt." But Pillsbury, who had predicted gloomily two days before the opening of the second conference that Negro enfranchisement was an impossibility, was a poor prophet. No one, Pillsbury least of all, could have foreseen the impact this pestilential periodical was to have on the colored world. By the end of its first year of publication, *The Crisis* could boast of more than 10,000 readers. By the end of its tenth year, its circulation was more than 100,000.[25]

[20]Mary White Ovington, *How the National Association for the Advancement of Colored People Began*, pamphlet (New York, 1914), p. 5.
[21] Du Bois to Walling, August 16, 1910, Du Bois Papers.
[22] Interview with Miss Richetta Randolph (Mrs. Frank Wallace), July 18, 1957. Miss Randolph had been secretary to Mary White Ovington when the latter was engaged in social work in Brooklyn before the formation of the NAACP. She informed the writer that the NAACP had no office staff from 1910 until 1918 save F. M. Turner, who acted as secretary to Dr. Du Bois and later as bookkeeper for the Association. During this period, Miss Randolph from time to time gave assistance to Miss Ovington and the volunteer workers while conducting a secretarial and stenographic service of her own. Due to a lack of office staff, records for this period, aside from the official board minutes, are almost nonexistent. Moreover, when Du Bois left the NAACP he took all his files with him. In 1918, Miss Randolph became office manager and private secretary to the executive secretary. She held this position until her retirement during Walter White's administration.
[23] Du Bois to Walling, August 19, 1910, Du Bois Papers.
[24] Du Bois to Walling, August 24, 1910, Du Bois Papers.
[25] Pillsbury to Du Bois, July 26, 1910, Du Bois Papers. In June, 1919, circulation went to 104,000. Board Minutes, NAACP, July 11, 1919. Average monthly circulation during 1919 was 94,908, with a total for the year of 1,138,900. *Crisis*, XIX (February, 1920), 198–99.

At Du Bois's urging, a special meeting of the Executive Committee was called at the new headquarters to give official approval to the proposed magazine. The subject matter was to deal with the race question and important news of the day. Du Bois estimated that the cost would be $50 a month for 1,000 copies. (The first issue contained only sixteen pages, about seven by ten inches in size.) The Committee decided that the first number should appear in November and that the copy should be submitted to all members of the Executive Committee for approval in order to establish a well-defined policy before presentation to the public.[26]

With the publication of *The Crisis* assured, Du Bois's journal, *The Horizon,* informed its subscribers that it was suspending circulation and that unexpired subscriptions would be filled by *The Crisis.*[27] Thus the new venture had the advantage of beginning with a small group of subscribers.

By the time of the regular meeting in October, Du Bois had mailed copies of proposed editorials of the first issue to the Committee, and the entire layout was ready for inspection. Villard made suggestions concerning the contents. To ensure firm control by the Executive Committee, he secured approval for the appointment of a subcommittee on publication (officers of the Association to be members ex officio) and of another subcommittee for dealing with the finances of the magazine.[28]

A prospectus, proclaiming *The Crisis* to be the official organ of the NAACP, listed six contributors in addition to the editor: Villard of the *Evening Post*; Charles Edward Russell, "the well-known magazine writer"; Kelly Miller, "author and critic"; Mrs. Mary Dunlop Maclean, a staff writer on the *New York Times*; J. Max Barber, former editor of *The Voice of the Negro*; and William Stanley Braithwaite, "poet and writer of international reputation."[29]

One thousand copies of the first issue of *The Crisis* were printed. Its expressed objective was "to set forth those facts and arguments which show the danger of race prejudice, particularly as manifested to-day toward colored people." It was to be first and foremost a news organ, with short articles, reviews of opinion and literature, and editorials standing for the rights of men, irrespective of color or race. *The Crisis* would be the organ of no clique or party and would avoid personal rancor of all sorts.

[26] Minutes, Executive Committee, special meeting, September 6, 1910, in Board Minutes, NAACP. Du Bois was still seeking estimates at the end of September. Du Bois to Robert A. Wood, printer, September 30, 1910, Du Bois Papers.
[27] F. Morris Murray to Du Bois, September, 1910, a printed postal card sent to subscribers of *The Horizon,* Du Bois Papers.
[28] Minutes, Executive Committee, October 11, 1910, in Board Minutes, NAACP. At this meeting John Haynes Holmes was elected vice-chairman of the Executive Committee.
[29] "The Crisis—Prospectus," pamphlet [New York, 1910].

The first issue described the movement that had resulted in the formation of the NAACP. It gave the names of the officers of the Association and made a plea for $10,000 to meet the expenses of the current year. It announced that the organization planned a systematic study of conditions among Negroes, that it would issue pamphlets and publish articles in magazines other than *The Crisis*, hold conferences and mass meetings, cooperate with other agencies working for the welfare of colored people, and help to discover and redress cases of injustice.

There were six "departments:" "Along the Color Line," a feature which had appeared in both *The Moon* and *The Horizon*; "Opinion"; "Editorial"; "The N.A.A.C.P." (brief notes concerning the activities of the Association); "The Burden," comprising descriptions of flagrant cases of injustice based on discrimination because of color; and "What to Read," a discussion of current books dealing with various aspects of the Negro problem.[30]

The first issue of *The Crisis* more than paid for itself and the Committee on Publication recommended doubling the number of pages.[31] Beginning with the second number, Mrs. John E. Milholland wrote a series of articles entitled "Talks About Women," in which she discussed the changing status of women in business, industry, and the professions. She urged colored women to expand their efforts and interests from their own circle and race and to join the larger movement—the struggle for women's rights and more particularly for the ballot.[32] Here again, after a lapse of many years, we see that the "new abolitionists" were interested, as were the old abolitionists, in other reform movements. One of Du Bois's first speeches in his official NAACP capacity was delivered at the Peace Conference at Greenacre, Maine.[33] In *The Crisis* and in his lectures, he did his best to bring the Negro movement into the main current of humanitarian reform.

RIVALRIES AND CONTROVERSIES

By November, the *Washington Bee*, a Negro newspaper, could no longer ignore the existence of the NAACP and its new periodical. The *Bee*, in an attempt to discredit the Association and Du Bois, pointed to the fate of former movements devoted to the advancement of the Negro. The editor sarcastically commented

---

[30] *Crisis*, I (November, 1910), 10, 12.
[31] "The Crisis," a printed circular for agents [New York, March, 1911], Du Bois Papers. This shows the increase in circulation as follows: November—1,000; December—2,500; January —3,000; February—4,000.
[32] *Crisis*, I (December, 1910), 28.
[33] Du Bois to the Reverend John B. Hayes, November 19, 1910, Du Bois Papers; Minutes, Executive Committee, November 29, 1910, in Board Minutes, NAACP.

that *The Horizon* had overshadowed *The Moon*, and that Du Bois was now confronted with a *Crisis*. The *Bee* accused Du Bois and his magazine of being under the control of a large committee of white people. He could talk only when this committee told him to talk, write only what this committee instructed him to write, and could go and come only when this committee told him to go and come.[34]

The Crisis had stated that first and foremost it was to function as a newspaper, and fear of a rival publication financed by white people had much to do with the tirade in the *Bee*.[35] The problem of white leadership and white control was to haunt the work of the Association for many years. Scarcity of positions of prestige for colored men in those days led to intense rivalry among Negroes "within the Veil,"[36] as Du Bois phrased it, as well as to resentment of white leadership. Jealousy of Du Bois led the *Bee* to appeal to race prejudice by alleging that Du Bois was a white man's lackey.

In addition to publishing *The Crisis*, Du Bois was active in other ways. He gave speeches in New York and other cities, wrote magazine and newspaper articles, published two pamphlets for the Association, and began planning a study of Negro education in the South. He also found time to develop a program for volunteer workers, in which members of the committee were invited to cooperate. They were to get subscriptions for *The Crisis*, write letters to newspapers and public men, write articles, correspond with white or colored persons in the South, do library research on the race problem, lead parlor talks and make speeches, help with the clerical work, collect significant clippings and information, conduct "missionary propaganda" among workers and the poor whites of the South, solicit funds, and make personal contributions.[37] By implementing this plan, the Association was able to mobilize and maintain over a period of years many volunteer workers of outstanding ability.[38]

To spread the movement as quickly as possible, the Executive Committee authorized mass meetings in Chicago, Cleveland, and Buffalo. In Cleveland, Charles Chesnutt told Walling that he could not think of a half-dozen white people who would take an active, not to say an aggressive, part in the movement. Nevertheless, the Chesnutts gave a reception in their home, and the Wallings met the leaders of Cleveland's Negro community there and discussed the possibility of organizing. Charles F. Thwing, president of Western Reserve University

[34] *Washington Bee*, November 5, 1910; November 12, 1910.
[35] *Crisis*, I (November, 1910), 12.
[36] Du Bois, *The Souls of Black Folk*, Premier Americana ed. (Greenwich, Connecticut, 1961), p. 153.
[37] Du Bois to the Reverend John B. Hayes, November 19, 1910, Du Bois Papers.
[38] Arthur B. Spingarn stated that in the early days all of the Board members gave freely of their time in the office, and he estimated that he contributed "half and probably more" of his own time to the cause. Interview with A. B. Spingarn, New York City, September 26, 1956.

and one of the signers of the 1909 Lincoln's Birthday "Call," invited the Wallings to repeat their talks at the University—presumably the first time the Association's program was formally presented to an American college audience.[39]

January 6, 1911, marked the one-hundredth anniversary of the birth of Charles Sumner, the abolitionist. The Sumner Centennial came close to causing serious dissension among race leaders. Du Bois had engaged Faneuil Hall for the January 6 celebration without consulting the Boston Committee. Nor did he seek the cooperation of Boston Negro leader Trotter, whose wrangling over the wording of the resolutions had been one of the chief causes of dissension at the 1909 conference. Trotter deeply resented Du Bois's action and was determined to hold a celebration of his own under the auspices of the New England Suffrage League, of which he was president. The Boston Committee decided that the matter was not worth arguing about and readily agreed to accept Trotter's offer to invite the National Committee to speak as guests at his meeting. Moorfield Storey and his group recommended that Trotter's invitation be accepted, or that the National Committee hold its own celebration in New York.[40]

This was a sensible solution to a trivial matter, but the three strong and difficult personalities involved, Du Bois, Trotter, and Villard, were either unwilling or unable to submerge themselves for the good of the cause. Throughout his career Du Bois found it almost impossible to work closely with his fellowmen, black or white. He and Villard had already clashed violently over the review of his book, and within a few years they were to fall out over the editorial policy of *The Crisis*. Eventually the friction between them led to Villard's withdrawal from active participation in the Association for many years. Trotter, always suspicious of whites and their motives, sulked on the outskirts of the NAACP. Perhaps his attitude was influenced by jealousy of Du Bois's prominence and success as a race leader. Trotter, too, was an individualist who had difficulty in getting along with other Negro personalities.

Villard was determined to challenge Trotter's leadership in the Boston area, but his uncle, Francis Garrison, warned him against making an issue of a small point and advertising another squabble among the race leaders, and Storey pointed out that harmonious cooperation among friends of the race movement was more important than celebrating the Sumner Centennial.[41]

---

[39] Minutes, Executive Committee, September 6, 1910; November 29, 1910, in Board Minutes, NAACP; Charles W. Chesnutt to Walling, October 13, 1910, quoted in Helen M. Chesnutt, *Charles Waddell Chesnutt: Pioneer of the Color Line* (Chapel Hill, 1952), pp. 239–40.
[40] Du Bois to Walling, August 16, 1910, fragment of a letter, Du Bois Papers; Moorfield Storey to Du Bois, October 29, 1910; November 19, 1910, Moorfield Storey Papers (in the possession of Mr. Charles Storey, Boston, Massachusetts); Garrison to Villard, November 19, 1910, Villard Papers.
[41] *Ibid.*; Storey to Du Bois, October 20, 1910; November 19, 1910, Storey Papers.

Since Garrison and Storey so strongly opposed challenging Trotter's leadership in Boston, there was little Villard and Du Bois could do but bow to their judgment. Villard yielded grudgingly, reluctant to establish what he considered a very dangerous precedent. He was convinced that sooner or later they would have to fight Trotter in his own territory.[42] The event was not to pass without further hostility.

In New York City there were no less than three anniversary meetings. One was the NAACP memorial celebration on January 6 at the Ethical Culture Society. John Lovejoy Elliot, an instructor at the Society and a descendant of Elijah P. Lovejoy the abolitionist, presided. A number of prominent sponsors (Vice-Presidents of the Meeting) were listed on the program,[43] among them philanthropists and business men who had long been supporters of Booker T. Washington and the Tuskegee Institute—Robert C. Ogden, Seth Low, Jacob H. Schiff, and Mr. and Mrs. J. G. Phelps-Stokes—as well as Charles W. Anderson,[44] who kept Booker T. Washington informed of what was going on.

Anderson had accepted Villard's invitation to act as a Vice-President of the Sumner meeting at the Ethical Culture Society with some hesitation and felt obliged to explain his action to Washington. He made it clear that he was doing all in his power to prevent defections to the new movement. "If the Atlanta crowd gets ahead of me, they will have the sweat brought to their brows," he wrote Washington. He reported that the hall was only two-thirds full. The speeches were monotonous, the applause was stinted, the entire meeting lacked fire and enthusiasm. He suspected that many of those present were there because Harry T. Burleigh, the famous Negro baritone, was to sing. According to Anderson, the names of only three or four Negroes appeared on the list of Vice-Presidents, and most of the white people whose names were on the list failed to attend the meeting. But he was worried that Jacob Schiff's "ringing telegram" to the meeting indicated friendliness to the movement.[45]

A rival meeting was held the same night at St. James' Church in Harlem. The organizer and chief speaker was Roscoe Simmons, a distant relative of Mrs.

---

[42] Villard to Garrison, November 21, 1910, Villard Papers.
[43] Blascoer to Joel E. Spingarn, December 27, 1910, in Joel Elias Spingarn Papers (Moorland Foundation, Howard University); *Crisis*, I (February, 1911), 5; "Programme—A Memorial Meeting to Charles Sumner, 1811–January 6, 1911," Du Bois Papers.
[44] *New York Sun*, December 27, 1910, clipping in a letter of Anderson to Booker T. Washington, December 29, 1910, Booker T. Washington Papers (Manuscript Division, Library of Congress). The other Vice-Presidents of the Meeting were: George McAneny, William G. McAdoo, Edward M. Shepard, Paul M. Warburg, Lillian D. Wald, V. Everit Macy, John Bigelow, Herman Rider, Dr. William H. Maxwell, Lincoln Steffens, Charles W. Anderson, John Haynes Holmes, Rabbi Stephen S. Wise, Major General Daniel E. Sickles.
[45] Charles W. Anderson to Washington, December 29, 1910; January 7, 1911, Washington Papers.

Booker T. Washington. He had earlier reported to Washington that the Negroes of New York had been entirely ignored by Villard and his "angels." They were "howling" because they were accustomed to making their own arrangements and intended to do so this time. Simmons informed Washington that there were 250 present at the "white folks' meeting," only 25 of whom were colored, but at his own meeting on the same night, the church was filled and every prominent Negro in town was present—except Anderson. Simmons wrote Washington that his slogan of "Negro leaders for Negro people" was heartily endorsed by the congregation, and "on all sides the colored men, those in the streets even, are beginning to pierce Villard's sham."[46]

A third New York gathering was held two days later in the afternoon and evening of January 8 at Reverdy C. Ransom's church. Du Bois spoke in the afternoon. "His crowd was not very large," Anderson reported. The *New York Times'* account was not flattering, and Anderson boasted that he had something to do with this, as the managing editor was a friend of his of long standing. He claimed that he had been able to counteract Ransom and Du Bois. "I am fully convinced . . . that however much these fellows may preach hysteria, the plain people are ready to receive sound doctrine." The Wizard, as Washington was called by his admirers, was delighted with Anderson's recital. He was interested to see "how this little crowd falls down every time it attempts to do some essentially big thing. . . . These fellows will be troublesome for a few months, but will soon wear themselves out."[47]

The antagonism centering around the Sumner celebration was just one more phase of the bitter controversy developing between the NAACP and Washington.

THE PINK FRANKLIN CASE AND OTHERS

In the meantime, the Association concerned itself with legal cases, involving peonage, extradition, and police brutality. Behind the scenes Villard found it expedient to call on Booker T. Washington for help in the solution of one of them.

The first case of real significance undertaken by the Association was the peonage case of Pink Franklin. At the time of the founding of the NAACP the majority of Negroes of the country lived in the South, and of these three-quarters

[46] Roscoe C. Simmons to Washington, December 27, 1910; January 9, 1911, Washington Papers. For the relationship of Roscoe Simmons to Mrs. Washington, see Anderson to Washington, June 5, 1911, Washington Papers. The *New York Age* reported few Negroes present at the NAACP meeting and maintained that the colored people were at the "other meetings." *New York Age,* January 12, 1911.
[47] Anderson to Washington, January 9, 1911; Washington to Anderson, January 4, 1911; January 10, 1911, Washington Papers. For political overtones see chapter on Booker T. Washington.

were landless, working for very low wages or under a sharecropping system that resulted in virtual bondage to creditors. It was difficult for Negroes to acquire land even if they had money. The dominant race considered land their only important capital investment and did not wish Negroes to enjoy the power that came from ownership of land in the South.[48]

Franklin was an illiterate Negro farmhand. A warrant had been sworn out for his arrest under a South Carolina statute making it a crime for a farm worker to leave his employer after receiving advances on his wages, although the Supreme Court of South Carolina had previously declared this statute to be in violation of the State Constitution and in conflict with the Thirteenth and Fourteenth Amendments to the Constitution of the United States.[49]

In serving the warrant, an officer named Valentine and his assistant went to Franklin's cabin before daylight with drawn revolvers and entered the bedroom occupied by Franklin, his wife Sad Franklin, and his small son, without announcing their purpose. Valentine was completely unknown to Franklin. A number of shots were fired and all save the child were wounded. Valentine died a few hours later. Pink Franklin and his wife narrowly escaped lynching and were indicted for murder. Two colored lawyers had charge of their defense. The woman was acquitted but Franklin was found guilty and sentenced to be executed. The case was appealed to the State Supreme Court, where the conviction was upheld. A writ of error was then obtained to the United States Supreme Court.[50]

At this point, the Constitution League asked Charles J. Bonaparte, former Attorney General of the United States under Theodore Roosevelt, to argue the case. Bonaparte found that the defense had been so inadequate and imperfect that he was afraid the Supreme Court would not find sufficient grounds to review the actions of the State Courts, but he agreed to take the case provided he had complete charge. The two Negro lawyers, however, refused to give up the case because of the publicity they hoped would ensue from arguing a case in the Supreme Court. Bonaparte thereupon withdrew, turning over to the Negro lawyers the brief he had already prepared.[51]

The first indication that the NAACP was interested was Villard's effort in March, 1910, to influence the Associated Press in publicizing the issues involved.

[48] C. Vann Woodward, *Origins of the New South 1877–1913*, Vol. IX of *A History of the South*, pp. 206–7; John Hope Franklin, *From Slavery to Freedom: A History of American Negroes*, 2d ed. (New York, 1956), p. 391.

[49] [Charles J. Bonaparte] to [Villard, August 1, 1910], Villard Papers. For date, Bonaparte's authorship, and Villard as recipient see Villard to Washington, August 4, 1910; Villard to John Palmer Gavit, March 25, 1910, Villard Papers. A brief summary of the case also appears in *Crisis*, I (November, 1910), 14; *Crisis*, I (December, 1910), 26.

[50] [Bonaparte] to [Villard, August 1, 1910], Villard Papers.

[51] Villard to Gavit, March 25, 1910; [Bonaparte] to [Villard, August 1, 1910], Villard Papers.

The importance of the case lay in forcing an opinion from the Supreme Court which, according to Villard, had for years evaded all questions relating to the rights of the Negro as a citizen, and in determining whether serfdom could be legally established in the United States.[52]

In May, 1910, however, the Supreme Court affirmed the decision of the lower courts, holding that Franklin had not been denied any of his constitutional rights. "This is a terrible blow," Villard confided to his uncle, "since it will encourage the whole South to go ahead with its peonage business."[53]

Time was fast running out for Pink Franklin. Pillsbury advised that a petition be prepared requesting commutation of the sentence, and Villard in desperation appealed to Booker T. Washington (whom he had formerly accused of misusing his political influence), to utilize his connections to help bring about a commutation of the sentence. "A word from Mr. Roosevelt would help," wrote Villard.[54]

Washington advised employing one of the strongest white lawyers in South Carolina to take the case directly to the governor, but Villard reported there was no money for this.[55] Washington also suggested seeking the help of the Reverend Richard Carroll, who, claimed Washington, had tremendous influence with Southern whites as well as with the mayors and state officials of South Carolina.[56]

Following this exchange of letters, Robert C. Ogden brought pressure to bear on the governor of South Carolina on behalf of Franklin. Since Ogden's correspondence with Washington shows that he sought and followed the latter's advice in matters concerning race relations in the South, it is hard to imagine that he would have taken this step unless Washington had suggested it or at least approved of the idea.[57]

Villard secured the help of Charles Dyer Norton, Assistant Treasurer of the United States, who had married into the Garrison family, in persuading President Taft to write a strong letter to Governor Martin F. Ansel, urging careful in-

[52] Villard to Gavit, March 25, 1910; Villard to "Aunt T" [Mrs. F. J. Garrison], April 22, 1910, Villard Papers.
[53] New York Evening Post, May 31, 1910; Villard to Garrison, June 1, 1910, Villard Papers.
[54] Pillsbury to Du Bois, July 26, 1910, Du Bois Papers; Villard to Washington, August 4, 1910, Villard Papers.
[55] Villard to Washington, August 12, 1910, Washington Papers. During the early years of the Association, it was not uncommon for white Southern attorneys to demand excessive fees. This was to be expected in the South, where risk of economic boycott, social ostracism, and even physical assault was high. Interview with A. B. Spingarn, New York City, July 27, 1956.
[56] Villard already knew Carroll, whom he had introduced to his uncle as "one of the most interesting colored men . . . I know." He suggested that Garrison ask Carroll "about his white father and relatives and his friendship with Senator Tillman." Villard to Garrison, November 21, 1905; Washington to Villard, August 9, 1910, Villard Papers.
[57] Crisis, I (February, 1911), 15. See the Ogden correspondence in Washington Papers.

vestigation to prevent a miscarriage of justice. Villard was also successful in getting several white lawyers in the South to intercede with the Governor.[58]

The colored lawyers again appealed, after Franklin was sentenced to death for the second time. This brought about a dilemma, for with Taft's intervention, Governor Ansel, whom Villard called "a humane man," would be likely to commute the sentence. If the lawyers insisted on appealing the case, however, the final decision would then be in the hands of the governor-elect, Coleman L. Blease, described by Villard as the worst kind of demagogue, elected on a base anti-Negro platform. It was a fearfully difficult decision, for Franklin's life was at stake in either case.[59] Villard consulted attorney Thomas Ewing, Jr., and William M. Wherry, Jr., counsel for the *Evening Post*.[60] As a result of these consultations Miss Blascoer went to South Carolina for the Association, persuaded Franklin's lawyers to withdraw, saw the governor, and employed counsel who were "persona grata to the powers that be." Before Governor Ansel left office, he commuted Franklin's sentence to life imprisonment. *The Crisis* commended the governor for his courage in the face of hostile public opinion but continued to argue that the life sentence was unjust and that Franklin should have been set free.[61]

One result of the Pink Franklin case was that Villard persuaded the Executive Committee to establish a legal redress department without delay. The problem of organizing the department and formulating a plan of action for the coming year was assigned to Villard's Committee on Program. At the same meeting (November 29, 1910) it was decided that the Association should be incorporated according to the laws of the State of New York, and this, too, was referred to Villard with full power to act.[62]

In reporting for the Committee on Program, Villard announced a very important policy of centralization and control by the national group which was to guide the NAACP in the conduct of its work for many years. This policy

[58] Villard to Charles Dyer Norton, August 28, 1910; Norton to Villard, September 1, 1910; Villard to William M. Wherry, Jr., October 21, 1910, Villard Papers.
[59] Villard to Wherry, October 21, 1910, Villard Papers.
[60] Thomas Ewing, Jr., was "one of the founders of the Association," nephew of General William T. Sherman, and later United States Patent Commissioner. Villard to Garrison, January 23, 1914, Villard Papers. Wherry and Ewing both worked on the Association's Legal Redress Committee.
[61] Minutes, Executive Committee, November 29, 1910, in Board Minutes, NAACP; Blascoer to Mary Church Terrell, November 16, 1910, Mary Church Terrell Papers (Manuscript Division, Library of Congress); *Crisis*, I (February, 1911), 12, 15. The NAACP did not let the case drop, however. It was reopened in 1915 (Board Minutes, NAACP, September 13, 1915; January 3, 1916), and finally in January, 1919, Governor Richard I. Manning granted Franklin parole. *The Crisis* reviewed "our first big case" and reported Franklin "now a free man." *Crisis*, XVII (March, 1919), 231. See also *Washington Bee*, February 22, 1919.
[62] Minutes, Executive Committee, November 29, 1910, in Board Minutes, NAACP.

stipulated that in the matter of memberships, members should belong to the national body, but that it would be well to form local groups which would take the nature of vigilance committees; all the actual work of the organization would be conducted through the central New York Executive Committee.[63] Almost immediately, these local vigilance committees in practice gave way to branches with legal committees to deal with cases of violence and racial discrimination.[64] In addition, the Executive Committee after the incorporation of the Association was supplanted by a Board of Directors; the work and control of the organization and its membership remained in the hands of the national body.

It was at this meeting that Joel E. Spingarn was elected to the Executive Committee,[65] an action of considerable moment to the NAACP. Joel Spingarn had been chairman of the Department of Comparative Literature at Columbia University and had left that institution over the issue of free speech. He was independently wealthy and after his election to the Executive Committee devoted most of his time and talents, which were considerable, to the Association, first as Executive Committee member, then as chairman of the Board of Directors. Upon the death of Moorfield Storey in 1929 Spingarn became president of the NAACP, holding this office until his death in 1939.[66]

When a local NAACP branch was organized in New York in January, 1911, Joel Spingarn became chairman. He was soon joined by his brother Arthur, able attorney and law partner of Charles H. Studin.[67] Arthur Spingarn became a member of the vigilance committee of the New York branch.[68] The purpose of this committee was to seek out, publicize, and prosecute cases of injustice to Negroes in the metropolitan area.[69]

Until 1913, the national body carried on its legal work by engaging counsel as the need arose and when funds permitted. At that time Arthur Spingarn and Charles Studin volunteered responsibility for this phase of the Association's work. After Studin's death, Arthur Spingarn continued to carry on the legal activities alone until, in 1935, William T. Andrews was engaged to assist him. In 1936,

[63] The Program Committee had been authorized at the October meeting and was appointed at the November 29, 1910, meeting. Villard was chairman and other members were Walling, the Reverend Joseph Silverman, the Reverend W. H. Brooks, Dr. Mossell, Mrs. Keyser, and Miss Ovington. Other committees appointed at this time were Finance—Milholland, chairman, Kennaday, the Reverend A. Clayton Powell, and Villard; Publication—J. H. Holmes, chairman, Dr. Bulkley, Mrs. Maclean, Miss Ovington, Russell, O. M. Waller, Walling, and Villard.
[64] Minutes, Executive Committee, March 7, 1911, in Board Minutes, NAACP.
[65] Spingarn was present at the meeting which elected him. Thomas Ewing, Jr., was elected to the Executive Committee at the same time. Minutes, Executive Committee, November 29, 1910, in Board Minutes, NAACP.
[66] New York Tribune, July 27, 1939, clipping in J. E. Spingarn Papers (Howard).
[67] Minutes, Executive Committee, March 7, 1911, in Board Minutes, NAACP.
[68] Interview with A. B. Spingarn, New York City, July 27, 1956.
[69] Crisis, II (August, 1911), 153.

Andrews was succeeded by Charles Houston as special counsel and Spingarn became chairman of the Legal Committee. This arrangement lasted until 1939, when Arthur succeeded his brother Joel as president of the NAACP and William H. Hastie became chairman of the legal Committee. Thurgood Marshall was then engaged as special counsel.[70]

It was the Steve Greene extradition case which first interested Joel and Arthur Spingarn in the NAACP.[71] The Association became involved in the case when Miss Blascoer and Walling were in Chicago arranging a drive for members.[72] The facts as told by Greene were published in *The Crisis*. Greene, a Negro, was born in Tennessee about 1862. He was illiterate and had never attended school. Since childhood he had worked as a laborer. He married and moved to Arkansas, choosing a place where his children could secure a common school education. In 1910, his landlord raised the rent, almost doubling it. Greene and the rest of the tenants moved out. The landlord sent word to Greene that if he did not work for him, he could not work in the county. One day, while Greene was working for a neighbor, his former employer rode by and shot him in the neck, left arm, and right leg. Greene ran to his house where he secured a rifle and killed his assailant. He fled, hiding out for three weeks on an island in the Mississippi. Friends supplied him with food, blankets, and ammunition, and finally raised $32 to help him escape. He arrived in Chicago on August 12 after a journey by foot and by train. There he was betrayed to the police, who arrested him on a fabricated charge of petty larceny. At the Garrison Street Police Station he was denied all food and drink during four days of questioning about the Arkansas shooting. In desperation Greene attempted suicide by eating matches. He became so ill he was placed in a hospital in a starving condition. There he was identified by the nephew of the man he had shot, who told him that a thousand persons were waiting to burn him in Arkansas.

The Negro Fellowship League under the leadership of Mrs. Wells-Barnett, learning of Greene's extradition, secured a writ of habeas corpus and telegraphed along the route to Arkansas, offering $100 to the sheriff who would intercept

[70] Ovington, *The Walls Came Tumbling Down* (New York, 1947), pp. 190, 271.
[71] Interview with A. B. Spingarn, New York City, July 30, 1956; Villard to J. E. Spingarn, October 17, 1910. This letter acknowledges the receipt of Spingarn's check for $100 for the Steve Greene case. Pencil note at the top of the letter in the handwriting of Mrs. Amy Spingarn reads: "JES's *first* interest in NAACP. He read of Steve Greene in the paper and sent a check to help—see Oct. 19 letter." The status of the Greene case as of that date is given in Villard to J. E. Spingarn, October 19, 1910. Both letters in J. E. Spingarn Papers (Howard). Arthur Spingarn says that Miss Ovington is in error when she says that Frances Blascoer "brought him to us in 1911, her great gift to the Association." Ovington, *The Walls Came Tumbling Down*, p. 110.
[72] Villard to Garrison, October 17, 1910, Villard Papers.

those who had Greene in custody. The sheriff of Cairo, Illinois, apprehended the party as they neared the state line, and Greene was returned to Chicago where counsel was engaged to defend him.[73]

A hearing was held, and Greene was set free on the grounds that there was a defect in the extradition papers. A few days later word came that the error in the papers had been corrected and that the sheriff from Arkansas was demanding the governor of Illinois to deliver Greene for extradition. Before another hearing could be held, Greene was spirited out of the country into Canada.[74]

Joel Spingarn was so incensed with what he had read about the Steve Greene case in the newspapers that he sent the NAACP a check for $100. At the same time he wired Edward H. Wright, one of the Negro attorneys engaged for Greene's defense, to ascertain and verify the facts, stating that he had placed money in the hands of the Association so that the defense might not be delayed or hampered for lack of funds.[75]

Wright answered with an appeal for more money, implying that voluntary subscriptions would not cover the expenses of the case. Mrs. Wells-Barnett was suspicious of the motives of the lawyers in trying to get more money from Spingarn. She reported to Villard that the Negro Fellowship League had already started Greene on his way to Canada. He had presumably reached his destination, but as he was illiterate, the group was uncertain as to his arrival and afraid to inquire. She assured Villard that a way would be found to communicate with Greene, and that if he needed money she would let Villard know.[76]

Villard passed this information on to Spingarn, commenting: "It is an unfortunate fact that the colored lawyers, as we have learned to our cost in the Pink Franklin case, usually take advantage of philanthropic interest of this kind to make money for themselves. . . . Either Mr. Wright is ignorant, or he deliberately seeks to mislead you on account of pelf." Villard thanked Spingarn

[73] *Crisis*, I (November, 1910), 14. Although *The Crisis* does not give credit to her, it was Ida Wells-Barnett who managed the Steve Greene case in Chicago. The Negro Fellowship League operated a reading room and social center for young people and tried to handle "all matters affecting the civil and legal affairs of the race." Ida Wells-Barnett to J. E. Spingarn, April 21, 1911, J. E. Spingarn Papers (Howard). Ida Wells-Barnett was a member of the NAACP Executive Committee.

[74] *New York Evening Post*, October 15, 1910. Interview with Arthur B. Spingarn, New York City, July 30, 1956. He gives the Association credit for getting Greene out of the country.

[75] Ida Wells-Barnett to Villard, telegram, n.d., quoted in Villard to J. E. Spingarn, October 19, 1910, J. E. Spingarn Papers (Howard).

[76] Edward H. Wright to J. E. Spingarn, October 17, 1910, J. E. Spingarn Papers (Howard); Ida Wells-Barnett to Villard, telegram, n.d., quoted in Villard to J. E. Spingarn, October 19, 1910, J. E. Spingarn Papers (Howard).

for his contribution and urged him to become active in the Association, informing him that his Columbia University colleague John Dewey was a sponsor.[77]
    Spingarn's interest in the advancement of the Negro had up to this time been
largely confined to an experiment in cooperation for social and economic improvement in Amenia, New York, the town where his summer home was
located.[78] His activity was now channeled into the newly formed organization
which dealt with the Negro problem in all its aspects. He was irresistibly drawn
to the little band of crusaders who were attempting to secure full economic,
political, and social rights for members of an oppressed minority. As a result
of Villard's urging, Spingarn became a member of the Executive Committee.[79]
    The NAACP undertook a third case during its first year. It concerned the
type of police brutality known as the third degree, sometimes inflicted upon
persons who had been arrested on suspicion of having committed a crime. The
case involved Thomas Williams, a Negro arrested early in November, 1910, and
charged with the murder of an 11-year-old white girl at Asbury Park, New
Jersey. According to news reports, there was danger that Williams might be
lynched. The NAACP investigated the case and concluded that the Public
Prosecutor did not have sufficient evidence to hold Williams. A writ of habeas
corpus was secured and at a hearing Williams was discharged when the State
failed to produce any evidence upon which he could be detained. Immediately
after the hearing, Williams was rearrested on a charge of having violated the
election laws of the State of New Jersey. The Association maintained that while
in jail the prisoner was subjected to the third degree in an attempt to fasten the
crime upon him. The case assumed more than local significance when the
NAACP wrote a recently constituted Congressional Committee appointed to
investigate use of the third degree, requesting permission to present the facts
of the Williams case.[80]
    The expense of these cases was a severe drain on the slender resources of the
Association. In order for the NAACP effectively to combat injustice on any one
of a number of fronts, Villard's estimate that $10,000 was urgently needed for
the year 1911 was not exaggerated.[81]

---

[77] Villard to J. E. Spingarn, October 19, 1910, J. E. Spingarn Papers (Howard). Arthur
Spingarn recalls, "There were few competent Negro lawyers in those days and they frequently attempted to charge the Association exorbitant fees." Interview with A. B. Spingarn,
New York City, July 27, 1956.
[78] Emmett J. Scott to J. E. Spingarn, August 14, 1910, J. E. Spingarn Papers (Howard).
[79] Minutes, Executive Committee, November 29, 1910, in Board Minutes, NAACP.
[80] Crisis, I (March, 1911), 15.
[81] The cost of the Pink Franklin case was $410.25. NAACP, The First Line of Defense: A
Summary of 20 Years' Civil Rights Struggle for American Negroes, pamphlet [New York,
1929]. Expenses for December, 1910, were $800, of which $266 related to the Thomas
Williams case. Minutes, Executive Committee, January 3, 1911, in Board Minutes, NAACP.

In its first year as a permanent organization, the NAACP had established a solid organizational structure and made plans for incorporation. It had set up an independent legal department which handled with some success three legal cases. It had engaged the leader of the radical faction in the Negro world and launched a periodical which was to be the voice of the Association. Financially it was still weak, but the combination of Du Bois's philosophy as enunciated in *The Crisis*, the organizational leadership of Villard, and the dedication of the early workers provided an alliance which triumphed over all obstacles.

Before continuing the story of the expansion of the NAACP and the conflicts that developed within the organization, it is necessary to describe the dramatic clash between the conservative forces of Booker T. Washington and the radical protest movement that in one short year had become focused in the NAACP.

CHAPTER IV

The NAACP and Booker T. Washington

At the time of the founding of the NAACP, the influence of Booker T. Washington was widespread and well entrenched. His philosophy, as set forth in his speech of 1895 known as the Atlanta Compromise,[1] had been acclaimed and accepted enthusiastically by politicians, Southern whites, and Negroes looking for guidance in overcoming their worsening status. He believed that economic opportunity was all-important for Negroes and that through vocational education, they would improve themselves, acquire property, and thus win the respect of white people. He sought to encourage Negroes in business enterprises by founding the National Negro Business League in 1900. His attitude toward business and labor conformed to the dominant philosophy of laissez-faire capitalism of the day. By preaching a doctrine of individualism, paternalism, and antiunionism,[2] he was successful in getting Andrew Carnegie, William H. Baldwin, Jr., and other white philanthropists to contribute to the development of Tuskegee Institute and to the promotion of other industrial schools. As a result of the Atlanta speech, he was looked upon with favor by national political leaders. Cleveland congratulated him for his speech, and President McKinley visited Tuskegee in 1898, as did Roosevelt in 1905. He was "intimate" with Roosevelt from 1901 to 1908. On the day Roosevelt took office, he invited Washington to the White House to advise him on political appointments of Negroes in the South.[3] This marked the high point of Washington's leadership and political power.

[1] Speech given at the International Cotton Exposition, September 17, 1895, quoted in Basil Mathews, *Booker T. Washington: Educator and Interracial Interpreter* (London, 1949), pp. 84–89.
[2] C. Vann Woodward, *Origins of the New South 1877–1913*, Vol. IX of *A History of the South*, ed. Wendell Holmes Stephenson and E. Merton Coulter (Baton Rouge, 1951), p. 367.
[3] Mathews, *Booker T. Washington*, pp. 91, 102, 229–30. For the significance of the career of Washington see August Meier, *Negro Thought in America, 1880–1915: Racial Ideologies in the Age of Booker T. Washington* (Ann Arbor, 1963).

The establishment of the NAACP evoked opposition from Washington. At first he confined his hostility to deft movements behind the scenes but as leaders of the Association such as W. E. B. Du Bois, John E. Milholland, Oswald Garrison Villard, and Joel E. Spingarn became impatient and began publicly to take him to task for his shortcomings, discord broke into the open.

When Du Bois left Atlanta University in the summer of 1910 to assume the position of Director of Publicity and Research in the NAACP, Washington was concerned. His chief antagonist was now in New York as the salaried official of an organization founded by prominent white liberals who counted in their inner circle no less a person than the grandson of William Lloyd Garrison. This man was wealthy and socially prominent; as an editor of the *New York Evening Post*, he was in a position to influence the white press. He could win many friends in high places for the new organization. He had been a friend of Washington's, and they had carried on an extensive correspondence. He had visited Tuskegee with Carnegie and had spoken at National Negro Business League meetings. If Villard and the NAACP were to become permeated with the philosophy and spirit of Du Bois, they might seriously menace Washington's position and leadership.

The clash of ideology between Washington and Du Bois was not new.[4] Though it came into the open in 1903, the pressures had been building up for three years. Du Bois agreed substantially with Washington before 1900, but after that time he began to stress the importance of higher education for Negroes.[5] In 1902, Du Bois considered going to Tuskegee to teach and conferred twice with Washington but without reaching a satisfactory agreement as to terms and conditions of the job. The interviews must have made both aware of their differences of philosophy. Washington had been "wary and silent."[6]

Du Bois declared himself, however, when in 1903 he published *The Souls of Black Folk*. In the chapter entitled "Of Mr. Booker T. Washington and Others," he criticized Washington for asking that Negroes give up political power, and insisted on civil rights and higher education for Negro youth. He objected to Washington's demand that they concentrate all their energies on industrial education, the accumulation of wealth, and the conciliation of the South, and he deplored the hushing of the criticism of honest opponents.[7]

[4] W. E. B. Du Bois, *Dusk of Dawn: An Essay Toward an Autobiography of a Race Concept* (New York, 1940), pp. 68, 71.
[5] Francis L. Broderick, *W. E. B. Du Bois: Negro Leader in a Time of Crisis* (Stanford, 1959), pp. 67–69.
[6] Du Bois, *Dusk of Dawn*, p. 78.
[7] Du Bois, *The Souls of Black Folk*, Premier Americana ed. (Greenwich, Connecticut, 1961), pp. 45, 48.

In January, 1904, a conference of about fifty persons took place in Carnegie Hall, called by Washington to "discuss fully all matters of interest to our race." Washington claimed that practically all the race interests were represented, and that both general and definite agreement as to future policy had been reached. Du Bois felt that the whole purpose of the conference had been the "lyric, almost fulsome praise of Mr. Washington and his work, and in support of his ideas."[8]

Out of this conference grew the Committee of Twelve for the Advancement of the Interests of the Negro Race, dominated by Washington and financed by Carnegie.[9] Du Bois was one of those appointed, but he resigned soon after, not wishing to appear to be endorsing policies enunciated by Washington as chairman. He believed that Washington was influencing men to do his will by "downright bribery and intimidation" and was seeking not the welfare of the Negro race but personal power.[10]

Thus the attempt to discuss all matters of interest to the race resulted in a clash of opinions. Time and time again after 1904 there were attempts to reach agreement but the underlying conflict was never resolved, and hostility ebbed and flowed until Washington's death in 1915. The conflict was based on the difference between the radical and the conservative approach to the solution of race problems. A strong personal jealousy developed, based on this difference. Du Bois stressed the importance of agitation for the rights of Negroes, while Washington was willing to accommodate to the Southern policy of suppression of Negroes' rights. Thus two rival factions developed, and the participants were classified as "Washington men," or "Du Bois men."

This contest hampered the work of the NAACP and frightened and frustrated Washington.[11] His public image as conciliator and compromiser did not change, and although Washington never swerved in his devotion to his own methods, there are indications that he was not as one-sided as he appeared to the public and that he secretly approved of the objectives of the radicals.[12]

[8] Du Bois, *Dusk of Dawn*, p. 81; *Washington Bee*, January 23, 1904; Booker T. Washington to J. C. Napier, December 18, 1903; Washington to William H. Baldwin, January 19, 1904, Booker T. Washington Papers (Manuscript Division, Library of Congress).
[9] Helen M. Chesnutt, *Charles Waddell Chesnutt: Pioneer of the Color Line* (Chapel Hill, 1952), p. 197; Washington to Baldwin, January 22, 1904; Charles H. Fearing to Washington, November 22, 1909; Washington to H. A. Franks, November 15, 1909; Washington to Andrew Carnegie, December 16, 1910, Washington Papers.
[10] Du Bois to Villard, April 20, 1905, Oswald Garrison Villard Papers (Houghton Library, Harvard University). Du Bois believed that Baldwin tried "to bribe him to change his opinion regarding Hampton and Tuskegee and myself." Washington to Robert Russa Moton, January 22, 1904, Washington Papers.
[11] August Meier traces Washington's opposition to the NAACP as revealed by his papers in "Booker T. Washington and the Rise of the NAACP," *Crisis*, LXI (February, 1954), 70.
[12] August Meier, "Toward a Reinterpretation of Booker T. Washington," *Journal of Southern History*, XXIII (May, 1957), 220–27, marshals evidence of Washington's maneuvers against

The principal causes of contention were control of the newspapers which reached the Negro public, political rivalry, personal attacks, and competition for public support in the United States and abroad. Because Du Bois was an officer of the NAACP and because the radical point of view won acceptance by the Association and was enunciated in the pages of *The Crisis,* the story of the maneuvers and clashes between the two factions became entwined with the story of the NAACP.[13]

PRESS RIVALRIES

One of Du Bois's proposals to the Carnegie Hall Conference of 1904 was for establishing a national Negro periodical. This became a source of rivalry. Washington, too, felt the need for a strong national Negro paper which would represent the interest of the race. To Washington it was a question of preempting the field or permitting his enemies to do so.[14] His first step was to buy out an already established newspaper.[15] Though his name was never mentioned in the contracts, there is evidence that, from 1903 on, Washington subsidized, directed, and by 1907 completed purchase of the *New York Age.* His influence over the Negro press was achieved by loans, advertising, printing orders, and political subsidies. He saw to it that critical papers received editorial material favorable to his cause and at times was even able to disrupt the distribution of such publications.[16]

segregation and disfranchisement. See also Oliver C. Cox, "The Leadership of Booker T. Washington," *Social Forces,* XXX (October, 1951), 91–97, for his philosophy of accommodation.

[13] Eric F. Goldman, *Rendezvous with Destiny: A History of Modern American Reform* (New York, 1952), pp. 176–83, places the Washington-Du Bois controversy in the American reform movement. Guy B. Johnson, "Negro Racial Movements and Leadership in the United States," *American Journal of Sociology,* XLIII (July, 1937–May, 1938), pp. 57–71, also discusses the Washington–Du Bois clash of ideas. Hugh Hawkins, *Booker T. Washington and his Critics: The Problem of Negro Leadership* (Problems in American Civilization; Boston, 1962), is a collection of essays expressing diverse views on the controversy.

[14] Du Bois to Kelly Miller, February 25, 1903, W. E. B. Du Bois Papers (now in the possession of Mrs. W. E. B. Du Bois, New York); Washington to Baldwin, January 19, 1904; Washington to T. Thomas Fortune, November 5, 1903, Washington Papers.

[15] August Meier, "Booker T. Washington and the Negro Press: With Special Reference to *The Colored American Magazine,*" *Journal of Negro History,* XXXVIII (January, 1953), 67–90, traces Washington's efforts at controlling the Negro press.

[16] Emmett J. Scott to Washington, January 18, 1907; Washington to Scott, January 22, 1907; Fortune to Scott, March 5, 1907; J. B. Peterson to Washington, May 9, 1907; Washington to Scott, May 3, 1905; July 27, 1905; July 28, 1904; July 29, 1904; August 7, 1905; Scott to Washington, August 3, 1905; July 23, 1905; August 10, 1905; Washington to John Mitchell, September 18, 1905; Washington to Whitfield McKinley, March 14, 1905; McKinley to Washington, March 20, 1905; May 15, 1905; August 9, 1905; Scott to R. C. Simmons, February 17, 1905; Washington to Anderson, October 16, 1905; Anderson to Washington, October 12, 1905; Anderson to Washington, October 16, 1905, Washington Papers.

Word of the negotiations with the *Age* leaked out, however, and in January, 1905, Du Bois publicly charged that $3,000 in "hush money" had been used to subsidize the Negro press in five leading cities.[17] Privately he claimed that this situation had been going on for three or four years and had become notorious among well-informed Negroes and was a subject of frequent comment.[18] There was an immediate denial in the *Age*, accompanied by efforts to force Du Bois to substantiate his charges. Soon the entire Negro press was issuing denials and denunciations of Du Bois.[19]

There was concern and consultation among members of the Garrison family at these charges and when Villard demanded explanation, Du Bois sent a number of "exhibits" as proof of his claims. Francis Jackson Garrison at first thought the evidence clear but later decided that his faith was not shaken in "Washington's purity of purpose and absolute freedom from selfishness and personal ambition." He compared Washington's calm, patience, and endurance to William Monroe Trotter's petty jealousy and spite and to the bitterness of the Butler Wilsons.[20]

Villard nevertheless challenged Washington on his activities with the press. At this time Villard still believed there were no essential differences between Washington and Du Bois. He explained to Du Bois that, though he believed in both industrial and higher education for Negroes, industrialism was the all-important question of the hour for the masses. In Washington's reply to Villard, he denied trying to influence people other than "in a manly, open manner" but admitted that his secretary, Emmett Scott, may have overstepped the bounds of propriety in attempting to keep Tuskegee before the public, Villard and Garrison were completely satisfied with Washington's answer.[21]

The length to which Washington was willing to go to discredit his enemies, both Negro and white, is evident in the story of the Cosmopolitan Club. This club was organized in 1906 as a medium for eradicating erroneous ideas about colored people.[22] In 1908 the club held an interracial dinner in New York at-

[17] Du Bois to Villard, March 24, 1905, Villard Papers; *Voice of the Negro*, IV (March, 1907), 110; Pauline E. Hopkins to Max Barber, April 18, 1905, Du Bois Papers.
[18] William Hayes Ward to Du Bois, February 18, 1905; Du Bois to Ward, March 10, 1905, Du Bois Papers.
[19] *New York Age*, January 19, 1905; February 16, 1905; February 23, 1905; March 9, 1905. These issues contain reprints of other newspaper reports.
[20] Villard to Garrison, April 6, 1905; Du Bois to Villard, March 24, 1905; Garrison to Villard, April 7, 1905; April 9, 1905, Villard Papers.
[21] Villard to Du Bois, April 18, 1905, Villard Papers; Garrison to Washington, May 8, 1905; Washington to Garrison, May 17, 1905; May 20, 1905; May 23, 1905, Francis Jackson Garrison Papers, in Schomburg Collection (New York Public Library, New York).
[22] Ovington to Villard, October 8, 1906, Villard Papers; *Voice of the Negro*, IV (May, 1907), 185–86.

tended by about a hundred persons, including Miss Ovington, Villard, Holt of *The Independent*, Max Barber of *The Voice of the Negro*, John Spargo, the socialist lecturer and writer, and A. B. Humphrey of the Constitution League. Villard found it a remarkable gathering of a very high order but was distressed at the reaction of the newspapers. In an editorial designed to rouse public opinion against socialism and against any kind of social relationships between Negroes and whites, the *New York Times* called attention to "forces of evil," "Socialistic propaganda," and "intermixing the races by marriage."[23] Other papers were even more vehement, and the after effects of the publicity were unpleasant. Miss Ovington received such obscene letters that she was compelled to have her letters opened by male relatives.[24]

It is clear that Washington had arranged for derogatory publicity and that he had helped to promote the lurid headlines. In January, 1911, a similar dinner was held by the Cosmopolitan Club. Learning that Du Bois and Milholland were scheduled to speak at the affair, Washington directed Charles W. Anderson to "get the same reporter who reported . . . a year or two ago" and to send copies of the printed announcement to "all city editors in advance." He was sure the *New York Times* would cooperate, since Anderson claimed a long-standing friendship with the managing editor. He was disappointed, however, that only two morning papers carried the story, though all had been "duly notified." The sensational headlines seemed to please Tuskegee. Scott wrote that one of the stories had been "a particularly savory article," and regretted only that there had not been more publicity for this "delectable function."[25]

POLITICAL RIVALRIES

When Du Bois left Atlanta for New York in 1910 to take up his new duties, Washington feared for the safety of his political prestige. Du Bois was interested in influencing Negroes to vote independently rather than to give blind allegiance to the Republican Party.[26] Feeling this threat, Washington urged Anderson to broaden the base of the Colored Republican Club of New York so as to include at least one representative of all the strong Negro organizations and

[23] Villard to Garrison, April 29, 1908; Villard to Ovington, April 29, 1908, Villard Papers; *New York Times*, April 29, 1908.
[24] Villard, "The Crumbling Color Line," *Harper's Magazine*, CLIX (July, 1929), 163; Villard, *Fighting Years: Memoirs of a Liberal Editor* (New York, 1939), p. 197.
[25] Washington to Anderson, telegram, January 21, 1911; Anderson to Washington, January 9, 1911; *New York World*, January 25, 1911, and *New York Press*, January 25, 1911, clippings in Anderson to Washington, January 25, 1911; Anderson to Washington, January 19, 1911; Scott to Anderson, January 28, 1911, Washington Papers.
[26] *Crisis*, I (November, 1910), 11. See Broderick, *W. E. B. Du Bois*, for the evolution of Du Bois's political thinking.

to make it a clearing house for these groups. The purpose was to give Anderson and the Washington forces a firm control over the Negro community that could quietly deal with any threat to the Tuskegee machine from Du Bois and the NAACP.[27] Charles W. Anderson was the recognized colored Republican leader of New York and an astute politician. He had worked for the election of Roosevelt in 1908 and was rewarded by being appointed Collector of Internal Revenue of the second district.[28]

Washington was worried about Taft's lily-white program and the waning of his own political influence through loss of the patronage he had enjoyed under Roosevelt. Taft announced in his inaugural address that he would not appoint Negroes as federal officials in the South where white people were opposed to them.[29] Even in the North, Washington felt the change. Anderson informed him that a rival candidate, opposed to the Washington forces, had received the appointment as United States District Attorney for Massachusetts. He commented ruefully, "Thus one by one our hopes fade away. Who will be next?"[30] William H. Lewis who had vacated that post had gone on to the position of Assistant Attorney General of the United States, but the Boston place was lost to the Washington clique and other appointments were not forthcoming.

During this period Villard, assuming that Washington would continue to get the political plums, tried to reach the ear of Taft through Charles Dyer Norton, Taft's private secretary.[31] He called attention to criticisms of Taft's policies in the *Age*. Norton was surprised, since policies outlined in the Inaugural Address represented Taft's "firm convictions of what [was] best for both races" and had been submitted to and approved by Washington, Anderson, and other prominent Negroes. Norton proposed an informal conference with a few editors and leaders, including Washington, and asked Villard for names of persons important in the Negro world, who were not office-seekers.

Villard tried to explain the two factions to Norton. He described Du Bois as one who had reached a greater intellectual height than perhaps any other colored man. Because Du Bois had insisted on fighting for the rights of Negroes set forth in the Thirteenth, Fourteenth, and Fifteenth Amendments and for opportunity to secure higher education, he had been accused of aspiring for social equality and being wholly antagonistic to Booker T. Washington. Villard explained to Norton that opposition to Washington was increasing, and that one

[27] Washington to Anderson, July 11, 1910, Washington Papers.
[28] James Weldon Johnson, *Along This Way* (New York, 1933), pp. 219–20.
[29] Du Bois, *Dusk of Dawn*, p. 233; Davis N. Lott (ed.), *Inaugural Addresses of the American Presidents: From Washington to Kennedy* (New York, 1961), pp. 195–96.
[30] Anderson to Washington, December 21, 1909, Washington Papers.
[31] Villard, *Fighting Years*, p. 191.

cause of Washington's diminishing prestige was that he had become office-broker for his race.

Norton professed to admire Du Bois as a scholar and writer, but failed to understand the difference between the two men. To Norton the words "social equality" meant intermarriage. Villard realized that this attitude would prevent Du Bois from securing Norton's support.[32]

It is clear that although Norton had married a Garrison and was on friendly terms with Villard, his fear of "social equality," the general anti-Negro bias of the Taft administration, and the secure position of Booker T. Washington as the leader and spokesman for the Negro made it impossible for Villard and the NAACP to influence Norton or Taft when it came to securing recognition and political appointments. Prejudice and the Tuskegee machine were too firmly ensconced.

It is true that Villard and the NAACP received the support of the Administration in the Pink Franklin case, but this did not involve recognition of a faction in opposition, and in this instance the Association, through Villard, had sought and secured the prior approval and cooperation of the Tuskegeean. Although Washington retained what little political influence was left for Negroes under Taft's lily-white program, he felt his power jeopardized when he learned that Villard and Du Bois were approaching Taft through Norton.

Following the November, 1910, elections Anderson suggested to Washington that the *New York Age* call attention to a circular sent out by Du Bois and Bishop Alexander Walters prior to the election, urging Negroes to vote the Democratic ticket if they wanted colored policemen and colored firemen in New York City and a colored regiment of soldiers in the State Guard. Anderson felt that since the Democrats had elected the Governor of the state and the Mayor of New York City and controlled the State Legislature, the *Age* should demand that they make good the promises in the Du Bois circular. He was sure they would not do so. It was his intention to show up the hypocrisy of the Negroes who prepared the circular, but Washington determined that it would be best to omit any reference to Du Bois and Walters lest publicity further their cause.[33]

Anderson and Washington were aware that *The Crisis* had urged Negro voters to cast their ballots for men and measures rather than to follow one particular party simply from habit.[34] If the Du Bois doctrine won acceptance and Negroes could no longer be depended upon to vote Republican, the power of the Tuskegee machine would be brought to an end.

[32] Norton to Villard, September 14, 1910; Villard to Norton, September 21, 1910; Norton to Villard, September 26, 1910; Villard to Garrison, October 31, 1910, Villard Papers.
[33] Anderson to Washington, November 15, 1910; Washington to Anderson, November 16, 1910, Washington Papers.
[34] *Crisis*, I (November, 1910), 11.

Meanwhile, Anderson believed that Milholland, who dabbled in Republican politics, was working overtime to get Du Bois political recognition, but that he would not be able to make Du Bois into a race leader with any real following. Anderson held that a leader must identify himself with the common man and the social and economic problems of the race. This he thought Du Bois could not do because he was considered an intellectual snob, far above the real scene of conflict. He predicted that the New York election would finish Du Bois, who would be unable to obtain patronage from the Democrats. Anderson claimed that Milholland was insincere and unscrupulous in advancing his own interest. He was sure that Milholland would provide no real threat either in politics or in promoting the cause of the race. It was most difficult, wrote Anderson, "in connection with the race question . . . to induce *big* white men [Carnegie] to take a real interest in it, and to prevent little, intriguing white men [Milholland] from doing so."[35]

Thus, the "Washington men" reassured themselves. In spite of Anderson's rationalizations, news of a secret meeting between Du Bois, Milholland, Dr. Felix Adler,[36] and President Taft must certainly have brought anxiety to Washington and Anderson. The disturbing news continued to reach them that the enemy had frequent access to the President and had convinced him that Booker T. Washington, in spite of denials, controlled the Negro press and had connived at criticism of the Administration by the *Age*. Washington was sure that neither Taft nor his secretary was familiar with the *Age*, and was afraid that the "Du Bois men" were giving the President the impression that the *Age* was against the Administration.[37]

THE "APPEAL TO EUROPE"

During this period of political maneuvering an episode occurred that caused increasing bitterness on the part of Booker T. Washington and his team, widened the gap between the two sides, and became a public controversy. In the fall of 1910 Washington traveled through Europe and England, referring in his speeches to the improvement of race relations in the United States with his customary optimism. He returned in October but not before the outbreak of a dispute, in which Du Bois and Milholland were identified as spokesmen of the NAACP.[38]

[35] Anderson to Washington, January 16, 1911, Washington Papers.
[36] Adler was the founder of the American Society for Ethical Culture and professor of social studies at Columbia University. Horace L. Friess, "Felix Adler," in Harris E. Starr (ed.), *Dictionary of American Biography: Supplement One* (New York, 1944), XXI, 13–14.
[37] *Washington Bee*, February 18, 1911; Anderson to Washington, June 5, 1911; Washington to Anderson, June 9, 1911, Washington Papers.
[38] John H. Harris to Washington, September 17, 1910; Washington to Harris, December 29, 1910, Washington Papers; Moton to Villard, November 15, Villard Papers.

In London, Washington delivered a speech to the Anti-Slavery and Aborigines Protection Society, and was interviewed by the *London Morning Post*. Milholland also in London at the time, wrote and distributed a circular letter of protest against Washington's statements,[39] and Du Bois published a leaflet which became known as the "Appeal to Europe."[40] It was signed by thirty-two prominent Negroes, and appeared in United States and English newspapers.[41]

The "Appeal" denied Washington's assertion that the condition of the Negro in America was being satisfactorily solved. It accused Washington, because of his dependence on philanthropists, of relating only what certain powerful interests would like to appear as the whole truth. Du Bois stressed the steady loss of the ballot by force and fraud and the determined and well-organized program to withhold common school education from colored children by denial of a fair share of school funds. He called attention to the widespread belief in the natural inferiority of the Negro race, to discrimination in housing, to poor health and labor conditions, to the crime of lynching and the failure of the courts to protect the Negro. Deploring the fact that anyone subject to daily insult and humiliation in America should consciously or unconsciously misrepresent the truth, Du Bois called for the moral support of England and Europe in a "crusade for recognition of manhood."[42]

The wide publicity given to the "Appeal" disturbed Washington, who asked Robert R. Moton to inquire whether the Du Bois movement had as its principal object "the discouragement of . . . the fundamentals of Hampton and Tuskegee." Moton reminded Villard that shortly after the first NAACP conference he had been assured that the new organization would not be anti-Washington. The circular distributed by Milholland in London while Dr. Washington was there, wrote

---

[39] *New York Age*, September 22, 1910; Washington to Villard, January 10, 1911, Washington Papers. In this letter Washington bitterly complained that Milholland's protest was issued the day *before* his first speech in England.

[40] Du Bois, *Race Relations in the United States: The Negro's Intolerable Condition Pointed Out by Professor Du Bois and Other Eminent Afro-Americans: Dr. Washington's Optimistic Utterances Repudiated. An Appeal to England and Europe*, pamphlet, 3 pp. (New York, 1910), Du Bois Papers. The title page, dated October 26, 1910, bears the following: "Headquarters—National Negro Committee, 20 Vesey Street, New York, U.S.A." According to Du Bois, the "Appeal" was sent to Europe on October 26. *Crisis*, I (January, 1911), 9–11, 16. However, Du Bois was still soliciting signatures to this protest as late as November 15, 1910. This probably accounts for the fact that it did not appear in the *New York Sun* until December 1, 1910. See Chesnutt to Du Bois, November 21, 1910, quoted in Chesnutt, *Charles Waddell Chesnutt*, p. 240. Washington sent to Moton a copy of "another" circular letter "more recently distributed in England." This, he pointed out, was dated at the headquarters of the new National Negro Committee and was signed by Du Bois as secretary. [Du Bois signed the circular as Secretary of the National Afro-American Committee.] Washington to Moton, November 22, 1910, Washington Papers.

[41] Washington to Villard, January 10, 1911, Washington Papers.

[42] *New York Sun*, December 1, 1910; Du Bois, *Race Relations in the United States*.

Moton, gave the appearance that the NAACP was actively engaged in discrediting Washington's philosophy. He implied that Villard himself was not entirely acquainted with the workings of the organization, and protested that Du Bois in Washington, D.C., and William English Walling in Chicago, had dwelt on Washington's shortcomings. He claimed that Washington and his followers hoped the NAACP would work along needed lines, and that both groups would accomplish the same results through different methods without antagonism. He professed a desire for uniting forces.[43]

Villard answered that he agreed with Milholland's views regarding Washington's role in politics and objected to Washington's philosophy of compromise and expediency and to his role as political broker for the Negro. Although he had worked to prevent the NAACP from being anti-Washington or pro-Du Bois, he assured Moton that the Association would not hesitate to protest any public statement of Washington's that was considered a betrayal of the race.[44]

Moton, on receiving this answer, felt that it was hopeless to attempt to come to an understanding with the NAACP. Washington, however, was never one to lose hope. He began a correspondence with Villard expressing concern that the forces working for the advancement of the Negro should be divided. He pointed out that the circular had been distributed in NAACP envelopes, calling this an evident attempt at deception on somebody's part.[45]

Villard informed Washington that the use of the envelopes was unauthorized. Nevertheless, he considered the protest valid. He had tried to prevent the NAACP from indulging in criticism of Washington's mistaken points of view, and assured Washington that he regarded him as sincere and honest and not subservient, either economically or politically, to the benefactors of Tuskegee. He reminded Washington that if his grandfather, William Lloyd Garrison had, on his trip to Europe in 1850, dwelt upon certain encouraging features of slavery and had cited the number of voluntary liberations and escapes to Canada as evidence that the institution was improving, he would have caused more harm than good. He warned Washington that an increasing number of Negro intellectuals were repudiating his leadership, and a number of white people as well. He urged Washington to refrain from speeches like the one he gave in London, since he, Villard, wanted to see Washington maintain his standing and reputation.

Continuing the controversy, Washington accused Milholland of falsehood and said that the circular had gone out before he had given any speeches in London. He claimed that his European speeches were no different from those he had given

---

[43] Washington to Moton, October 24, 1910, Washington Papers; Moton to Villard, November 15, 1910, Villard Papers.
[44] Villard to Moton, November 23, 1910, Washington Papers.
[45] Moton to Washington, December 2, 1910, Washington Papers; Washington to Villard, December 11, 1910, Villard Papers.

at home, and he rejected Villard's attempt to compare what Garrison, the abolitionist, had done with what he was doing. Garrison's work had been to destroy a great evil; Washington was trying to show that "the progress the Negro has made in America justified the word and work of your grandfather." He was convinced that Villard was in contact with only those Negroes who were sour, dissatisfied, and unhappy, who had not been successful, and who had been opposing him since his speech at the opening of the Atlanta Exposition in 1895 (an obvious reference to Du Bois). He refused to believe that he was losing influence with intellectuals. His experience and observation convinced him otherwise.[46]

Villard responded by defending Milholland as a tried friend of human liberty and refused to be led into criticism of him. He resented Washington's assertion that he was in contact only with "sour" and "unhappy" Negroes. Washington's speeches, Villard said, were all right "as far as they go, but they do not go far enough to satisfy any Garrison. Perhaps this is a fault of the Garrisonian temperament."

The Negro leader, never letting fall the thin mask of amiability, expressed amazement at Villard's willingness to gloss over Milholland's misrepresentations and refused to give an inch in regard to his own policy. He was unwilling to bend to Villard's will, Garrison or no Garrison. Those possessing the "Garrisonian temperament . . . may be disposed to be more impatient with others because they do not do what they would have them do."[47]

PERSONAL ATTACKS

Following this exchange of letters, the *New York Age*, which had always shown deference and respect for the Garrisons and Villard, now subjected Villard to attack, impugning his sincerity by accusing him of not hiring Negroes above the custodial level, a thrust which irritated and angered Villard. He insisted that Washington call off the villainous attacks in papers like the *Age*, but Moton explained that Washington was able to influence the *Age* only in a personal and friendly way.[48]

When the NAACP decided not to merge with the Constitution League, Villard notified Washington so that he would not hold the Association liable for any actions taken by the Constitutional League. Washington took this to mean that Villard and Milholland had fallen out or that they had "agreed between them to

[46] Villard to Washington, December 13, 1910, Villard Papers; Washington to Villard, January 10, 1911, Washington Papers.
[47] Villard to Washington, February 7, 1911; Washington to Villard, February 11, 1911, Washington Papers.
[48] *New York Age*, March 9, 1911; Villard to Moton, April 5, 1911; Moton to Washington, April 17, 1911, Washington Papers.

let the Constitutional League do the dirty work and use the other organization to inveigle our friends into believing in their sincerity."[49]

The effectiveness and extent of activity of Du Bois as the Association's Director of Research and Publicity was another area that demanded attention from the Washington team. In his first six months, Du Bois estimated that he talked to 21,000 persons in the 58 lectures he gave in the New York area, Chicago, the East, and the South.[50] To "monopolize the 'speaking business' and shut out the opposition," Anderson suggested that the Governor (former Lieutenant Governor P. B. S. Pinchback of Louisiana) prepare for use on short notice several good speeches on the race question.[51] Anderson had highlighted the difficulty the Tuskegee machine was having in trying to counter the Association's activity in the field of information and public relations. Du Bois was highly educated, young, vigorous, on fire for the cause, and could devote his entire time and energy to writing and speaking. The Washington forces had no one with prestige, save possibly Pinchback, who was now aging and living largely on his past reputation. Washington, Anderson, and Moton, all able men, were occupied in other spheres of activity and could enter this field only from time to time.

The indefatigable Anderson kept track not only of Du Bois's movements and activities but also those of other NAACP Board members and reported to Washington. Through the *New York Age* Washington sought to mold and direct public opinion and to discredit the NAACP, Du Bois, and other race leaders who supported the new movement. The *Age*, trying to make it appear that Du Bois was deliberately building up tensions, noted that he advocated agitation for the next twenty-five years. William English Walling, who was appearing as defendant in a sensational breach of promise suit, was the next victim. Villard mourned that the affair had about ruined Walling's usefulness for a long time to come. In Boston Francis Garrison, arranging for the third annual conference of the NAACP, tried to avoid linking the Association with the scandal by not announcing that Villard had taken Walling's place as chairman.[52]

[49] Villard to Washington, January 19, 1911, Villard Papers; Washington to Anderson, January 23, 1911, Washington Papers.
[50] Du Bois, "Report of the Department of Publicity and Research," March, 1911, in Du Bois Papers; *Crisis*, I (April, 1911), 17. The Director's office also served as a clearinghouse for information on the race question, and his outgoing correspondence on this matter reached a total of 2,949 letters in the period covered by his report. In addition, he wrote magazine articles, letters to newspapers and press associations, supervised the publication of five pamphlets for the NAACP, and edited *The Crisis* as well.
[51] Anderson to Washington, January 25, 1911, Washington Papers.
[52] Anderson to Washington, February 27, 1911, Washington Papers; *New York Age*, March 2, 1911; Villard to Garrison, February 27, 1911; Garrison to Villard, March 6, 1911, Villard Papers.

The story was not to be overlooked, however, by the other side. Washington asked Anderson to get Fred Moore, editor of the *Age*, "to burn Walling up." In righteous indignation, the *Age* pointed to Walling as the type of leader "that some people are trying to foist upon the colored people." Such a man, said the *Age*, had presided over meetings where such colored women as Mrs. Mary Church Terrell were present. "We hope that no colored man or woman will in the future disgrace our race by inviting Mr. Walling in their home or ask him to speak at any public meeting."[53]

PEACE NEGOTIATIONS

Three weeks later another scandal erupted into headlines, bringing about a temporary lull in hostilities between the two camps. Booker T. Washington was assaulted by Albert Ulrich, a white carpenter, who alleged that Washington had made improper advances toward his wife. The assault occurred on Sunday evening, March 19, 1911, under mysterious circumstances in a section of New York City of unsavory reputation. Washington explained that he was in the area looking for the home of the auditor for Tuskegee.[54]

Several days later Villard talked on the telephone with Washington, who was overwhelmed with expressions of sympathy from people whom he had considered his worst enemies. He asked Villard to help him bury the hatchet and bring about a cordial union of both factions on a mutually satisfactory basis. Villard was delighted with this opportunity.[55]

Since the first of the year, the NAACP had been preparing for the third annual conference. There had been difficulty in securing moral and financial support from prominent and wealthy Bostonians. Those interested in the cause of the Negro were for the most part under the influence of Washington and supported Hampton and Tuskegee. At first some of these people refused either to join or to allow their names to be used as sponsors of the conference. Garrison was afraid that Washington might block all efforts to enlist support, and Villard was sure that Washington's "active or tacit opposition" would be forthcoming. He suggested that the NAACP "saw wood and say nothing." Nevertheless the committee in charge of local arrangements, composed of such prominent Bostonians as Moorfield Storey, Albert Pillsbury, Francis Jackson Garrison, and Horace Bumstead, were so successful in the home of abolitionist activity that they were worried lest either Milholland or Du Bois say something that might antagonize their new supporters. Garrison was convinced that if Washington

---

[53] Washington to Anderson, March 3, 1911, Washington Papers; *New York Age*, March 9, 1911.
[54] *New York Age*, March 23, 1911.
[55] Villard to Garrison, March 24, 1911, Villard Papers.

could have got at them, he would have cautioned many of the sponsors not to sign. Once "in print" they were less likely to be alienated and stampeded, provided the conference were wisely conducted. When Washington was assaulted in New York, Villard tried to impress upon Du Bois and Milholland that any criticism of the Negro leader would reflect on the whole race.[56]

As evidence of conciliation, Washington wanted the NAACP to send a delegation to the annual meeting of the National Negro Business League. Villard had in mind a resolution of sympathy and confidence in Washington to be adopted at the NAACP conference. He was afraid this would be hard to get past some people, but he hoped the prestige of some of the Boston members would hasten peace negotiations. Villard knew that Washington's failure to endorse the work of the Association had been harmful, and that if a truce could be brought about, the assault upon Washington would prove to be "one of the best things that ever happened."[57]

Opinions of the Boston members, as Garrison communicated them to Villard, were varied. Bumstead was willing to vote a resolution of sympathy, but not of confidence, until Washington could substantiate his version of the story. Butler Wilson, long a critic of Washington's pronouncements and policies, felt that, regardless of differences of opinion, it was the duty of members of his race to stand by the Tuskegeean. As a lawyer he was aware of the weakness of Washington's explanations and he was fearful that Monroe Trotter might use the *Guardian,* and especially the business session of the conference, to voice violent opposition to the resolution, and that the sensational press might jeopardize the attempt at reconciliation. Pillsbury believed that Washington's version of the assault was either misrepresentation or a pure invention. He was convinced that the educator had something to conceal and that his move for reconciliation was transparent because he was in trouble and anxious for every endorsement.

They finally agreed to suggest that Washington write Villard a letter to be read at the conference, expressing his interest in and general approval of the work of the NAACP. This would open the way for a resolution of sympathy from the conference. They were cautious as to an expression of confidence until Washington's statements concerning the unfortunate incident had been proved beyond a doubt.[58] NAACP leaders in the meantime would try to control and limit one of their most consistently hostile members, Monroe Trotter.[59]

[56] Garrison to Villard, March 15, 1911; Villard to Garrison, March 16, 1911; Garrison to Villard, March 17, 1911; Villard to Garrison, March 20, 1911, Villard Papers.
[57] Villard to Garrison, March 24, 1911, Villard Papers.
[58] Garrison to Villard, March 25, 1911; March 26, 1911; Villard to Washington, telegram, March 27, 1911, Villard Papers.
[59] Storey to Trotter, March 29, 1911, Moorfield Storey Papers (in the possession of Mr. Charles Storey, Boston, Massachusetts). As to Trotter's membership in the NAACP at this time, see Villard to Garrison, January 6, 1911, Villard Papers.

Washington sent word to the *Age* to pursue the cause of reconciliation. Anderson, of course, fell in with Washington's strategy. "For us to decline the olive branch would be to expose us to the charge of being narrow, and it would give the scoundrels . . . an excuse for wielding the dirty weapons, which they know so well how to use."[60]

Washington's wire to Villard left nothing to be desired in cordiality.

I shall be glad to work in friendly cooperation with all the workers for the general advancement of the colored people especially along constructive directions. . . . While we necessarily may in the future as in the past work along different lines, we still may work together in harmony, sympathy and mutual understanding. . . . The time has come when all interested in the welfare of the Negro people should lay aside personal differences and personal bickerings . . . and keep in mind only rendering the service which will best protect and promote the race in all of its larger interests. . . . I am sure that all of my friends everywhere will happily cooperate with you in the directions that I have mentioned.[61]

The resolution passed by the NAACP conference was severely correct by comparison.

Resolved, that we put on record our profound regret at the recent assault on Dr. Booker T. Washington in New York City, in which the Association finds renewed evidence of race discrimination and increased necessity for the awakening of the public conscience.[62]

Following the conference, Villard wrote to Moton urging that all Negroes present a united front and expressing the hope that this would be the beginning of friendly relations between the two factions. In his reply Moton tried to convince Villard that Washington was not opposed to any progressive movement, and Villard pressed Washington to send a fraternal delegation from the National Negro Business League to the next conference of the NAACP.[63] For a time the personal relationship between Villard and Washington improved,[64] but the era of good feelings was short-lived. Du Bois's editorial in the June *Crisis* was so sharply critical of Washington that Storey saw *The Crisis* making enemies for the Association instead of winning friends. Villard was inclined to excuse

[60] Washington to Anderson, March 28, 1911; Anderson to Washington, March 29, 1911, Washington Papers.
[61] Washington to Villard, telegram, March 30, 1911, Washington Papers.
[62] Villard to Washington, telegram, March 31, 1911, Washington Papers.
[63] Villard to Moton, April 5, 1911; Moton to Washington, April 17, 1911; Villard to Washington, April 10, 1911, Washington Papers.
[64] Washington to Villard, April 6, 1911; April 19, 1911; Villard to Washington, April 11, 1911; Garrison to Villard, April 27, 1911, Villard Papers; *New York Age*, April 20, 1911.

Du Bois on grounds of temperament, but Storey, who hated the factionalism and personal animosities among those fighting for the same cause, became so exasperated as to write that sometimes the difficulty seemed to him to be "almost racial."[65]

The basic philosophies of neither side had changed. In spite of all the protestations of sincerity and reconciliation the so-called truce could not last.

FURTHER CONFLICT

During the summer of 1911, the NAACP officially challenged Booker T. Washington's philosophy on the international scene. In July the Association sent four delegates[66] to the First Universal Races Congress at London. Only a few months had elapsed since Washington's trip to England and the controversy stirred up by Du Bois's "Appeal to Europe." It is indicative of the Executive Committee's interest in the international aspects of race relations that $650 was earmarked for the expenses of the delegation at a time when money was coming in so slowly as to make continued existence of the Association doubtful. The money was Milholland's contribution.[67] He and Du Bois succeeded in securing official sanction for the trip.

The object of the Races Congress was the development of closer understanding and cooperation between white and colored peoples of the world. Chairman of the affair was Lord Weardale, a leader in the World Peace Movement. Fifty racial groups were represented. The idea for such a Congress had originated with Felix Adler. It was organized by Gustave Spiller of the London Ethical Culture Society, who spent several years preparing for the Congress and named Adler co-secretary. Du Bois was to handle plans for a United States representation.[68]

To facilitate Du Bois's trip, Spiller wrote to the Anti-Slavery and Aborigines Protection Society, a conservative English group that had opened doors for Washington by obtaining financial help for Tuskegee from British aristocrats.[69] Here Washington once more subtly sabotaged Du Bois. Through his influence the Anti-Slavery and Aborigines Protection Society stipulated as a condition of

[65] *Crisis*, II (June, 1911), 62–64; Storey to Villard, October 20, 1911; October 17, 1911, Storey Papers.
[66] Du Bois, Milholland, Mary White Ovington, and Dr. W. A. Sinclair of Philadelphia. Ovington, *The Walls Came Tumbling Down* (New York, 1947), p. 131; *Crisis*, II (October, 1911), 234.
[67] Minutes, Executive Committee, January 3, 1911, in "Minute Book of the Board of Directors of the National Association for the Advancement of Colored People" (now in the Manuscript Division, Library of Congress; hereafter referred to as Board Minutes, NAACP).
[68] *Crisis*, II (September, 1911), 200–2. The World Peace Foundation financed the publishing of the report of the proceedings of the Races Congress. Du Bois, *Dusk of Dawn*, p. 230.
[69] Mathews, *Booker T. Washington*, pp. 257, 271.

their aid that they must have in advance "typed interviews" for publicity and that they would not support any undertaking which would engage in an attack on Booker T. Washington.[70]

The Tuskegee faction was represented at the Races Congress by Moton. He was convinced that there was a determined effort on foot to lessen Washington's influence in both the United States and Europe. He had heard rumors that Miss Ovington, Milholland, and Du Bois were discussing ways in which they could "down" Booker Washington. Moton felt that it was his duty to attend the Congress to prevent them from undoing the good that Washington had accomplished the year before.[71]

In London, however, Moton was wooed by Du Bois and Milholland, and on his return to New York he praised them for their conservative and optimistic speeches, which he claimed were entirely different in tone from their "Appeal to Europe" of 1910. Moton was sure that the two factions would come together and work for the common good of humanity. Washington reacted somewhat differently to Du Bois's address, when it was printed and circulated some months later in the official report of the Congress. He could not find any of the "bubling [sic] optimism," of which Moton had written.[72]

Before many months had passed, Moton had again given up hope of being able to cooperate with Du Bois. He thought the NAACP had tremendous possibilities under the proper management, but Du Bois was not the man to manage the organization. On the other hand, he was afraid that any attempt to tell Villard that Du Bois was unsuited to lead the Association would be interpreted as an attempt to oust him from his job.[73]

Through the years Washington continued to get news of the internal dissensions which wracked the NAACP. He observed the resentment engendered by white men assuming to lead and control the colored people and agreed with Bishop Walters to use his influence in the Negro press to emphasize Negro leadership for Negroes. At one point, thinking the NAACP near disintegration, the Tuskegee people saw an opportunity to soften Villard and perhaps split

---

[70] John H. Harris to Washington, December 1, 1910; Washington to Harris, December 28, 1910; January 9, 1911; January 23, 1911; Harris to Washington, January 13, 1911, enclosing copy of letter, Harris to Du Bois, January 13, 1911; Harris to Milholland (copy sent to Washington, March 22, 1911), Washington Papers.

[71] Moton to Washington, May 13, 1911; Moton to Scott, May 20, 1911, Washington Papers.

[72] New York Age, August 10, 1911; August 17, 1911; Moton to Washington, July 23, 1911; August 11, 1911; Scott to Moton, December 26, 1911, Washington Papers. See Gustav Spiller (ed.), Papers on Inter-Racial Problems Communicated to the First Universal Races Congress Held at the University of London, July 26–29, 1911 (London, 1911), pp. 348–64. Du Bois's article, "The First Universal Races Congress," Independent, LXXI (August 24, 1911), 401–3, dealt with "race" from a scientific point of view.

[73] Moton to Scott, January 15, 1912, Washington Papers.

him off from Du Bois's influence altogether. They professed to believe that Villard was being deceived by Du Bois and others in the Association.[74] Villard had in fact resigned as Chairman of the Board in a dispute with Du Bois over *The Crisis* and the authority of the chairman. Joel Spingarn, the new chairman, had been severely critical of Washington.

Moton therefore proposed a meeting between Fred Moore and Villard, think-ing that Villard and Du Bois were afraid of the *New York Age*, and anxious for Moore's cooperation. The Tuskegee group was shocked by Villard's uncom-promising answer. He was doubtful that a conference with Moore would be of value because the *Age* was essentially the organ of Dr. Washington. Villard admitted that Spingarn's public criticism had been severe, but he deplored Washington's silence while one civil right after another was being taken away from the colored people. Washington believed he was the leader of his people, but he did nothing about the segregation in Washington, in Baltimore, and in nine other Southern cities. Villard shocked Moton by comparing Washington to Nero.[75]

Moton termed the comparison to Nero odious and called on Emmett Scott for a suitable reply with "a few strong quotations" to prove that Washington was not silent about segregation. There followed a flurry of letters between Moton, Moore, Scott, and Washington, as they sought to reassure themselves but refused to admit that the Tuskegee program was anything but "sane."[76] Their efforts ended as before in an impasse.

Nevertheless, there was a subtle change of tone. With the failure of the attempt to woo Villard, the Tuskegee machine redoubled its efforts to propagandize its own program in order to counteract the growing influence of the NAACP. Moton urged that Washington "strike right out from the shoulder on what we are trying to do to help the Negro." This theme was stressed at a public meet-ing in New York in April, 1914, and again at the annual meeting of the National Negro Business League in the fall, at which Washington urged Negroes to get off the defensive and begin an aggressive and constructive progressive policy.[77]

Meantime, Villard was not content to leave vocational education entirely to Washington. His experience as a member of the Board of the Manassas In-dustrial School had convinced him that reforms were necessary. In 1913, he called a conference of the small rural industrial schools in the South to meet at NAACP headquarters for an exchange of ideas and experiences, discussion of

[74] Washington to Scott, January 16, 1914; Moton to Moore, March 5, 1914, Washington Papers.
[75] Moton to Moore, March 5, 1914; Villard to Moton, March 9, 1914, Washington Papers.
[76] Moton to Scott, March 11, 1914; Scott to Moore, March 18, 1914; March 24, 1914, Wash-ington Papers.
[77] Moton to Washington, April 8, 1914, Washington Papers; *New York Age*, September 3, 1914.

educational and business procedures, public relations, fund raising, and the problems of substandard schools.[78]

Washington considered this an effort to undermine his influence in industrial education. He had learned that Thomas Jesse Jones, Director of the Phelps-Stokes Fund, was about to investigate the entire school system in the South. There were signs, too, that Tuskegee itself was coming in for criticism by academics because its type of education was not preparing its students for life in a changing industrial world.[79] Washington's adviser, Robert E. Park, urged that the Negro should be represented in all reform movements in the South and that Tuskegee should play as large a role as possible.[80]

Washington at first ignored Villard's call for a conference. Later he agreed to send a representative from Tuskegee, provided the meeting were held at some place other than the headquarters of the NAACP. He considered it a mistake to identify educational problems of the South with the work of the Association and inferred that Villard was encroaching on Tuskegee's domain. Washington felt sure that the real purpose of this conference on schools was to spread the impression through *The Crisis* that the NAACP was taking over the problems of education in the South and that they had drawn Dr. Hollis B. Frissell, principal of Hampton Institute, and himself into the organization.[81]

Villard called Washington's refusal to attend cowardly, but to meet the objection of association with the NAACP, arranged for the conference to be held elsewhere. Neither Moton nor Washington would attend, however. Moton thought the meeting was not "big enough" to take up Washington's time. Villard accused Washington of throwing cold water on his plans, but Washington replied that the whole project was a duplicate of the Stokes Fund survey, which was already under way in 1914, and he continued to undermine Villard's efforts.[82]

[78] Villard to Washington, February —, 1913, Washington Papers; NAACP, *Third Annual Report 1912* (New York, 1913), p. 29.

[79] Jacob H. Hollander to Julius Rosenwald, November 5, 1912, Washington Papers. Professor Hollander of The Johns Hopkins University suggested to Rosenwald an evaluation of Tuskegee's program by means of a study of the "economic usefulness" of its alumni.

[80] Robert E. Park to Washington, December 16, 1912; Villard to Washington, June 3, 1914, Washington Papers. Park, a sociologist, was architect of a number of Washington's policies and programs at Tuskegee, including the curriculum, and helped him to write many of his books and articles. Park to Washington, January 1, 1906; October 5, 1911; and *passim*, Washington Papers; J. E. Spingarn to Washington, February 25, 1913; Scott to Spingarn, March 1, 1913, Joel Elias Spingarn Papers (Moorland Foundation, Howard University).

[81] Washington to Villard, February 27, 1913; March 21, 1913; April 8, 1913; Washington to Moton, March 21, 1913; Washington to Scott, March 21, 1913, Washington Papers.

[82] Board Minutes, NAACP, April 1, 1913; Villard to Moton, March 31, 1913; Moton to Scott, April 11, 1913; Villard to Washington, May 21, 1914; Washington to Villard, May 27, 1914; Washington to Alfred T. White, June 1, 1915, Washington Papers.

RECONCILIATION: THE AMENIA CONFERENCE

With Washington's death at the end of 1915, the Tuskegee faction was without a leader. Moton, who had long desired and worked for unity and peaceful relations, became head of the Tuskegee school, but he could not fill Washington's place as leader.

Du Bois suggested that the regular annual meeting of the NAACP in 1916 be postponed because a memorial meeting for Booker T. Washington was to be held on the same date. He wrote Spingarn that a meeting at that time would not only be an anticlimax but would appear to be a counter attraction, and a basis for further antagonism. He proposed instead a "get-together" meeting of the leaders of the Negro race and their friends, including the heads of all large Negro organizations. This led to the Amenia Conference held in August, 1916, at Joel Spingarn's estate, Troutbeck, at Amenia, New York.

Plans for the conference and the guest lists were drawn up with reconciliation in mind. The names in Du Bois's confidential index of conferees were classified "Niagara Movement Man," "Washington Man," or "?" They were about equally divided. He wanted a full and free discussion as to the next step to be taken in a number of different lines of advance and agitation. In working out the program he avoided discussion leaders who might crystallize the conference into two hard groups at the start, and he avoided appearing on the program himself. Two sessions were devoted to education and industry. Other discussions centered around the Negro in politics, civil and legal discrimination, social discrimination, and a working program for the future.[83]

James Weldon Johnson recalled many years later that half a hundred of the country's most influential and progressive Negroes and white people interested in the cause of Negro rights participated.[84] They drew up a series of resolutions, agreeing: that all forms of education are desirable for the Negro; that in common with all other races, the Negro race cannot achieve its highest development without complete political freedom; that organization and a practical working understanding among race leaders were necessary for that development; that antiquated subjects of controversy, ancient suspicions, and factional alignments must be eliminated and forgotten; and that there was a special need of understanding between leaders in the South and in the North.[85]

[83] Du Bois, "Memorandum to Chairman of the Board, the Treasurer and the Secretary," December 14, 1915, in Joel Elias Spingarn Papers (James Weldon Johnson Collection, Yale University); Roy Nash to Spingarn, August 16, 1916; Amenia Conference "Programme" in J. E. Spingarn Papers (Howard).
[84] Johnson, *Along This Way*, p. 308.
[85] Amenia Conference, "Report of the Committee on Resolutions," August 26, 1916, in J. E. Spingarn Papers (Yale). See also Du Bois, *The Amenia Conference: An Historic Negro Gathering* (Troutbeck Leaflets, VIII; Amenia, New York, 1925), pp. 14–15.

The conference was held with a minimum of publicity. Without Washington's overpowering personality, and with Du Bois in the background, leaders of all schools of thought were able to agree upon fundamental lines of action. Reaction from both sides was favorable. Charles Bentley, a former Niagara man, called it the beginning of a welding process of the radicals and conservatives; J. C. Napier, a Washington man, called it a wise and discreet step; and the *New York Age* reported that it marked the birth of a new spirit of united purpose and effort.[86]

During the twenty years between the Atlanta Compromise speech of 1895 and his death in 1915, Booker T. Washington had reached the height of his career. His policy of conciliation to the South had brought him acclaim. It had satisfied Southern whites. His pronouncements on labor had given him access to Northern philanthropists. He had achieved prestige in politics, power in the Negro press, supremacy in the field of industrial education, and a position of leadership in the Negro world.

But Washington's philosophy was entirely unsatisfactory to Du Bois and many of his "talented tenth." Though Du Bois lost out at the Carnegie Hall conference of 1904, this minority realized how ineffective Washington's policy was against the growing segregation and denial of rights to Negroes. To the "Du Bois men" only a policy of agitation and protest would do. The NAACP provided an effective and permanent organization for carrying out this policy.

The Amenia Conference was held at a time of great opportunity for the Negro and of great danger too. Though not officially sponsored by the NAACP, it was nevertheless carried out by NAACP men. Its success in achieving a basis of unity among Negro leaders made it possible to fight more effectively for an extension of democracy at home during the years when the nation was fighting a war on foreign soil "to make the world safe for democracy."

[86] Board Minutes, NAACP, January 2, 1917; Charles E. Bentley to J. E. Spingarn, August 29, 1916; J. C. Napier to J. E. Spingarn, September 7, 1916, J. E. Spingarn Papers (Howard); *New York Age*, September 14, 1916.

CHAPTER V

Internal Organization and Policy

The name of the Association caused dissastisfaction and led to frequent discussion and debate during the first six or seven years. From March, 1909, to March, 1910, the founders spoke of themselves as the Committee on the Negro, the Committee on the Status of the Negro, or (after the first conference, May— June, 1909) as the National Negro Committee. The Committee on Permanent Organization headed by Oswald Garrison Villard proposed the name "National Association for the Advancement of Colored People," and this was accepted by the second annual conference in May, 1910.

Prior to incorporation in 1911, complaints and suggestions regarding a change of name were received from prominent members of the Boston group—Francis Jackson Garrison, Horace Bumstead, and George G. Bradford. Villard defended the name because of the "astounding amount of publicity" received following the Boston conference in 1911. He said the Boston group could use another name, such as the Boston Liberty League, provided it made clear it was a branch of the national organization.[1]

Discussion of the question continued but in May, 1911, the Executive Committee voted not to change the name. This led Moorfield Storey to urge Villard to hold the matter open as both he and Albert Pillsbury thought the title long and cumbersome. Pillsbury, in fact, became so disgruntled when the Association took no further steps to change its name that he refused for a time to continue his annual contribution of $500.[2]

[1] Francis Jackson Garrison to Oswald Garrison Villard, April 7, 1911; Villard to Garrison, April 7, 1911, Oswald Garrison Villard Papers (Houghton Library, Harvard University); Minutes, Executive Committee, April 11, 1911, in "Minute Book of the Board of Directors of the National Association for the Advancement of Colored People" (now in the Manuscript Division, Library of Congress; hereafter referred to as Board Minutes, NAACP).
[2] Minutes, Executive Committee, May 2, 1911, in Board Minutes, NAACP; Moorfield Storey to Villard, May 12, 1911, Moorfield Storey Papers (in the possession of Mr. Charles Storey, Boston, Massachusetts); Villard to Garrison, March 21, 1912, Villard Papers.

NAACP

In 1913, the agenda for the Annual Meeting included an item for considering "changing or modifying the name of the Association with a view to shortening it." At that meeting, a Committee on the Change of Name offered five substitutes:

The Emancipation League
The Garrison Association for the Advancement of Colored People
The Lincoln Association for the Advancement of Colored People
The Association for the Advancement of Colored People
The League for the Advancement of Colored People

After much debate the question was referred to the Board of Directors for report to the annual conference in the spring. The Board again decided, however, that a change of name was "not now advisable." [3]

This did not settle the matter. In 1916, members were once more asked for suggestions for a name. The replies were studied by a committee headed by John Haynes Holmes, who reported that most members would be in favor of a change if the right name could be found. Those who objected to a change did so on the grounds that it would take too much time to establish a new name, and that a name representative of the Association's uncompromising radicalism might alienate some of its Southern friends.[4]

This was probably the reason why the designation "New Abolition Movement" did not catch on, though it was used frequently by Joel Spingarn and by *The Crisis* during 1913 and 1914. At one point the *Chicago Evening Post* commented that "new abolitionism" fitted the movement exactly, "for it is fiery abolitionism, as against the calm meliorism of Booker T. Washington, that this society preaches."[5] When the name "Garrison-Douglass Association" was proposed in 1916, it was turned down by the Board. This was the last official action taken on the subject.[6]

The active leaders of the "New Abolition Movement," like their contemporaries who led the Progressive Movement, were young men and women.[7] According to Mary White Ovington, the average age of the five incorporators was thirty-five.[8]

[3] Minutes, Annual Meeting, January 21, 1913, in Board Minutes, NAACP; Board Minutes, NAACP, March 11, 1913.
[4] Storey to Roy Nash, October 26, 1916, Storey Papers; Board Minutes, NAACP, November 13, 1916; December 11, 1916.
[5] Quoted in *Crisis*, VII (March, 1914), 227. See also Solomon Porter Hood to Spingarn, January 6, 1913, and John W. Day to Spingarn, January 24, 1914, Joel Elias Spingarn Papers (Moorland Foundation, Howard University).
[6] Board Minutes, NAACP, December 11, 1916. This was one of the few times that a vote is recorded. The first motion that the name might "advantageously" be changed passed, 6 to 5; but the next motion to use the "Garrison-Douglass Association," was defeated, 9 to 3.
[7] Richard Hofstadter, *The Age of Reform: From Bryan to F.D.R.* (New York, 1955), pp. 166–67.
[8] Mary White Ovington, *The Walls Came Tumbling Down* (New York, 1947), p. 107.

90

Complementing the young leaders were the elder statesmen, whose lives embraced the two abolition movements. They were the Garrisons, Fanny Garrison Villard, the second William Lloyd Garrison (who died shortly after the first conference), Francis Jackson Garrison, Moorfield Storey, and Albert E. Pillsbury.

It was Pillsbury who drew up the bylaws for the Association, which were presented to the first meeting of the incorporators on June 20, 1911, and unanimously approved.[9] The bylaws provided for a Board of thirty directors to be elected at the first meeting of the corporation in January, 1912. Officers of the corporation were to be elected from the Board: a president, two or more vice-presidents, a chairman of the Board, a secretary, and a treasurer. Thus, the Executive Committee was supplanted by a Board of Directors.

The Board was authorized to appoint a Director of Publicity and Research and other officers, and provision was made for committees on finance, legal redress, publications, and memberships, as well as a general advisory committee.[10]

The first meeting of the Board of Directors was held immediately following the incorporators' meeting and the three present, Villard, Miss Ovington, and Walter Sachs, constituted the quorum. (Later the quorum was changed to six.) They proceeded to nominate as officers: Moorfield Storey, president; John E. Milholland and Bishop Alexander Walters, vice-presidents; Villard, chairman of the Board; Mary White Ovington, secretary; and Walter Sachs, treasurer. W. E. B. Du Bois was appointed Director of Publicity and Research.[11]

On January 4, 1912, three meetings were held. First the old Executive Committee met and presented a slate of thirty Board members for nominations and adjourned. Then the Board (authorized by the incorporators) met and voted that members of the General Committee (Committee of One Hundred) should be asked to serve on the new Advisory Committee. Finally the Annual Meeting of Members was held, and the thirty Board members were elected. Villard presided at all three meetings. There were at that time 329 members of the Association.[12]

At the first regular meeting of the Board in February, 1912, the officers who had been nominated at the time of incorporation were elected, and two vice-presidents were added, the Reverend John Haynes Holmes and the Reverend

---

[9] "First Meeting of the Incorporators of the NAACP," June 20, 1911, in Board Minutes, NAACP. Miss Ovington, Villard, and Walter W. Sachs were present, and Du Bois and John Haynes Holmes sent proxies. The Articles of Incorporation were drawn up and signed on May 25, 1911. They were approved June 9, and filed in the office of the Secretary of the State of New York on June 16, and with the County Clerk of New York County on June 19, 1911.

[10] Bylaws of the National Association for the Advancement of Colored People, in Board Minutes, NAACP, June 20, 1911.

[11] Board Minutes, NAACP, June 20, 1911.

[12] Board Minutes, NAACP, January 4, 1912. See Appendix E for first Board of Directors.

Garnett R. Waller. Martha Gruening, a volunteer social worker, and Paul Kennaday were appointed as assistant secretaries.[13]

INTERNAL STRIFE

Dissension within the organization caused a great deal of trouble for the new Association. Though internal organizational conflict is not unknown in institutional life, there were times when Negroes and whites alike blamed the disruptive element on race. Booker T. Washington once expressed regret that all his friends could not seem to work harmoniously and naively commented, "In this respect white people excel us very much." Villard, when he first started working with the Negro problem, was distressed by the "way the colored people fight among themselves." Moorfield Storey was concerned with the differences among colored leaders and frequently tried to stop William Monroe Trotter from emphasizing points of difference.[14]

It is true that there were few places of prestige open to Negroes, and the rivalry for status was keen. The most extreme individualists occasionally withdrew. Mrs. Ida Wells-Barnett felt slighted when Villard called a meeting of the Chicago branch at Hull House without notifying her. She complained that Villard and Du Bois wanted Jane Addams to "mother" the movement, although she had neither the time nor the strength to lead this new crusade. Mrs. Wells-Barnett resented the patronizing assumptions of the academic few who wanted to keep the organization in their own hands. She had been given to understand at a meeting of the Executive Committee in New York that she was not expected to do anything save to be a member. For this reason she limited her active participation in the development of the Chicago branch. Even Miss Ovington came in for denunciation. Mrs. Wells-Barnett declared that Miss Ovington's attitude was all right theoretically, but that she was not in sympathy with the colored people as a whole. She accused Miss Ovington of having special pets and claimed that her restrictive policy of admission by ticket had limited the number of people attending the New York annual meeting in 1912—in marked contrast to the Boston conference, where there were no restrictions. On the other hand, Mrs. Wells-Barnett counted William English Walling and Joel Spingarn among her few real friends in the movement; they had the "truest conception" of the work.[15]

[13] Board Minutes, NAACP, February 6, 1912.
[14] Washington to Daniel Murray, March 6, 1904, Booker T. Washington Papers (Manuscript Division, Library of Congress); Villard to Garrison, October 23, 1906, Villard Papers; Storey to Trotter, April 11, 1911, Storey Papers.
[15] Ida Wells-Barnett, "The National Association for the Advancement of Colored People," *Fellowship* (organ of the Negro Fellowship League of Chicago), January 17, 1912, n.p., clipping in Du Bois Papers (now in the possession of Mrs. W. E. B. Dubois, New York City); Ida Wells-Barnett to Joel Spingarn, April 21, 1911, J. E. Spingarn Papers (Howard).

William Monroe Trotter, always jealous of any invasion of his National Equal Rights League, remained a member of the NAACP until 1913, but by 1914 he had drifted out of the NAACP and was attacking both Du Bois and Washington with equal fury.[16]

If Negro leaders were inclined to be as temperamental as prima donnas, each seeking his own place in the limelight, the rank and file tended to be apathetic, indolent, and supine. Jessie Fauset, the novelist, felt that the average colored man was "too near the traditions of slavery not to esteem nominal freedom and fleshpots above their real value." Francis J. Garrison thought it would take five to ten years for the prosperous Negroes to assume their moral and financial obligation of supporting the Association, but he was confident that in time they would accept the responsibility of fighting for their own freedom.[17]

Even Negro intellectuals could not see the problem in its entirety at times. John Hope admitted that, shut off as Negroes were, they were apt to take an isolated and very personal attitude toward their problems. He acknowledged his debt to Joel Spingarn and Charles Edward Russell for helping him to see what he called the bigger, world side and the human significance of the Negro.[18]

Jessie Fauset urged Spingarn to "prod us, prick us, goad us on by unpleasant truths to ease off this terrible outer self of sloth and acceptance. . . . Some of us need to be told that we should be men. . . . Teach us, hammer into us that expediency is not all, that life is more than meat. And don't give us up. . . . For we are worth it."[19]

But the causes of friction within the Association were by no means confined to one race. White and Negro members were involved equally. In March, 1911, Miss Blascoer, disagreeing vehemently with Du Bois on all issues, resigned as "secretary" of the Association and became a member of the Executive Committee. A short time later she accepted an appointment to field work. Storey provided $1,200 for her salary for the first six months and the Association underwrote her expenses. As organizer, she was to spend a month each in Boston, Philadelphia, and Chicago, working with the branches. She became dissatisfied, however, with the arrangements concerning her expenses and before the middle of May gave up the work and returned to New York. According to Villard, she refused to be governed by simple business rules in regard to her expenses. She had

[16] Garrison to Villard, November 5, 1911, Villard Papers; Trotter to Spingarn, January 2, 1913, J. E. Spingarn Papers (Howard); Storey to Bumstead, March 10, 1914, Storey Papers.
[17] Jessie Fauset to Spingarn, February 12, 1913, J. E. Spingarn Papers (Howard); Garrison to Villard, January 29, 1913, Villard Papers.
[18] John Hope to Spingarn, February 28, 1913, J. E. Spingarn Papers (Howard).
[19] Jessie Fauset to Spingarn, February 12, 1913, J. E. Spingarn Papers (Howard).

already clashed with Du Bois over *Crisis* finances, refusing to show him the vouchers when their accounts did not balance.[20]

Miss Blascoer was apparently ill at this time. Villard spoke of her as a trying person to work with, though the first year of their association had been pleasant. Arthur Spingarn later recalled that she had a mental breakdown from which she never recovered. Her resignation was accepted but she remained on the Executive Committee for one more month. When she sent word that she could not attend meetings, she was asked to remain on the Committee of One Hundred.[21]

Miss Ovington took over the secretarial work without pay. To Villard, she was a perfect official, always unruffled, a "most ladylike, refined and cultivated person." Because of her other obligations on behalf of colored people, Miss Ovington was able to give only part time to the secretarial work. In May, 1912, she resigned and was elected a vice-president of the Association. May Childs Nerney, a young woman of executive ability, a former librarian who had worked in the State Library in Albany and in the Newark Public Library, was hired to take over the secretarial duties.[22]

Friction in the national office continued. After less than a year, Miss Nerney threatened to resign, accusing Du Bois's secretary of insolence and impertinence. According to Villard, this young woman had for a long time merited dismissal, but Du Bois, preoccupied with other matters, refused to let her go. Villard thought the only solution was to move Miss Nerney to separate quarters.

Villard got along with Du Bois by letting him go his own way, but he became irritated with the Negro leader when he discovered he was writing a book on NAACP time. He also resented Du Bois's attitude toward *The Crisis*, which Du Bois, according to Villard, considered his own property and his own creation. They clashed over Villard's suggestion that *The Crisis* publicize crimes perpetrated by Negroes as well as those committed against them. The Board straddled the issue by voting that Du Bois could publish information on the crimes of Negroes as he saw fit.[23]

Following this clash, Du Bois wrote to Villard, stating that he considered the Board of Directors his authority, and himself a fellow officer, not a subordinate

[20] Minutes, Executive Committee, March 7, 1911; April 11, 1911; May 2, 1911, in Board Minutes, NAACP; Garrison to Villard, April 8, 1911; Villard to Garrison, May 12, 1911, Villard Papers; Du Bois to Villard, April 11, 1911, Du Bois Papers. For NAACP secretaries, see Appendix F.

[21] Villard to Garrison, May 12, 1911, Villard Papers; A. B. Spingarn to writer, September 5, 1958; Minutes, Executive Committee, May 16, 1911; June 6, 1911, in Board Minutes, NAACP.

[22] Villard to Garrison, May 17, 1911; March 21, 1912, Villard Papers; *Crisis*, IV (July, 1912), 125.

[23] Villard to Garrison, February 7, 1913; February 11, 1913, Villard Papers; Board Minutes, NAACP, March 11, 1913.

receiving orders. He admitted the right of a Board member to criticize his work and to offer suggestions, but he resented Villard's implication that his independence of action was a breach of discipline or a personal discourtesy.[24]

Villard, however, thought of the chairman of the Board as *the* executive of the Association, with authority over paid employees, whether editors or clerks. He disclaimed any personal animosity toward Du Bois; the situation was the result of putting a paid employee on the Board of Directors. He left it to the Board to determine the relationship between officers of the Association, but he proposed that Joel Spingarn should soon succeed him as chairman of the Board.[25]

Du Bois cheerfully withdrew anything offensive he might have said in the heat of the argument, but a month later in April, 1913, there was another clash at the Board meeting and as a result Villard asked Du Bois to remove his name from the list of contributing editors of *The Crisis*.[26]

In an attempt to secure greater efficiency and better cooperation a committee, consisting of Miss Ovington, Charles Studin, Francis Batchelder,[27] and Walter Sachs, was constituted to inquire into the functioning of the national office. In addition, a *Crisis* advisory committee was appointed, consisting of Joel Spingarn, Dr. William Henry Brooks, and Miss Ovington.[28]

The friction continued, however, and to these personal irritations of Villard's was added a feeling that other Board members were not shouldering their responsibilities. Villard was also impatient with the Philadelphia members and complained of having to struggle "with the colored people and their easily hurt feelings," not only in NAACP work but also at Board meetings of the Manassas School. Working so close to Association headquarters meant that he was frequently called on four and five times a day, and his work for the *Evening Post* suffered accordingly.[29]

In November, 1913, Bishop Walters, a Board member, resigned because Villard publicly accused him of advocating segregation, and Sachs resigned as treasurer.[30]

---

[24] Du Bois to Villard, March 18, 1913, Villard Papers.
[25] Villard to Spingarn, March 20, 1913, Villard Papers.
[26] Du Bois to Villard, March 18, 1913, Villard Papers; Villlard to Du Bois, memorandum, April 2, 1913, in Board Minutes, NAACP. See also Du Bois to Villard [April 3, 1913]; Villard to Du Bois, April 3, 1913, Du Bois Papers.
[27] Francis Batchelder, a certified public accountant, audited the Association's books from the time of incorporation for many years. He was the brother of Margaret Batchelder, Miss Ovington's secretary, who became an officer of the New York branch.
[28] Board Minutes, NAACP, April 1, 1913.
[29] Board Minutes, NAACP, May 6, 1913; Villard to Garrison, February 7, 1913; March 14, 1913; October 23, 1913, Villard Papers.
[30] Villard to Garrison, September 23, 1913, Villard Papers; Board Minutes, NAACP, November 6, 1913; *New York Age*, November 6, 1913. Sachs resigned from the Board in 1914. Board Minutes, NAACP, October 6, 1914.

THE CRISIS OVER *THE CRISIS*

Further trouble with *The Crisis* precipitated Villard's resignation as chairman of the Board. Du Bois had remained defiant and insubordinate in regard to *The Crisis*, and Villard had accused him of refusing to recognize it as an organ of the Association. Villard reluctantly put up with Du Bois's independence because Du Bois was a Board member, but he was unable to accept the same attitude from a subordinate, Augustus G. Dill, business manager of *The Crisis*, who refused to obey official instructions.

Villard was no longer willing to continue as chairman unless the functions of that position were clearly defined. He recommended that the staffs of *The Crisis* and the Association be promptly separated. To Miss Ovington he expressed a fear that he might eventually be carrying the organization alone, since he had had no support whatever on the financial side from other members of the Association.[31]

Miss Ovington hinted that he took too much of the burden on himself and suggested that he leave all the executive work to Miss Nerney. To Mary White Ovington, Villard's withdrawal meant "a confession to the world that we cannot work with colored people unless they are our subordinates. . . . It puts us back five years."[32]

Du Bois met with Miss Ovington and Joel and Arthur Spingarn, to try to iron out the difficulties concerning *The Crisis* and the Association. He suggested three plans for the possible reorganization. Under the first, *The Crisis* would be completely separated from the NAACP and operated by an independent organization, The Crisis Associates, and Villard would continue as chairman of the Board. If this arrangement should go into effect, Du Bois promised a complete and thoroughgoing effort at cooperation with Villard and the Board. The second plan proposed that Miss Ovington become chairman of the Board and that a young colored man be selected as secretary and organizer. Du Bois would be under legal contract with the Board to edit and manage *The Crisis*; his other work would be voluntary, as in the case of other members of the Board. The third plan, which Du Bois professed to like least of all, proposed that the offices of Director of Publicity and Research and of Secretary be combined; Du Bois would become "executive secretary" working under the Board, and under the chairman between meetings. He proposed hiring an organizer, a managing editor for *The Crisis*, and with the first increase in revenue, a lawyer and an advertising agent.[33]

[31] Villard to Board of Directors, November 19, 1913; Villard to Ovington, November 21, 1913, Villard Papers.
[32] Ovington to Villard, November 21, 1913; November 25, 1913, Villard Papers.
[33] "Memorandum to Mr. J. E. Spingarn, Mr. A. B. Spingarn, and Miss Ovington from W. E. B. Du Bois," n.d. [November, 1913], Du Bois Papers.

Du Bois envisioned *The Crisis* as a separate entity with himself in charge, although his third plan, by way of contrast, was suggestive of the proposal at the 1910 conference to bring him into the Association as executive secretary, a proposal which had been defeated by Villard and Miss Blascoer. In spite of his protestations to the contrary, his failure to be appointed executive secretary may well have been the basic cause of Du Bois's friction with the Association.

The Board, however, did not accept any of Du Bois's proposals and as a first step in countering his moves to withdraw *The Crisis* from the aegis of the Association they adopted a resolution that each issue of the magazine should clearly and prominently state the aims and objectives of the NAACP, and the duty of *Crisis* readers to become members of the National Association. This was followed by steps to copyright *The Crisis* and its contents in the name of the Association.[34]

In January, 1914, Villard retired as chairman of the Board and became treasurer and chairman of the finance committee. In spite of past differences, Du Bois complimented Villard in *The Crisis*, saying that no other person had done more for the new abolition movement: "He took it when it was nothing but an idea and left it a nation-wide movement, with 24 branches and 3,000 members, out of debt, aggressive and full of faith."[35]

Villard's retirement and the election of Joel E. Spingarn as chairman of the Board failed to bring peace to the Association. All through the year 1914 one episode followed another. Du Bois's comments in *The Crisis* antagonized both individuals and groups. One source of friction was Du Bois's failure to give general recognition to what Trotter and his associates in the National Independent Political League were doing in the battle against segregation during the Wilson Administration. Moorfield Storey was so concerned over the resulting disharmony that he wrote at length to Villard and Spingarn in an attempt to get *The Crisis* to take a broad and catholic view of all that was being done for the common cause. At Spingarn's behest, Du Bois printed an explanation of the omission, but Trotter considered the explanation inadequate and far from convincing.[36]

Early in 1914, the NAACP moved into larger quarters in the "educational building" at 70 Fifth Avenue.[37] Although Du Bois insisted that there would be no additional expense in the move, which gave *The Crisis* more room and con-

[34] Board Minutes, NAACP, December 2, 1913; February 3, 1914; Nerney to Du Bois, February 6, 1914, Du Bois Papers.
[35] Board Minutes, NAACP, January 6, 1914; *Crisis*, VII (February, 1914), 188. For NAACP Board Chairmen, see Appendix G.
[36] Storey to Villard, January 8, 1914; January 13, 1914; Storey to Spingarn, January 15, 1915, Storey Papers; Trotter to Spingarn, January 28, 1914, J. E. Spingarn Papers (Howard).
[37] Nerney to Charles T. Hallinan, December 22, 1913, NAACP Files (formerly in NAACP offices, New York; now in Manuscript Division, Library of Congress).

venience, running expenses at the new office increased $700 a year at a time when *The Crisis* was still not self-supporting. Villard, however, was relieved and glad NAACP staff were no longer his tenants, for they had been "hard to please."[38]

To Villard, the new chairman of the Board, Joel Spingarn, was a firebrand who started off with a violent attack on Booker T. Washington. Villard had no faith in Miss Nerney's ability to carry on the executive work. He complained that Du Bois had again irritated many on the Board with a wanton attack on *The Survey*,[39] and that the mounting expenses made the Association's financial outlook appear ominous. Unwittingly, he gave a clue to his own personality (and to one cause of the clash with Du Bois) when he wrote of *The Nation*, "It is going to be a broad, fine paper with O. G. V. as absolute dictator of the policy."[40] But Villard was entirely correct when he predicted that Du Bois was precipitating an inevitable crisis with *The Crisis*. Within the next few months, Du Bois was to attack not only Trotter but the Negro press, white philanthropy, the colored clergy, and Negro higher education.

A number of Negro editors showed deep resentment when Du Bois said that Negro papers were poorly written and the Negro press as a whole was unreliable, incomplete, and venal.[41] Was this his method of guiding them "towards better methods and ideals?"[42]

Du Bois's harsh criticism of Robert C. Ogden, at the time of his death, was interpreted by the *New York Age* as an ungrateful attack upon white philanthropy. Du Bois wrote that "a self-conscious, self-helping Negro was beyond Mr. Ogden's conception. . . . He wanted Negroes to be satisfied and do well in the place . . . he was sure they . . . ought to occupy." In spite of Ogden's sincerity and unselfishness, he had become a captive of the white South, and the activities

---

[38] Spingarn to Du Bois, October 24, 1914, Joel Elias Spingarn Papers (James Weldon Johnson Collection, Yale University; hereafter referred to as the Johnson Collection). Villard to Garrison, March 1, 1914, Villard Papers.

[39] Villard to *Crisis* Committee, January 23, 1914, NAACP Files; *Crisis*, VII (February, 1914), 187. *The Survey* was published by the Charity Organization Society of the City of New York and was sympathetic to the cause of the Negro. *The Survey* had asked Du Bois for an article, but had refused to accept it. Du Bois claimed Villard and Miss Nerney had "discredited" him behind his back, and he took a "last fling at the Survey" which disturbed Board members anxious to keep *The Survey* open to material about the Association. Du Bois to Spingarn, October 28, 1914, Johnson Collection.

[40] Villard to Garrison, March 1, 1914, Villard Papers.

[41] *Crisis*, VII (March, 1914), 239–40. The *New York Age*, March 12, 1914, includes reprints from the *Atlanta Independent* and the *Richmond Planet*. The *Washington Bee* counterattacked the "insult to the Negro press" by accusing *The Crisis* of clipping its news from the Negro weeklies. *Washington Bee*, March 7, 1914.

[42] Du Bois, Memorandum to Board on Objects and Methods of the Organization, n.d. [1913], Du Bois Papers.

of the Southern Education Board had become a movement for white people only.[43]

Du Bois also aroused a storm of protest from W. S. Scarborough, president of Wilberforce University, by his article on "The New Wilberforce," in which he praised the new state-supported college and indirectly criticized the older church-related school. Scarborough claimed that the article through misrepresentations and distortions had greatly stirred up the alumni.[44]

The colored clergy were criticized and denounced in a "Church Number" of *The Crisis*. The Negro church was censured for not reaching the mass of middle-class Negroes and for not choosing honest and efficient leaders. Alexander Walters, Bishop of the African Methodist Episcopal Zion Church and an NAACP Board member, was embarrassed because *The Crisis* reported that his was the only one of the four leading Negro churches which had not responded to a request for an article for the "Church Number." Du Bois's comment on the need for radical reform in the financial affairs of the Zion Church enraged Bishop Walters and probably contributed to his rapprochement with Booker T. Washington.[45]

The president of the Baltimore NAACP branch reported to national headquarters that the position of *The Crisis* had caused much trouble and urged the Association to court, rather than criticize, the Negro press and ministry. This Du Bois would not do, and a Boston member urged Spingarn to do his best to eliminate from *The Crisis* "those bitter and sarcastic expressions that have created so many enmities."[46]

In an attempt to overcome these problems, a new policy was hammered out by the Association through the spring and summer of 1914. A new constitution and bylaws drawn up by Charles Studin were approved by the Board in July, 1914.[47]

Although the duties of officers were defined, Villard was not satisfied with the way the office of treasurer was presented and again found himself up against Du Bois. The new bylaws provided that the treasurer should receive regular reports, inspect the books, and audit the accounts of all departments and bureaus. Villard

---

[43] *New York Age*, April 23, 1914; *Crisis*, VII (April, 1914), 274–75. For a discussion of Ogden and the Southern Education Board, see the excellent study by Louis R. Harlan, *Separate and Unequal: Public School Campaigns and Racism in the Southern Seaboard States 1901–1915* (Chapel Hill, 1958), pp. 75–101.
[44] *Crisis*, VIII (August, 1914), 191–94; W. S. Scarborough to Villard, September 8, 1914; Villard to Scarborough, September 10, 1914; Nerney to Spingarn, September 11, 1914; Scarborough to Spingarn, September 18, 1914; Spingarn to Scarborough, September 19, 1914, in J. E. Spingarn Papers (Howard).
[45] *Crisis*, IV (May, 1912), 24–25, 28–33; R. W. Thompson to E. J. Scott, April 18, 1913, Washington Papers.
[46] Dr. Francis N. Cardozo to Spingarn, December 18, 1914; George G. Bradford to Spingarn, December 2, 1914, J. E. Spingarn Papers (Howard).
[47] Board Minutes, NAACP, April 17, 1914; April 28, 1914; July 7, 1914.

thought the treasurer should supervise all the financial affairs of the organization, including *The Crisis*. Failure to run the magazine in an efficient manner meant that the Association had to pay part of the expenses as well as the editor's salary. Villard thought *The Crisis* should produce a profit, which could be used to extend the work of the Association. His business experience in the publishing field made him conscious of the need for a trained business manager, and for accurate advertising records or statements to show the exact cost per issue and the exact returns. Information concerning the number of agents in arrears, totals of bad debts, and analysis of paper costs was also needed.[48]

During the discussions of the proposed bylaws, Du Bois offered a resolution further defining the duties of officers and this was accepted as an amendment to the constitution being evolved. The treasurer, according to Du Bois, should, with the advice and cooperation of the Finance Committee, raise funds for the support of the Association. This made the treasurer the money-raising officer of the Association with little or no policy-making functions and with no control in financial affairs.

The chairman of the Board was also shorn of executive powers. The Du Bois resolution provided for an executive committee, consisting of the chairman of the Board, the treasurer, the secretary, and the Director of Publications and Research (a change of title from "Director of Publicity and Research").[49] This executive committee was to have general supervision over the work and finances of the Association and all its departments and was to report to the Board. Though the chairman was to have general control and supervision of the Association between meetings, his decisions and appointments were subject to the approval of the Board and the executive committee.[50] The secretary was to be limited in authority and function to keeping records, supervising the branches, the annual meetings and annual conference, conducting the press and lecture bureau, acting as secretary of the executive committee, and collecting and disbursing dues and general funds of the Association.

[48] Board Minutes, NAACP, July 7, 1914; Villard to Spingarn, April 16, 1914, J. E. Spingarn Papers (Howard).
[49] This "executive committee" was a committee of the Board in contrast to the "Executive Committee" which was the governing body of the Association before incorporation.
[50] This procedure is in direct contrast to a report on "methods of organization and administration" submitted in 1912 by an unidentified "Mr. Morgan." In order to avoid and overcome "many of the difficulties which have been encountered in the past," Morgan divided the organization into three functional areas: the advisory function, the executive function, and machinery for carrying out details. He recommended as "fundamental" to a successful organization that the executive function should be in the hands of one person, and that this director "must be the same person who follows it up and sees that it is done." This work could not be done by a Board of Directors or an Executive Committee. "Memorandum by Mr. Morgan of Organization Work," August 23, 1912, Du Bois Papers.

The Director of Publication and Research, with the advice and cooperation of the Publication Committee of the Board, was given power to edit and manage *The Crisis*, collect and disburse *Crisis* monies, make reports to the treasurer, edit and issue all other publications of the Association, and direct the Bureau of Research and Information.

Villard's opposition to Du Bois's plan found support in Florence Kelley, who thought the carte blanche proposed for his department was staggering. Nor could she accept his idea of the duties of the secretary, commenting that no sane person would undertake the task as Du Bois had outlined it.[51]

Nevertheless, the Board adopted Du Bois's resolution, along with the article naming the officers. The chairman of the Board did not become the center of authority that Villard had maintained was necessary. The secretary was in no sense an executive officer, and all power and authority, save that which it chose to delegate, lay with the Board of Directors and its subordinate executive committee.[52]

In so defining the duties of the officers, the Board at this time upheld Du Bois's contention as to his role as an equal on the Board with the chairman, the treasurer, and the secretary. The Board, in refusing to subject the finances and business management of *The Crisis* to the scrutiny and control of the treasurer, also defeated another move by Villard for control over Du Bois's activities. Villard's vision of a single, autocratic, efficient executive officer lost out to Du Bois's reliance on consensus of the group, over which he could wield influence.

Miss Ovington wrote Spingarn that she had warned Du Bois of the strong desire of some Board members to get rid of him. She had cautioned him against Villard, who had "always been opposed" to their choice of Director of Publicity and Research, and against Miss Nerney, who seemed also to be opposed to his being there. She told Spingarn of pleading with Du Bois not to give any of his opponents the slightest handle against him, and not to go to extremes in his speaking or writing in any way that would endanger his position.[53]

THE "COLOR LINE"

Though Villard would have denied it vehemently, to Du Bois the conflict between them was one more evidence of the color line. This becomes clear in an exchange which developed between Du Bois and Joel Spingarn, whom he later called a knight.[54] As chairman of the Board, Spingarn, too, found it difficult to work with Du Bois. This time it was Du Bois who felt the tension and made

[51] Florence Kelley to Spingarn, June 8, 1914, J. E. Spingarn Papers (Howard).
[52] Board Minutes, NAACP, July 7, 1914.
[53] Ovington to Spingarn, November 7, 1914, J. E. Spingarn Papers (Howard).
[54] Du Bois, *Dusk of Dawn: An Essay Toward an Autobiography of a Race Concept* (New York, 1940). The dedication is "To keep the memory of Joel Spingarn, scholar and knight."

what was for him an exceptional effort at reconciliation. He felt that the new chairman doubted his honesty and did not meet him in a straightforward manner but approached him "warily and cautiously watching for his dodging and deception." Hoping it was only his imagination, Du Bois, who rarely confided his inmost thoughts, confessed in a letter to Spingarn that the feeling had become so poignant that it demanded—and almost forced—an expression.[55]

Perhaps this was the opening which Spingarn had been waiting for. In any case, he took the opportunity to write a frank letter, assuring Du Bois that there was no question of his honesty, but that he had an extraordinary unwillingness to admit a mistake and that he would find or even invent reasons and quibbles to prove that he was not wrong. This was nothing, however, compared with the atmosphere of antagonism surrounding Du Bois, not just with Villard, Miss Nerney, and the Board, but in the whole colored world, where even his best friends felt a mingled affection and resentment. Spingarn went on to accuse Du Bois of mistaking obstinacy for strength of character. Many were sure that he, Du Bois, was the only source of the disorder and lack of unity in the organization, and that for the Association to work together effectively and without friction, Du Bois must be eliminated. Though Spingarn disagreed with that point of view because of his faith in Du Bois's character and talents and because he believed it was a matter of temperament, he agreed that Du Bois's talents must be subordinated to the general welfare of the organization. He made it clear that the rift between the departments was closed. "There can be no Crisis, no non-Crisis; the war of dividing our work has failed; both must be one." Without this cooperation, Spingarn concluded, the Association was doomed.[56]

A few days later Du Bois replied to Spingarn. He denied that he was obstinate. He blamed his temperament on the peculiar education and experiences to which he had been subjected because of his color and asked for a chance to work unhampered. He looked upon *The Crisis* as one of the world's great journals, a means of educating and training the Negro masses. Not until the journal achieved a circulation of 100,000 would the machinery of the NAACP be perfected.

Here again was the conflict as to whether they should first perfect the organization or should proceed at once with widespread propaganda. Du Bois believed that the "great blow—the freeing of ten million" would not be possible until the support of the Negro masses had been enlisted. Internal friction within the NAACP was a minor matter for which he refused to take the blame. His explosion over the matter of publicizing Negro crimes had been the result of piled-up slights and unkindnesses on the part of Villard. Two weary years of that had

[55] Du Bois to Spingarn, October 23, 1914, Johnson Collection.
[56] Spingarn to Du Bois, October 24, 1914, Johnson Collection.

put his nerves on edge. He had had little disagreements with Miss Nerney over office regulations, but Miss Nerney had a violent temper and was depressingly suspicious of his motives. She had elbowed him out of all connection with the general work of the NAACP, and he had been right in refusing to allow her to interfere with *The Crisis*.

The basis of all this friction, Du Bois explained to Spingarn, was the "color line." There was not a shadow of the thing in either Spingarn or Miss Ovington. As for Miss Nerney, though she had no conscious prejudice, "her every step [was] unconsciously along the color line." Du Bois found Villard even worse. (It is true that Villard's letters, in spite of his good intentions, often show a patronizing attitude toward the Negro. It was something that Booker T. Washington could tolerate, but it must have been extremely trying to Du Bois, who was sensitive enough to observe every "shadow.")

No organization of this type, Du Bois continued, had ever succeeded, because it became either a group of white philanthropists helping the Negro or a group of colored folk freezing out their white co-workers by insolence and distrust. Since everything broke along the so-called color line, Du Bois tried to evolve a scheme whereby Negroes and whites could work together on the same level of authority and cooperation by having two branches of the same work, one with a white head and one with a colored. In short the Association would work best with a white secretary, or chairman, while Du Bois kept complete control of *The Crisis*.

He recommended that, first of all, the rift of the color line be fully recognized. Secondly, he demanded a chance to complete his work without chains and petty hampering. He asked to be trusted with power, and to be allowed the same right as a white man to succeed or to make mistakes on his own merits. Then if the Association should decide that he was standing in the way of its success, he would leave.[57]

Spingarn brought the matter into the open at the November, 1914, Board meeting, a move which distressed Miss Ovington, who had worked steadily for five years to prevent this lining up of personalities. She became very angry when Spingarn claimed that the friction centered about a single individual, whom he described as childish and insubordinate. To Spingarn's charge that she idolized Du Bois, she answered that she did worship genius. The other Board members were able journeymen, but Du Bois was the master builder. She defended Du Bois's criticism of Miss Nerney's temper, admitting that she had confined herself to working on *The Crisis* because of Miss Nerney's ill will toward her in the office.[58]

[57] Du Bois to Spingarn, October 28, 1914, Johnson Collection.
[58] Ovington to Spingarn, November 4, 1914; November 7, 1914, J. E. Spingarn Papers (Howard).

As a result of these events, Du Bois sent a new proposal to Spingarn, suggesting that the office and his salary as Director of Publication and Research be abolished and that he give full time to *The Crisis*, which would continue as the official organ of the NAACP. A committee would exercise a veto over editorials and have the right to publish in each issue five pages of material concerning the Association.[59]

To gain support for his proposal Du Bois went to Boston and discussed the plan with Storey. Storey wrote Villard that Du Bois had created *The Crisis* and should be permitted to carry it on, although privately he was doubtful that Du Bois would be able to succeed alone.[60]

BYLAWS AND REVISIONS

At the December, 1914, meeting the Board reversed its July decision. The executive committee was abolished and the chairman of the Board was made the executive officer, with full authority over heads of departments between meetings of the Board. Employees, however, were subject to the authority of heads of departments and not to the chairman of the Board. Department heads were to be hired and fired only with the consent of the Board. The Director of Publication and Research, having the rank of a department head, was to be responsible for the administration of the *Crisis* Fund and formulation of policy for *The Crisis*, limited only by the advice of a *Crisis* committee, consisting of the chairman of the Board and two others. He was to report monthly to the Board. Voting with Du Bois against the majority report were Kennaday, George W. Crawford, Verina Morton-Jones, and Mary White Ovington. Twenty were present at the meeting.[61]

Further revisions of the bylaws gave the Board chairman greater control and full authority over all officials and employees between Board meetings. In spite of Du Bois's efforts, the Association had not relinquished control of *The Crisis*. Not only did his attempt to reduce the power of the Board chairman fail, but the chairman regained some control of *The Crisis* by means of his mandatory position on the *Crisis* committee. Steps were taken to incorporate *The Crisis* and the committee decided a lawyer should edit the legal notes appearing in the journal.[62]

[59] Du Bois, "Memorandum to Mr. J. E. Spingarn and Mr. O. G. Villard," November 10, 1914, Johnson Collection.
[60] Storey to Villard, November 19, 1914; November 21, 1914, Storey Papers.
[61] Board Minutes, NAACP, December 1, 1914. Dr. Morton-Jones was head of the Lincoln Settlement in Brooklyn, and one of few Negro women physicians. She was elected to the Board in 1913 to fill the unexpired term of Mrs. Mary Dunlop Maclean. Board Minutes, NAACP, January 21, 1913.
[62] Board Minutes, NAACP, February 2, 1915.

The new bylaws also tightened control of nominations of directors, requiring that the nominating committee submit nominations sixty days before the annual meeting, and that they be published in *The Crisis* at least thirty days prior to the meeting. Independent nominations required the signature of at least fifteen members to be turned in sixty days in advance and published in *The Crisis*.[63] The original bylaws had permitted nominations from the Board ten days before the annual meeting and nominations from the membership twenty days before.[64]

In 1915, with Florence Kelley as chairman, the nominating committee established a policy that new Board members be "selected on grounds of substantive services to the colored race" and in particular to the NAACP. They decided that present members should be continued unless they wished to withdraw, had moved too far away to be available, or for reasons obvious to the Board had become useless or injurious. They refused to elect L. M. Hershaw because he was a government employee and in danger of suffering reprisals if he should protest Administration policies.[65]

In 1917 it was decided that at least sixteen Board members must live in the vicinity of New York so that they could easily attend Board meetings. It was also stipulated that the nominating committee be biracial. Again the question of service and active work for the Association was emphasized.[66]

In 1918 a move got under way to increase the Board from thirty to forty and this amendment was added to the bylaws at the 1919 annual meeting.[67] A standing nominating committee was appointed to recommend names from time to time until the ten extra places should be filled.[68]

In 1919, John E. Milholland was dropped from the list of vice-presidents, because he had not been an active Board member for some time. Though the office was largely an honorary position, policy required usefulness to the Association.[69] Also in 1919, in response to pressure from the members for greater representation, the whole constitution came under review again. A study was undertaken of the relationship of branches to the national Board and to the nominating and electing of officers. Following this re-evaluation, the nominating

[63] Board Minutes, NAACP, December 1, 1914. Some changes in bylaws were adopted at the October 6, 1914, Board meeting. Others were tabled, and adopted at the December 1, 1914, meeting.
[64] Bylaws, in Board Minutes, NAACP, June 20, 1911.
[65] Board Minutes, NAACP, September 13, 1915; Kelley to Spingarn, October 23, 1915, J. E. Spingarn Papers (Howard).
[66] Minutes, Annual Meeting, January 2, 1917, in Board Minutes, NAACP.
[67] Board Minutes, NAACP, November 11, 1918; Minutes, Annual Meeting, January 6, 1919, in Board Minutes, NAACP.
[68] Board Minutes, NAACP, February 10, 1919. The committee consisted of Holmes, Morton-Jones, and Charles H. Studin.
[69] Board Minutes, NAACP, January 6, 1919.

committee sought to add strength to the Board by asking the Chicago branch to recommend someone of national reputation from that area.[70]

FINANCIAL MATTERS

Another item of business at the December, 1914, meeting was the adoption of the "retrenchment program" which had been presented by Villard in October. Adding to the interoffice tension that existed throughout the early years was the continual state of crisis created by the precarious financial condition of the Association. As the program expanded, expenses increased. Though some Board members contributed generously, Villard fretted because the Board as a whole did not assume its financial obligations. As chairman and later as treasurer, he often went "begging" for money at the end of the month to meet the bills, the rent, and the salaries, complaining to his uncle that he was carrying the whole Association on his shoulders, an opinion probably not shared by some other Board members.[71]

Throughout 1913 and 1914, salaries and bills were often unpaid. Villard frequently made loans, as did Spingarn, and money was borrowed from the various special funds. The retrenchment program adopted in December, 1914, was a six-month plan to reduce expenses, while Board members increased their efforts to raise money. These measures were so successful that Villard, in February, 1915, could speak of a "nest egg" for the summer and a reserve in the bank for operating expenses.[72]

Although the largest contributions to the NAACP ranged from $500 to $2,000, they were small when compared to the typical philanthropies of the day. For instance, Julius Rosenwald gave $1,000 in 1915,[73] but in 1912 he had donated $5,000 to Tuskegee Institute and later became a major contributor to education for Negroes in the South.[74] In 1914, more than half the income of the NAACP came from eighteen individuals, but by 1918 the bulk of support came from small contributions. From 1912 to 1917, annual income ranged between $11,000

[70] Minutes, Annual Meeting, January 6, 1919, in Board Minutes, NAACP; Board Minutes, NAACP, November 10, 1919.
[71] Board Minutes, NAACP, October 6, 1914; December 1, 1914; Minutes, Annual Meeting, January 21, 1913, in Board Minutes, NAACP; Villard to Garrison, February 20, 1911; September 21, 1911, Villard Papers.
[72] Villard to Garrison, January 28, 1913; October 6, 1914; January 15, 1915; February 26, 1915, Villard Papers; Board Minutes, NAACP, April 1, 1913; September 2, 1914; October 6, 1914; December 1, 1914; Treasurer's Reports for March, June, and December, 1913, and for May, June, July, September, October, November, 1914, in Board Minutes, NAACP.
[73] Board Minutes, NAACP, July 12, 1915.
[74] John Hope Franklin, *From Slavery to Freedom: A History of American Negroes*, 2d ed. (New York, 1956), p. 380.

and $15,000. In 1919, when more than 62,300 persons contributed to the Association, it was over $44,000.[75]

A SPATE OF RESIGNATIONS

In the fall of 1915, trouble over *The Crisis* and its editor flared up again. Villard took offense at an item in the magazine, and Walling challenged Du Bois's expense account. In November another move was made to limit Du Bois's activities to the editing of *The Crisis*. A committee was appointed to bring in a plan defining and delimiting the work of executive officers, and the entire problem was made the special order of business for the December, 1915, meeting—just one year after the last analysis of executive functions.[76]

Du Bois took advantage of the fifth anniversary of *The Crisis*, in November, 1915, to publicize his version of the relationship between the magazine and the Association.[77] It certainly must have enraged Villard to read Du Bois's statement that though the Association was the journal's legal owner, it had never expended a single cent for its publication. The Association, claimed Du Bois, had undertaken no financial responsibility; he, as editor, had been personally responsible for every debt, and had used his own salary and borrowed money to meet emergencies;[78] therefore, there were both precedent and moral right that legal ownership, in whole or in part, should reward such financial risk. What Du Bois failed to mention was the fact that *The Crisis* had been subsidized from the beginning, since the Association had paid his salary and allowed him to devote the greater part of his time and efforts to it.[79]

Du Bois, by this move, had taken the fight to the *Crisis* readers and to the Board members directly, in an attempt to enlist sympathy and support for him-

[75] *Crisis*, IX (April, 1915), 297–98; XVII (November, 1918), 18; XIX (April, 1920), 320; V (November, 1912), 39; NAACP, *Third Annual Report 1912* (New York, 1913), pp. 31–32; "Fifth Annual Report 1914," *Crisis*, IX (April, 1915), 298; "Seventh Annual Report 1916," *Crisis*, XIII (February, 1917), 167; *Eighth and Ninth Annual Reports 1917–1918* (New York, 1919), pp. 13, 14, 73–75; *Tenth Annual Report 1919* (New York, 1920), pp. 84–86; *Eleventh Annual Report 1920* (New York, 1921), pp. 73–74; *Twelfth Annual Report 1921* (New York, 1922), p. 80; *Thirteenth Annual Report 1922* (New York, 1923), pp. 59–60; *Fourteenth Annual Report 1923* (New York, 1924), pp. 47–48.
[76] Ovington to Villard, August 10, 1915; Villard to Ovington, August 11, 1915, Villard Papers; Board Minutes, NAACP, October 11, 1915; November 8, 1915.
[77] *Crisis*, XI (November, 1915), 25–27.
[78] Du Bois to Spingarn, October 20, 1915, Johnson Collection; copy of signed personal two-year note for $484.05, bearing 4% interest, Du Bois to Mrs. Frances E. Hoggan, M.D., London, England, December 14, 1912, in *Crisis* material, Du Bois Papers; copy of signed personal three-year note for $250.00, bearing 5% interest, Du Bois to Mary W. Ovington, August 5, 1913, in *Crisis* material, Du Bois Papers.
[79] *Crisis*, XI (November, 1915), 27; Minutes, Annual Meeting, January 3, 1916, in Board Minutes, NAACP.

self. He not only wanted complete personal control of *The Crisis*, but he also wanted to be an executive officer on a level with other Board members in directing the work of the Association. Yet his personal antagonisms prevented his working with most Board members and staff. As various solutions to the problems were proposed, he appeared to acquiesce, but there was trouble again and again.

The Board was ambivalent, trying at times to limit Du Bois's activity to *The Crisis*, and at other times to force him to give more of his energy to the NAACP program. Because of the tremendous influence of his writings and his philosophy, they were unwilling to let personal antagonisms bring about a complete break from the Association. Villard, on the other hand, came to the conclusion that the "National Association will never do its duty to itself until it removes a man of Dr. Du Bois's spirit from all connection with it!"[80]

The report of the 1915 committee to delimit the work of executive officers recommended specifically that Du Bois's activities be limited to *The Crisis* and Association business. Any other activity should require permission of the Board, although this was tempered with a policy "to allow all possible freedom of action consistent with the needs of the Association's work." The finances of *The Crisis* were to be assigned to a business manager selected by, and directly responsible to, the Board. In a startling move, however, the Board voted that it was inexpedient to approve the committee's report.[81] The refusal of the Board to adopt the report led Spingarn and Villard to announce their intention to resign. Miss Nerney wrote that the treasurer's resignation had been received "nine hundred and ninety nine times"; she was distressed that the epidemic had spread, and that Spingarn was now playing with the idea of resigning.[82]

Miss Ovington, writing to Spingarn, conveys the tension of the meeting and the division among friends: "Now that this vote is over, won't you forgive us all around? It's dreadful to have you come in and turn away from our section of the room as though we were under suspicion." According to Miss Ovington, the only possible replacement for Spingarn as chairman would be a radical. Joseph Loud of the Boston branch unwittingly agreed with her when he wrote Spingarn that it would be disastrous if Milholland or Miss Ovington should come to the fore as a result of his resignation. He was afraid that the withdrawal of Spingarn and Villard would bring about complete collapse of the organization.[83]

[80] Villard to Spingarn, November 3, 1915, J. E. Spingarn Papers (Howard).
[81] Board Minutes, NAACP, December 13, 1915.
[82] Villard to Garrison, December 31, 1915, Villard Papers; Joseph Loud to Spingarn, December 24, 1915; Nerney to Spingarn, n.d. [1915], J. E. Spingarn Papers (Howard).
[83] Ovington to Spingarn, December 13, [1915]; Loud to Spingarn December 24, 1915, J. E. Spingarn Papers (Howard).

Loud believed that Negroes should direct the affairs of the Association and he considered Archibald Grimke the Negro best qualified for chairman,[84] but he doubted that Grimke would be able to work with Du Bois any better than the others. He firmly opposed Du Bois as chairman of the Board, or a figurehead under Du Bois's control, and he did not believe that Du Bois could serve effectively as both secretary and Director of Research, as Du Bois himself had proposed. Yet he recognized that Du Bois was making a signal contribution to the work of the Association and that a way must be found of allowing him as much freedom as in the past, limited only as to the general policy as adopted by the Board. (Miss Ovington also urged that a way be found to use Du Bois and his "obstinacy" under conditions where he could work naturally and happily.)

The Association, thought Loud, was at a critical period of its existence, and he agreed with Miss Nerney that a program of constructive work must be formulated and put into action lest internal dissension result in loss of interest in the NAACP and its objectives.

Other members protested when they learned that Villard and Spingarn planned to refuse reelection at the end of their three-year terms. Butler Wilson pointed out the progress made by the Association, its growth of membership, and the publicity brought by its opposition to the motion picture "The Birth of a Nation." He appealed to Spingarn's idealism, reminding him that the "cause is human justice. The task is tremendous. What cause is more worthy of any man's steel? Who better than you to lead it? My friend, you must not quit us now. Never mind if the colored people have not rallied as you have reason to believe they should. Give them time. They are sure to come and we are sure to win."[85]

From the deep South William Pickens, a Negro educator who had graduated from Yale with Phi Beta Kappa honors, wrote Spingarn of his distress at learning of the proposed resignations. Dr. William A. Sinclair of Philadelphia wrote that Springarn had "the talent, tact, temperament, character, enthusiasm, earnestness and a happy combination of conservatism and radicalism—conservatism

[84] Archibald and Francis Grimke were sons of Henry Grimke of South Carolina and Nancy Weston, "a beautiful family slave." When their father died, they were cared for by their white half-brother and their aunts, Sarah Moore Grimke and Angelina Emily Grimke, the antislavery crusaders. Archibald graduated from Lincoln University and from Harvard Law School. His brother Francis was a clergyman in Washington, D.C. Edward M. Hinton, "Archibald Henry Grimke," in Allen Johnson and Dumas Malone (eds.), *Dictionary of American Biography* (New York, 1931), VII, 632–33. Both Archibald and Francis were members of the original Committee of Forty. *Proceedings of the National Negro Conference 1909: New York May 31 and June 1*, p. 225; *New York Evening Post*, June 2, 1909.

[85] Ovington to Spingarn, November 7, 1914; Loud to Spingarn, December 24, 1915. J. E. Spingarn Papers (Howard).

on non-essentials and radicalism whenever principle is involved—the qualities so necessary in a great leader in a great propaganda."[86] Meanwhile Du Bois was busy rallying support for himself. He elicited from Moorfield Storey assurance, as he had the year before, that if *The Crisis* were to become self-supporting, Du Bois would take entire charge and sever all nominal connections with the Association.[87]

Using as an excuse that certain members of the Board were unable to attend meetings regularly and thus were not fully informed, Du Bois sent out a "Statement" to the Board in December, 1915, asserting that the real basis of the difficulties within the NAACP was the question of power and control. He had come to the Association with the understanding that he was to be an executive officer, responsible directly to the Board, and that he was to have as much freedom as possible in working for the Association. He had consistently refuted the contention that the chairman was chief executive officer and that the editor of *The Crisis* was responsible to him. The new chairman, the statement went on to say, had reasserted the idea of the executive function of the chairman, but this time an agreement had been reached whereby Du Bois was assigned the specific work of editing and publishing *The Crisis,* together with some general duties, while the chairman was given general supervision over all other areas of the Association. Du Bois interpreted this action of the Board to mean that the chairman was "a sort of arbiter in cases of dispute . . . or where the whole machinery of the organization must act as a unit." He claimed to have abided by this agreement, but suddenly, to his great surprise, came a series of recommendations aimed at still more radical changes in his duties and in his relations to the Board. This proposal would have removed most of his control over *The Crisis* and still further subordinated him to the chairman.

The recommendations had been rejected by a vote of twelve to two, but this had not solved the problem. Du Bois, claiming to have been on the verge of resigning four times, demanded a clear understanding that he was an executive officer, independent of other executive officers, and responsible directly to the Board. This time, he insisted in his statement, the editing and management of *The Crisis* must be recognized as his job, and any other duties he performed would be on the same voluntary basis as the work of other members of the Board.[88]

The January, 1916, annual meeting was an airing of grievances from all sides. Spingarn paid tribute to Du Bois's work outside the Association, his books, articles, and activities in other organizations such as the Races Congress, the New

---

[86] Butler Wilson to Spingarn, December 28, 1915; William Pickens to Spingarn, January 11, 1916, J. E. Spingarn Papers (Howard); *Crisis,* XIX (April, 1920), 334–36; Sinclair to Spingarn, January 4, 1915, Joel Elias Spingarn Papers (Howard).
[87] Storey to Du Bois, December 27, 1915, Storey Papers.
[88] Du Bois, "A Statement," n.d., [December, 1915], Du Bois Papers.

York Emancipation Exposition, and the Horizon Guild. But while these activities indirectly stimulated interest in the cause, Spingarn held that the Association would profit by receiving more of the time of its most highly paid official. He blamed the Board for failing to make clear the understanding on which Du Bois had been induced to come to New York—a point on which Du Bois himself, incidentally, was perfectly clear.

Spingarn acknowledged Du Bois's role in creating without initial capital a magazine with a circulation of over 30,000, reaffirming that *The Crisis* was the official organ of the NAACP, and that the editorials were necessarily the expressions of the personality that gave them shape. But Spingarn admonished Du Bois (and warned the membership as well) when he said that the editor must "interpret our cause nobly [and] never sink to the level of petty irritation, insulting personalities or vulgar recrimination [or] meet insult with insult and injustice with injustice."

In rebuttal, Du Bois reported that he considered his main usefulness to the objectives of the Association was forwarding certain pioneer movements and general methods of uplift. Three times he had prepared general programs for the guidance and reorganization of the Association. Because funds had not been made available he had been unable to establish what he had planned in the way of research and publication in the name of the NAACP. He now proposed a Publications and Research Fund of $2,500, implying that *The Crisis* would then be self-supporting and that the money which had been used to pay his salary would go to this fund. With it, he would publish a number of small bulletins.

Miss Nerney's report at the January, 1916, meeting was also full of complaints. She worried about the lack of activity of committees of the Board, especially the Publications and Research Committee, which had never met. She compared her own work of expanding the organization with that of Du Bois. Publishing a magazine, she said, had offered subscribers an immediate and steady return on their money, whereas the most she could offer to an American public which had not yet developed a social consciousness was lofty principles. White people were either ignorant of, or antagonistic to, her work; the masses of colored people did not know the organization; and the words "Civil Rights," "Democracy," and "The New Abolition" meant nothing to them. She warned that unless some great crisis should arise, they could not hope for material results for a long time. Though she offered no reason for her resignation, the heavy work of the secretary's job as well as the unsettled status of the officers caused a great strain on her. (She was irritated to learn later that Du Bois, the cause of much of her problem, had suggested she was leaving because of her health, and wrote Spingarn, "That's putting effect for cause.")[89]

[89] Minutes, Annual Meeting, January 3, 1916, in Board Minutes, NAACP; Nerney to Spingarn, January 6, 1916, J. E. Spingarn Papers (Howard).

Villard, too, presented his formal resignation from the Board in January, but despite lengthy discussion, the annual meeting took no action on the resignations. At the Board meeting on January 10, 1916, Miss Ovington once again became acting secretary, replacing Miss Nerney, but Spingarn, Storey, and Du Bois retained their posts, and Villard was unanimously reelected treasurer.[90]

The job of finding a new secretary was not easy. Miss Nerney, who believed that Negroes should be given positions of leadership in the Association, proposed Jessie Fauset and several others. A white man, however, Royal Freeman Nash, became the new secretary and remained in that post until he left for war duty in 1917.[91]

In another move to tie *The Crisis* to the Association, the *Crisis* committee suggested that a list of officers and a statement of the purposes of the Association be printed in a prominent place opposite the first page of reading material.[92]

VILLARD OR DU BOIS?

The compromises resulting from the January "resignations" were only temporary. By April, 1916, Du Bois was once more in trouble, this time with the proper Bostonians for using what they called an unpleasantly suggestive cover on *The Crisis*. When Villard protested the misuse of the cover, Du Bois "calmly left the room without excusing himself . . . a fine attitude for an employee of the Association." The Board voted its disapproval but referred the matter to the *Crisis* committee for action, a move which guaranteed no action at all.[93]

It was equally difficult to control Du Bois in other matters. When a *Crisis* supplement was issued describing a particularly atrocious lynching at Waco, Texas, Du Bois reluctantly altered his text to meet the objections of Charles Studin, chairman of the Legal Committee. Arthur Spingarn considered the pamphlet libelous, however, and it was necessary for the secretary to appeal to the chairman of the Board for a ruling before Du Bois would agree to additional changes. Nor was it possible for Du Bois to avoid rancor and personal thrusts in his editing of *The Crisis*, and letters continued to come to Spingarn urging a spirit of unity and a concentration of effort in the fight against "the real enemy."[94]

[90] Board Minutes, NAACP, January 10, 1916.
[91] Nerney to Spingarn, January 6, 1916, J. E. Spingarn Papers (Howard); Board Minutes, NAACP, February 14, 1916; March 13, 1916; May 8, 1916; September 17, 1917. Miss Ovington called Nash "a writer." Ovington, *The Walls Came Tumbling Down*, p. 147.
[92] Board Minutes, NAACP, March 13, 1916.
[93] Garrison to Villard, April 27, 1916; Villard to Garrison, April 28, 1916; Villard to Garrison, May 10, 1916, Villard Papers; Board Minutes, NAACP, May 8, 1916.
[94] Royal F. Nash to Joel Spingarn, June 14, 1916; George W. Cook to Spingarn, December 19, 1916, J. E. Spingarn Papers (Howard).

At the 1917 annual meeting, Miss Ovington revealed that Du Bois had a number of times made editorial changes to conform to what the *Crisis* committee considered to be the best interests of the Association. In reply to criticisms she explained that the policy of the committee had been to strike a balance between editorial freedom and restraint, lest the editor become a rabid propagandist and convert no one. Nevertheless, she praised Du Bois's work and commented that the yearly increase in the readership of *The Crisis* was the best comment on its management. The committee recommended that his salary be increased, a move approved by the Board, after postponing it for more than a year because of financial difficulties and continued friction.[95]

The new secretary, meanwhile, was not measuring up to his responsibilities. Royal F. Nash had begun work in February, but by the middle of November he was still without a program, apparently lost in office routine. He was undecided as to whether the greatest need of the Association was for a lawyer or a publicity man, a matter which chilled Villard and Studin when they conferred with him.[96] Moreover, the Board found his plan for a financial campaign unsatisfactory and wasteful. Nash then requested the Board to appoint a committee to aid him in drawing up a program for 1917. On this committee were Miss Ovington, John Haynes Holmes, Villard, Du Bois, and James Weldon Johnson, who was hired in November as field secretary, the new title for "national organizer."[97]

Though Villard had accepted reelection as treasurer at the time of the annual meeting, a week later at the regular Board meeting he asked to be relieved of his duties as treasurer and Board member because of ill health. Meanwhile, his uncle, Francis Jackson Garrison, died in December, 1916, ending the twenty years of correspondence between the two men which reveals so much of the inner history of the NAACP, Villard's attitudes, and his work in behalf of the colored people. In May, 1917, Paul Kennaday agreed to serve as assistant treasurer to relieve Villard of some of his duties.[98]

The perennial question confronting the Board was: Villard or Du Bois? Villard frequently made it clear that if Du Bois were out of the way he would again be available as chairman of the Board, a possibility against which Miss Ovington and Du Bois were constantly on guard. In May, 1917, Spingarn and Nash entered officers training camp, leaving Miss Ovington as acting chairman

[95] Minutes, Annual Meeting, January 2, 1917, in Board Minutes, NAACP; Board Minutes, NAACP, November 13, 1916; "Report of Committee delimiting the work of Executive Officers," in Board Minutes, NAACP, December 13, 1915.
[96] Villard to Spingarn, November 20, 1916, J. E. Spingarn Papers (Howard).
[97] Board Minutes, NAACP, December 11, 1916; Cook to Spingarn, January 16, 1917, J. E. Spingarn Papers (Howard).
[98] Board Minutes, NAACP, January 8, 1917; May 14, 1917; Loud to Spingarn, December 15, 1916, J. E. Spingarn Papers (Howard).

and James Weldon Johnson as acting secretary. When Spingarn talked of resigning, Du Bois observed that Villard had his eye fixed upon a possible vacancy.
Miss Ovington warned Spingarn that it was evident Villard wanted to return to
control things.[99]

In September, 1917, Nash, who had been on leave since May, sent in his
resignation and it was necessary to find a new secretary. Roger Baldwin was
ruled out because he was a pacifist and looked on with disfavor by the government. This action irritated Villard because he considered himself even more
a pacifist than Baldwin and very much out of favor with the government.
(An unspoken reason for Baldwin's rejection by the Board may have been that he
and Villard were old friends and had once been schoolmates.)[100]

As a member of the selection committee Villard then proposed Owen Lovejoy,
general secretary of the National Child Labor Committee, but Miss Ovington
objected to Lovejoy. She feared he would assume command and alienate the
colored people, who had been won with such great effort. She observed that white
members of the Board received little support from Negroes who resented direction. She looked forward to the day when a Negro capable of the secretaryship
would become available. She considered James Weldon Johnson a man of excellent ideas, but not aggressive enough. She thought he needed someone to keep
him stirred up. On the other hand, any white man selected as secretary would
need great tact and the ability to work with his colleagues on a basis of equality.[101]
This was an obvious reference to Villard, the autocrat, and to the type of person
he himself would choose as secretary. Miss Ovington had scolded him for his
criticisms at a time when he was not actively in touch with the work, and he had
again lashed out at Du Bois and threatened to resign as treasurer. Conscious of
his own prestige, Villard had said he would not lend his name to the organization unless it were efficient. "The first step toward that efficiency and public
confidence," he reiterated, would be "the removal of Dr. Du Bois as editor." [102]

At the January 7, 1918, meeting Lillian Wald and Florence Kelley presented the
name of John R. Shillady, an experienced social worker who had been employed
in the Department of Charities and Corrections in Westchester, New York, and
the Board voted to engage Shillady as secretary. As assistant secretary it
selected Walter White, an active member of the Atlanta branch who worked for

[99] Board Minutes, NAACP, May 14, 1917; Du Bois to Spingarn, September 25, 1917, Johnson
Collection; Spingarn to Board of Directors, May 1, 1917; Ovington to Spingarn, November
24, 1916; September 26, 1917; September 29, 1917, J. E. Spingarn Papers (Howard).
[100] Board Minutes, NAACP, September 17, 1917; October 8, 1917; Villard to Ovington,
October 6, 1917; Villard to Garrison, March 14, 1913, Villard Papers.
[101] Ovington to Spingarn, July 5, 1917; September 26, 1917; September 29, 1917, J. E.
Spingarn Papers (Howard); Ovington to Villard, October 5, 1917, Villard Papers.
[102] Villard to Ovington, October 6, 1917, Villard Papers.

an insurance company. Both men were to contribute new vigor to the Association.[103]

Villard's contention that the Association could use a well-trained social worker was borne out by the efficiency demonstrated by the new secretary in organizing the work. Shillady was engaged with the stipulation that he must raise money. At the first Board meeting he attended he brought plans for a membership drive —the Moorfield Storey drive—which turned out to be the catalyst in a startling increase in membership. James Weldon Johnson later wrote of Shillady's great ability as a systematizer and organizer, and Miss Ovington commented on his businesslike manner. Walter White also lost no time in proving his fitness and adaptability for the work.[104]

In 1918, Spingarn again asked to be released as chairman, and Du Bois suggested that he propose Miss Ovington as his successor in order to evade "the usual unpleasant candidate" (meaning Villard). Miss Ovington was elected January 6, 1919, in time to face another crisis over *The Crisis*. The irrepressible Du Bois had published an issue without first submitting its editorials to the *Crisis* committee, and even Miss Ovington found it necessary to discipline the editor after having defended him for so many years. When the committee met with Joel Spingarn as its new chairman, it decreed that *Crisis* matters should be discussed at the weekly staff conferences instituted by Shillady. The committee reaffirmed that its function was to approve the editorials and to pass on all matters of policy affecting *The Crisis*.[105]

The recurring crises over the Association's journal were too much for Oswald Garrison Villard. He finally resigned as treasurer and as Board member, giving as his reasons the pressure of his duties on the *Evening Post* and *The Nation*. They were legitimate reasons, but it is clear that Villard saw no end to Du Bois's career in the Association now that Miss Ovington had "come to the fore." In October, 1919, the board elected Joel Spingarn treasurer in his place and made Villard a vice-president, after praising him for his long service.[106]

[103] Board Minutes, NAACP, November 12, 1917; January 7, 1918; *Crisis*, XV (March, 1918), 219; Walter White, *A Man Called White: The Autobiography of Walter White* (New York, 1948), pp. 28, 33–40.
[104] Board Minutes, NAACP, January 14, 1918; February 11, 1918; James Weldon Johnson, *Along This Way* (New York, 1933), p. 329; Ovington, *The Walls Came Tumbling Down*, p. 148.
[105] Du Bois to Spingarn, January 12, 1918; August 15, 1918, Johnson Collection; Board Minutes, NAACP, January 6, 1919; May 12, 1919.
[106] Shillady to Spingarn, May 21, 1919, J. E. Spingarn Papers (Howard); Board Minutes, NAACP, October 13, 1919.

CHAPTER VI

Growth of Branches and Membership

Little time was lost in carrying the Association to areas outside of New York. In the beginning, Executive Committee members from Boston, Chicago, and Philadelphia organized local committees, which became branches. The early branches presented problems and difficulties that had to be met successfully before the Association could expand on a national scale. Policy decisions made during the early days of growth in large measure prevented disintegration or dissipation of energies in factionalism or in purely local objectives and personal aggrandisement.

The concept of the "vigilance committee" was used for a while in the attempt to promote expansion of branches. In a "call to arms" the Association announced its purpose to federate local vigilance committees among colored people in every community in the United States. Although the original New York branch was called the Vigilance Committee, and for a time the Washington branch was called the National Vigilance Committee,[1] the term did not endure, and when procedures were regularized for admitting local groups, the model bylaws required that each group be known as that community's branch of the National Association for the Advancement of Colored People.[2]

In March, 1911, when Villard reported that NAACP membership was small and not representatively national, Miss Ovington and Mrs. Maclean proposed that the colored members of the Association and of the Executive Committee be called together to recommend responsible colored people throughout the country to act on a finance committee. Moorfield Storey too was disturbed at the small

---

[1] *Crisis*, VI (May, 1913), 27–29; XI (March, 1916), 258; NAACP, *Third Annual Report 1912* (New York, 1913), p. 24.
[2] "Constitution for Branches: for local organizations affiliated with the N.A.A.C.P." [1911], W. E. B. Du Bois Papers (now in the possession of Mrs. W. E. B. Du Bois, New York City).

membership, a total of 179, and at the meager resources available for attacking the formidable evils which the Association had been formed to combat. He expressed surprise that colored people had not taken greater interest in the work.[3]

By 1913, however, the Board felt it necessary to advise all branches and groups applying for admission that they must include white members in order to conform with the requirements of the Association.[4] In the drive to increase memberships and branches, local Negro organizations were often drawn into the NAACP in a body. Some Negro leaders lost ground in this way and, fearing loss of status in the Negro community, rebelled against what they considered to be white interference. Nevertheless, the Association was constantly on the alert to find outstanding colored people for positions of leadership and responsibility in the local organizations as well as on the national Board. This was the reason that the nominating and other committees were biracial. On the local level, this led to honest misunderstandings and to deliberate misinterpretation of the NAACP's interracial activities, as demonstrated in the Cosmopolitan Club dinner affair.

There were three reasons why the Association wanted to enlist the interest of prominent white people: first, to build prestige and to secure money; second, to counterbalance prevailing white Southern attitudes; and third, to promote interracial understanding and to acquaint white people with distinguished Negroes (Du Bois called this "cooperation").

The New York branch in 1914 and 1915 tried to "educate" white people by holding a series of so-called parlor meetings. Because whites generally would not attend the Association's mass meetings, small integrated groups were brought together in private homes of people like Mrs. Walter Lewisohn, Mrs. Max Morgenthau, Jr., C. R. Lowell, and Fanny Garrison Villard, Villard's mother.[5]

Sometimes the national office forced a branch to take in white members. The Philadelphia group was willing to have whites act in an advisory capacity without

[3] Minutes, Executive Committee, March 7, 1911, in "Minute Book of the Board of Directors of the National Association for the Advancement of Colored People" (now in the Manuscript Division, Library of Congress; hereafter referred to as Board Minutes, NAACP); Moorfield Storey to Oswald Garrison Villard, November 3, 1911, Moorfield Storey Papers (in the possession of Mr. Charles Storey, Boston, Massachusetts); Francis Jackson Garrison to Villard, November 6, 1911, Oswald Garrison Villard Papers (Houghton Library, Harvard University).

[4] Board Minutes, NAACP, February 4, 1913.

[5] May Childs Nerney to Joel E. Spingarn, July 30, 1914, Joel Elias Spingarn Papers (Moorland Foundation, Howard University); Crisis, IX (January, 1915), 135; Board Minutes, NAACP, June 14, 1915. Interracial parlor meetings in New York were used as early as 1911 by Mrs. John Dewey to foster the women's suffrage movement. This was in accord with NAACP policy to reunite the two reform movements. Villard to J. E. Spingarn, February 28, 1911, J. E. Spingarn Papers (Howard).

118

becoming members but did not want a white man for president. In other areas the colored people insisted on white leaders.[6]

In January, 1917, Boston member George G. Bradford requested the Association to alter the wording of its statement of purpose from "It believes colored men and women must organize" to "It believes American citizens white and colored must organize and fight for the full rights of colored citizens and all other native-born American citizens."[7] The policy of biracialism was reaffirmed and strengthened at the 1917 annual meeting by a vote recommending to the Board that the nominating committee be composed of both races.[8]

During the membership drive in 1918, Bradford again warned that an association for the advancement of colored people would not naturally attract white people and that there was danger it would become a society of colored citizens exclusively, which might bring about the false charge that it was a selfish racial organization. He urged that a special effort be made to bring all racial elements into the membership. Many new immigrant groups were moving into the North, and Bradford thought it was essential to the success of the organization that it win the sympathy and active membership of even a small percentage of the other racial elements of the community. The possibility of including a few white members in the Southern branches was not to be overlooked, but he questioned the wisdom of emphasizing this at the time.[9]

From the beginning the Association was highly centralized and the national body maintained control over branches and membership. The 1911 bylaws provided that application for membership must be submitted in writing and approved by the Board of Directors. Branches were under the authority of the Board, and the Board required approval of each branch constitution.[10] Membership in the branch included membership in the national organization. Eligibility was based on belief in the brotherhood of man as a practical present ideal and willingness to work for it. Dues were fixed by the national Board, but a portion was kept by the local group to meet its own expenses. The branch could also raise money by other means. Close contact with the national office was maintained by monthly reports of the branch secretary, while the national secretary in turn reported to the branches on the work of the Association and offered suggestions for cooperation. Members were pledged to extend the circulation of *The Crisis* as the official organ of the Association. The work of organizing the

[6] Kathryn M. Johnson to Royal F. Nash, July 11, 1916, NAACP Files (Manuscript Division, Library of Congress).
[7] *Crisis*, XIII (January, 1917), 123. It is likely that the original statement of purpose was written by Du Bois, since his Niagara Movement was primarily for Negroes.
[8] Minutes, Annual Meeting, January 2, 1917, in Board Minutes, NAACP.
[9] George G. Bradford to James Weldon Johnson, March 13, 1918, NAACP Files.
[10] Bylaws of the National Association for the Advancement of Colored People, June 20, 1911, in Board Minutes, NAACP.

branches was at first assigned to the secretary, but in 1916 the field secretary took over this work, and in 1918 the Department of Branch Affairs was created with Miss Ovington as its first full-time director.

Activities of the branch were to include: the lessening of racial prejudice; the advancement of colored people; legal redress for colored persons unjustly persecuted; the setting up of a local bureau of information; mass meetings, parlor meetings, and memorial exercises; the study of local racial conditions; efforts to influence the press; efforts to lessen race discrimination and to secure full civil rights and political rights to colored citizens and others; and the establishment of a civic center for the work. The local program was in the hands of the branch, but general policy was under the control of the parent organization.[11]

BOSTON AND NEW YORK

The Boston branch started in 1909 as a small, select, somewhat aristocratic committee consisting of abolitionists and descendants of abolitionists together with a few Negro intellectuals (the Butler Wilsons, Clement G. Morgan, and for a brief time, William Monroe Trotter). This group helped raise money for the national office and agreed to act as hosts for the third annual conference of the Association in 1911. The conference gave authority to the Boston group to become a branch of the Association, but George Bradford, Francis Jackson Garrison, and Horace Bumstead objected to the elaborate and burdensome provisions for branches that was contemplated by the national office. They thought that such regulations would weaken the prestige of the branch and its power for effective influence in emergencies and urged that the proposed bylaws be modified. The Boston group wanted to function as an emergency committee, which would act only when a crisis arose. Garrison was for an enrollment of sympathizers rather than a membership organization, but Villard's will and central control prevailed.[12]

To further the tie between abolitionism and the new movement, the Boston group observed the one hundredth anniversary of the birth of Wendell Phillips in November, 1911, and in February, 1912, the branch was organized with fifty-six members, including the majority of the sons and daughters of the most noted New England abolition leaders.[13]

[11] "A Constitution for Local Organizations Affiliated with the N.A.A.C.P." [1911], Du Bois Papers; Board Minutes, NAACP, July 7, 1914; Crisis, XVII (November, 1918), 19.
[12] Garrison to Villard, January 22, 1911; January 28, 1911; April 5, 1911; April 7, 1911; April 8, 1911; Horace Bumstead to Villard, April 6, 1911; Villard to Garrison, April 7, 1911, Villard Papers; Crisis, II (June, 1911), 61; J. P. Loud, "Report of the Committee on Organization of the Boston Branch of the NAACP" [February, 1912], NAACP Files.
[13] Garrison to Villard, September 3, 1911; September 22, 1911; Villard to Garrison, September 11, 1911, Villard Papers; Loud, "Report of Committee on Organization of the Boston Branch" [February, 1912], NAACP Files; Board Minutes, NAACP, February 6, 1912;

In 1913 the Boston branch won what it called a quick and decisive victory against exclusion of Negro men and boys from YMCA swimming pool facilities.[14] A mass meeting in Fanueil Hall in the same year protesting segregation in the departments of the federal government was hailed as a great awakener to the colored people. This, together with the activity of Butler Wilson (who was the "real life" of the branch according to Garrison) and Mrs. Wilson's program of parlor meetings, resulted in winning the support of a number of the colored people of Boston.[15]

In 1914 the branch forced the Boston School Committee to hold a public hearing and to withdraw a song book used in the school system which contained the words "darky," "nigger," and "massa."[16] The branch spent nearly $1,000 fighting the film *The Birth of a Nation*, under the slogan "Assassination of a Race." Though David Wark Griffith and his counsel successfully maintained their right to show the film, continued agitation by the branch eventually resulted in the passage of a new state law concerning censorship. The executive committee of the branch approached local problems under the principle "that reasoning with, persuading, and appealing to the sense of justice is far more likely to cure evils than is a policy of attack."[17]

In New York for the first few years, the local group constituted a Vigilance Committee and concerned itself with problems of legal redress. It was run by liberal whites and Negroes such as Joel E. Spingarn, Charles H. Studin, Gilchrist Stewart, Arthur B. Spingarn, and Mary White Ovington. In 1910, Miss Ovington made an effort to build a Greater New York auxiliary membership of the National Association. On January 27, 1911, the New York branch was

---

Butler Wilson to Mary White Ovington, February 9, 1912, NAACP Files; *Crisis*, III (March, 1912), 203. The executive committee of the branch included Loud, Bumstead, Miss Adeline Moffatt, Clement Morgan, Miss Maria L. Baldwin, and Mrs. Joseph P. Loud.

[14] Butler Wilson, "Boston, the Banner Branch," *Branch Bulletin*, I (March, 1917), 25–26. Butler Wilson, Mrs. McAdoo, and Garrison were largely responsible for this victory. Garrison to Villard, November 4, 1913; November 12, 1913, Villard Papers. Although this move opened up the YMCA, several months later Booker T. Washington observed that colored people did not use YMCA facilities throughout the country unless they had a special building and that even in Boston less than a dozen colored men out of a population of some twelve or fifteen thousand had any practical connection with YMCA activities. Washington to William C. Graves, August 6, 1914, Booker T. Washington Papers (Manuscript Division, Library of Congress).

[15] Garrison to Villard, December 25, 1913; January 18, 1914, Villard Papers. Garrison wrote that Wilson was bearing the brunt of the labor, that he was going "personally to all Masonic bodies of colored men and stirring them up." Garrison to Villard, November 9, 1913, Villard Papers. In addition, Mrs. Wilson in the year 1915 held 150 parlor meetings. Minutes, Annual Meeting, January 3, 1916, in Board Minutes, NAACP.

[16] Wilson, "Boston, the Banner Branch."

[17] Garrison to Villard, April 8, 1915, Villard Papers; Wilson, "Boston, the Banner Branch."

organized with Joel Spingarn as chairman so that the national organization could devote all its energies to the national program.[18]

Miss Ovington tried to keep officers of the national Association off the Executive Committee of the New York branch in an effort to transfer responsibility to New York people not involved in the national work. Knowing that Villard liked to keep closely in touch with local affairs, she proposed that he and Miss Blascoer be the only ex officio members of the branch.[19] Nevertheless, the New York Vigilance Committee and the branch which succeeded it suffered from the fact that many of the officers were members of the national Board. Even after this situation had been corrected, the mere fact that national headquarters was located in New York tended to overshadow the development of an effective local organization.

In April, 1911, Miss Blascoer attended a meeting of the New York branch and criticized its lack of purpose and looseness of organization. She complained that the speakers had not mentioned the function of the Association, the legal work, or the recent annual conference. She was annoyed that Du Bois had deprecated the efficacy of meetings as a means of solving the problem and reminded Villard and Spingarn that the colored press had criticized the Association for being a movement of talkers instead of doers.[20]

In answer to Miss Blascoer's criticism, Du Bois proposed that the branch should have an investigator and organizer to examine cases, to raise funds for permanent headquarters, and to develop a forum for discussion. Gilchrist Stewart, former attorney for the Constitution League, was chosen to fill this role and he became chairman of the New York Vigilance Committee. Trotter considered Stewart a young man of ability. He would willingly have traded the aging dignitaries of the Boston branch for some of the men responsible for what he described as the "live, thorough-going, radical, courageous activity" of the New York group.[21]

The purpose of the Vigilance Committee was the immediate investigation and relief of all cases of outrage or discrimination against colored people in Greater New York and its vicinity. In the fall of 1911 a branch headquarters was opened in Harlem, where colored people could report any cases of injustice before the law.[22]

---

[18] Minutes, Executive Committee, June 7, 1910; March 7, 1911, in Board Minutes, NAACP; *Crisis*, II (August, 1911), 152.

[19] Ovington to Spingarn, February 22, 1911, J. E. Spingarn Papers (Howard); Minutes, Executive Committee, March 7, 1911, in Board Minutes, NAACP; *Crisis*, IV (August, 1911), 152.

[20] Blascoer to Villard, carbon copy enclosed in Blascoer to Spingarn, April 7, 1911, J. E. Spingarn Papers (Howard).

[21] Du Bois to Spingarn [1911]; William Monroe Trotter to Spingarn, February 12, 1912; Minutes, New York branch, March 11, 1912, J. E. Spingarn Papers (Howard); Minutes, Executive Committee, June 6, 1911, in Board Minutes, NAACP.

[22] *Crisis*, II (August, 1911), 153; Minutes, Executive Committee, November 14, 1911, in Board Minutes, NAACP.

During the first six months the New York group handled three cases involving police brutality inflicted on innocent Negroes. In one of these a policeman was put on trial and as a result suspended for three months.[23] The next attack was aimed at discrimination against Negroes in public places of amusement and recreation. Section 514 of the New York Penal Law made it a crime to exclude citizens from public places on account of color. In October, 1911, two Negroes were refused permission to occupy orchestra seats in the Lyric Theatre. In spite of the backing of the so-called theatrical trust, the management of the theater was convicted and fined, and the appeals court upheld the decision. Credit for the outcome of the case went to Gilchrist Stewart and to Charles Studin, whose legal advice was valuable because of his previous work in the office of the District Attorney.[24]

As a result of this success, the branch decided to adopt a militant policy toward New York theaters and break up the pattern of theater segregation. Under the leadership of Joel and Arthur Spingarn it was arranged that colored men were to secure orchestra tickets for six different theaters on the evening of March 18, 1912, and seek to gain admission. A white person was to accompany each party. The Lyric Theatre, having been prosecuted, admitted the Negroes without question. In two instances they were challenged at the door but not disturbed when they brushed past theater attendants and took their seats. Two of the other groups were sent to the manager, who tore up the tickets. Joel Spingarn was with one of these groups. When he tried to intervene, the manager was arbitrary and discourteous, and threatened him with "summary ejectment." Both cases were turned over to the District Attorney for action.[25]

Another case concerned the Palisades Amusement Park, which refused admission to a Negro family. This case was settled out of court. The NAACP attorneys advised that since the company had offered to yield the principle involved, the family should accept $300 and season tickets to the Park in settlement.[26]

In spite of these activities, the New York branch was plagued by a lack of stability. In December, 1913, the Board decided that the New York Vigilance Committee should be completely reorganized and that it should be a money-raising agency in the New York area for the national Association. The legal work formerly handled by the Vigilance Committee was turned over to the national office, which now had a full-time lawyer. Stewart protested this move and stressed the need for instant legal redress. He felt that colored agencies should be

[23] Minutes, Executive Committee, June 6, 1911; October 16, 1911, in Board Minutes, NAACP; *Crisis*, II (August, 1911), 152.
[24] *Crisis*, III (March, 1912), 205; *New York Age*, February 6, 1913.
[25] Minutes, New York Branch, March 11, 1912, J. E. Spingarn Papers (Howard); Board Minutes, NAACP, April 4, 1912.
[26] Board Minutes, NAACP, October 16, 1911; June 4, 1912; NAACP, *Third Annual Report 1912* (New York, 1913), p. 9.

in control of the work among colored people in New York City and that a full-time lawyer in the national office was a poor substitute when it came to enforcing the colored man's rights.[27]

The first New York branch failed to prosper, and when the Sixth Annual Report was published early in 1916, it was not listed. The original charter had been lost. Since there was no record of its date of issue, a new charter dated November, 1917, was granted when James Weldon Johnson succeeded in organizing a Harlem branch.[28]

CHICAGO AND PHILADELPHIA

The Chicago group was dominated for some time by supporters of Booker T. Washington—Julius Rosenwald, Jenkin Lloyd Jones (a Unitarian clergyman)[29] and others who thought the NAACP too radical and outspoken in its demands for civil, political, and economic rights for Negroes. In contrast to these were the liberal whites and Negroes, Jane Addams, Celia Parker Woolley, Willoughby G. Walling, brother of William English Walling, Dr. Charles E. Bentley, an old Niagara man, and for a time Mrs. Wells-Barnett.

The Association held its annual conference in Chicago in 1912 to build membership and interest there. Prior to the conference, Jane Addams called an organizational meeting of those interested in the NAACP. Villard described Miss Addams as the moving spirit of the whole enterprise and wrote his uncle that the Association was fortunate to have such warm friends as "Saint Jane" and her fellow social worker, Miss S. P. Breckinridge.[30] Mrs. Wells-Barnett, however, was critical, claiming there had been insufficient notice of the meeting.[31]

Du Bois met with the Board of the Chicago branch before the conference and helped them form a Chicago Vigilance Committee and a program of propaganda. Dr. Bentley wrote to Spingarn that it was the most enthusiastic meeting yet

[27] Board Minutes, NAACP, December 2, 1913; Gilchrist Stewart to Spingarn, December 1, 1913, J. E. Spingarn Papers (Howard).

[28] NAACP, "Sixth Annual Report 1915," in Crisis, XI (March, 1916), 245–64; Crisis, XII (June, 1916), 89; Board Minutes, NAACP, June 12, 1916; January 8, 1917; October 8, 1917; October 13, 1919; April 12, 1920; Ovington to Villard, October 5, 1917, Villard Papers.

[29] Jenkin Lloyd Jones was editor of Unity magazine and published a series of radical Sunday school leaflets for use by liberal churches, stressing "evolution, mythical analogies, and the ethical harmony of the great world religions." He was a member of Henry Ford's Peace Ship Mission in 1915, and he signed the 1909 NAACP "Call." Charles H. Lyttle, "Jenkin Lloyd Jones," in Dumas Malone (ed.), Dictionary of American Biography (New York, 1933), X, 179–80.

[30] Minutes, Executive Committee, November 14, 1911, in Board Minutes, NAACP; Villard to Garrison, January 17, 1912, Villard Papers. Sophonisba P. Breckinridge was a cousin of Villard's wife.

[31] Ida Wells-Barnett, "The National Association for the Advancement of Colored People," Fellowship, January 17, 1912, clipping in Du Bois Papers.

held by the Chicago group. They had at last begun to realize how to proceed. Julius Rosenwald's secretary was present at the meeting, which delighted Charles Bentley, as he was sure the fulfillment of their plans depended to a large extent on contributions from Rosenwald. Villard made several trips to Chicago in an effort to keep Rosenwald interested,[32] but the national office was worried about the influence exerted on the Board of the Chicago branch by the annual Rosenwald visits to Tuskegee. Bentley wrote Spingarn of the hypnotic spell that these visits seemed to cast on the Chicago members who took the trip with Rosenwald. Even the president of the branch, Judge Edward O. Brown, had been overwhelmed by what he saw. To overcome the Washington influence, Bentley saw the need of missionary work among the directors to make them aware of the whole picture.

By 1915, Du Bois was writing to Spingarn that he was "more and more convinced that the Chicago Branch [should] make a decisive step and get itself loose from such people as Mr. Rosenwald and Jenkin Lloyd Jones, who do not agree with us and will not whole-heartedly support our aims."[33]

The first Association meeting in Philadelphia preliminary to organization was held in the Friends Meeting House on Race Street on February 22, 1911. Villard claimed that he was honored to be placed in Lucretia Mott's famous seat and attempted to arouse the old Quaker abolitionist spirit in support of the Association.[34] He was disappointed. The Society of Friends, outspoken opponent of slavery in pre-Civil War days, was strangely silent and apathetic toward the New Abolition Movement, and Villard's efforts to rekindle a concern among Quakers for the new slavery failed, except in a few instances. White leadership in the new movement, not only in Philadelphia but elsewhere, was in a large measure composed of Jewish and Unitarian clergymen and laymen.

Factionalism among Negro leaders and between the NAACP and the Constitution League almost prevented the formation of a Philadelphia branch. The 1913 annual conference was held in Philadelphia, and Board member Dr. N. F. Mossell, superintendent of the Frederick Douglass Memorial Hospital, informed the Board that he and other Philadelphians would raise the funds necessary to cover the expenses of the conference. Villard discovered, however, that Mossell and Sinclair, another physician at the Douglass Hospital and national field secretary of the Constitution League, had "conspired" with Milholland to raise $1,200

[32] Charles E. Bentley to Spingarn [April 29, 1912], J. E. Spingarn Papers (Howard); Charles T. Hallinan to Nerney, April 7, 1913, NAACP Files.
[33] Bentley to Spingarn, March 29, 1915, J. E. Spingarn Papers (Howard); [Du Bois] to Spingarn, April 2, 1915, Joel Elias Spingarn Papers (James Weldon Johnson Collection, Yale University; hereafter refered to as the Johnson Collection).
[34] Minutes, Executive Committee, March 7, 1911, in Board Minutes, NAACP; *Crisis,* I (March, 1911), 15; Villard to Garrison, February 23, 1911, Villard Papers. Lucretia Mott was a Philadelphia Quaker, a champion of women's rights, and an abolitionist orator.

for the conference, of which $900 was to go to Milholland's Constitution League. Villard argued that this was obtaining money under false pretenses, since the Association had severed all connection with the League.[35]

In addition, Villard claimed that Drs. Mossell and Sinclair were causing endless trouble. The hospital group wished to dominate the conference and according to Villard were assailing Richard Wright, editor of the Philadelphia *Christian Recorder*, "by innuendo." As a result, the Board voted to send Miss Nerney to Philadelphia for a month to arrange details of the conference. "Nearly one half of Miss Nerney's and my time," moaned Villard, "is spent in trying to reconcile these jealous or scheming black brothers, and the work suffers in consequence."[36]

Nevertheless, Villard was pleased with the conference. He persuaded the Mayor to give the opening address and obtained a contribution of $500 from Samuel Fels. For the first time the Association engaged a professional newspaperman, Allen R. Eckman of the *Philadelphia Evening Telegram*, to handle publicity for its annual conference.[37]

The Reverend K. E. Evans, minister of the Girard Avenue Unitarian Church, became chairman of the organizing committee for the Philadelphia group, with the task of reconciling the warring factions. He pledged himself to solve the difficult situation by agreeing to the admission of the Douglass hospital group (with cash in hand) as charter members. He was confident this would "leave almost everyone good natured."

Villard succeeded in interesting two prominent Quakers in the Philadelphia branch: Ellwood Heacock, secretary of the Pennsylvania Abolition Society, who became branch president, and Henry W. Wilbur, secretary to the Friends general conference and president of the Pennsylvania Abolition Society, who spoke at the conference.[38] However, it was a Jewish soap manufacturer who was the principal contributor from the area, and it was a Unitarian minister who succeeded in bringing the rival factions together. The Douglass Hospital group of Negro professional men, already organized as the Constitution League, became the base of the Philadelphia branch.

WASHINGTON AND BALTIMORE

The growth of the Washington and Baltimore branches could be attributed to the rapid extension of segregation. A strong local organization was needed in the

[35] Board Minutes, NAACP, January 7, 1913; February 4, 1913; March 11, 1913; Villard to Garrison, March 31, 1913, Villard Papers; Arthur Gary, "Sketch and History of the Constitution League of the United States," typed MS., 6 pp., W.P.A. Writers Project, Roi Ottley, ed., May 26, 1939, Schomburg Collection (New York Public Library, New York).
[36] Villard to Garrison, March 14, 1913, Villard Papers; Board Minutes, NAACP, March 11, 1913.
[37] Board Minutes, NAACP, April 1, 1913; Villard to Garrison, March 31, 1913, Villard Papers.
[38] Nerney to the Reverend K. E. Evans, May 1, 1913, NAACP Files; Evans to Spingarn, June 7, 1913, J. E. Spingarn Papers (Howard); *Crisis*, VII (March, 1914), 248.

District of Columbia to guard against hostile legislation and provide an effective lobby in Congress for the rights of the American Negro. It was in Washington that the policy was established that not only the officers of the national body but also those of local branches must refrain from using the Association for, or committing it to, partisan politics. Here, too, the national office set the precedent of exercising close supervision over local bodies by suspending recognition of the branch. The cause of the suspension was J. Milton Waldron's attempt to use the prestige of the branch presidency to obtain a political appointment. The national office thereupon organized a probationary group to guide the selection of local officers.[39]

In spite of this situation, money poured in from the Washington membership, under the leadership of Archibald Grimke. The issue of government jobs solidified the branch. Upper level appointments, such as Recorder of Deeds, were being closed to Negroes, and federal clerks were being segregated into Jim Crow divisions. This was not only humiliating but severely limited opportunities for advancement. Few Negroes were hired as replacements. Thus it was not a case of being asked to give allegiance to vague principles, it was a case of bread and butter—a personal involvement. Members might not be concerned when one Negro failed to get a political appointment to a high place in government, but rank-and-file clerks now found their opportunities slipping away. Because of this type of discrimination, the District of Columbia branch was galvanized into action. By the end of 1913 membership had jumped to 400 and $3,000 had been raised for the national office.[40] In the fall of 1915 the national Board of Directors voted to present a trophy to the branch in recognition of its work for the Association. It had become the largest branch in the Association, with an enrollment of 1,500. The total national membership was then 8,266.[41]

In connection with the organization of the Baltimore branch, Villard stated a cardinal principal of the Association: that it would not resort to force or violence to gain its ends but would use only peaceful and constitutional means. The Baltimore branch was chartered in April, 1912, with the stipulation that its advisory board should include prominent white members. Following the pattern of holding the annual conference where it would bring public attention to specific issues and stimulate membership growth in a particular area, the Asso-

---

[39] Board Minutes, NAACP, May 6, 1913; July 1, 1913; October 7, 1913; *Crisis*, III (May, 1912), 22–23; VII (November, 1913), 342–43; VII (March, 1914), 250; Ovington to Nerney, May 17, 1913; Nerney to Spingarn, July 2, 1913; Spingarn to Nerney and Charles H. Studin, July 28, 1913; Villard to Spingarn, July 31, 1913, J. E. Spingarn Papers (Howard); *Washington Bee*, January 24, 1914. Waldron was also national organizer and chairman of the campaign committee of the National Independent Political League. J. Milton Waldron to Spingarn, July 12, 1913, J. E. Spingarn Papers (Howard).
[40] *Crisis*, VII (February, 1914), 193.
[41] Board Minutes, NAACP, September 13, 1915; *Crisis*, X (September, 1915), 289.

ciation held its sixth annual conference in Baltimore in 1914, the "furthest South" that the conference had met.[42]

ST. LOUIS AND ELSEWHERE

At the end of 1912 there were eleven branches with eleven hundred members, but this was by no means enough, and Board members increased their efforts to expand the organization.[43] After he became Board chairman, Joel Spingarn made two Western trips at his own expense in 1914 and in 1915, visiting a dozen or more cities on each trip. In his speeches he attacked segregation and discrimination in all its forms—residential, political, and economic, using as his title, "The New Abolitionism."[44] His militant tone inspired his listeners and excited both favorable and unfavorable reactions. Some were "jubilant" in describing the "glorious" meetings. Spingarn "swayed them." He "stiffened the fibre in many a spinal cord." But some understood him to be advocating violence and questioned his use of the word "gunpowder." Even the term "abolitionism" was construed as a harking back to past bitterness, more apt to kindle anger and destruction than to further the constructive work of the Association.[45]

Spingarn's open criticism of Booker T. Washington brought on a tilt with Roger Baldwin at the Chicago meeting[46] that created a flutter among the Washington cohorts, brought satisfaction to the old Niagara group, and caused Villard distress. The Negro press was critical of the attack on Washington. The *New York Age* launched a counterattack on the Association, calling attention to the preponderance of white leaders in the NAACP and pointing out that Negroes held offices of limited importance and were allowed to participate only in minor deliberations.[47]

Certain of the cities visited by Spingarn presented unique problems. At St. Louis, where there was no branch, the National League on Urban Conditions Among Negroes (commonly known as the Urban League) was strong and, according to Miss Nerney, kept the Association from getting a foothold. Roger

[42] Board Minutes, NAACP, April 4, 1912; August 5, 1913; *Crisis*, IV (May, 1912), 23; *Crisis*, VII (June, 1914), 86.
[43] Board Minutes, NAACP, January 21, 1913; April 1, 1913.
[44] "Dr. Spingarn's Trips," n.d., in NAACP Files; *Crisis*, IX (April, 1915), 286; *New York Age*, January 1, 1914. Spingarn had used this term a year earlier at Jersey City, New Jersey, January 1, 1913.
[45] G. K. Williams to Nerney, January 16, 1914; H. J. Nichols to Nerney, January 16, 1914, in NAACP Files; H. O. Cook to Spingarn, January 18, 1914; John W. Day to Spingarn, January 24, 1914; Trotter to Spingarn, January 28, 1914, J. E. Spingarn Papers (Howard). Trotter was especially pleased with Spingarn's fighting spirit and congratulated him on his speaking tour.
[46] Bentley to Nerney [January, 1914], NAACP Files.
[47] *Washington Bee*, January 24, 1914; February 28, 1914; *New York Age*, February 26, 1914; March 5, 1914; letter in *New York Age*, March 5, 1914.

Baldwin, leader of a powerful group of white people in St. Louis and prominent in the work of the Urban League, expressed the hope that a branch of the NAACP would be established there. Miss Nerney, however, considered Baldwin too conservative and thought him inclined to hold back the colored people. She labeled him "a devoted friend of Mr. Washington's."[48]

Booker T. Washington and Robert R. Moton were both sponsors of the Urban League, which was created in 1911 by merging three organizations: the National League for the Protection of Colored Women; the Committee on Urban Conditions Among Negroes, which had been set up to coordinate the various programs of social work for Negroes in New York City; and the Committee for Improving Industrial Conditions of Negroes in New York, founded in 1905 by W. L. Bulkley and William J. Schieffelin (Miss Ovington and Villard also belonged to this group). Other founders and sponsors of the Urban League who were involved with the NAACP were E. R. A. Seligman, who became the League's first president, Felix Adler, Mrs. William H. Baldwin, Jr., John Haynes Holmes, Dr. W. H. Brooks, Kelly Miller, and Jacob W. Mack. Like the NAACP, the Urban League was created by liberal whites and its national and local boards were biracial.

The Urban League's primary objective was to secure jobs for Negroes. It stressed equal salaries for equal jobs, and equal opportunities for promotion. During the great migration of Negroes to Northern industrial centers in the early years of the century, the League played a significant role in helping Negro migrants adjust to urban life.[49]

In Columbus, Ohio, there was what Miss Nerney called a local committee of one hundred of the most representative colored men, but efforts to organize an NAACP branch had been frustrated by jealousy and rivalry. In Springfield, Ohio, the committee on organization was composed entirely of colored ministers, and efforts to enlist white support had not been successful. The Omaha group was dominated by a prominent white man who was determined to run things on his own terms. In Detroit, Miss Nerney had found on an earlier visit that women were not admitted to the branch; she had "laughed them out of this," but warned Spingarn that the women who had joined did not seem to be working. At Indianapolis, on the other hand, the membership had been composed entirely of women, mostly schoolteachers, and the colored men of the city were incensed

[48] Nerney to Spingarn, "Notes on Branches for Dr. Spingarn" [January, 1914]; Baldwin to Villard, January 21, 1914; Nerney to Kathryn M. Johnson, July 30, 1915, NAACP Files.
[49] New York Age, July 12, 1906; October 19, 1911; Proceedings of the National Negro Conference 1909: New York May 31 and June 1, pp. 67, 89, 227; National League on Urban Conditions Among Negroes, Report 1910–1911 (n.p., n.d.), passim; John Hope Franklin, From Slavery to Freedom: A History of American Negroes (2d ed.; New York, 1965), pp. 440–42; Gunnar Myrdal, An American Dilemma: The Negro Problem and Modern Democracy (New York, 1944), pp. 837–42.

because they were not represented. The branch was directed to admit both men and women, but only two or three men submitted applications. Meantime, a group of men were taking steps to organize a separate branch, and Miss Ovington and Du Bois were afraid they were trying to use it for political purposes.[50]

The year 1915 saw the adoption of the policy of suspending branches because of lack of activity, their members being retained as members-at-large of the Association. In order to lessen the chance of new branches failing, another policy was adopted—that organizing groups would first receive recognition as provisional committees or "locals," which, if successful, would at the end of a year be chartered as branches. A model constitution for locals was worked out to supplement that for branches.[51] The purpose of this move was partly to give new groups time to grow and strengthen themselves, and partly to reorganize branches already in existence. Spingarn had noticed the sudden flush of feeling at the time a branch was born, when people were enthusiastic after attending a mass meeting, or indignant at some local injustice. How to make this mood of excitement continuous without excessive and expensive supervision from headquarters was the problem.

A RESIGNATION

When Miss Nerney left the Association at the end of 1915, she was proud of having successfully dealt with the problem of working with groups of people who had no habits of cooperation. In many cases she had had to take advantage of a situation in which a group was just emerging from a welter of personal and factional fights to help them understand the rudiments of organized effort. She had felt a sense of satisfaction when such people began to read and think of the race question in terms of democracy.[52]

Board members were jolted and depressed, however, by her report at the time of her resignation. She concluded that nowhere was the NAACP beginning to cope with the undeniable increase in prejudice and discrimination. In cities with large numbers of Negroes who had migrated from the South, the feeling for the NAACP ran the gamut from indifference and incredulity to open hostility. Many Negroes did not want to disturb the pattern of segregation, believing it conferred economic opportunity. Miss Nerney was convinced that this group did not really object to other forms of discrimination, as the Association claimed. She had discovered that when Southern Negroes with a conservative point of view infiltrated a branch, they loaded the executive board with people who

---

[50] "Schedule: NAACP Tour," annotated, January, 1915, J. E. Spingarn Papers (Howard); Nerney to Spingarn, "Notes on Branches for Dr. Spingarn" [January, 1914], NAACP Files.
[51] Board Minutes, NAACP, January 5, 1915; May 10, 1915; June 14, 1915; Ovington to Kathryn M. Johnson, September 14, 1915, NAACP Files.
[52] Minutes, Annual Meeting, January 3, 1916, in Board Minutes, NAACP.

would discourage active work, thus nullifying the effectiveness of the Association's program.[53]

Field worker Kathryn M. Johnson supported Miss Nerney's contention, observing that intelligent colored people everywhere were backward about taking part in the NAACP for bread-and-butter reasons. What they needed more than anything, she wrote, was a campaign of education to imbue them with the idea that they were men and women. Until they could be made to realize this and to resist the insults heaped upon them, the colored people would not support the work of the Association.[54]

These reports gave Miss Ovington "the blues." Miss Nerney's chief achievement had been the creation and running of branches, and the getting of money out of these branches, an achievement which Miss Nerney herself now seemed to consider questionable.[55]

At the 1916 Annual Meeting, Miss Nerney, as former secretary, summarized some of the problems and difficulties facing the organization. She was pessimistic about the future of the NAACP because of the failure of either its program or *The Crisis* to reach the masses of colored people. The illiterate and lowly of the race "do not speak our language," she said. At the same time, she recommended a course of action that went to the heart of many of the problems confronting the NAACP. A full-time promoter should be employed to organize the work of the branches, relieving the secretary of this work. A first-class lawyer should be engaged to supervise the legal work of the branches. Local cases of discrimination, wherever possible, should be in the hands of colored lawyers working under the supervision of the Association's attorney, and the costs should be assumed by the branch. The attorney, with the advice of the Board's Legal Committee, should have charge of all cases that might become of national importance.[56]

Field work had convinced the former secretary that both white and colored members desired a more definite and practical program. They were not so interested in legal disabilities as in economic opportunities. Where a definite task could be handled with no threat to economic security, a branch was almost always successful and active, but waiting for the legal process of a case to work itself out would not in itself keep a branch alive. A definite practical program in the social-economic field was a necessity for the branches.[57] Miss Nerney proposed that branches should have small committees that would make persistent

---

[53] Ovington to Spingarn, December 13 [1915], J. E. Spingarn Papers (Howard); Board Minutes, NAACP, December 6, 1915; Minutes, Annual Meeting, January 3, 1916, in Board Minutes, NAACP.
[54] Kathryn M. Johnson to Nash, August 19, 1916, NAACP Files.
[55] Ovington to Spingarn, December 13 [1915], J. E. Spingarn Papers (Howard).
[56] Minutes, Annual Meeting, January 3, 1916, in Board Minutes, NAACP.
[57] "Report of Secretary's trip," December 6, 1915, in Board Minutes, NAACP.

131

efforts to secure professional and industrial opportunities for Negroes and that these committees should make every effort to reach and influence manufacturers, professional and business men, and labor unions.

Joel Spingarn rejected Miss Nerney's suggestions on the grounds that the purposes of the NAACP would require more exact definition if the branches were to undertake work other than that of the fight for civil rights, and if they were at the same time to avoid competing with other organizations or duplicating their work.[58]

The problem of overlapping efforts on the part of the NAACP and the Urban League had arisen several times. George Haynes, sociologist from Fisk University, had dismayed Miss Ovington with his plan to form a national organization in the areas of employment and philanthropy, a plan that took a large field of "advancement" out of the NAACP program. She soon realized, however, that there was a need for two organizations, one less militant, to raise money and concern itself with employment—a business in itself. By an informal conference the leaders of the two organizations were able to bring about a mutually satisfactory arrangement as to the division of their respective activities.[59]

In response to the need for a continuing program for NAACP branches, Spingarn suggested that intellectual and artistic activities would help to bridge the gaps between the spasmodic intervals of excitement that were bound to occur in the struggle for equal rights, and for a time the Association experimented with a "forum circuit" idea.[60]

It was obvious that the work of organizing and supervising the branches was a full-time job, but lack of money for a reasonable salary led to various compromises on a part-time basis.[61] Members of the Committee on Branches helped the secretary, but the field work done by Miss Blascoer and by Miss Nerney until her resignation in 1915 took them away from the office, and the need for a competent organizer or field agent was often voiced.

[58] Minutes, Annual Meeting, January 3, 1916, in Board Minutes, NAACP.
[59] Ovington, *The Walls Came Tumbling Down* (New York, 1947), p. 112; Villard to Garrison, May 25, 1914, Villard Papers; Minutes, Annual Meeting, January 3, 1916, in Board Minutes, NAACP.
[60] Board Minutes, NAACP, May 8, 1916; July 9, 1917; September 9, 1918; September 17, 1917; October 8, 1918.
[61] In 1912 Dr. M. C. B. Mason was added to the staff as a "paid organizer." He was to be "on the road" holding meetings to build up interest in the NAACP and to raise money to cover his salary and traveling expenses. Board Minutes, NAACP, October 1, 1912. Dr. Mason was the first Negro to hold an executive position in the Methodist Episcopal Church. He had also been active in the Afro-American Council. *Crisis*, V (February, 1913), 191. From 1914 to 1916 Kathryn M. Johnson worked as a "field agent" receiving a commission on memberships and *Crisis* subscriptions and an expense allowance. Board Minutes, NAACP, September 1, 1914; February 2, 1915; September 11, 1916. Martha Gruening and Nettie Asbury also did field work and organizing during these years.

NEW BLOOD

At the Amenia conference in August, 1916, Spingarn's attention was drawn to James Weldon Johnson, a writer for the *New York Age*. Roy Nash considered Johnson an excellent choice for field secretary and organizer, better than John Hope or William Pickens, who had also been considered. "He is not academic," wrote Nash, "is a good mixer with a social bent that Du Bois and Hope lack, he is free from the stigma of religion, is a good talker, and would offend no group nor any audience."[62]

Johnson's background led to questions about his choice from some Board members. He had in truth been a "Washington man." In New York he was a close friend of Charles W. Anderson and had been president of the colored Republican Club of New York City. Washington's influence with Elihu Root had resulted in Johnson's appointment as United States Consul at Puerto Cabello, Venezuela, in 1906. In recommending Johnson for the position, Charles Anderson had stressed Johnson's stainless character and his "ripe scholarship . . . against whom nothing can possibly be said, except that he is a member of 'Ethiopia's blameless race.' "[63]

Returning to New York in 1914, Johnson, thanks to Anderson, was offered an editorship on the *New York Age*. Washington was delighted to have someone of Johnson's ability on the staff of the *Age* at a time when he feared that *The Crisis* might become the mouthpiece of the Negro.[64]

As editorial writer for the *Age*, Johnson displayed moderation and independent thought without straying from the Washington camp. He cautiously followed the policy Washington had laid down and avoided mentioning the name of the Association in his editorials. He supported Washington's pronouncements, had high praise for Charles W. Anderson when he retired, and expressed resentment over Du Bois's *Crisis* editorial on the death of Washington.[65]

Johnson's name had already been associated with the NAACP. As early as 1912 he had spoken at a meeting in Washington, D.C., under the auspices of the Association. In 1916 he became vice-president of the newly reorganized New

[62] Nash to Spingarn, October 27, 1916, J. E. Spingarn Papers (Howard). John Hope, president of Morehouse College, turned down Spingarn's tentative offer because he was unwilling to leave his college work. John Hope to Spingarn, October 21, 1916, J. E. Spingarn Papers (Howard).

[63] Charles W. Anderson to Washington, January 12, 1906; Washington to Anderson, February 28, 1906, Washington Papers.

[64] James Weldon Johnson, *Along This Way* (New York, 1933), pp. 302–3; Fred R. Moore to Booker T. Washington, October 7, 1914; Lester A. Walton to Washington, December 14, 1913; Washington to Moore, October 3, 1914, Washington Papers.

[65] *New York Age*, November 19, 1914; April 8, 1915; December 16, 1915; January 13, 1916; *Crisis*, XI (December, 1915), 82.

133

York City branch, and in August at the Amenia conference he was one of the speakers on the panel "A Working Programme for the Future." Spingarn, impressed with Johnson's contribution to the unity and harmony of the conference, wrote Nash: "It will seem strange to have us go to Fred Moore's office for a man, but I rather think that would be a coup d'etat."[66]

Du Bois agreed that Johnson would be an asset to the NAACP staff. To Miss Ovington's accusation that Johnson was hopelessly reactionary on labor and other problems, Nash countered that the American Negro was not yet ready for anything radical in any line. All he wanted was "a chance to live without a rope around his neck . . . Johnson will not shy at the essentials."[67]

Johnson responded affirmatively when approached. Spingarn indicated that the job was not easy, that it demanded exercise of executive ability and tact and above all, unswerving loyalty to the main purpose of the Association, but that the right man could become one of the greatest forces for good in the Afro-American world. Johnson accepted the challenge, and in December, 1916, was appointed field secretary and organizer of the NAACP.[68]

Increases in membership and in the geographical spread of the organization called for a closer relationship between branches and the national office. At the annual meeting in 1917, a separate session was given over to reports of branches and to a discussion of means of effecting closer ties. A publication to further this relationship had already been established—the *Branch Bulletin*, which first appeared in December, 1916.[69] Another innovation was the district conference, proposed by the Cleveland branch in 1916. The Great Lakes District Conference was organized in May, 1916, as a permanent body consisting of the branches in Cleveland, Pittsburgh, Columbus, Detroit, Toledo, Buffalo, Dayton, and Springfield.[70]

Johnson's field work in the South early in 1917 led to the organization of the Dixie District, which added 13 branches and 738 members to the Association. The NAACP, until then an essentially Northern organization, now faced the enemy at close range. Johnson, who had been born and raised in Jacksonville, Florida, spoke of the new spirit he encountered among Negroes in the South.[71]

[66] Board Minutes, NAACP, April 4, 1912; *New York Age*, December 21, 1916; Amenia Conference, "Programme" (Amenia, New York, August 24–26, 1916); Spingarn to Royal F. Nash, n.d., attached to Johnson to Spingarn, October 21, 1916, J. E. Spingarn Papers (Howard).
[67] Nash to Spingarn, October 27, 1916, J. E. Spingarn Papers (Howard).
[68] Spingarn to Johnson, October 28, 1916, Johnson Collection; Johnson to Spingarn, November 5, 1916, J. E. Spingarn Papers (Howard); Board Minutes, NAACP, December 11, 1916.
[69] Board Minutes, NAACP, November 13, 1916; December 11, 1916.
[70] Board Minutes, NAACP, May 8, 1916.
[71] Board Minutes, NAACP, February 13, 1917; April 9, 1917; May 14, 1917; *Crisis*, XIV (May, 1917), 19. The branches added were Atlanta, Tampa, Richmond, Savannah, Columbia, Jacksonville, Athens, Raleigh, Charleston, Augusta, Greensboro, Norfolk, and Durham.

With the reduction of the staff during the war, Johnson became acting secretary and accomplished a great deal—"in his quiet way" (according to Miss Ovington, who wrote Spingarn that she was glad he had overruled her in the matter of Johnson's coming to the Association).[72] With Johnson fully engaged at the national office, it was essential to find someone to help with the mushrooming branch work. Accordingly, Johnson entered into correspondence with Walter White. Twenty-four years old and a recent graduate of Atlanta University, White was secretary of the Atlanta NAACP branch, which had been organized by Johnson on his trip through the South. He was a man of engaging manners and a pleasing personality. Moreover, he was able to "pass" as white because of his blue eyes, blond hair, and fair skin, a factor which made him especially valuable to the Association as an investigator of such manifestations of mob violence as rioting and lynching. He came to the Association in February, 1918.[73]

TENTH ANNIVERSARY GAINS

Membership rolls for 1918 made previous statistics look pale. For more than a year there was a steady and spectacular rise in income as well as membership. The Moorfield Storey drive, honoring Storey's seventieth birthday, was John Shillady's first major effort on becoming secretary of the NAACP. The drive started in April, when there were 9,869 members and 85 branches. By the middle of May, 11,300 new members had joined the Association and 18 new branches had been organized. By December, 1918, there were 165 branches in 38 states (of these 85 were new branches), and the Association proclaimed that it was not only a national but an international organization, with branches in Canada and in Panama. The membership at the end of the year was 43,994, an increase of 34,712 over that of the previous year. Membership in the South alone was 18,701, double the total membership of the association for 1917, and there were branches in all the Southern states. The largest branch was Washington, D.C., with 6,843 members.[74]

Notwithstanding the energetic work of the field agents and Board officers, much of this spectacular growth was spontaneous, effected without any assist-

[72] Ovington to Spingarn, September 26, 1917, J. E. Spingarn Papers (Howard).
[73] Johnson, *Along This Way*, pp. 316–17; Ovington, *The Walls Came Tumbling Down*, p. 148; Ovington, *Portraits in Color* (New York, 1927), pp. 110–11; Walter White, *A Man Called White: The Autobiography of Walter White* (New York, 1948), p. 3; White to Johnson, October 10, 1917; Johnson to White, December 12, 1917; December 15, 1917; January 5, 1918; January 15, 1918; January 22, 1918, Johnson Collection.
[74] Board Minutes, NAACP, March 11, 1918; April 8, 1918; May 13, 1918; July 8, 1918; September 9, 1918; *Crisis*, XVI (August, 1918), 172–74; XVI (October, 1918), 274; NAACP, *Eighth and Ninth Annual Reports 1917 and 1918* (New York, 1919), pp. 17–19, 82, 87.

ance from the national office other than by correspondence.[75] It was a reaction to the wave of lynchings and mob violence throughout the nation, which was to reach its peak in the "Red Summer of 1919."

The year 1919 witnessed the first effort on the part of the branches to elect to the national Board Negroes who had demonstrated leadership in the affairs of local units. E. Burton Ceruti, a prominent attorney of Los Angeles, represented the West.[76] The Washington branch sent Neval H. Thomas, who had been active in the fight against segregation in government departments.[77] From the South came Robert R. Church, the first distinctively Southern member elected to the Board to represent this vast territory and large membership. Church, a wealthy Negro businessman and powerful Republican politician of Memphis, Tennessee, was Mrs. Robert Terrell's father.[78]

In 1919 the Pennsylvania branches took steps to perfect a statewide organization. There were other manifestations of interest at the state level. *The Crisis* urged branches located at state capitals to enlist their governors as supporters of the work. Following the Cleveland conference, the committee on organization recommended that such branches keep close watch over proposed state legislation affecting the Negro and report such legislation to the state branches and to the national office, just as the Washington branch did in regard to proposed national legislation.[79] Both district and state levels of organization were manifestations of a grass-roots desire for a geographical unit intermediate between the national and the local levels.

At the time of the Cleveland conference in 1919, on the tenth birthday of the NAACP, there were 220 branches and 56,345 members, and the circulation of *The Crisis* stood at 100,000 copies. The NAACP proclaimed proudly that it was "without peer, the greatest fighting force for Negro freedom in the world. . . . The Negro who is not a member of it finds himself on the defensive. The white man who does not believe in it does not believe in American democracy."[80]

A determination on the part of the Southern delegates to fight for the ballot was evident at the Cleveland conference. This aggressiveness caused such apprehension among conservative and timid members that *The Crisis* felt called upon to explain that the words FIGHT and VOTE meant not bloodshed but the determination to secure the right to vote. In the same spirit the conference warned

[75] *Crisis*, XVI (October, 1918), 274.
[76] Board Minutes, NAACP, September 9, 1918; June 9, 1919; John Haynes Holmes to Charles H. Studin, April 10, 1919, in Arthur B. Spingarn Papers (now in the Manuscript Division, Library of Congress).
[77] Roscoe Conkling Bruce to Studin, March 22, 1919, A. B. Spingarn Papers.
[78] *Crisis*, XVII (January, 1919), 122; Paul Lewinson, *Race, Class, and Party* (New York, 1932), pp. 139ff., 172n., 175.
[79] Board Minutes, March 10, 1919; April 14, 1919; October 13, 1919; *Crisis*, XVII (April, 1919), 284.
[80] *Crisis*, XVIII (June, 1919), 59; Board Minutes, NAACP, June 9, 1919.

against what appeared to be an attractive program offered to Negroes by Bolshevism. Resolutions adopted by the conference demanded an investigation of the treatment of Negro soldiers, the end of segregation in the armed forces and civilian life, federal legislation to prevent lynching, and a fair share of federal funds for aid to education. The convention called on Negro voters "in the better civilized parts of the country" to see that their representatives in Congress implemented these demands.[81]

By the end of 1919 there were 310 branches and 91,203 members organized into 8 districts, three of which were in the Far West. Of these the fastest growing was the Pacific District. For the first time Southern membership exceeded that of the North, 42,588 to 38,420. It was estimated that about nine-tenths of the members were colored and one-tenth white. Reflecting the geographical shift to the South, the Board decided to hold the 1920 conference in Atlanta, Georgia. This was not done without misgivings and even opposition from some branches, notably Boston.[82]

It took courage to call an interracial conference south of the Mason-Dixon line, where abolitionists still were anathema.[83] Atlanta had been the scene of terrible riots in 1906, and in the intervening years lynching and mob violence had reached a peak rather than abated. In Austin, Texas, the Association's white secretary had been attacked and beaten in broad daylight while investigating a case. Who knew but that the Red Summer of 1919 would be repeated in 1920?

[81] *Crisis*, XVIII (August, 1919), 190–93.
[82] Board Minutes, NAACP, June 9, 1919; July 11, 1919; September 8, 1919; October 13, 1919; November 10, 1919; December 8, 1919.
[83] Spingarn to L. H. Hammond [December, 1912], J. E. Spingarn Papers (Howard).

CHAPTER VII

Propaganda and Publicity

In the early days of the Association the most effective means of reaching the masses was the lecture platform. The NAACP made use of anniversaries such as the birthdays of the abolitionists Charles Sumner, Wendell Phillips, and William Lloyd Garrison, and the anniversary of the signing of the Emancipation Proclamation. Mass meetings celebrating these events provided a link with the old abolition movement and attracted public attention to the new abolition movement, which had as its goal the completion of emancipation.[1] Nearly all the Board members traveled extensively in the early days, but with the growth of the branches, the expansion of the circulation of *The Crisis,* and the increased use of salaried field workers, the lecture platform became less essential to the growth of the Association.

Du Bois estimated that during his first ten years with the organization he traveled in nearly every state and in several foreign countries and delivered 424 lectures to a total of almost 200,000 people. When the Board chided him in 1919 for spending too much time on lectures that had no direct relation to the work of the Association, he replied that after expenses his income from lectures totaled $2,050, an average of $228 a year. He assured the Board that his lectures had been for purposes of propaganda and not for profit.[2]

Du Bois was interested in other propaganda methods as well. In the spring of 1912, he met with a group of writers in an effort to interest them in the Negro as a source of literary material and to persuade them to present the truth re-

[1] Notice of Annual Meeting, January 21, 1913, in "Minute Book of the Board of Directors of the National Association for the Advancement of Colored People" (now in the Manuscript Division, Library of Congress; hereafter referred to as Board Minutes, NAACP).
[2] Board Minutes, NAACP, July 11, 1919.

garding the race, rather than fictionalized accounts of a sentimental or sensational character.[3]

Still another approach to the problem of propaganda was Du Bois's research activity. He had come to the NAACP with the idea of continuing his research and providing objective, scientific facts with which to carry on the propaganda work. He was handicapped, however, by the Association's lack of funds for such activities, and from time to time sought appropriations from other agencies to finance studies of special phases of the Negro problem.[4] He conducted researches into African history through the years 1913, 1914, and 1915, and undertook what he called smaller researches on Negro folklore and folk songs, which were presented in the form of papers at the Brooklyn Institute and Columbia University. He also carried on an investigation of land grant colleges and made a study of lynching.[5]

Du Bois hoped that all research into the condition of the American Negro being carried on in Negro colleges and universities would be centralized at the NAACP with himself as director, and that other leading universities would be invited to cooperate with the Association in studying the social and political problems of segregation, disfranchisement, Negro schools, and lynching. He tried to interest the Slater Fund in financing such a project, but without success.[6]

Other efforts to secure publicity included the printing and distribution of the proceedings of the annual conferences, of speeches given by Board members, and of the annual reports of the Association. Later *The Crisis* published calendars, pictures, and Christmas cards with Negro themes. The object of this was not only to obtain publicity for the NAACP but also to stimulate pride in Negro achievements.[7]

A more serious effort to foster pride in Negro accomplishments was the establishment by Joel Spingarn of a gold medal (the Spingarn Medal) to be awarded

[3] Form letter [April, 1912], W. E. B. Du Bois Papers (now in possession of Mrs. W. E. B. Du Bois, New York City) ; Board Minutes, NAACP, May 4, 1912.
[4] After he came to the NAACP in 1910, Du Bois continued to work on a series of studies started at Atlanta University, financed by the Slater Fund and the University, and published by the University: *The College Bred Negro American* (1910), *The Common School and the Negro American* (1911), *The Negro American Artisan* (1912), *Morals and Manners Among Negro Americans* (1914).
[5] Board Minutes, NAACP, May 6, 1913; Minutes, Annual Meeting, January 3, 1916, in Board Minutes, NAACP.
[6] Board Minutes, NAACP, September 3, 1912; Minutes, Annual Meeting, January 3, 1916, in Board Minutes, NAACP.
[7] Minutes, Executive Committee, April 11, 1911; Minutes, Annual Meeting, January 3, 1916, in Board Minutes, NAACP; Charles Edward Russell, *Leaving It to the South* (New York, 1912). A calendar of Negro biography was published for 1917. For 1919, 12,500 copies of a "calendar of [Negro] war heroes" was issued. Board Minutes, NAACP, December 12, 1916; January 8, 1917; February 10, 1919; February 9, 1920.

annually by the NAACP for "the highest and noblest achievement of an American Negro." This award brought the attention of white people to Negro Americans who each year made significant contributions in many fields of endeavor, and—what was even more important—gave the Association publicity among colored people. In 1915 an award committee was set up by the Board, consisting of Oswald Garrison Villard, James H. Dillard, Bishop John Hurst, of the African Methodist Episcopal Church, John Hope, and ex-President Taft. The public was invited to make nominations.[8]

From the thirty nominations submitted, the first Spingarn Medal was awarded to Ernest Everett Just of Howard University for his research in biology.[9] The award was presented in February, 1915, by Governor Charles S. Whitman of New York at a public mass meeting following the annual meeting of the NAACP. The second Spingarn Medal went to Major Charles Young for his work in organizing the constabulary in Liberia, and the third, in 1917, to Harry T. Burleigh, the singer.[10]

The awarding of the Spingarn Medal at once became a major event for the NAACP and the Negro world. Prior to the announcement of the first winner, there was much excitement and speculation, and one newspaper, attempting a scoop, wrongly announced that it had been awarded to William Monroe Trotter.[11] The Association tried to attract publicity to the event by having a state governor or some person of prestige make the award. In 1918, the medal was won by the poet William Stanley Braithwaite, and was presented by Governor R. Livingston Beeckman of Rhode Island.

In recognition of his organization of the Washington branch, of his fight against segregation in the federal service, and of his work with congressional legislative committees, Archibald Grimke received the medal in 1919; and at

[8] Board Minutes, NAACP, March 11, 1913; October 7, 1913; NAACP, *Ninth Annual Report 1918* (New York, 1919), p. 69; *Washington Bee*, May 24, 1913; *New York Age*, February 18, 1915. Dillard was director of the Anna T. Jeanes Foundation and a member of the Southern Education Board. Anson Phelps-Stokes, "James Hardy Dillard," in Schuyler and James (eds.) *Dictionary of American Biography: Supplement Two*, XXII (New York, 1958), 150–51.
[9] *Crisis*, IX (April, 1915), 284. Some of the others nominated were Howard Drew, holder of the world's record for the one hundred yard dash; Mrs. Meta Warrick Fuller, a sculptress; William Monroe Trotter, "the intrepid agitator"; Heman Perry, founder of the first Negro old-line life insurance company; William Stanley Braithwaite, the poet; R. R. Moton; Isaac Fisher, "essayist of Tuskegee Institute"; and Cornelia Bowen, principal of the Mt. Meigs School in Alabama.
[10] *New York Age*, February 18, 1915; *Washington Bee*, February 20, 1915; February 26, 1916; May 12, 1917; May 26, 1917; Minutes, Annual Meeting, January 2, 1917, in Board Minutes, NAACP.
[11] *Amsterdam News* (New York), February 12, 1915, cited in *New York Age*, February 18, 1915.

the Atlanta conference in 1920, Moorfield Storey presented the coveted award to Du Bois for his work in organizing the Pan-African Congress.[12]

The fiftieth anniversary of the Emancipation Proclamation in 1913 was made the occasion for demonstrating the progress of the Negro over half a century. After failure to obtain federal sponsorship of a Negro Exposition, the NAACP persuaded the New York State Legislature to appropriate funds for an Emancipation Exposition. Du Bois, appointed by the governor as one of nine commissioners to plan the celebration, wrote and directed for the Exposition a historical pageant of the Negro race, "The Star of Ethiopia." About 30,000 persons visited the Exposition. According to Du Bois, this was the "largest assemblage of colored people ever held in the city."[13]

A few years later, the NAACP Board supported Du Bois's proposal for a celebration of the tercentenary of the landing of the Negro in America at Jamestown, Virginia, in August, 1619. Du Bois also planned to publish an *Encyclopedia Africana* to mark the commemoration, but neither the celebration nor the publication materialized. The death of Mme. C. J. Walker, treasurer of the committee on arrangements, ended the possibility of securing financial support from one of the few very wealthy Negroes in America. Du Bois, chairman of the committee, left for France in 1919 with other representatives of the press to report the Peace Conference to *Crisis* readers, and his four-month absence greatly handicapped the committee. When he returned, his bitter arraignment of Robert R. Moton and Emmett J. Scott for failing to look after the interest of Negro soldiers in France seriously divided the Negro community. And, finally, the upheavals of the summer of 1919 produced a climate of public opinion unfavorable to a large-scale celebration. The national office, however, drew up and distributed literature and a general program on the tercentenary that could be adapted to local branch needs. There was also a special tercentenary issue of *The Crisis*, and 12,500 copies of a tercentenary calendar were printed and sold.[14]

THE BIRTH OF A NATION

Not only did the Association attempt to glorify the role of the Negro in the past and in the present, it also tried to combat the harmful portrayal of the

[12] Board Minutes, NAACP, April 8, 1918; May 13, 1918; NAACP, *Ninth Annual Report 1918*, p. 69; *New York Age*, June 28, 1919; *Washington Bee*, June 5, 1920.
[13] Board Minutes, NAACP, February 6, 1912. See also Senate Report Number 311, "Semicentennial Anniversary of the Act of Emancipation," 62d Congress, 2d Session, I, 1–7; [NAACP] "Annual Report of the Director of Publicity and Research," January 5, 1913 [1914], Du Bois Papers.
[14] Board Minutes, NAACP, September 9, 1918; October 14, 1918; January 13, 1919; Minutes, Annual Meeting, January 3, 1916, in Board Minutes, NAACP; NAACP, *Ninth Annual Report 1918*, p. 57; NAACP, *Tenth Annual Report 1919*, p. 67; *Crisis*, XVIII (September 1919); *Crisis*, XVIII (August, 1919), 183.

Negro as depicted in the motion picture, *The Birth of a Nation,* released in 1915. This film, based on Thomas Dixon's novel *The Clansman,* characterized the Negro, according to *The Crisis,* as an "ignorant fool, a vicious rapist, a venal and unscrupulous politician, or a faithful but doddering idiot."[15]

The film, which brought fame to its director, David Wark Griffith, heralded a great advance in motion picture art and technique. It was an enormous success, and numerous revivals over the years have attested to its popularity and longevity. But without question it was a potent force for implanting in Northern minds the Southern conception of the Negro. At a time when mob violence was increasing and Negroes were migrating to the North in great numbers, the film inflamed public opinion. In the St. Louis area, real estate agents, as part of their campaign for the introduction of residential segregation ordinances, distributed copies of their trade journal, *The Home Defender,* to audiences as they left the theater. In Lafayette, Indiana, a white man "without provocation" shot and killed a fifteen-year-old Negro boy immediately after seeing the picture.[16]

The problem of combatting the evil effects of the picture presented the liberal leadership of the NAACP with a dilemma. Inez Milholland, representing those who were opposed to censorship, objected to suppressing the bad as a means of establishing the good and defended the right of the individual to judge for himself. She pointed out the value of the discussion of the Negro problem, which had been precipitated by the film. Her advice was to protest vigorously but not to suppress.[17]

Spingarn defended freedom of expression but argued that it was the Association's right and duty to see that the National Board of Censorship in Moving Pictures acted with fairness and justice. The fight, therefore, at first centered in an effort to have the picture suppressed by the National Board of Censorship. At the request of the NAACP, and with the friendly intercession of some of the Censorship Board members whom Spingarn was able to reach personally, this Board met and withdrew its prior sanction of the film. However, at a subsequent meeting they again reversed themselves by a small majority. The NAACP, acting upon the advice of Storey, Villard, and others, then retained the legal services of a Southerner, James O. Osborne, to represent them in legal action against the producers and owners of the film, but the case was indefinitely postponed, and the producers were successful in securing injunctions restraining city authorities from interfering with the showing of the picture everywhere in the South.[18]

[15] Thomas Dixon, Jr., *The Clansman: An Historical Romance of the Ku Klux Klan* (New York, 1905); *Crisis,* X (May, 1915), 33.
[16] Mary White Ovington, *The Walls Came Tumbling Down* (New York, 1947), p. 127; Board Minutes, NAACP, September 13, 1915; *Chicago American,* April 24, 1916, quoted in *Crisis,* XII (June, 1916), 87.
[17] Inez Milholland, "Censorship," *Crisis,* XIII (January, 1917), 116–17.
[18] Minutes, Annual Meeting, January 3, 1916, in Board Minutes, NAACP; *Crisis,* X (May, 1915), 33; May Childs Nerney to Board Members, March 17, 1915; March 18, 1915, in

Villard refused to accept advertising for the film in the *New York Evening Post*. The NAACP undertook to persuade film exhibitors to boycott the picture. They tried to organize a protest in the form of a manifesto signed by a number of well-known Southerners, but these steps were ineffective. Of greater value was Miss Ovington's carefully prepared leaflet on certain points raised by the film, such as the Black Codes and the role of the Ku Klux Klan. The leaflet was distributed in cities where the film was being shown. In New York City nearly 8,000 of these circulars were distributed at the doors of theaters.[19]

Also in New York City, at Lillian Wald's suggestion, a dignified procession of about 500 representatives of New York organizations interested in the welfare of the Negro marched to attend a hearing on the film at the Mayor's office. These efforts and those of Charles W. Anderson (who succeeded in reaching Mayor John Purroy Mitchel ahead of the NAACP) resulted in the elimination or modification of some of the most objectionable scenes.[20]

During 1915, the national office was flooded with requests for help in suppressing *The Birth of a Nation*. A number of branches tried with varying degrees of success to build up sentiment against the picture in advance of its showing. The Boston branch, as we have seen, waged a significant fight against the film.[21]

As a final measure, the NAACP attempted to produce its own motion picture, to counteract Griffith's film without attacking it by portraying the Negro and Reconstruction historically. (The idea of using a motion picture to present the Association's message to the public was first recommended by Miss Nerney in 1913.) A committee of the Board consulted novelist James Oppenheim, who was already working on a scenario for a film to counteract *The Birth of a Nation*. At the same time Villard independently arranged to have a scenario

---

Board Minutes, NAACP; Oswald Garrison Villard to Dillard, March 18, 1915, Oswald Garrison Villard Papers (Houghton Library, Harvard University); Board Minutes, NAACP, September 3, 1915.

[19] Villard to Dillard, March 18, 1915; Dillard to Villard, March 17, 1915; March 19, 1915; Frissell to Villard, December 9, 1916, Villard Papers; Board Minutes, NAACP, September 13, 1915; Ovington, *The Walls Came Tumbling Down*, pp. 130–31.

[20] Nerney to Board Members, March 18, 1915, in Board Minutes, NAACP, March 23, 1915; Nerney to "Our Members in New York and Vicinity," March 29, 1915, in John E. Bruce Papers (Schomburg Collection, New York Public Library, New York); *Crisis*, X (May, 1915), 33; Charles W. Anderson to Booker T. Washington, March 31, 1915, Booker T. Washington Papers (Manuscript Division, Library of Congress). Washington made efforts to stop the showing of the picture, but was concerned lest these efforts should advertise the picture rather than suppress it. Washington to Anderson, April 10, 1915, Washington Papers.

[21] Board Minutes, NAACP, June 14, 1915; September 13, 1915; Minutes, Annual Meeting, January 3, 1916, in Board Minutes, NAACP. The national office and branches also had to fight two other pictures which were produced to compete with and capitalize on the popularity of *Birth of a Nation*. They were *The Nigger* (1915), and *Free and Equal* (1918), but they were both imitative and did not capture Griffith's wide audience. Board Minutes, NAACP, April 13, 1915; January 14, 1918.

written by a writer for the Universal Film Company, one of three large movie companies planning to produce a film to rival Griffith's.[22]

Universal eventually produced a scenario entitled *Lincoln's Dream*, which it offered to make it into a twelve-reel film on a scale comparable to *The Birth of a Nation*, provided the NAACP would raise at least $10,000 of the estimated $60,000 cost of production. The profits, if any, were to be equally divided between the NAACP and the company until the $10,000 was repaid. Miss Ovington considered this the one big constructive piece of work that had yet been given the Board to do. Nothing else had come near it in importance, but it had to be done at once to be effective. Despite strenuous efforts, it was impossible to raise the money, and the production had to be abandoned. Nevertheless Villard reported that the steps taken to make a film had so frightened the producers of *The Birth of a Nation* that they had sent him a threatening letter, alleging that he was attempting blackmail.[23]

In an attempt to counter the influence of Griffith's movie, the NAACP spent several hundred dollars to help produce a "race play" called *Rachel*, written by Angelina Grimke, the daughter of Archibald Grimke. It was performed in Washington and New York, but it reached no white audiences and did not meet expenses.[24]

After America's entry into the World War, the Association appealed to all governors and to State Councils of National Defense asking them to ban the picture on the grounds of its being detrimental to the war effort, because it fostered race hatred and disunity in a time of crisis. The Governor of Ohio, James M. Cox, and the West Virginia Council of National Defense had already suppressed the picture in those states, and, following the Association's appeal, several other states took steps to ban it.[25] The fight against *The Birth of a Nation* undoubtedly advertised and gave publicity to the film, but it also provided an opportunity for presenting the aims of the NAACP to the public.

PUBLICITY, 1909–19

Originally the founding group planned for a committee of volunteers to provide publicity for the Association. There were a number of newspaper people and writers in the group—Paul Kennaday, Mrs. Mary Dunlop Maclean, James F. Morton, Jr., William English Walling, Charles Edward Russell, and Mary

[22] Nerney to Board Members, May 7, 1915, in Board Minutes, NAACP; Board Minutes, NAACP, November 6, 1913; June 14, 1915; Ovington to Villard, April 17, 1915, Villard Papers.
[23] Ovington to Villard, June 6, 1915, Villard Papers; Board Minutes, NAACP, June 14, 1915; September 13, 1915; November 8, 1915; Minutes, Annual Meeting, January 3, 1916, in Board Minutes, NAACP.
[24] Board Minutes, NAACP, March 13, 1916; April 9, 1917; May 14, 1917.
[25] Board Minutes, NAACP, October 14, 1918; February 10, 1919.

White Ovington. In January, 1911, Villard's committee on program recommended the establishment of a Bureau of Information to supply the daily press, magazines, and individuals with unbiased information on all questions pertaining to the Negro. A few months later, a Press Committee of thirty members was organized under Morton of the *Chicago Public* to reply or to comment upon, all editorials and news items obnoxious to the colored people.[26]

These volunteer methods did not function very well, and Villard continued to stress the need for a first-rate publicity man. A professional newspaper man was engaged to take charge of publicity for the fifth annual conference in 1913, otherwise the secretary handled publicity. Miss Nerney, in 1913, not only conducted the investigation of segregation in government departments and provided an abstract of her investigation to the press services, but sent the full report to 600 daily papers, various secular magazines, 50 religious publications, the Negro press, and the so-called radical press. All Congressmen, except those from the South, and other interested individuals also received the report. As a result, Villard was satisfied that in this case the NAACP had been given an unusual amount of publicity.[27]

To 600 Southern newspapers Miss Nerney also sent an article by Villard on the Jim Crow car and a portion of an address of Professor W. O. Scroggs of Louisiana on the same subject, delivered before the Southern Sociological Congress. The NAACP often tried to influence Southern public opinion by selecting Southerners of prominence and prestige to serve on committees, write articles, or handle legal cases in the South. At the same time they tried to avoid types of publicity that would irritate Southern opinion.[28]

It was unreasonable to assume that the secretary could or should continue to be responsible for publicity in addition to organizing duties and the routine work of the national office. Miss Nerney tried to persuade the Board to engage Charles T. Hallinan of the *Chicago Evening Post* to organize a publicity bureau at the national office on a temporary basis under her charge. (It was at this time that Villard recommended that Du Bois's title be changed from Director of Publicity and Research to Editor of *The Crisis,* so that confusion would be avoided if the Association should engage a publicity manager.)[29]

---

[26] Report of the Preliminary Committee on Permanent Organization, in Minutes, National Negro Committee, May 5, 1910; Minutes, Executive Committee, January 3, 1911; May 2, 1911; Minutes, Annual Meeting, January 21, 1913, in Board Minutes, NAACP; *Crisis,* V (December, 1912), 89; NAACP, *Third Annual Report 1912* (New York, 1913), p. 13.

[27] Villard to Moorfield Storey, September 10, 1913, Villard Papers. Villard listed the *Washington Post,* the *Washington Star,* the *Philadelphia North American,* the *Boston Transcript,* and the *Boston Advertiser* as among the newspapers doing "splendid work" in publicizing the NAACP. Villard to Roscoe C. Bruce, October 29, 1913, Villard Papers.

[28] Board Minutes, NAACP, November 6, 1913; Nerney to Joel E. Spingarn, January 16, 1913, Joel Elias Spingarn Papers (Moorland Foundation, Howard University).

[29] Villard to Board of Directors, November 19, 1913, Villard Papers; Board Minutes, NAACP, November 6, 1913.

Hallinan was engaged to write publicity for the Baltimore conference, but Miss Nerney continued to handle the routine press work. In 1914 she sought advice from a professional newspaperman, Malcolm W. Davis of the *Evening Post*, on how to publicize Spingarn's Western trip. Davis instructed her in the technique of sending advance notices, followed by a more complete story, and, finally, by a third-spread story, which resulted in good press coverage of the trip.[30]

Another means of publicizing the work of the NAACP was through the national conventions of the various social agencies. Miss Nerney made it a practice to send such agencies information about the Association. For example, the Russell Sage Foundation was supplied with a statement of purposes of the NAACP for a pamphlet on the interrelation of social movements. In 1914, a steadily increasing number of invitations was received, requesting that the Association send delegates to meetings and conventions of other organizations, evidence that the NAACP was becoming increasingly well known in professional circles.[31]

A further indication of the large amount of publicity work handled by the secretary can be seen by the 5 lists of 289 newspapers compiled for use by the national office: 50 leading Negro papers, 92 Northern and 44 important Southern papers, 66 friendly white newspapers, and 37 papers published in foreign countries. While it was impossible for Miss Nerney to set up a systematic weekly news service, all of these newspapers received stories of particular racial interest.

A clipping service supplied the national office with excerpts from sixty-five papers, all of which carried extended accounts and editorials on the Waco, Texas, lynching. More than twenty-five carried the story of the NAACP appeal to Congress for additional Negro regiments in the United States Army. These figures indicated only a fraction of the total publicity, since no clipping bureau covered the entire white press, and none covered the Negro press.[32]

At the end of 1916, Villard again pressed for a full-time publicity manager with newspaper training. The question was discussed at length at the Board meeting, but the finances of the Association would not permit such an addition to the staff.[33]

[30] Board Minutes, NAACP, December 2, 1913; June 2, 1914; Malcolm W. Davis to Nerney, December 23, 1913, NAACP Files (Manuscript Division, Library of Congress).
[31] Board Minutes, NAACP, September 3, 1912; October 1, 1912; November 12, 1912; June 2, 1914. Among the first groups to invite the NAACP to address their meetings were the National Association of Cosmopolitan Clubs and the National Forum of Bahaists. Board Minutes, NAACP, January 7, 1913; December 31, 1915.
[32] Minutes, Annual Meeting, January 3, 1916; January 2, 1917, in Board Minutes, NAACP.
[33] Royal F. Nash to Spingarn, December 6, 1916, J. E. Spingarn Papers (Howard); Board Minutes, NAACP, December 11, 1916.

It was at this time that the *Branch Bulletin* was launched. Since *The Crisis* was not a house organ in the usual sense, and since the space allotted to "NAACP Notes" (written by the secretary) was not deemed adequate for items of information, advice, and suggestions to branches of a more intimate character, the *Branch Bulletin* was initiated as a monthly medium of communication between the national office and the branches. By 1919, its circulation had reached 27,439, but increases in postal rates, paper cost, and printing soon brought an end to its publication.[34]

By the end of 1917, the troubles of the Negro were increasing in number and tempo. Villard became so concerned that he once more urged the Board to secure adequate publicity. The Board complied by voting that in exceptional cases, such as the favorable decision of the Supreme Court in the Louisville segregation case, a professional publicity man should be engaged to secure as wide a circulation of the story as possible. In addition, the Board voted to engage Ernest Gruening at $100 a week to gather and disseminate to both the white and colored press news regarding Negro troops in the war zone. James Weldon Johnson, in the hope of securing more attention in daily and weekly papers, began mailing a clip sheet from *The Crisis* to all Negro newspapers and to friendly white papers.[35]

John R. Shillady, when he became secretary in 1918, expanded and further systematized the press coverage, setting up a regular press service and enlarging the clipping service, which had previously covered only those articles in which the name of the Association appeared. The new service covered all references to lynchings appearing in New York City newspapers and in the papers in areas where the lynchings occurred. In addition, clippings were ordered on all legislative matters that would affect the Negro. Shillady also initiated the practice of sending copies of press releases to the secretaries of the various branches for discussion at branch meetings, to keep the membership adequately informed of activities of the national office. In connection with the anti-lynching drive organized by Shillady in 1918, about 130,000 pieces of literature were distributed. Branches were given leaflets and pamphlets at less than cost so that they might make a profit on their sale.[36]

[34] NAACP, *Ninth Annual Report 1918*, pp. 51–52; *Crisis*, XIX (March, 1920), 244. There is no complete file of the *Branch Bulletin* at the national office.
[35] Board Minutes, NAACP, November 12, 1917; December 10, 1917. Ernest Gruening (Martha Gruening's brother), while managing editor of *The Nation* during the 1920's, guided the NAACP in its successful effort to bring about withdrawal of the United States forces from Haiti. Ernest Gruening to author, April 5, 1966. He later became governor, then United States Senator from Alaska. *New York Times*, July 15, 1958; April 6, 1959.
[36] Board Minutes, NAACP, February 11, 1918; April 8, 1918; NAACP, *Ninth Annual Report 1918*, pp. 50–52.

During 1918, in spite of the predominance of war news, an unusual number of favorable editorials appeared as a direct result of the Association's increased publicity. While "unfriendly" papers did not print the releases sent to them, the effect of this publicity was nevertheless reflected on their editorial pages. By this time the Negro press was usually appreciative of news from the NAACP.[37]

Herbert Seligmann, a reporter for the *New York Evening Post* was engaged to take charge of the publicity for the national conference on lynching in April, 1919. His work pleased the Board, which then sent him to investigate lynchings in Mississippi. Villard published Seligmann's report in *The Nation*. This marked the beginning of Seligmann's association with the NAACP; in September, 1919, he became the first Director of Publicity.[38]

During his first month with the Association, his articles were accepted for publication by the *New Republic, Current Opinion,* and *The Nation.* He also issued in pamphlet form four articles previously published by staff members, wrote thirteen press stories, and sent letters to selected newspapers. By the end of the year, the Publicity Department had distributed 427,000 pieces of literature, an increase of nearly 300,000 over the previous year. In addition, 134 press releases were sent out, and special articles of a publicity nature were written by Seligmann, Walter White, and Miss Ovington.[39]

TEN YEARS OF *THE CRISIS*

The Crisis was the principal means of propaganda and publicity of the NAACP. It began publication in November, 1910, with an initial edition of 1,000 copies. In six months circulation reached 10,000; at the end of two years, 24,000. Total income for the first two years was $17,374.51. This phenomenal growth led the editor to boast in 1912 that the magazine had the largest net circulation of any periodical devoted to the Negro race in America.[40]

When compared to *The Voice of the Negro* (1904–7), the only other Negro periodical that had had a national audience, *The Crisis* was an amazing triumph.

[37] Board Minutes, NAACP, May 13, 1918; NAACP, *Ninth Annual Report 1918,* pp. 51–52.

[38] Board Minutes, NAACP, May 12, 1919; July 11, 1919; Herbert Seligmann, "Protecting Southern Womanhood," *Nation,* CVIII (June, 1919), 931, 938–39. Seligmann's first contact with the NAACP was through Du Bois and James Weldon Johnson, who met him during the summer of 1917 at a conference of the Inter-Collegiate Socialist Society at Belleport, New York, which he was reporting for the *Evening Post.* Seligmann's write-up of the paper delivered by Johnson received worldwide publicity, appearing in American, European, Australian, and South African journals and papers. Board Minutes, NAACP, October 8, 1917; James Weldon Johnson, *Along This Way* (New York, 1933), pp. 326–27.

[39] Board Minutes, NAACP, October 13, 1919; *Crisis,* XIX (March, 1920), 244.

[40] At the end of 1911, there were 4,000 subscribers. A staff of 223 agents had disposed of over 11,000 additional copies and 60 books on the Negro problem. "Report of Publicity and Research, September 1, 1910, to January 1, 1912"; "Total Cash of *Crisis,* November 1, 1910, to November 1, 1912," Du Bois Papers; *Crisis,* V (November, 1912), 28.

The Voice of the Negro reached the height of its circulation in May, 1907, when 15,000 copies were sold; its average monthly income was between $400 and $500.[41]

The contribution of the NAACP to the support of *The Crisis* had been considerable. From November, 1910, until May, 1912, the Association paid the salaries of the editor, his secretary, the bookkeeper, and the stenographer, in addition to rent, light, heat, telephone, and cleaning bills. Du Bois estimated that editing *The Crisis* took about two thirds of his time and that it had been a total expense to the NAACP of less than $4,000 for the first two years. But he warned the Board that competition could at any time challenge his monopoly in the field of race journalism. His objective was to build so good and so popular and indispensable a publication that it could meet any competition.[42]

The chief problem as to circulation was one of distribution, since ordinary channels for distributing periodicals could not be used. *The Crisis* had to rely chiefly upon its own agents, who were "largely missionaries in a crusade." It was Du Bois's belief that when the magazine achieved a circulation of 50,000, its permanence and independence would be guaranteed.[43] He estimated that out of about one million literate Negro families in America, at least 100,000 could in time be induced to subscribe to *The Crisis*. In determining the make-up of the magazine and its editorial policy, he kept in mind the fact that eighty per cent of all *Crisis* readers were Negroes. The journal's varied audience included what he described as "educated, hypercritical reformers of refined taste," as well as people who could scarcely read or write. Its editorial policy was to impart reliable news and information. Du Bois considered that Negro periodicals as a whole had neither sought out the facts nor presented them properly. *The Crisis*, he felt, should discuss problems affecting the Negro in a frank and fearless manner. Its format should appeal to people who were starved for warmth and color. If *The Crisis* and some of its contents savored of the "penny dreadful," this was necessary to reach the Negro masses. As to purely editorial discussion, Du Bois was determined to present strong, thought-provoking, frank material on

[41] J. Max Barber to Du Bois, March 2, 1912, Du Bois Papers. *The Voice of the Negro* was edited by J. W. E. Bowen and J. Max Barber. It was published in Atlanta, Georgia, from January, 1904, to July, 1906, when it was driven out by whites, incensed over its coverage of the Atlanta riot. The magazine moved to Chicago, where it resumed publication for nearly a year. In January, 1907, it appeared under the title *The Voice*, with Barber as sole editor. Reasons given for the change of the title were the hostility the journal had aroused among Southern whites, the fact that some Negroes seeking to identify themselves with America objected to the word "Negro" in the title, and lastly, the shorter title, which was less cumbersome and therefore better for business reasons.

[42] "Annual Report of Director of Publicity and Research for 1912," Du Bois Papers; Board Minutes, NAACP, April 4, 1912. On May 1, 1912, separate bank accounts were set up for *The Crisis* and the NAACP. At this time the Association had a deficit of $1,200.

[43] *Crisis*, V (November, 1912), 28.

the Negro problem, because Negroes were surfeited with flabby generalities. He urged that he be allowed reasonable freedom for the full development of his ideas.[44]

It is impossible to tell from Du Bois's published reports and private papers the exact status of *The Crisis* at any one time. This is due to his failure to supply complete figures as to cost, salaries, NAACP subsidies, and net paid circulation. From May, 1912, through January, 1913, the number of copies printed monthly remained static (about 22,000), whereas there was a slight increase in "total cost"—a term which was never clarified.[45] In his formal financial reports to the Board for the first two years, Du Bois did not account for such matters as the periodical's share of the rent, heat, light, telephone, janitor service, or that portion of his salary or those of the clerks that was met by the NAACP. Only after this omission had been repeatedly brought to his attention did Du Bois admit these charges in his verbal and informal reports to the Board. It is evident from an examination of the records that Villard's criticism of Du Bois's business methods was justified.

By 1913 *The Crisis* was expanding so rapidly that Du Bois decided he must have more assistance to carry on the additional work. Mary Dunlop Maclean, a feature writer for the *New York Times*, who had been Du Bois's managing editor and had worked closely with him on *The Crisis* as a volunteer from its inception, had died in July, 1912.[46] To replace her, Du Bois engaged an editorial assistant. Since the 30,000-copy summer editions of the magazine were producing an income of about $1,300, he felt safe in persuading Augustus G. Dill, his successor at Atlanta University, to join the staff of *The Crisis* as its business manager. These additions to the staff entailed further expense, as they made "imperative" a remodeling of the *Crisis* office at NAACP expense.[47]

In less than a year, citing the growth of business and the fact that the magazine now had a staff of one part-time and seven full-time employees in addition to the editor, Du Bois blithely announced that *The Crisis* was compelled to seek larger quarters. He also reported the partial fulfillment of another dream—that

---

[44] "Annual Report of Director of Publicity and Research for 1912," Du Bois Papers. Even in 1916, white readership was estimated at only twenty per cent, which caused Spingarn to urge that a "concentrated effort" be made to increase the circulation among whites. Minutes, Annual Meeting, January 3, 1916, in Board Minutes, NAACP.

[45] "Crisis Balance Sheet, December 31, 1912," Du Bois Papers.

[46] She was "an unusually capable newspaper woman, brilliant and attractive." A. B. Spingarn to writer, September 5, 1958; *Crisis*, IV (August, 1912), 184–85; Board Minutes, NAACP, August 6, 1912.

[47] The February, 1913, issue of 24,000 copies sold out in three days. Thirty thousand copies were printed for March, and the net paid circulation was about 28,000 copies. "The normal circulation," Du Bois reported, "would seem to be above 25,000 . . . and the increase is continuous." Board Minutes, NAACP, March 11, 1913; April 1, 1913; September 2, 1913.

The Crisis would soon publish books and pamphlets about the Negro which ordinarily would have difficulty in finding a publisher.[48]

The book-publishing project ran into legal difficulties and was abandoned when Studin pointed out that the name *Crisis* belonged to the Association and could not be used in the private business contemplated by Du Bois. The nearly $1,000 which Du Bois had to borrow to start the publishing venture and the $500 debt he had incurred in moving *The Crisis* office were additional reasons for forcing him out of this project at a time when the Association was in great financial difficulties.[49]

As we have seen, during 1913 the Board was severely critical of the contents of *The Crisis,* and Du Bois had to defend his policy and program for the magazine by citing its growth in circulation and by pointing out that a magazine which was merely a house organ and a mouthpiece of the Association and which contained only official reports and accounts of NAACP work would not be read to any extent, nor would it pay its own expenses. His reply to criticism that *The Crisis* did not contain much about the NAACP was that "a propaganda magazine never does its work so completely and deftly as when it does so indirectly" and that readers would quickly tire of it if the NAACP's work jumped at them from every page. Accordingly, his objective had been to found a magazine that would "ring true on the problem of human rights to all men, be beautiful, be entertaining, and also incidentally give this Association the widest publicity of any similar organization in the world." Du Bois was convinced that without *The Crisis* as an organ of publicity, the National Association for the Advancement of Colored People could not have survived. The Association was not popular with white philanthropists; it was largely unknown to colored people; but because of *The Crisis* "100,000 of the most intelligent" Negroes in the country now knew about the NAACP and were "as soil being prepared for the seed of permanent organization."[50]

Securing advertising to help pay for *The Crisis* was a problem. White suppliers of goods and services had not yet discovered the market possibilities of ten

[48] "Annual Report," January 5, 1913 [1914], Du Bois Papers. The books published were Maude Cuney Hare, *Norris Wright Cuney* (New York, 1913); Ovington, *Hazel: The Story of a Little Colored Girl* (New York, 1913). Two pamphlets were published: *Gyp the Mixed Breed* (1912); Henry E. Baker, *The Colored Inventor* (1913). Two pamphlets were "taken over for sale after publication," Julia L. Henderson, *A Child's Story of Dunbar* (1914); *A Memento of the Emancipation Exposition of the State of New York* (1914). Another book, George W. Crawford, *Prince Hall and His Followers* (1914), was published. Minutes, Annual Meeting, January 3, 1916, in Board Minutes, NAACP.
[49] Du Bois to Villard, August 14, 1914, NAACP Files; Du Bois to Charles H. Studin, August 21, 1914; August 24, 1914, A. B. Spingarn Papers (now in the Manuscript Division, Library of Congress); Nerney to Du Bois, February 6, 1914, Du Bois Papers; Board Minutes, NAACP, February 3, 1914; June 2, 1914; September 1, 1914.
[50] "Annual Report," January 5, 1913 [1914], Du Bois Papers.

million Negro consumers, and few Negro enterprises were of national or even regional significance. Moreover, some of the advertising obtainable was of an objectionable nature, scarcely suitable to a magazine dedicated to the advancement of the race. But income from advertising rose slowly with the growing circulation. Kennaday and Villard, who had connections with the newspaper world, made efforts to secure advertising accounts. In 1918 the advertising income had reached nearly $6,000, and in 1919, the year of the magazine's greatest circulation, it had almost doubled.[51]

In 1915 Du Bois announced that *The Crisis* was sold in every state and territory, in Mexico, South America, Hawaii, the West Indies, Asia, Europe, Africa, and the South Seas. Analysis of the circulation revealed, however, that it was concentrated in the East, North Central, Middle Atlantic, and South Atlantic states. States with the largest circulation were Illinois, Pennsylvania, Ohio, and New York. Relatively few copies went to towns with a population under 5,000, indicating that it was largely read by upper-class urban Negroes and that it seldom reached the rural Negroes of the deep South. It was not until 1917, when Johnson made his organizing tour of the South, that a field agent, F. J. Calloway, was engaged on a commission basis to spearhead a four-month circulation drive in the region.[52]

In the meantime, Du Bois announced that as the result of five years of effort he had established a self-supporting magazine. When the circulation reached 37,000 in 1916, the large debt of *The Crisis* was liquidated. The Waco lynching supplement helped circulation to skyrocket in 1917. It doubled in 1918 and by June, 1919, reached its peak monthly circulation of 104,000 copies. This was the year of returning veterans, the "Red Summer" of violence, and *The Crisis* carried a message.[53]

Nevertheless, expenses mounted, and Du Bois warned that as a business proposition the magazine had too narrow a margin between income and expenses. In spite of a large number of agents selling *The Crisis* in the field, circulation dropped rapidly and in eight months was down to 72,000. Du Bois blamed the strike of paper handlers and printers which had delayed publication several months, so that the agents had to dispose of three issues at once, which ordinarily would have been sold separately. In addition, rising costs had necessitated an increase in the price of the magazine.[54]

[51] Board Minutes, NAACP, June 2, 1914; July 7, 1914; March 9, 1915; May 10, 1915; July 11, 1919; *Crisis*, XIX (February, 1920), 198–99.
[52] Minutes, Annual Meeting, February 12, 1915, in Board Minutes, NAACP; Minutes, NAACP, May 10, 1915; November 12, 1917; December 10, 1917; *Washington Bee*, March 9, 1918.
[53] Board Minutes, NAACP, December 13, 1915; November 3, 1916; Minutes, Annual Meeting, January 2, 1917, in Board Minutes, NAACP; *Crisis*, XIX (February, 1920), 198–99.
[54] Board Minutes, NAACP, July 11, 1919; September 8, 1919; November 10, 1919; December 8, 1919; February 9, 1920; July 12, 1920.

Not all NAACP members subscribed to *The Crisis*, and not all *Crisis* readers belonged to the NAACP, but *The Crisis* and the NAACP were both vehicles for expression of the same philosophy. Both intended to present reliable factual information to combat false racial attitudes, and both protested against injustices dealt to Negroes. The NAACP Board, while recognizing Du Bois's value in formulating and expressing its philosophy, refused to relinquish control of the magazine and maintained that one of its functions was the propagation of the organization. The reasons for the spectacular rise in membership of the Association and in circulation of *The Crisis* were closely allied to the violence and mistreatment of Negroes which reached a crescendo in 1919.

The sanction and extension of segregation within the government during the Wilson administration set the tone for the entire country and was a factor in the increasing discrimination and violence throughout these years.

CHAPTER VIII

The NAACP and the Wilson Administrations

The Presidential election of 1912 caused grave concern among Negroes and the leaders of the NAACP. Disappointed because of Taft's policy of refusing to appoint Negroes to federal offices in the South, W. E. B. Du Bois at first threw his support to Theodore Roosevelt and the Progressive Republican movement. Although the NAACP officially took no part in the election, four directors participated in the Progressive Convention. Du Bois drafted a plank calling for the repeal of unfair discriminatory laws and the right to vote on equal terms with other citizens. Joel E. Spingarn, Jane Addams, and Henry Moskowitz worked in vain for inclusion of the plank in the party platform.[1]

Roosevelt's strategy was to lure Southern Democrats into the ranks of the Progressives by organizing a lily-white party in the South. According to Roosevelt, the Progressive Party would secure the enfranchisement of the Negro by appealing to the sense of honor and justice in the best men of the South,[2] but when the convention met in Chicago, Negro delegates from the South were barred from taking their seats.[3]

As a result there was much mental anguish among Negroes and their friends. Jane Addams, accepting Roosevelt's argument of political expediency, stayed with the party and seconded his nomination. Charles Bentley and others of the Chicago group were dismayed, certain that the overwhelmingly anti-Roosevelt

---

[1] W. E. B. Du Bois, *Dusk of Dawn: An Essay toward an Autobiography of a Race Concept* (New York, 1940), pp. 232–33.
[2] Theodore Roosevelt, "The Progressives and the Colored Man," *Outlook*, CI (August 24, 1912), 909–12.
[3] Arthur S. Link (ed.), "Correspondence Relating to the Progressive Party's 'Lily White' Policy in 1912," *Journal of Southern History*, X (November, 1944), 480–90; "The Negro as a Factor in the Campaign of 1912," *Journal of Negro History*, XXXII (January, 1947), 96–97.

feeling of the Negroes would produce votes for the other candidates. Roosevelt's attitude toward the Negro was regarded by one leading white paper as more brutally frank than that of the other candidates, because he not only spoke as though the Negro were out of politics, but acted promptly and vigorously as if it were the fact.[4]

The Negro press, radical and conservative, was largely against Roosevelt and the Progressives because of their refusal to admit Negro delegates to the convention. They were agreed that this would favor the Republicans in the presidential election in those states in which a large Negro population was accustomed to vote. Du Bois claimed that a vote of 600,000 could determine the electoral vote of Illinois, Indiana, Ohio, and New York, and he asked his readers, "Now Mr. Black Voter . . . what are you going to do about it?"[5]

Du Bois turned to the Democratic Party as he had in 1908 when he, Bishop Alexander Walters and J. Max Barber had urged the election of Bryan. At that time he hoped the weight of the Negro vote would break the exasperating impasse in the Democratic Party caused by the "impossible alliance of radical socialistic Democracy at the North with an aristocratic caste party at the South." The Democratic Party, once freed from its enslavement to the reactionary South, could return to its pre-Civil War creed of the widest possible participation of American citizens in the government. After the 1912 Progressive Convention, Walters, who was president of the National Colored Democratic League, approached Du Bois, proposing that *The Crisis* support Wilson if they could secure from him assurances of fair dealing for Negroes.[6]

Wilson already had Villard's support. The two men had met in 1895, when Villard went to Philadelphia to attend a university extension course in which Wilson lectured on American history, and they had locked horns over the latter's discussion of the abolitionists. A closer relationship developed in 1910 when both men were passengers on a steamer to Bermuda, and Villard had promised *Evening Post* support for Wilson's candidacy for Governor of New Jersey. Wilson thought enough of Villard to consult him in his choice of a secretary after his election as governor. When Wilson announced his candidacy for President, Villard was convinced that Wilson had become a truly liberal leader, and once more gave him support. During the campaign, Villard met regularly with

[4] Charles E. Bentley to J. E. Spingarn, August 13, 1912, Joel Elias Spingarn Papers (Moorland Foundation, Howard University); *Boston Evening Transcript*, August 7, 1912, clipping in W. E. B. Du Bois Papers (now in the possession of Mrs. W. E. B. Du Bois, New York City).
[5] *Independent*, LXXIII (September 19, 1912), 688; *Crisis*, IV (September, 1912), 236.
[6] *New York Age*, April 2, 1908; Du Bois, "The Negro Vote, Talk Number Four," *Horizon*, IV (September, 1908), 4–5; Du Bois, *Dusk of Dawn*, p. 234.

William F. McCombs, Wilson's campaign manager, and William G. McAdoo, a lawyer and railroad executive, to plan the strategy of the campaign.[7]

In spite of Villard's enthusiasm for Wilson, his uncle, Francis Jackson Garrison, was filled with foreboding; Garrison feared that the door of the White House would be closed to all colored guests by Wilson and his "Georgian wife." He predicted that Wilson's democracy would not meet the test on such questions as the Negro, women's rights, and Philippine independence.[8]

Villard, on the other hand, was delighted with Wilson's attitude on the Negro problem. Wilson had told him at a conference in Trenton, New Jersey, that he intended to be "President of all the people" and that he would make appointments solely on the basis of merit. He made it clear that the only place where he and Villard might differ would be as to the point where the entering wedge should be driven; also, he would not appoint Negroes in the South because it would increase race antipathy. Villard reported that Wilson said he would have no power as President to help the colored people in the matter of lynching, but would speak out against it. He promised a statement on the Negro question which could be used in helping his candidacy.[9]

In the meantime, the president of the Washington NAACP branch, J. Milton Waldron, who was also leader of a Negro Democratic club, obtained an interview with Wilson. Waldron's memorandum on the interview stated that Wilson desired the support of Negroes. There was nothing to fear from a Democratic Congress, he assured Waldron, because he as President would veto hostile legislation, administer the laws impartially, and would not exclude Negroes from office on the basis of color.[10]

At the end of July a group of New Jersey Negro Democrats were received by Wilson at Sea Girt. His remarks to this group were substantially the same as those reported by Waldron. Villard called Wilson's statement a fine utterance, which pleased Du Bois and the *Crisis* friends tremendously. McAdoo absolutely approved of it. (Villard sarcastically added that McAdoo's only fear was that Wilson would go too far in the direction of friendliness to the colored people.)[11]

[7] Oswald Garrison Villard, *Fighting Years: Memoirs of a Liberal Editor* (New York, 1939), pp. 216–18, 220–22. For a discussion of the campaign of 1912, see Arthur S. Link, *Wilson: The Road to the White House* (Princeton, 1947), I.

[8] Francis Jackson Garrison to Villard, July 16, 1912, Oswald Garrison Villard Papers (Houghton Library, Harvard University).

[9] Villard to Garrison, August 14, 1912, Villard Papers.

[10] Villard to Woodrow Wilson, August 14, 1912, Villard Papers; *Crisis*, IV (September, 1912), 216–17.

[11] "Excerpt from Governor Wilson's address to the negroes; as reported by the delegates," n.d., enclosed in Villard to Garrison, August 9, 1912; Villard to Wilson, August 28, 1912, Villard Papers.

The day after the Sea Girt meeting, Villard forwarded Waldron's memorandum to Wilson, asking for an official statement similar to the remarks Wilson had made to Waldron. He wanted to see this published in *The Crisis* and the *New York Evening Post* and released to the Associated Press, for he knew this was the kind of assurance Negroes desired.[12]

Wilson expressed amazement at Waldron's memorandum. He wanted the colored people to be assured they had nothing to fear from a Democratic President and Congress, but he had not conferred with party leaders on this question, nor had he promised to veto hostile legislation. Neither had he given any assurances about patronage, except that Negroes need not fear discrimination. He denied saying he needed Negro support or that he had given promises for the sake of obtaining it. He asked Villard to aid him in formulating a statement in conformity with what he had written, for he wanted "these people to be reassured."[13]

Villard promptly forwarded the draft of a statement he and Du Bois had prepared, declaring that the Democratic Party made no distinction between citizens based on race or caste, that it sought the votes of all Americans, that the Party was opposed to legislation which discriminated against any class or race, that qualifications for voting should be the same for all citizens, and that if Wilson were elected the Negro would not be barred from holding office.

At the same time Villard expressed concern over the disagreement between Waldron and Wilson as to the nature of the assurances given to the Negro leaders. He warned that the Party could make no headway with the colored people without a quotable utterance from Wilson. Villard pointed out that Negroes were suspicious of Wilson personally. While he was president of Princeton, the University was closed to Negro students. Moreover, he was a Southerner, as were McAdoo and McCombs, and they feared that the policy of injustice and disfranchisement in Southern as well as in many Northern states would receive a great impetus by the presence of a Southerner in the White House. Negroes, wrote Villard, particularly wanted assurance they would not be entirely excluded from holding federal office, because the bulk of their race were absolutely deprived of any self-government on the local level, even in such matters as schools and the making of town ordinances.[14]

Wilson, however, was not prepared to go along with this more temperate statement. In fact, no authorized statement was ever given to Villard for

[12] Villard to Wilson, August 14, 1912, Villard Papers. For this and subsequent Villard and Moorfield Storey correspondence with Wilson, see also the Woodrow Wilson Papers (Manuscript Division, Library of Congress).
[13] Wilson to Villard, August 23, 1912, Villard Papers.
[14] Villard to Wilson, August 28, 1912, Villard Papers.

publication. Nevertheless, in September *The Crisis* published Waldron's memorandum, perhaps with the thought of forcing Wilson's hand.[15]

In the meantime, NAACP Board member Alexander Walters tried to persuade Wilson to address a mass meeting at Carnegie Hall. Wilson declined but wrote Bishop Walters that he earnestly wanted to see justice done to the Negroes of the country, "not mere grudging justice, but justice executed with liberality and cordial good feeling." He noted the progress made by the colored people and professed his long-standing sympathy. Should he become President, they could count on him for absolute fair dealing and for help in advancing the interests of their race in the United States.[16] The words "fair dealing" convinced Villard that Wilson had finally issued an excellent letter to the colored people, and with this assurance *The Crisis* espoused the cause of the Democratic candidate. In spite of all political risks and in the face of disconcertingly vague promises, Du Bois urged the election of Wilson to "prove once for all if the Democratic Party dares to be Democratic when it comes to black men."

Villard's uncle, Frances Garrison, was again pessimistic, pointing out that Wilson's letter, while smooth enough, had carefully avoided precise terms such as lynching, disfranchisement, and Jim Crow.[17]

THE NATIONAL RACE COMMISSION

Villard, having helped Wilson win the election, hoped for great accomplishments. Soon after the election, the Board of Directors of the NAACP authorized him to formulate a plan with Du Bois for a National Race Commission to study the race question in the United States. The idea for the Race Commission originated with a Southerner, R. H. Leavell, Associate Professor of Economics at the Agricultural and Mechanical College in Texas, who had formerly been at the Wharton School of the University of Pennsylvania. Villard took up Leavell's suggestion with great enthusiasm and won the support of Walter Hines Page, expatriate Southern progressive, hoping to organize the Race Commission along the lines of Roosevelt's Rural Life Commission, of which Page had been a member. Villard wanted to raise $50,000 for the project before approaching Wilson in order not to have to go to Congress for support. He was afraid that his radicalism would make it difficult to get money from Rockefeller and other philanthropists who usually contributed through the conservative General Education Board, but he hoped to interest Jacob Henry Schiff and

---

[15] Villard to Garrison, October 7, 1912, Villard Papers; *Crisis*, IV (September, 1912), 216–17.
[16] Wilson to Alexander Walters, October 16, 1912, copy in Du Bois Papers. See also Alexander Walters, *My Life and Work* (New York, 1917), pp. 194–95; and *New York Age*, October 24, 1912.
[17] Villard to Garrison, October 27, 1912; Garrison to Villard, October 31, 1912, Villard Papers; *Crisis*, V (November, 1912), 29; Du Bois, *Dusk of Dawn*, pp. 234–35.

Julius Rosenwald. He was cautious in sounding out people for membership on the Commission for fear of interference from members of the General Education Board or the Southern Education Board, who would inevitably use their influence either to kill the scheme or to take it into their own hands.[18]

Villard wanted a Southern white man for chairman, but people like James H. Dillard or Hollis B. Frissell of Hampton Institute were either under the control of the General Education Board, or were fearful of bringing harm to their "education work." He avoided naming a chairman but, after canvassing the NAACP Board, recommended five Southern whites, five Northerners, and five Negroes.[19]

Leavell's naive suggestion—to try to enlist the sympathy of demagogue James K. Vardaman of Mississippi through family connections—was rejected by Villard, who also turned down a suggestion for including a representative of organized labor. He preferred not to introduce another controversial issue. Neither Du Bois nor Booker T. Washington was included, because, said Villard, they could not work together, and to put either of them on the Commission would at once prejudice half the race. He hoped, however, that Du Bois would be employed as one of the Directors. He also expected President Wilson to make suggestions of his own. Rosenwald's appointment, he was sure, would solve the financial problem and would placate Booker T. Washington.[20]

Villard was anxious to secure immediately the services of Leavell as his lieutenant to aid in arousing interest in the plan. He anticipated that Leavell would make the investigations for the Commission after it was organized, but he was unable to raise funds for Leavell's salary. He was further handicapped when Walter Hines Page was appointed Ambassador to the Court of St. James, for he had counted on Page's intimacy with Wilson to put the project through. As to the possibility of Wilson's rejecting the project entirely, Villard wrote,

[18] Villard to R. H. Leavell, December 19, 1912; December 31, 1912, Villard Papers
[19] May Childs Nerney to Spingarn, January 4, 1912, J. E. Spingarn Papers (Howard).
[20] Villard to Leavell, December 31, 1912; May 8, 1913, Villard Papers. The proposed membership of the Commission as finally formulated by Villard and the NAACP was composed of five Negroes (R. R. Moton of Hampton Institute; Kelly Miller of Howard University; Archibald Grimke; John Mitchell, Jr,, editor of the *Richmond Planet*; and W. Ashbie Hawkins), five Southerners (Dillard; Mrs. Desha Breckinridge, whose husband was a newspaper editor of Lexington, Kentucky; Alfred H. Stone of Mississippi; Dr. J. G. Snedecor, secretary of the Colored Evangelization of the Presbyterian Church, South; and James H. Slayden, congressman from Texas), and five Northerners (Jane Addams, Albert E. Pillsbury, Joel Spingarn, Julius Rosenwald, and Villard). NAACP, *A Proposal for a National Race Commission to be Appointed by the President of the United States* [New York, 1913], leaflet, 5 pages.

Storey had advised Villard not to include Pillsbury because many people felt that "his manner and attitude" made it "impossible to work with him." Storey respected Pillsbury, but admitted that it was not always easy to get along with him. Storey to Villard, September 11, 1913, Villard Papers.

"I shall not be altogether downcast, but shall try to think up another scheme, or try to go ahead without presidential sanction." This attitude was not borne out by subsequent events.[21]

In May, 1913. the plan was formulated, printed, and personally presented by Villard to Woodrow Wilson at the White House. It called for the appointment of a National Race Commission by the President of the United States to engage in "a non-partisan, scientific study of the status of the Negro in the life of the nation, with particular reference to his economic situation." Areas proposed for study were physical health and efficiency, homes and property, work and wages, education, religious and moral influences, citizenship, legal status, and participation in government. The methods of work suggested included the publishing of a report indicating the progress of the Negro during his half-century of freedom, the obstacles to progress in the past and future, and practical suggestions as to the Negro's future welfare. Besides listing the possible personnel of the Commission, the proposal also named a number of organizations or groups that would support the plan: the Federal Commission on Industrial Relations; Southern agencies, such as the Southern Sociological Congress; Negro agencies, colleges, and fraternal bodies; independent organizations concerned with the welfare of the Negro, including the Urban League and the NAACP; and philanthropies such as the Jeanes, Slater, Southern Education, General Education, Hand, Peabody, and Phelps-Stokes funds.[22]

Villard was jubilant with his reception at the White House, the most satisfactory he had ever had with Wilson. He came away with the impression the President was convinced as to the necessity of such an inquiry, and ready to appoint the Commission, if it became clear that his relations with the Senate and Congress would allow it. The decision was to be deferred until Villard returned from Europe in July.[23] Before sailing, Villard instructed John Gavit, the *Evening Post* representative in Washington, "to keep steadily at" Wilson's secretary, Joseph P. Tumulty, in order to win him over to the idea of the Race Commission.[24]

By the middle of July, when Villard returned to America, the Negro community was in a furor over the official introduction of segregation by members of

[21] Villard to Leavell, April 11, 1913; May 8, 1913; Leavell to Villard, April 16, 1913, Villard Papers.
[22] Villard to Garrison, May 13, 1913, Villard Papers; NAACP, *A Proposal for a Race Commission.*
[23] Maude E. Lacey (Villard's secretary) to Garrison, May 15, 1913, Villard Papers. In a statement written many years later for the NAACP archives, Villard gives no indication that Wilson was at any time other than hostile to his proposal. He mistakenly gives the date of the presentation as May, 1912. Villard to Walter White, June 6, 1946, NAACP Files (Manuscript Division, Library of Congress).
[24] Villard to John P. Gavit, May 16, 1913, Villard Papers.

the Wilson Administration in several government departments in Washington—the Bureau of the Census, the Bureau of Printing and Engraving, and the Treasury and Post Office Departments. Villard immediately drafted an emphatic protest to the President. He disliked doing so for fear of interfering with the Race Commission project, but he felt that the segregation issue was more important than his project.[25]

From this point on, the question of the appointment of a Race Commission and the fight against segregation in government departments became closely linked. The NAACP, through Villard, continued to urge the appointment of the Commission, as well as the assignment of capable Negroes to certain offices to counter the very great dissatisfaction of the colored people at the treatment they were receiving at the hands of the Wilson Administration. It was alleged in at least one segment of the Negro press that segregation in government departments had been instigated by Mrs. Woodrow Wilson after a visit to several of the departments, where she was surprised and disgusted to find that colored clerks were working in the same room as white clerks. According to the press, she was even more upset when she discovered that colored clerks and white clerks ate their lunches in the same room.[26]

Appealing to Wilson's idealism, Villard tried to convince the President that the situation engendered by the policy of segregation in government departments was hurting the cause of good government and that John Purroy Mitchel's reform ticket would not receive a single colored man's vote in Harlem and New York, where Mitchel was regarded as the New York representative of the Wilson Administration. He pointed out that *The Crisis*, which had supported Wilson's campaign, was now being criticized for its silence in the face of these discriminatory practices by men it helped put in office. Moreover, Negroes who had worked and voted for Wilson in the belief that their status as American citizens was safe in his hands were deeply cast down. Villard feared the loss of what had been gained by splitting the Negro vote and teaching a part of the race to vote nationally without regard to its own immediate interests. He reminded Wilson that, as the first Southern-born President of the United States since the Civil War, he had a wonderful opportunity to win the confidence and interest of those people who had been thrilled with Wilson's "New Freedom" and the belief that his democracy was not limited by race or color.[27]

Villard wrote not only as a friend who had supported Wilson, in season and out, but also as chairman of an organization whose membership was greatly

[25] Villard to Garrison, July 17, 1913, Villard Papers.
[26] Villard to Wilson, August 18, 1913; August 27, 1913, Villard Papers; *New York Age*, September 11, 1913. Photographs of the original order of July 16, 1913, segregating toilets in the Treasury Department are in Villard Papers.
[27] Villard to Wilson, July 21, 1913; September 18, 1913, Villard Papers.

stirred up over what they considered to be the hostile attitude of the Administration. He tactfully suggested that the segregation policies might have been introduced on the initiative of subordinate officials.[28]

Wilson replied that the segregation had been initiated at the suggestion of several department heads and had been carried out with the approval of several influential Negroes, for the purpose of removing the friction—or rather the discontent and uneasiness—which had prevailed in many government departments.[29] It was not, according to Wilson, a movement *against* Negroes. He believed it to be in their interest and was dismayed that those who interested themselves most in the welfare of Negroes should misjudge this action. He believed that "by putting certain bureaus and sections of the service in the charge of negroes we are rendering them more safe in their possession of office and less likely to be discriminated against."[30]

Villard spent an hour at the Executive Offices with Tumulty in an attempt "to get him in line" because of the secretary's influence with the President. Villard warned of mass demonstrations, loss of the Negro vote, and an attack from the NAACP unless a prompt end was brought to segregation in government offices. He brought up the question of Negro appointees to federal office, urging that Wilson fight it out with Hoke Smith of Georgia and James K. Vardaman, who were opposing the nomination of Adam E. Patterson to succeed J. C. Napier as Register of the Treasury. Tumulty agreed with Villard and arranged a conference with Wilson the following week with the understanding that Villard would bring the draft of a letter for Wilson's signature, authorizing Villard to raise funds for the Race Commission.[31]

At the August, 1913, meeting of the NAACP Board, Villard outlined a course of future action, and the Board authorized him to send an official letter of protest

[28] Villard to Wilson, July 21, 1913, Villard Papers.
[29] The question of segregation had been discussed in a cabinet meeting on April 11, 1913. Albert S. Burleson, the Postmaster General, had conferred with "Bishop Walters and other prominent negroes," some of whom had approved of the plan. When Burleson suggested that "segregation was best for the negro and the Service," no cabinet member objected. Wilson claimed that he had "made no promises in particular to negroes, except to do them justice." According to one cabinet member present, Wilson did not want the Negro's "position" reduced, but wanted the segregation "matter adjusted in a way to make the least friction." Josephus Daniels' "Diary," April 11, 1913 (Josephus Daniels Papers, Manuscript Division, Library of Congress), quoted in Arthur S. Link, *Wilson: The New Freedom* (Princeton, 1956), II, 247. See also George C. Osborn, "The Problem of the Negro in Government, 1913," *The Historian: A Journal of History*, XXIII (May, 1961), 338.
[30] Wilson to Villard, July 23, 1913, Villard Papers.
[31] Villard to Garrison, July 31, 1913, Villard Papers. The following year at the NAACP conference in Baltimore, Villard publicly branded Smith, Vardaman, and Benjamin R. Tillman of South Carolina as "political demagogues risen to eminence on the backs of the negro," and condemned them as both "violent" and "the most reactionary of our public men . . . at Washington" and therefore "our chief enemies." *New York Times*, May 6, 1914.

to the President in the name of the Association if it were needed.[32] Also in August, Booker T. Washington expressed his approval to Villard of an *Evening Post* editorial on the segregation situation, assuring him that it conveyed the feeling of all Negroes in the United States. He was deeply disappointed in the new President. "I have never seen the colored people so discouraged and bitter as they are at the present time, he confided to Villard."[33]

The conference arranged with the President failed to materialize. Villard asked Tumulty bluntly if Wilson had changed his mind. When after five more days there was no reply, Villard wrote Tumulty that he assumed Wilson did not care to discuss the problem with him, especially as during this interval he had appointed a white man as Minister to Haiti. He indicated that on the following day an official protest on behalf of The National Association for the Advancement of Colored People would be released to the Associated Press for publication.[34]

This communication brought an immediate reply from Tumulty to the effect that it was impossible to arrange an interview because of the Mexican situation and the legislative program. He asked Villard to send him a memorandum which the President could consider late in the evenings, when his mind was comparatively free. This Villard took to be a clear-cut refusal, and he forwarded the NAACP protest to President Wilson, the Associated Press, and to members of the Association, requesting them to write to the President and to their senators and congressmen.[35]

On the day the NAACP letter appeared in the morning papers Villard once more renewed his suggestion that Wilson approve the plan for a Race Commission and authorize him to attempt to raise money for financing its investigations. Such approval in principle would not commit the President to the persons suggested for membership in the Commission or to any program beyond an impartial, nonpartisan investigation of the race situation by a joint commission of colored and white men and women.[36]

In the meantime, Wilson wrote Villard a charming and disarming letter of apology for his failure to arrange an interview. Calling him an understanding

[32] Board Minutes, NAACP, August 5, 1913, "Minute Book of the Board of Directors of the National Association for the Advancement of Colored People" (now in the Manuscript Division, Library of Congress; hereafter referred to as Board Minutes, NAACP).
[33] Washington to Villard, quoted in Villard to Joseph P. Tumulty, August 15, 1913, Villard Papers. The original was forwarded to Wilson with Booker T. Washington's permission. Villard to Washington, August 8, 1913; Villard to Garrison, August 19, 1913, Villard Papers. A slightly different version of the letter in Washington's handwriting is to be found in the Booker T. Washington Papers (Manuscript Division, Library of Congress).
[34] Villard to Garrison, August 8, 1913; Villard to Tumulty, August 13, 1913, Villard Papers.
[35] Tumulty to Villard, August 14, 1913; Villard to Garrison, August 15, 1913, Villard Papers; NAACP, *A Letter to President Woodrow Wilson on Federal Race Discrimination*, pamphlet (New York, August 15, 1913), in the Arthur B. Spingarn Papers (now in the Manuscript Division, Library of Congress).
[36] *New York Times*, August 18, 1913; Villard to Wilson, August 18, 1913, Villard Papers.

friend, who would instantly comprehend the situation, Wilson again pleaded absorption in the complications of the Mexican situation and currency matters. But a few days later a second letter dashed all hope for the appointment of the Commission. The delicacy and difficulty of the situation in Washington with regard to the Negro, wrote Wilson, was such that he was absolutely blocked by the sentiment of senators, not only those from the South, but also those from other parts of the country. This situation would be exacerbated by any systematic inquiry into conditions because of the feeling that there was some sort of indictment involved in the inquiry itself. He considered it would be a blunder to give his approval to the project.[37]

Villard found Wilson's decision difficult to understand, first, because of his campaign pledge to assist in advancing the interests of the race, and second, because the procedure for the Race Commission as outlined involved no appeal to the all-powerful senators for financial aid and left Wilson free to lay the report before Congress or not as he saw fit. He questioned Wilson's intimation that an indictment was implicit in such an inquiry. If that were true, wrote Villard, "should we who search for truth only hold off, particularly when, as you yourself told me, you felt that it was needed and the right thing to do?" He requested Wilson to discontinue segregation policies in Washington and asked if he would continue to refuse to appoint any Negro to public office. He was concerned lest Wilson be maneuvered into a position where Negroes and their supporters could say he had broken his promise.[38]

Wilson replied that he "honestly thought segregation to be in the interest of the colored people as exempting them from friction and criticism in the departments." He reiterated that a number of colored men with whom he had consulted had agreed with him in this respect. He was willing to admit that in several instances the matter had not been handled tactfully, but he had tried to set it right and in more than one instance had succeeded "very pleasantly." Concerning the Race Commission, Wilson said that he was thinking of the efficiency of the work and of the effects that the report would have. He did not want to set in its way prejudices which might shift the whole discussion from the findings of the Commission to the method in which it had been set up.[39]

SEGREGATION IN THE GOVERNMENT

Villard at once took note of the reference in Wilson's letter to "a number of colored men"[40] who had been consulted concerning the segregation in Wash-

---

[37] Wilson to Villard, August 19, 1913; August 21, 1913, Villard Papers; see also copy in A. B. Spingarn Papers; Villard to Garrison, August 27, 1913, Villard Papers.
[38] Villard to Wilson, August 27, 1913, Villard Papers.
[39] Wilson to Villard, August 29, 1913, Villard Papers.
[40] A recent analysis of the Wilson papers indicates that of the several hundred letters from Negroes on segregation, less than ten per cent favored the policy, while over ninety per cent

ington and wrote that he had had many demands for the names of these consultants. It was rumored that Bishop Walters[41] was one of the group, and Villard pointed out to Wilson that if the names of these people became generally known "they would be driven out of the communities in which they reside, or at least held up to the scorn of the race, as has been the man Patterson whom you nominated for Register of the Treasury."[42]

Wilson's reply was a plea for an understanding of the real situation and a realization that what the President was trying to do could be accomplished only through the cooperation of those associated with him in the government. He had faith in the slow pressure for argument and persuasion and was convinced that nothing could be accomplished if a bitter agitation was inaugurated and carried to its natural conclusion. He appealed to Villard for help in keeping things "at a just and cool equipoise" until he could determine whether a solution could be evolved.[43]

At the September, 1913, meeting of the Board of Directors of the NAACP it was reported that numerous editorials and comments had appeared in the press as the result of the Association's official letter to the President. Results of the appeal to the membership to register protest with the White House were described as magnificent, but Villard was afraid that the letters would never reach Wilson's desk.[44]

Charles Anderson complained to Booker T. Washington that the letter to Wilson was not wholly accurate concerning segregation. Still more serious was its failure to mention "the reflex influence of the Administration's attitude towards us." This Anderson considered to be more hurtful than all of the removals, demotions, and segregation put together, because it inspired enemies of the Negro all over the country to run amuck at any time without fear of punishment and notified the oppressor that oppression was safe and protected by the highest authorities in the land. The NAACP protest, according to Anderson, was

---

bitterly denounced it. Negro government employees showed the greatest opposition. Osborn, "The Problem of the Negro in Government, 1913," p. 344.

[41] It was this issue which brought about Walters' resignation from the NAACP Board when Villard publicly accused him of supporting Wilson's segregation policy. It seems clear that Villard must have heard from Tumulty, or someone close to the cabinet, that Burleson had named Walters, since no defense of Walters was offered by the Board. Board Minutes, NAACP, November 6, 1913; *New York Age*, November 6, 1913; *Washington Bee*, December 13, 1913.

[42] Villard to Wilson, September 18, 1913, Villard Papers. Adam E. Patterson was held up to scorn by Negroes because as soon as "'opposition to his confirmation developed in the Senate" he "withdrew his name," thus freeing Wilson of the necessity of clashing with Southern senators. William G. McAdoo to Villard, October 27, 1913, Villard Papers.

[43] Wilson to Villard, September 22, 1913, Villard Papers.

[44] Board Minutes, NAACP, September 2, 1913; Villard to Garrison, September 10, 1913, Villard Papers.

also unsatisfactory because of its failure to mention the number of men who once held presidential appointments and who had been removed from office.[45]

William Monroe Trotter was critical of the NAACP because Villard, Du Bois, Storey, and others had urged Negro voters to support Wilson in the presidential campaign. He challenged the NAACP letter to the President on the ground that segregation in government departments had not begun under Wilson. Nevertheless, he invited Storey to speak at a meeting of the National Independent Political League in order to present the NAACP point of view. Storey, unable to attend, sent a long letter of defense.[46]

By September, as a result of the adverse publicity, the Treasury Department had removed the offensive signs in the toilet rooms. Nevertheless, Hershaw, a clerk in the department, revealed to Garrison, that although the signs had been removed, the Negro clerks "who took this as a rescinding and returned to the regular toilets were sharply reprimanded and warned."[47]

Anderson was unsuccessful in his efforts to persuade the editor of the *Amsterdam News* not to print a story that gave credit for the removal of the signs to Villard, Du Bois, and their committee. The *New York Age* countered by reporting that the obnoxious signs had been removed as a result of interviews with McAdoo by Walters and Napier. In the meantime, Miss Nerney had conducted an investigation for the NAACP that received unexpected press coverage, and members of Congress requested copies. The *Age* jealously commented that they found nothing new in the investigation.[48]

Since Wilson had avoided the issue at every point and had refused him a conference, Villard asked Storey to join him in demanding a hearing from the President. Storey agreed but did not expect success, as he was convinced that Wilson was a man of Southern antecedents with the usual fashionable race

[45] Charles W. Anderson to Washington, August 19, 1913, Washington Papers. By September, 1913, the following had been removed from office by the Wilson Administration: W. H. Lewis, Assistant Attorney General in charge of Immigration Affairs; Ralph W. Tyler, Auditor for the Navy Department; James C. Napier, Register of the Treasury; Henry W. Furniss, Minister to Haiti; J. X. E. Bush, Receiver of Public Moneys, Little Rock, Arkansas; Nathan H. Alexander, Register of the Land Office, Montgomery, Alabama; Robert Smalls, Collector of Customs, Beaufort, South Carolina; Joseph E. Lee, Collector of Internal Revenue, Jacksonville, Florida; S. Laing Williams, Assistant U.S. District Attorney, Chicago, Illinois. Emmett J. Scott to Anderson, September 4, 1913, Washington Papers. In addition P. B. S. Pinchback had resigned, "undoubtedly requested to do so." Anderson to Washington, August 19, 1913, Washington Papers.
[46] Storey to William Monroe Trotter, September 16, 1913; Storey to Villard, September 25, 1913, Moorfield Storey Papers (in the possession of Mr. Charles Storey, Boston, Massachusetts).
[47] Villard to Storey, September 10, 1913; Garrison to Villard, September 11, 1913, Villard Papers.
[48] Board Minutes, NAACP, November 6, 1913; December 2, 1913; NAACP, *Segregation in Government Departments* (Mary Dunlop Maclean Memorial Fund Publication No. 1; n.p., November 1, 1913); *Washington Bee*, November 22, 1913; Anderson to Washington, September 26, 1913, Washington Papers; *New York Age*, August 28, 1913; December 11, 1913.

prejudices. Storey tried to influence the Assistant Secretary of the Treasury, whom he knew to be a sympathetic if not "very combative" person.[49]

In the meantime, Villard heard from John P. Gavit, who had seen Wilson. Gavit's analysis of Wilson's position is significant. Two utterly incompatible ideas, he thought, were the point of conflict. The first was that the Negro should be treated upon his individual merits, exactly as if he were white. The other view maintained that the Negro was of a different and inferior race and was to be treated with justice and all possible consideration, but was to be kept apart and compelled to make his progress on different, though parallel, lines. Wilson appeared to favor the second point of view; but in any case he had to deal with a Congress in which both houses were dominated by men to whom this view was fundamental. In addition, said Gavit, the Southerners had the tacit support of a large proportion of men from the North and West. If Wilson should oppose this viewpoint, he would bring the legislative program to a complete stop. Gavit was convinced that the Senate would not confirm the nomination of a Negro for any position in the federal service in which he would be in command of white people—especially white women.

Gavit thought the Republicans had merely pretended to believe in the first point of view to capture the Negro vote in some Northern states, and that the extent of segregation in government offices was much exaggerated. Nevertheless he knew beyond question that the spirit, the desire, and the intention to discriminate existed in varying degrees, even though no formal policy had been adopted. No Cabinet officer had issued any instructions as Villard and others had surmised; the initiative had come from subordinates, some of them newly appointed Southerners.

Gavit himself was not certain as to what action Wilson should take. He considered the problem the most difficult, the most delicate, and perhaps the most perilous confronting the President. As Washington representative of the *New York Evening Post*, he was simply presenting the facts and elements of the problem and leaving the expression of opinion to the editorial page.[50]

Gavit had convinced Wilson, however, that it had been a blunder not to meet and talk frankly with Villard, and on October 7, 1913, Villard was invited to lunch at the White House. Villard, completely disheartened by Gavit's report, nevertheless accepted the invitation.[51]

Three days later Villard reported the interview in detail to Garrison. Wilson told him that he "hoped . . . to accomplish something" for the colored people but

[49] Villard to Storey, September 10, 1913, Villard Papers; Storey to Villard, September 11, 1913, Storey Papers.
[50] John P. Gavit to Villard, October 1, 1913, Villard Papers.
[51] Wilson to Villard, October 3, 1913; Villard to Garrison, October 10, 1913, Villard Papers. See also Villard to William G. McAdoo, October 9, 1913, Villard Papers.

was frustrated by the attitude of Northern as well as Southern senators. He had to overcome "prejudice among Congressmen and Senators" concerning himself since he had the stigma of being "a schoolmaster, a taskmaster." He had done much to change their attitudes and believed that in time they would allow him to "guide them in this negro matter." Until this time arrived, he could not authorize the Race Commission.

When Villard proposed that the scope of the Commission be enlarged to study race conflict in Oregon and California, Wilson maintained that this might upset the "extremely delicate situation with Japan." He was "in a cruel position . . . at heart working for these people," but unable to make a public statement because that would "betray" his "plan and method to the Senators, and make impossible any accomplishments." He claimed that white men had been chosen as ministers to Haiti and Santo Domingo, because they were "peculiarly fitted" for "certain specific things which Bryan wanted accomplished," but that "within a year" they would be recalled, and Negroes would be appointed to the positions. On the other hand he emphasized again that he would "never appoint any colored man in the South, because that would be a social blunder of the worst kind." As to segregation in the government offices, he stated that "there was a social line of cleavage which, unfortunately corresponded with a racial line."

Villard stressed the significance of the precedents that Wilson and McAdoo were establishing, and their unawareness of the manner in which their subordinates were handling segregation within the departments. "Because you are a Southerner, and your Administration is largely Southern," he told Wilson, "your subordinates are going about it in a high-handed way." He read parts of Miss Nerney's report of her investigations, and Wilson asked for a copy declaring that he would "draw the teeth" and "put a stop to that sort of thing."

When Villard appealed again for a hearing. Wilson promised to give it his consideration but added, "I would rather do something than talk, but what to do I do not know." Villard proposed that Wilson "do what Grover Cleveland did and what Theodore Roosevelt did . . . continue to send nominations to the Senate and leave the responsibility of the rejection upon the Senate." Discouraged by the interview, he confided to his uncle that the only net result was that he had placed his personal relations with Wilson on such a basis that they would not be affected by his publicly taking the Administration to task, as he planned to do at NAACP mass meetings in Baltimore and Washington. He urged Garrison to make certain that the Boston branch send a telegram of protest that same night, and he would have the Baltimore group do the same. He believed that the Administration was feeling the pressure of these protests.[52]

---

[52] Villard to Garrison, October 10, 1913, Villard Papers. Villard's letter contains direct quotations of Wilson's statements. Secondary quotation marks have been omitted for the sake of clarity.

Tumulty had given Villard to understand that there would be no further extension of segregation, but NAACP leaders were not convinced. Storey urged that the Association should not abate its efforts and that the educational campaign of publicity was most effective.[53]

Villard wanted to apply pressure on the Administration by branch activities and mass meetings that would adopt protesting resolutions and forward them to the President. During October and November, in addition to meetings held in Baltimore, Washington, and Boston, mass meetings took place at Providence, Tacoma, Portland, Topeka, and Northern California, and members were urged to write to their congressmen and senators.[54]

Villard now shifted his attack to Secretary of the Treasury William G. McAdoo. McAdoo and Villard were well acquainted. In 1910 McAdoo had accepted Villard's invitation to act as a sponsor of the NAACP Sumner celebration. They had also worked together for Wilson's election to the presidency, and (according to Villard) McAdoo sought Villard's help in persuading Wilson to give him the Cabinet position.[55] When it was reported that the new Collector of Internal Revenue at Atlanta had said he would discharge all Negroes employed at that office, Villard asked McAdoo to act at once in the name of fair play and justice. He demanded a sharp rebuke and removal of the Collector for his outrageous utterance.[56]

When McAdoo denied that the Collector had made such statements to the press, Villard answered that he was concerned more with the Collector's opinions than with the specific interview in question. McAdoo assured him that faithful colored employees would not be deliberately turned out on charges preferred and tried by Internal Revenue Collectors. Nevertheless, Villard felt he must take action and informed McAdoo that he intended to speak critically of the Secretary and the President at the NAACP protest meetings.[57]

In his reply, McAdoo denied that there was a segregation issue in the Treasury Department but admitted that there had been an effort to remove causes of complaint and irritation in cases in which white women had been forced to sit at desks with colored men. He branded as untrue Villard's statement that Negro women in the Bureau of Printing and Engraving were forced to eat in the toilet rooms. "There is no truth in this statement," wrote McAdoo. "They eat at

[53] Storey to Villard, December 17, 1913, Storey Papers.
[54] Board Minutes, NAACP, November 6, 1913; December 2, 1913.
[55] *New York Sun*, December 27, 1910, clipping in letter, Anderson to Washington, December 29, 1910; Anderson to Washington, January 7, 1911, Washington Papers; "Programme— A Memorial Meeting to Charles Sumner, 1811, January 6, 1911," Du Bois Papers; Villard, *Fighting Years*, pp. 222–23.
[56] Villard to McAdoo, October 9, 1913; November 21, 1913, Villard Papers.
[57] Villard to McAdoo, October 20, 1913; October 25, 1913; McAdoo to Villard, October 22, 1913, Villard Papers.

separate tables in the same dining room with white people." McAdoo stoutly maintained that he was without prejudice and that his desire to help had been made clear by his appointments. But, he declared, "I shall not be a party to the enforced and unwelcome juxtaposition of white and negro employees when it is unnecessary and avoidable without injustice to anybody."[58]

Villard read McAdoo's letter at the NAACP meeting in Washington. Two thousand people packed the church, he claimed, and another three thousand were turned away. At the close of his speech he received a standing ovation which lasted several minutes, and he took satisfaction in writing McAdoo that the audience had laughed derisively at his letter. He accused McAdoo of being ignorant of what went on in his Department, saying that he, Villard, had been scrupulously truthful and that his information had been based on the report of an investigator, on Gavit's report, which had been carefully checked, and on reports from segregated persons themselves.[59]

A short time later Villard obtained one of the original segregation notices dealing with toilet facilities issued by order of the Secretary of the Treasury and sent it to him. He told McAdoo that certain church groups such as the Congregational Church Conference in Kansas City and the Unitarian Conference in Norfolk were voicing disapproval of his policy, and that McAdoo and the Postmaster General were antagonizing the country and injuring the President.[60]

Trouble again flared up over the Collector of Internal Revenue at Atlanta. This time Villard sent an official NAACP protest to McAdoo because the new Collector had discharged six colored men and was replacing them with white men from his own rural district, none of whom were eligible to fill the positions, all of which were in the classified list. There had been no complaints or criticisms filed against the discharged men during the thirteen-year period of the two previous Collectors. Villard charged that the Negroes were removed for political reasons and reminded McAdoo that the discharged men were supposedly under the protection of the Civil Service Commission. Moreover, he had been able to secure a sworn affidavit attesting to the authenticity of a statement by the Collector that he would discharge all Negroes in his office. If McAdoo did not promptly disavow this violation of law and gross act of racial injustice, the NAACP would present the matter to the President publicly or ask the Civil Service Reform Association to take action.[61]

Villard now called on Pennsylvania Congressman A. Mitchell Palmer, later Attorney General in the second Wilson Administration, appealing to him as a Quaker, as a Swarthmore graduate, and as a descendant of those who freed the

[58] McAdoo to Villard, October 27, 1913, Villard Papers.
[59] Villard to McAdoo, October 28, 1913, Villard Papers; Villard, *Fighting Years*, p. 240.
[60] Villard to McAdoo, November 3, 1913, Villard Papers.
[61] Villard to McAdoo, November 21, 1913, Villard Papers.

slaves, to use his influence to halt the anti-Negro policies of the government—but without success.[62] He also tried to focus public attention on the problem. In an article for *The North American Review* he took Wilson to task for a democracy limited "both by the sex line and the color line," and warned that to establish two classes of citizens and two kinds of Government employees would lead to "convulsing anew this land of liberty."[63]

Villard's threat of obtaining action by the Civil Service Reform League failed. He was told that the question of segregation in government agencies did not fall within the scope of the League. When he tried to persuade Charles W. Eliot, the League's president, that Negro clerks were being denied promotion because of their color, and that John Skelton Williams, whom he called the "anti-negro" Assistant Secretary of the Treasury, was responsible, Eliot replied that he believed in the social separateness of Negroes. He expounded his view that in a democracy "civilized white men" would not be comfortable living beside "barbarous black men." Negroes and whites must live in harmony, but without the social contacts which would promote intermarriages.[64]

The introduction of anti-intermarriage bills in Northern state legislatures and in Congress was part of the wave of attempted anti-Negro legislation, segregation, and discrimination which followed Wilson's election. It was at this time that the Association began efforts to engage a lobbyist (in the best sense of that term) to promote the interests of the race in Congress by watching for legislation inimical to the rights of the Negro.[65]

Early in 1913, anti-intermarriage bills were introduced in New York, Michigan, Kansas, and other Northern states. Villard used the arguments William Lloyd Garrison had used in seeking the repeal of the Massachusetts law against miscegenation. To block a similar measure proposed for New York, he wrote to State Senator Franklin D. Roosevelt, urging him to vote against the bill because it would be an infringement upon the right of human choice and would encourage "concubinage." Few intermarriages took place, even in those states which had no laws to prevent them, wrote Villard, and the passage of such legislation would subject Negro women to prostitution by making them helpless victims of white men.[66]

---

[62] Villard to A. Mitchell Palmer, November 20, 1913, Villard Papers.
[63] Villard, "The President and the Segregation at Washington," *North American Review*, VI (December, 1913), 800–07.
[64] Villard to Eliot, September 29, 1913; November 10, 1913; Eliot to Villard, November 11, 1913, Villard Papers; Board Minutes, NAACP, November 6, 1913.
[65] Minutes, Annual Meeting, January 21, 1913, in Board Minutes, NAACP; Board Minutes, NAACP, October 21, 1913.
[66] Villard to Garrison, January 29, 1913; Villard to Franklin D. Roosevelt, January 29, 1913, Villard Papers; Board Minutes, NAACP, February 4, 1913. For state laws forbidding miscegenation, see Pauli Murray (ed.), *States' Laws on Race and Color* (Cincinnati, 1950) and Jack Greenberg, *Race Relations and American Law* (New York, 1959).

The increase of Southern influences in the government caused some Booker T. Washington supporters to join NAACP groups. For example, Roscoe Conkling Bruce, fearful of losing his position as assistant superintendent of schools in Washington, D.C., became an active member of the District of Columbia branch.[67] Accused of disloyalty, Bruce felt it necessary to reaffirm his friendship with the Tuskegeean and his hostility to Du Bois. Nevertheless, he acknowledged the good work being done by the NAACP, declaring, "Who does not wish such a work success has lost his mind. I am Mr. Washington's friend and admirer; I am also a loyal supporter of the essential principles for which Mr. Villard stands."[68]

Washington claimed he had been able "to get into a little working touch with President Wilson," and had used his influence to bring about Judge Robert H. Terrell's appointment to the Municipal Court of the District of Columbia. This appointment led Villard to congratulate Wilson for flinging down the gauntlet to unreasonable senators, and to urge Wilson to keep Terrell's nomination before the Senate for the sake of the principle involved.[69]

All efforts were unsuccessful, however, when it came to reappointing Charles W. Anderson as Collector of Internal Revenue for the Second District of New York. Both Booker T. Washington and Villard did their best. Du Bois praised Anderson's work in *The Crisis*. (Anderson was chagrined to find that no other Negro publication had done so.) When Anderson was dismissed early in 1915, Villard and Du Bois asked Tumulty to intercede with the Commissioner of Internal Revenue to accept Anderson's application for another position, but this effort also failed.[70]

Discrimination culminating in dismissals continued in the Post Office Department, spreading from Washington to Philadelphia and the railroad mail service. In Washington, Villard and Archibald Grimke tried to get a delegation of twenty-five postal clerks (or, failing that, a group of the most influential Washington citizens) to demand an interview with Wilson. Both attempts failed, although

[67] Villard to Roscoe Conkling Bruce, October 29, 1913; Villard to Garrison, October 30, 1913. Bruce was the son of Blanche K. Bruce, United States Senator from Mississippi during Reconstruction. Roscoe Bruce was a graduate of Harvard and had been head of the academic department at Tuskegee. Through the efforts of Washington, he had gotten his job with the Washington schools, a political appointment. *Washington Bee*, January 28, 1905; June 21, 1919; "Success of Negroes at Harvard," *New York Tribune*, July 5, 1903.
[68] Bruce to Fred R. Moore, March 20, 1914, Washington Papers.
[69] Washington to Anderson, April 2, 1914, Washington Papers; Villard to Wilson, March 5, 1914, Villard Papers. For the fight over Terrell's confirmation, see *Congressional Record*, 63d Cong., 2d Sess., 7621, 12003–4.
[70] Anderson to Scott, March 28, 1914, Washington Papers; *Crisis*, VIII (May, 1914), 15; Villard to Tumulty, March 23, 1915; Tumulty to Villard, March 24, 1915; July 8, 1915; Villard Papers.

Grimke and the Washington branch succeeded in securing some reinstatements in cases in which Negro postal workers had been unfairly dismissed.[71]

On November 12, 1914, William Monroe Trotter, heading a delegation from the National Independent Political League, personally presented a petition to President Wilson, protesting discrimination against Negroes in the federal service. Wilson took offense at Trotter's language and attitude and curtly dismissed the group, alleging rudeness and lack of courtesy. Garrison considered the incident a setback to the cause. He blamed Wilson for his defiant stand for segregation but maintained the President was right in resenting Trotter's threat of voting against him and the Democrats. "Otherwise," said Garrison, "Trotter was sound and the President insulting and condescending."[72] The incident produced a number of editorials in New York newspapers such as the *World, Post, Globe,* and *Tribune,* protesting discrimination in the government departments as a grave injustice.[73]

R. R. Moton and other supporters of Booker T. Washington sought to use the incident for political gain, believing that they would now be able to make an impression on Wilson. With this in mind, Moton wrote the President that Negroes generally did not in any way approve of Trotter's conduct. He informed Wilson that Trotter had at one time been jailed in Boston for attempting to break up a meeting, which Booker T. Washington was holding in the interests of racial cooperation.[74]

Washington himself was careful not to become involved in the Trotter episode, but Villard took it up with Tumulty, who replied that the segregation issue was receiving the most earnest attention of the White House. Tumulty admitted that Trotter's speech to Wilson was one of the most eloquent he had ever heard, and that the President had confided to his secretary after the interview that he was sorry he had lost his temper, and that he had made a great mistake.[75]

By the end of December, Anderson was referring to Wilson as "our friend." He had informed Tumulty that the Tuskegee group was responsible for prevent-

[71] Villard to A. Mitchell Palmer, November 20, 1913; Villard to Garrison, November 5, 1913, Villard Papers; Board Minutes, NAACP, July 7, 1914; July 12, 1915.
[72] *New York Age,* November 13, 1914; *Crisis,* IX (January, 1915), 119–20; Garrison to Villard, November 13, 1914, Villard Papers.
[73] Cited in Anderson to Washington, November 14, 1914, Washington Papers. See also *Crisis,* IX (January, 1915), 129.
[74] Moton to Washington, November 23, 1914; Anderson to Washington, November 14, 1914; Washington to Anderson, November 18, 1914; Moton to Wilson, November 16, 1914, Washington Papers.
[75] Charles E. Mason to Washington, November 28, 1914, Washington Papers; Tumulty to Villard, November 18, 1914; Villard to Tumulty, November 23, 1914; Villard to Garrison, December 11, 1914, Villard Papers.

ing Trotter from holding a protest meeting in New York, and wanted Wilson to know that they were able to serve in this connection.[76] Washington praised Wilson for his speech to the Southern University Commission on Race Problems, in which he had said his object was "to know the needs of the Negro and sympathetically help him in every way that is possible for his good and our good." Wilson said that "as a Southern man" he knew "how sincerely the heart of the South desires the good of the Negro and the advancement of his race on all sound and sensible lines." Washington, as quoted in *The Crisis*, thought that the President's words indicated a growing liberal sentiment on the part of an increasingly large group of Southern white people.[77]

Du Bois, on the other hand, wrote in the same issue of *The Crisis* that he could not see how any clear-minded American could now doubt the insincerity of President Wilson regarding the American Negro. "Fed on quiet assurances of good will," Du Bois had at first thought it "impossible that so high-minded and scholarly a man could repudiate the . . . plain straightforward words . . . that he would treat the Negro with absolute fairness." Du Bois was completely disillusioned when the President, "not daring or not caring to utter clear, strong words for or against ten million people, contents himself with shifty and unmeaning platitudes." His words had become the "most grievous disappointments that a disappointed people must bear."[78]

Villard had already written in *The Nation* that the growing race friction was almost wholly overlooked by governmental agencies. The nation's statesmen were indifferent to the problem. The President, in his readiness to tackle every other problem and to offer constructive solutions, was content to pass this problem by, and the two leading political parties were willing to shirk the issue. The government had set up a new agency whose exclusive concern was with the children of the nation; even the forests had been given their special federal guardian, but no agency was charged with the scientific study of the race problem, which Villard called the least solved and the least understood of all social problems.[79]

When Congress adjourned on March 4, 1915, without having passed a single anti-Negro bill, the officers of the NAACP felt a great sense of relief. Du Bois wrote that the Congress, which would long be remembered for its Negro-baiting, had never so engrossed the attention of the NAACP as it had during the first two months of 1915. During this period six Jim Crow streetcar bills had been introduced in the House for the District of Columbia. In addition the House

---

[76] Anderson to Washington, December 29, 1914; Washington to Anderson, January 2, 1915, Washington Papers.
[77] *Crisis*, IX (February, 1915), 172.
[78] *Crisis*, IX (February, 1915), 181.
[79] Villard, "The Race Problem: Its Dangers and Opportunities," *Nation*, XCIX (December 24, 1914), 738–40.

had passed an anti-intermarriage bill for the District without reference to, or consideration by, the appropriate committee. Though Villard was assured by the legislative agent now employed by the NAACP that the bill would not pass the Senate, he nevertheless considered this an ominous portent and a forerunner of attempts to pass such legislation for the entire country.[80]

Another cause for concern had been the attempt by anti-Negro forces to get Congress to exclude Negro aliens from the United States, regardless of their ability to meet the literacy test. Such a provision was introduced into the Senate as an amendment to the Immigration Bill and was passed by a vote of twenty-nine to twenty-five.[81]

NAACP headquarters and the branches, particularly the Washington branch under the leadership of Archibald Grimke, sought to bring all possible pressure to bear to prevent the House from adopting a similar amendment by sending letters, petitions, and telegrams, and by appearing at hearings. A seven-point brief was drawn up and placed on the desks of all members of Congress, and NAACP members made a door-to-door canvass of the House Office Building to secure support against the amendment. Defeat of the amendment, 252 to 75, was hailed as a great victory for the NAACP.[82]

The Association was not alone in fighting the amendment. Booker T. Washington was actively at work and his efforts contributed substantially to its defeat. Both the *New York Age* and the *Washington Bee* took the NAACP to task for claiming credit for the maneuver.[83]

There is no doubt, however, that the two experienced newspapermen engaged by the Association to report all bills hostile to Negroes were of great value. Spingarn reported to the annual meeting in 1916, that the burden of vigilance had been particularly onerous during the two years when the South was in the saddle. Because of the reduced Democratic majority in the new Congress and its preoccupation with military preparedness, he anticipated that the next two years would be less difficult, but since there was always the danger of a bill slipping through unobserved, the Association planned to continue to employ a legislative agent.[84]

[80] Board Minutes, NAACP, March 9, 1915; *Crisis*, IX (March, 1915), 246; *New York Age*, February 20, 1915; Villard to Garrison, January 15, 1915, Villard Papers.
[81] *Crisis*, IX (February, 1915), 190. A similar policy of excluding Negroes had been in effect in Canada, the one-time terminus of the underground railroad, and the NAACP had protested to Lord Bryce, British Ambassador to the United States. Minutes, Executive Committee, March 7, 1911, in Board Minutes, NAACP.
[82] *Crisis*, IX (March, 1915), 246; Archibald Grimke to Spingarn, January 8, 1915, J. E. Spingarn Papers (Howard).
[83] *New York Age*, February 4, 1915; *Washington Bee*, January 23, 1915. See Immigration Bill file and Moton file in regular correspondence for 1915, Washington Papers.
[84] Minutes, Annual Meeting, January 3, 1916, in Board Minutes, NAACP.

To ascertain the attitude of the new Congress, the Association sent question-naires to all candidates of the Democratic, Republican, and Progressive Parties, asking for their views on abrogation of the Fourteenth and Fifteenth Amendments, and on lynching, segregation, reduction of Southern representa-tion, and anti-intermarriage laws.[85]

One writer describing the American scene in 1915 considered it undeniable that the Negro was less popular in the North than thirty years earlier, when segregation of Negro clerks by the government would have caused a tornado of protest. "Now," he wrote, "it passes almost unnoticed."[86] Moorfield Storey thought the country ripe for agitation. He stressed again and again the need for a new anti-slavery crusade to overcome the crass indifference which permitted "a growing tendency to legislate against . . . colored citizens, in regard to their dwelling places, the lands which they may own, their transportation in public conveyances, their employment in public offices, their right to vote at public elections, their opportunities for education, and now their domestic relations." In an effort to arouse the public conscience, he wrote an open letter—To the People of the United States—appealing for justice.[87]

Even though Villard had quarreled with Wilson over the Negro question, he heard from Tumulty that Wilson had requested his suggestions for a successor to William Jennings Bryan, who resigned as Secretary of State in 1915. Villard's "first choice" was Moorfield Storey. One wonders whether the fact that Storey was president of the NAACP had any bearing on Wilson's selection of Robert Lansing, Villard's second choice.[88] Villard followed up this contact by pointing out to Tumulty that, if Wilson would accept an invitation to address the annual meeting of the NAACP at Carnegie Hall on Lincoln's birthday, he would have an unsurpassed opportunity to speak on the Negro question. Villard called his attention to the fact that in Indiana, Ohio, and Illinois the Negro held the balance of power.[89]

Wilson, replying personally, said that Villard was very much mistaken in assuming that he was not interested in the Negro and the Negro vote, though he conceded that he and Villard did not agree as to the best way in which to promote the welfare of the colored people. He declined the invitation on the grounds that his duties required his presence in Washington and that, for the present, he must limit his speaking to pressing national questions chiefly of a nonpartisan sort.[90]

[85] Nerney to Moore, September 26, 1914, Washington Papers; *Washington Bee*, October 3, 1914; Board Minutes, NAACP, October 6, 1914; November 4, 1914.
[86] Paul L. Haworth, *American In Ferment* (Indianapolis, 1915), p. 136.
[87] Storey to Nerney, February 11, 1915; Storey to Villard, March 30, 1915; Storey to Du Bois, March 30, 1915, Storey Papers; *Crisis*, X (June, 1915), 78–80.
[88] Villard, *Fighting Years*, pp. 277–78.
[89] Villard to Tumulty, October 26, 1915, fragment of a copy, Villard Papers.
[90] Wilson to Villard, October 28, 1915, Villard Papers.

THE SECOND WILSON ADMINISTRATION

The 1916 election led to increased activity on the part of some NAACP Board members. Moorfield Storey urged that the segregation issue be given a political turn by letting politicians know that friends of the NAACP would not vote for any office-seeker who would not promise in advance to oppose segregation. He was convinced that the election would be close, and desired to see the vote made effective. In a magazine article, he reproached Wilson for his stand on segregation in the federal service, but concluded by supporting Wilson's reelection.[91]

On behalf of the NAACP, both Villard and Du Bois attempted to bring pressure on the Wilson administration by writing to Henry Morgenthau, who was high in party councils.[92] Du Bois pointed out that intelligent Negroes considered the habit of voting Republican unwise and dangerous. The 1912 election had provided an opportunity to break the pattern of Negro voting, because Taft was not popular with Negro voters and the Progressive Party had repudiated them. Wilson had pledged fairness but had persistently and thoroughly violated his pledge by his wholesale dismissal of Negro officeholders and by sponsoring their humiliation and segregation in ways both legal and illegal. In addition the President persistently refused to address colored people. In what Du Bois termed matters of larger policy affecting the Negro, Wilson had failed to speak out against lynching. He had refused to appoint a Commission to study the Negro problem. He had refused to appoint Negro Americans to deal with the problem of Haiti, but instead had placed that country in the hands of the navy, the "seat of Southern influence and of anti-Negro hatred." Wilson's actions and those of his subordinates had left those Negroes who supported him— at the risk of considerable unpopularity—without a leg to stand on.[93]

Villard, in a letter to Henry Morgenthau, called Wilson the most selfish public man he had met in his twenty years as a journalist, and the most arrogant and the least willing to take advice. He enumerated what he considered to be Wilson's failures in handling foreign and domestic matters and his failure to keep his campaign pledge to the Negro.[94]

---

[91] Storey to Villard, March 30, 1915, Storey Papers; Storey to Villard, February 4, 1916, Villard Papers; Storey, "President Wilson's Administration," *Yale Review*, V (April, 1916), 449–73.
[92] Another member of the Morgenthau family, Mrs. Max Morgenthau, Jr., had been on the NAACP Board of Directors since 1913. Minutes, Annual Meeting, January 21, 1913, in Board Minutes, NAACP.
[93] Du Bois to Henry Morgenthau, April 10, 1916, copy in Villard Papers.
[94] Villard to Henry Morgenthau, April 10, 1916, Villard Papers. Villard was particularly stung by Gavit's report that Wilson had said he "despised the *Evening Post*."

The next move of the Association was an attempt to influence politicians to insert a strong plank on the Negro in the Democratic and Republican platforms. A special Board meeting was called for the drafting of a model plank to be submitted to the major parties at their conventions in 1916,[95] pledging the parties: to establish equal congressional representation through apportioning seats in Congress in accordance with the voting population; to end lynching through federal legislation; to end segregation, especially in interstate commerce and in the District of Columbia; to suppress peonage; to secure equal facilities in public office and public service, including the armed forces; and, finally, to repeal all statutory recognition of race for residents of this country.[96]

At once Board members began to seek sponsors for the platform among the prominent and influential members of the two major parties. Theodore Roosevelt gave his endorsement and John Milholland secured the promise of Nicholas Murray Butler, president of Columbia University, to present the plank to the resolutions committee of the Republican Convention. Alexander McKelway of the National Child Labor Committee and sociologist Samuel McCune Lindsay worked to reach the platform-makers. Lillian Wald contacted the wealthy Chicago manufacturer and Wilson supporter, Charles R. Crane. Colonel Edward M. House, confidant of the President, was reached by a friend of the Association, Sidney E. Mezes, president of the College of the City of New York, and former president of the University of Texas.[97]

At Storey's suggestion, the Board wrote a letter to Charles Evans Hughes, Republican candidate for President, asking for his position on the Negro problem. It emphasized that Wilson's failure to live up to his promises had left Negroes with an indifferent choice, since nothing could be found in Hughes's writings or speeches as to his policy on the Negro.[98] The letter received no answer from Hughes beyond a formal acknowledgement, nor was there any response to a telegram requesting an answer in time for the November issue of *The Crisis*. In spite of this rebuff, Du Bois, disillusioned with Wilson and the Democratic Party, came out in favor of Hughes.[99]

[95] Mary White Ovington, Charles H. Studin, and A. B. Spingarn to Board of Directors, May 29, 1916, in Board Minutes, NAACP.
[96] Board Minutes, NAACP, June 1, 1916. On the committee which drafted the platform were Du Bois, William English Walling, and A. B. Spingarn.
[97] Royal Freeman Nash to Spingarn, June 2, 1916, J. E. Spingarn Papers (Howard); Carlton L. Brownson, "Sidney Edward Mezes," Dumas Malone (ed.), *Dictionary of American Biography* (New York, 1933), XII, 588–89. Mezes and House were brothers-in-law.
[98] Storey to Nash, August 4, 1916, Storey Papers; Board Minutes, NAACP, September 11, 1916; NAACP to Charles Evans Hughes, copy, n.d., Villard Papers; *Crisis*, XIII (November, 1916), 16–17. It was signed by J. E. Spingarn, Villard, Du Bois, and Archibald Grimke.
[99] Board Minutes, NAACP, October 9, 1916; *Washington Bee*, November 4, 1916.

Another device to bring political pressure on the Republican and Democratic Parties was the suggestion of Inez Milholland that the NAACP provide leadership in organizing a Negro Party along the same lines as the Woman's Party. She advocated that the Negro Party enter the 1916 campaign.[100] This strategy was approved by the Board and warmly championed by Du Bois in *The Crisis*. He held that the Democratic Party could only be effective with the help of its Southern wing and therefore could never, as a party, effectively bid for the Negro vote. The Republican Party, as the party of wealth and big business, was the natural enemy of the working people to whom the mass of Negroes belonged. Therefore, there was little choice between parties. Du Bois pointed out, however, that the parties were represented by individual candidates and that colored people could have a voice in selecting these candidates. As he saw it, the only effective method would be to organize in every congressional district as a Negro Party, and to endorse the candidates of whatever party seemed most likely to aid the cause of the Negro in that district. If no candidate measured up, Negroes should then nominate a candidate of their own and give that candidate their solid vote. If this policy could be effectively and consistently carried out by Negro voters, unaffected by the bribe of petty office and money, the Negro vote would be one of the most powerful and effective in the country. Even though this was a move toward separateness and segregation, Du Bois saw no other way out: "The American Negro must either vote as a unit or continue to be politically emasculated."[101]

Shortly before the election the *New York Evening Post*, after a period of wavering, came out in favor of Wilson's reelection. As a result, Villard was attacked by numerous Negro newspapers, which demanded his resignation as an officer of the NAACP. The *New York Age*, however, in the post-Amenia era of cooperation, sprang to his defense. Noting that the *Evening Post* was not a one-man affair and that the *Age* had not always agreed with Villard and had never been an ardent supporter of the NAACP, it nevertheless considered Villard a sincere and honest friend of the Negro, and the *Evening Post* a champion of the Negro cause.[102]

Legislation hostile to Negro Americans continued to be introduced into Congress in 1916: five anti-intermarriage bills, three Jim Crow streetcar bills for the District of Columbia, and a bill to make it unlawful to appoint Negroes as commissioned or noncommissioned officers in the army or navy. Other measures that indirectly affected Negroes were the bill to exclude Negro immigrants and an attempt to disfranchise Puerto Ricans through the Civil Government

[100] Nash to J. E. Spingarn, July 22, 1916, J. E. Spingarn Papers (Howard).
[101] Minutes, Annual Meeting, January 2, 1917, in Board Minutes, NAACP; *Crisis*, XII (October, 1916), 268–69.
[102] *New York Age*, December 14, 1916.

Act. This new wave of anti-Negro bills was climaxed by the introduction of a resolution in Congress by Senator Vardaman of Mississippi, calling upon the Attorney General to have the United States Supreme Court pass upon the validity of the Fourteenth and Fifteenth Amendments. None of these measures was passed by Congress in 1916, perhaps because the fact that it was a presidential election year made members of Congress cautious. Meanwhile the NAACP legislative agent continued to alert the National office and the Washington branch to hostile legislation. The Washington branch was successful in securing hearings on the anti-intermarriage and Jim Crow streetcar bills and in having the testimony printed. Southern members of the committee indignantly refused to attend the hearings.[103]

By 1918, discrimination in the federal bureaus in Washington was a settled policy, further perfected by requiring applicants for civil service positions to file photographs, a procedure first reported to the Association in 1914. Inquiries as to the reasons for the order at first brought only evasive answers, but finally the president of the Civil Service Commission gave assurances that the Commission was prepared to take measures to prevent the order from being used to discriminate against colored citizens. Nevertheless, cases came to the attention of the NAACP of Negroes who, having passed civil service examinations, were directed by telephone to report for duty, only to be informed upon reporting that an error had been made and that there were no vacancies. The Association was convinced that the "errors" in these cases had been made by clerks who had failed to learn that the persons so urgently needed to "win the war" were colored, and therefore not so urgently needed as had been supposed when it was believed they were white.[104]

Segregation in government was extended to the Senate lunchroom in the United States Capitol building and to the galleries of the United States Senate. The NAACP registered an emphatic protest and asked the branches to write to their representatives in both houses of Congress. When the Association learned that the restaurant in the District of Columbia court building was discriminating against Negroes, protests were sent to Supreme Court Justice Walter I. McCoy, who ordered that the discrimination should cease. The Association also protested to the chairmen of the Senate and the House Committees on the Library against the introduction of segregation in the restaurant and lunchroom of the Library of Congress. The NAACP was informed that the policy had been put

---

[103] Minutes, Annual Meeting, January 2, 1917, in Board Minutes, NAACP; Board Minutes, NAACP, January 8, 1917.
[104] Board Minutes, NAACP, June 2, 1914; July 7, 1914; August 4, 1914; NAACP, *Ninth Annual Report 1918* (New York, 1919), p. 44.

into effect by a new superintendent, an appointee of President Wilson. The Association wrote to Wilson, but he did not reply.[105]

The *New York Tribune* published the Association's letter to Wilson but twisted the facts to substantiate its contention that the NAACP was seeking to secure the right of Negroes to eat with whites.[106] James Weldon Johnson replied in the *Age* that this was the perverting of a legitimate protest.[107]

Many Negroes of education and culture were depressed and discouraged by their worsening status under the Wilson Administration. Dr. C. B. Purvis of Brookline, Massachusetts, a trustee of Howard University, wrote to Judge Terrell revealing his disillusionment. "In the American heart there is no love for the black brother. Segregation is not repugnant to him—it really suits his taste, his prejudices. . . . As I read *The Crisis* my heart sickens. I grow more and more skeptical as to the healing power of love and justice."[108]

The advent of the first Southern administration since the Civil War, in spite of the lofty idealism and fine promises of its leader, marked the opening of a new and bitter phase in the struggle against discrimination. The pattern of segregation sanctioned and extended within the federal government by the Wilson Administration was to set a precedent for the nation.

[105] Board Minutes, NAACP, July 9, 1917; December 8, 1919; *Washington Bee*, November 3, 1917; December 6, 1919; December 20, 1919.
[106] As reported in *New York Age*, December 6, 1919.
[107] *New York Age*, December 6, 1919.
[108] Dr. C. B. Purvis to Robert H. Terrell, September 30, 1916, Terrell Family Papers (Manuscript Division, Library of Congress).

CHAPTER IX

Segregation, Discrimination, and Jim Crow

In 1909, patterns of segregation were widely accepted by Negroes and whites, in the North as well as in the South. The principle of "separate but equal" had been established by the Supreme Court of the United States in 1896. Legal sanction was thus given to segregation, though little was done to implement the concept of equality of accommodations.[1] The aim of the NAACP was to protest and fight against all types of segregation and discrimination. Even before the founding group had given itself a name or broadcast the "Call" it had visited the commissioner of police in New York City to urge the end of discrimination in the appointment of policemen, citing other cities where colored policemen were doing satisfactory work.[2]

RESIDENTIAL SEGREGATION

On December 10, 1910, Baltimore, Maryland, enacted the first city ordinance in the United States providing for the segregation of Negroes in residential areas. The Negro population of cities had swelled by the movement of Negroes, first from country to town in the South following Reconstruction, then from the South northward to the Border states and to Northern urban centers. The white popula-

[1] E. Franklin Frazier, *The Negro in the United States* (rev. ed.; New York, 1957), pp. 161–62; Rayford W. Logan, *The Negro in American Life and Thought* (New York, 1954), pp. 159, 233; *Plessy v. Ferguson*, 163 U.S. 537 (1896). Harry E. Groves, "Separate But Equal—The Doctrine of *Plessy v. Ferguson*," in *Phylon*, XII (First Quarter, 1951), 66–72, discusses the effects of this case. For an account of the origin of segregation legislation in the South and the factors involved, see C. Vann Woodward, *The Strange Career of Jim Crow* (rev. ed.; New York, 1957).
[2] Oswald Garrison Villard to General Theodore A. Bingham, February 2, 1909, Oswald Garrison Villard Papers (Houghton Library, Harvard University).

tion reacted with hostility to the great migrations between 1910 and 1920. Segregation by city ordinance merely legalized the established practice of keeping Negroes within residential boundaries.

When the Baltimore ordinance was passed in 1910, it was fought by the Baltimore NAACP branch. Through the efforts of attorney W. Ashbie Hawkins, the Supreme Court of Maryland declared the ordinance unconstitutional. A second ordinance, enacted April 7, 1911, and reenacted May 15 of the same year, was declared unconstitutional in June, 1913. A third ordinance was then introduced which came under review of the Court of Appeals, where final decision was deferred pending the decision of the Supreme Court of the United States in the case of *Buchanan* v. *Warley* known as the Louisville, Kentucky, Segregation Case.[3]

Other cities in Border and Southern states were quick to follow the example set by Baltimore. In North Carolina, Mooresville and Winston-Salem enacted ordinances requiring residential segregation in 1912, and Asheville the following year, but these were held invalid by the state courts. In 1913, segregation ordinances were adopted by three Virginia cities—Richmond, Norfolk, and Roanoke—while similar laws were passed in Atlanta, Georgia, and Madisonville, Kentucky. The Louisville, Kentucky, ordinance became effective in May, 1914. Birmingham, Alabama, passed a residential segregation ordinance later the same year. By 1916, St. Louis, Missouri, Dallas and other Texas cities, and cities in Oklahoma had followed suit. Officials of St. Louis and some other cities, according to Miss Nerney, had written to Baltimore for copies of the "improved segregation ordinance."[4]

The organization of the Baltimore NAACP branch was hastened by the passage of the segregation ordinances,[5] and in the autumn of 1913, after the third ordinance was passed, the tension erupted in violence and rioting. Four white men were wounded when a Negro, defending his home, fired into a mob. Villard reported that residents in areas where there had been rioting were armed with stones, bricks, and firearms.[6]

[3] W. Ashbie Hawkins, "A Year of Segregation in Baltimore," *Crisis*, III (November, 1911), 27–30; Villard to Garrison, December 23, 1913, Villard Papers; *Crisis*, XV (December, 1917), 69–73.
[4] Board Minutes, NAACP, June 4, 1912; August 4, 1914; April 10, 1916; June 9, 1916, in "Minute Book of the Board of Directors of the National Association for the Advancement of Colored People" (now in the Manuscript Division, Library of Congress; hereafter referred to as Board Minutes, NAACP); *New York Age*, November 8, 1917; May Childs Nerney to Joel E. Spingarn, "Notes on Branches for Dr. Spingarn" [January, 1914], NAACP Files (Manuscript Division, Library of Congress); *Crisis*, IX (February, 1915), 188; Minutes, Annual Meeting, January 2, 1917, in Board Minutes, NAACP.
[5] Francis Jackson Garrison to Villard, February 6, 1911, Villard Papers; *Crisis*, IX (March, 1915), 249.
[6] Villard to Garrison, October 23, 1913, Villard Papers. There was violence in other cities. For example, the Association received a request for legal help from Negro home owners

The Baltimore branch with the cooperation of the national office decided to bring a test case under the new ordinance, and a mass meeting was called for October 20, 1913, when the tension was at its height. Villard delivered his "segregation speech," which urged peaceful rebellion and revolution against discrimination, and constant agitation that would keep the country in turmoil until the grievances of nine million united people were adjusted.[7] But Villard was distressed by the militant tone of the meeting and took umbrage at Joel Spingarn for countering his advice that the colored people use only peaceful methods. When Spingarn protested that peaceful methods were contrary to those of William Lloyd Garrison, Villard interrupted and set him right, but the crowd was with Spingarn.[8]

Villard was pleased with the publicity the Chicago and Boston papers gave his speech, although he observed that there was only a very brief notice in the Baltimore press. The segregation issue aroused new interest in the NAACP throughout the country, especially among Negroes, and Villard predicted, correctly, that the issue would bring the Association money as well as friends.[9]

It was not the Baltimore segregation ordinance, however, that the Association fought through to the Supreme Court of the United States, but that of Louisville, Kentucky. The NAACP was convinced that the Louisville ordinance furnished the best opportunity to test the whole movement of residential segregation in the cities.[10]

Considerable work was required in organizing and strengthening a Louisville branch before this step could be taken. Preliminary legal studies were conducted

---

in Kansas City whose homes had been dynamited. The Association took up the case and found that there was no segregation ordinance, and whites had moved into a neighborhood formerly occupied largely by Negroes. The whites began to exert various types of pressure upon the Negroes to make them move. The Association's approach to the governor of the state brought about a police investigation of the situation. *Crisis*, III (February, 1912), 160–62.

[7] Board Minutes, NAACP, October 7, 1913; Villard, *Segregation in Baltimore and Washington: An Address Delivered before the Baltimore Branch of the National Association for the Advancement of Colored People, October 20, 1913* (n.p., n.d.), 12, 14.

[8] Villard to Garrison, October 23, 1913, Villard Papers. Francis Cardozo had especially urged Spingarn to attend the meeting because the people could "approach" him "so informally." Cardozo to J. E. Spingarn, September 23, 1913, Joel Elias Spingarn Papers (Moorland Foundation, Howard University).

[9] Villard to Garrison, October 23, 1913, Villard Papers; *Chicago Tribune*, October 21, 1913; *Chicago Inter-Ocean*, October 23, 1913; *Boston Evening Transcript*, October 21, 1913. It was at this time that John P. Gavit, who was "heart and soul interested in this question," became the managing editor of the *New York Evening Post*, replacing "an anti-negro Southerner." This was "gratifying" to Villard, as there were "very few people" in the *Evening Post* office who were in sympathy with his policies except the editorial writers. Villard to Garrison, October 25, 1913, Villard Papers.

[10] Board Minutes, NAACP, January 6, 1914; February 3, 1914; July 7, 1914; February 2, 1915; Minutes Annual Meeting, January 3, 1916, in Board Minutes, NAACP.

by the Association's attorney, J. Chapin Brinsmade. Joel Spingarn, then chairman of the Board, together with William Pickens, conducted a mass meeting in Louisville and organized a branch for the purpose of fighting segregation. A year later, in the midst of the fight Miss Nerney was obliged to visit Louisville to reorganize the branch, which was torn by factions and by charges that funds collected for the segregation case had not been properly accounted for. Even though residential segregation in the cities was becoming more menacing, the colored people at times found it difficult to work together. St. Louis was an illustration of dissipation of effort. There two groups were at work, the local branch of the NAACP, which was seeking to challenge the constitutionality of the law, and a group of Negro clergymen who sought to enjoin the election commissions from holding a referendum on the law.[11]

The Louisville segregation case, known as *Buchanan* v. *Warley*, proceeded under the direction of Clayton B. Blakey of Louisville to the Kentucky Court of Appeals, which upheld the ordinance. The decision was then appealed to the Supreme Court of the United States. W. Ashbie Hawkins, on behalf of the Baltimore branch, filed a brief as *amicus curiae*. In support of the ordinance, briefs as *amicus curiae* were filed on behalf of the mayor and city council of Baltimore and the city of Richmond, Virginia.[12]

Moorfield Storey conducted the case before the Supreme Court, presenting his final arguments at the end of April, 1917. Storey had offered to bear the entire expense of the case so as not to put a strain on the NAACP budget, but the Association not only paid his expenses but sent an appeal to the branches to help defray the deficit of $334.92 resulting from the case.[13]

Early in November, 1917, the Supreme Court reversed the Kentucky Court of Appeals, ruling that the ordinance was not merely regulatory but in effect "destroyed the right of the individual to acquire, enjoy, and dispose of his property" and hence was in violation of the due process clause of the Fourteenth Amendment. Although the Court had previously held "separation of the races" on public carriers to be valid, it had done so on the basis of equal accommodations. Moreover, other courts of high authority had held that separate schools

[11] Board Minutes, NAACP, January 6, 1914; July 7, 1914; July 12, 1915. In the segregation cases in Richmond and Ashland, Virginia, the Association had been obliged to postpone action because the "representative colored people in both cities could not agree on any definite plan of action." Minutes, Annual Meeting, January 3, 1916, in Board Minutes, NAACP. The Richmond case was finally ended as the result of the United States Supreme Court ruling in the Louisville case. *New York Age*, December 22, 1917.

[12] *Buchanan* v. *Warley*, 245 U.S. 60 (1917); *Crisis*, XIV (June, 1917), 67–70; Mary White Ovington, *The Walls Came Tumbling Down* (New York, 1947), p. 116.

[13] Moorfield Storey to Royal F. Nash, April 4, 1917, Moorfield Storey Papers (in the possession of Mr. Charles Storey, Boston, Massachusetts); Nash to J. E. Spingarn, April 5, 1917, J. E. Spingarn Papers (Howard); Board Minutes, NAACP, April 10, 1916; April 4, 1917; May 14, 1917.

were legal where equal privileges existed. Under the Fourteenth Amendment, however, such legislation had its limitations, and the Court held that the segregation ordinances had exceeded the limitations imposed by Amendment.[14]

To secure publicity, the national office wrote all branches asking that they celebrate the victory. In New York the colored clergy were urged to make known to their congregations the importance of the decision and the role played by the NAACP. In addition, the Board issued a pamphlet giving the story of the cases in Baltimore, St. Louis, Richmond, and Louisville.[15] The victory, however, was more apparent than real, for although segregation by city ordinance was outlawed, the same objective was achieved by the writing of restrictive covenants into deeds.

Late in 1913, it came to the attention of the Board that Clarence Poe of North Carolina, editor of *The Progressive Farmer*, an influential Southern agricultural journal, was advocating that segregation be extended to the farms of the South. The Board considered this campaign extremely serious, and tried to rally opposition among Southerners. In an attempt to bring publicity to bear on this new move to extend segregation patterns, the Board proclaimed "Segregation" as the theme of the public mass meeting which followed the annual business meeting in January, 1914. When leading newspapers failed to publicize the meeting and Du Bois's speech on farm segregation in the South, the national office got a number of "representative members" to write letters to the editors. The NAACP also issued four pamphlets dealing with segregation—on the farm, in the cities, in government, and in the trades.[16]

SEGREGATION IN EDUCATION

Early in its existence, the NAACP turned attention to segregation and discrimination in secondary and higher education. The chief objective was to secure equal opportunity in public schooling for Negro youth in the South through a fair apportionment of the public funds allotted to education. The Association consistently maintained that not only was the uneducated Negro child at a disadvantage, but also that an uneducated Negro population was a menace to the welfare of the nation.[17]

[14] *Buchanan* v. *Warley*, 245 U.S. 60 (1917).
[15] Board Minutes, NAACP, November 12, 1917.
[16] Villard to George Foster Peabody, January 23, 1914, Villard Papers; Board Minutes, NAACP, December 2, 1913; February 3, 1914.
[17] Minutes, Executive Committee, January 3, 1911, in Board Minutes, NAACP. Important studies of the problem by NAACP members are: Du Bois, *The Negro Common School* (Atlanta University Publications, No. 6; Atlanta, 1901); Du Bois and Augustus G. Dill (eds.), *The Common School and the Negro American* (Atlanta University Publications, No. 16; Atlanta, 1911). A more recent study of the problem is Louis R. Harlan, *Separate and Unequal: Public School Campaigns and Racism in the Southern Seaboard States 1901–1915* (Chapel Hill, 1958).

When the twentieth century began, the school system in the South lagged far behind school systems elsewhere. Contributing to this condition was the poverty of the region and a dual school system with grossly unequal support. The great proportion of the Southern population was rural and scattered, and the majority of Negroes in the United States lived in the rural South, where there was very little taxable income to provide for public instruction. Rural teachers were poorly trained, poorly paid, and inadequately supervised. Conditions were not much better in the cities. School terms were shorter in the South than in the rest of the country, and fewer children of school age attended regularly. Few high schools existed even for whites. As a result illiteracy was high among whites, and more than half the Negroes in the South could neither read nor write.[18]

Between 1901 and 1911, Northern philanthropy did much to bring about an educational awakening in the South. Established philanthropies such as the Slater and Peabody Funds, founded to aid Southern education, were joined by the Jeanes and Phelps-Stokes Funds. John D. Rockefeller endowed the General Education Board for the advancement of public education throughout the country. Julius Rosenwald's interest in Tuskegee led him to provide money for the construction of school buildings for Negroes. The Southern Education Board was founded in 1901 by Robert C. Ogden, a wealthy New Yorker, to coordinate Southern leadership and Northern philanthropy to stimulate local support for public education. This group believed that education was the answer to problems stemming from poverty, ignorance, and racism. All these philanthropic agencies except the Phelps-Stokes Fund became closely linked with one another through interlocking boards of directors, a system then prevalent in the world of big business. Nearly all philanthropic aid for Southern education passed through these boards.[19]

To make the crusade a purely Southern one and to remove any suspicion of Northern interference, Southern leadership was enlisted at state and local levels. The Northern philanthropists were careful not to interfere with the pattern of segregated schools for fear of jeopardizing the success of the movement. Discrimination in education was fundamental to all patterns of segregation in Southern life. Southern whites from landowner to poor white feared the emancipation that education would bring to Negroes. However, the philanthropists believed that by improving the general level of education in the South, the white

---

[18] C. Vann Woodward, *Origins of the New South 1877–1913*, Vol. IX of *A History of the South*, pp. 398–99; Harlan, *Separate and Unequal*, pp. 22–28.
[19] Woodward, *Origins of the New South*, pp. 400–03; Harlan, *Separate and Unequal*, pp. 79, 85–87; John Hope Franklin, *From Slavery to Freedom: A History of American Negroes* (2d ed.; New York, 1965), pp. 378–80.

supremacy movement would be undermined, and the Southern white would eventually become tolerant in matters of race.[20]

By 1910, the educational awakening had brought about both a decline in illiteracy and a marked increase in revenues, length of school terms, and number of high schools. Nevertheless, in spite of this great advance, education in the South remained far behind that of the rest of the country, and there was a growing tendency to allocate more and more of the available money to white schools. Disfranchisement left the Negro helpless to stop the widening gap between the amount of money spent on white children and that spent on Negroes.[21]

One of the first publications issued by the NAACP concerned education in the South for both races and was based on the 1909 report of the United States Commissioner of Education. Horace Bumstead, author of the pamphlet, emphasized the wisdom of giving the Negro an adequate education to increase his productive power and to enhance the prosperity of the state. He noted that the great disparity between the number of Negroes and whites in secondary schools and colleges existed not because Southern whites were by nature unjust, but because they had deviated so far from a true conception of democracy as to be convinced that an entire race or class could be safely entrusted with deciding what educational opportunities another race or class should have.[22]

In line with this philosophy, federal aid to education was the subject of John Milholland's address at the 1911 annual conference and was the object of one of the four resolutions adopted at that time. In January, 1911, the Executive Committee invited Dr. William H. Maxwell, Superintendent of Schools of New York City, to discuss with them the formation of an independent national committee to study and work for federal aid to education. It was felt that an independent committee would avoid identification with a pressure organization working for the advancement of the Negro. A preliminary group, consisting of Moorfield Storey, Albert E. Pillsbury, and Charles J. Bonaparte, worked with Maxwell but with little success. Of the twenty-four persons invited to participate in the study, only six accepted, and of these four were NAACP Board members.[23]

Not until February, 1912, did Maxwell's committee meet and formulate plans to study methods used by foreign governments to distribute national funds to aid local educational programs. The purpose was to draw up a bill to be intro-

---

[20] Woodward, *Origins of the New South*, p. 404; Harlan, *Separate and Unequal*, pp. 39–40, 79–81, 92–93.
[21] Woodward, *Origins of the New South*, pp. 405–06; Harlan, *Separate and Unequal*, pp. 252–58.
[22] Horace Bumstead, *Secondary and Higher Education in the South for Whites and Negroes* (New York [1910]), p. 3. For earlier statements see Ovington to Villard, May 29, 1908, Villard Papers, and John Milholland, *The Nation's Duty* (n.d., n.p.), reprint of a speech given April 30, 1907.
[23] *Boston Evening Transcript*, March 30, 1911; *Crisis*, III (May, 1911), 24–25; Minutes, Executive Committee, January 3, 1911; June 6, 1911, in Board Minutes, NAACP.

duced in Congress. During 1912 and 1913, however, efforts to establish a working committee failed. Both William English Walling with an NAACP Board committee and Milholland, who took over Maxwell's committee, were unsuccessful. The committees were merged by the Board in 1913, with negligible results.[24]

The founders also took an interest in agricultural extension legislation and in federal aid for vocational education in public secondary schools.[25] The NAACP was uncompromisingly hostile to the agricultural extension measure, known as the Smith-Lever bill, because of its discriminatory features. The measure was introduced in 1911 but was not passed until 1914.[26]

In April, 1913, Hoke Smith again introduced his agricultural extension bill, and a separate bill for the training of vocational teachers, as well as a joint resolution calling for a commission to investigate the entire problem of vocational education. This led Milholland to offer the NAACP Board $1,000 to establish an office in Washington so that former Senator Henry W. Blair of New Hampshire could lobby in the name of the NAACP for the passage of an appropriate measure authorizing federal aid to education.[27]

When Congress approved Hoke Smith's resolution for a Commission on National Aid to Vocational Education, the NAACP attempted to have Florence Kelley appointed to the Commission. By background, training, and experience she was admirably qualified. Both Jane Addams and Lillian Wald wrote to President Wilson, urging the appointment, but possibly because of Mrs. Kelley's role in the NAACP, and also because of the feud between Villard and Wilson at

[24] "Report of Committee on Federal Aid to Education," February 24, 1912, in Board Minutes, NAACP, March 5, 1912; Board Minutes, NAACP, January 7, 1913.
[25] For the background of this legislation and the role of Hoke Smith, see Dewey W. Grantham, Jr., *Hoke Smith and the Politics of the New South* (Baton Rouge, 1958), pp. 254–67. August Meier, "The Vogue of Industrial Education," *Midwest Journal*, VII (Fall, 1955), 241–66, has a stimulating study of the vocational education movement.
[26] *Washington Bee*, March 7, 1914; Villard to Garrison, March 1, 1914, Villard Papers. For a résumé of the terms of the Smith-Lever bill, see James H. Dillard *et al., Twenty-Year Report on the Phelps-Stokes Fund: Trends in Negro Education 1915–1930* (New York, 1932), p. 41.
[27] Board Minutes, NAACP, May 6, 1913. In 1906, Blair had served as a paid lobbyist on a retainer basis for Booker T. Washington, who used Archibald Grimke as an intermediary. Grimke to Washington, May 25, 1906; June 1, 1906; Washington to Grimke, June 2, 1906; June 8, 1906, Booker T. Washington Papers (Manuscript Division, Library of Congress). Blair's job at that time was to try to prevent the insertion into the Railroad Rate bill of anything hostile to the Negro. He was the author of the ill-fated bill for federal aid to education, which provided that funds be distributed on the basis of illiteracy; although segregation was to be maintained, there was to be no discrimination in the use of the appropriations. The bill passed the Senate in 1884, 1886, and 1888, but never came before the House for a vote. Later as a representative, Blair continued to work on behalf of federal aid to education. *Congressional Record*, 48th Cong., 1st Sess., 3204; 49th Cong., 1st Sess., 2105; 50th Cong., 1st Sess., 1223; 51st Cong., 1st Sess., 2161–66.

this time over the Race Commission and segregation in government departments, she was not appointed. Florence M. Marshall, principal of the Manhattan Trade School for Girls, was chosen instead.[28]

The NAACP was active in presenting its point of view on the Smith-Lever bill. Its discriminatory features led Moorfield Storey to write Miss Nerney that it "ought to be fought at every point," and to remark gloomily that "our enemies seem to gain in audacity constantly." Villard, too, was concerned because in providing for rural agricultural aid, Congress was making it easy for the South to exclude every colored farmer from the benefits of the bill.[29]

J. Chapin Brinsmade drafted an amendment that would have divided federal funds between Negro and white agricultural colleges. It was introduced by Senator Wesley L. Jones of Washington and was violently attacked by Smith and Vardaman. Brinsmade and Du Bois compiled a memorandum in support of the amendment for use by senators friendly to the Association and held interviews with a number of senators to inform them of the Association's work and the NAACP position on the Smith-Lever bill. Although the Jones amendment was finally rejected, Brinsmade boasted that the NAACP had caused a two-day debate in the Senate and that the role of the NAACP in introducing the amendment had been well publicized. Moreover, Jacob H. Gallinger, Republican senator from New Hampshire, read to the Senate a letter of protest from the Association and called attention to the caliber of the NAACP Board members, mentioning Storey and Jane Addams by name. John D. Works of California read a telegram from the California branch opposing the bill.[30]

Villard was delighted with the results of the publicity and with the NAACP's splendid fight. The editor of the *Washington Bee* called the NAACP a modern abolition movement, which had wielded a tremendous influence in molding public opinion in efforts to secure for the Negro a fair share of federal funds for agricultural extension work. As a final gesture, the Association sent an open

---

[28] *Congressional Record*, 63d Cong., 1st Sess., 57, 1838–39, 2238; Board Minutes, NAACP, February 16, 1914; Grantham, *Hoke Smith and the Politics of the New South*, p. 265, n. 32. Florence Kelley was the first and only woman to hold the position of state factory inspector until Governor Alfred E. Smith in 1928 appointed Frances Perkins to a similar position for the state of New York. Josephine Goldmark, *Impatient Crusader: Florence Kelley's Life Story* (Urbana, 1953), p. 36.

[29] Storey to Nerney, January 31, 1914, Storey Papers; Villard to George Foster Peabody, January 23, 1914, Villard Papers.

[30] Board Minutes, NAACP, February 3, 1914; *Crisis*, VII (March, 1914), 247–48; *Congressional Record*, 63d Cong., 2d Sess., 2929–48, 3031–46, 3115–24. J. Chapin Brinsmade, "The Smith-Jones Bill," *Crisis*, VII (April, 1914), 291–92. Grantham says that Works opposed the bill on the grounds that he considered it "class legislation." Grantham, *Hoke Smith and the Politics of the New South*, p. 260. Nowhere does Grantham mention the NAACP or the role it played in marshaling opposition to the measure.

letter to Wilson urging that he veto the Smith-Lever bill on the ground that it discriminated against the Negro farmer in the South.[31]

The NAACP committee on federal aid to education tried in vain to persuade New York members of the Commission on Vocational Education to advocate federal aid.[32] The recommendations of the Commission, which became known as the Smith-Hughes bill, did, however, provide for federal support of vocational training and for the preparation of teachers in agricultural, industrial and domestic arts in secondary schools. The NAACP supported the Smith-Hughes bill as did educators, labor, and other progressive organizations, and it became a law in 1917.[33]

In February, 1916, Walling revived the merged committee, renewing contact with those whom the NAACP had earlier tried to interest in the cause of federal aid to education. He wanted to take advantage of a meeting in New York on "National Education Preparedness" to publicize once more the need for federal aid to education. Walling was spurred on by the preparedness debate in Congress, in the course of which Hoke Smith introduced an amendment to the Army reorganization bill providing vocational education for soldiers in order to prepare them for return to civilian life—a measure of great importance to the Negro.[34]

In June, 1916, the revived committee drew up a statement of objectives, demanding federal aid to state governments to provide for vocational and agricultural education, the upgrading of rural schools, the elimination of illiteracy, and an Americanization program for immigrants. The NAACP Board endorsed this platform, and by autumn Walling was able to report that the committee had an executive body of fifteen, including Florence Kelley and John Milholland, whom Walling called a splendid enthusiast. NAACP secretary Roy Nash was secretary-treasurer. Walling recommended that the revitalized committee become an independent body, since Southern cooperation was necessary for the enactment

---

[31] Villard to Garrison, March 1, 1914, Villard Papers; *Washington Bee*, March 7, 1914; *Crisis*, VIII (July, 1914), 124; Board Minutes, NAACP, June 2, 1914.

[32] Board Minutes, NAACP, April 28, 1914. Du Bois drafted the "Memorandum" which was presented to the Commission. Minutes, Annual Meeting, January 3, 1916, in Board Minutes, NAACP.

[33] Board Minutes, NAACP, June 2, 1914; June 1, 1916; *Congressional Record*, 63d Cong., 2d Sess., 9503–5; *Report of the Commission on National Aid to Vocational Education Together with the Hearings Held on the Subject made Pursuant to the Provisions of Public Resolution No. 16, Sixty-Third Congress* (S. J. Res. 5) (Washington, D. C., 1914); Grantham, *Hoke Smith and the Politics of the New South*, pp. 265–66. For a brief summary of the terms of the Smith-Hughes bill, see Dillard *et al.*, *Twenty-Year Report of the Phelps-Stokes Fund*, p. 41.

[34] Board Minutes, NAACP, June 2, 1914; July 7, 1914; March 13, 1916; Grantham, *Hoke Smith and the Politics of the New South*, pp. 294–95.

of legislation. For this reason, the NAACP Board discharged its own committee and turned over the balance of its Federal Education Fund to the group.[35]

Nash threw himself with such vigor into the work of the Federal Aid Committee, that Miss Ovington was led to observe that more than half his time was devoted to it. Consequently, the Board insisted that Nash resign as secretary-treasurer, though he continued to cooperate with the committee and several associated groups.[36]

In March, 1918, the Board learned that James H. Dillard had proposed a method of national aid to Negro education which had the approval of the Department of Superintendents of the National Education Association. Dillard's plan envisioned federal aid to fifteen Southern and Border states for salaries to public school teachers in all grades. He proposed that aid be graduated according to amounts previously spent on Negro education from public funds without diminishing state or local support. He proposed to place the administration of the aid in the hands of a committee composed of the state superintendent of education, the state agent for Negro rural schools, and the president of the leading Negro state institution.[37]

Du Bois was jubilant, claiming that this was the greatest piece of constructive statesmanship that had come out of the South in fifty years, and he recommended that the NAACP push this proposal in every way possible. However, several Board members were also active on the National Child Labor Committee, and at their instigation, the Committee formulated a plan for federal aid to education. Due to the insistence of Florence Kelley, Walling, and Paul Kennaday, the NAACP Board withheld approval of Dillard's proposal until the two plans could be harmonized. The Association took no action during 1918; at the annual meeting in January, 1919, Mrs. Kelley impressed upon her colleagues that the NAACP must take the initiative if any progress were to be made toward federal aid to education within the next five years.[38]

Education for the Negro was of primary interest to the NAACP. The Board believed the only way Negroes would get a fair share of educational opportunities was with the support of federal money impartially distributed, but when it came

[35] Board Minutes, NAACP, June 1, 1916; November 13, 1916; William English Walling to Spingarn, August 27 [1916], J. E. Spingarn Papers (Howard); Minutes, Annual Meeting, January 2, 1917, in Board Minutes, NAACP.

[36] Ovington to Spingarn, February 28, 1917, J. E. Spingarn Papers (Howard); Board Minutes, NAACP, February 13, 1917; March 12, 1917; April 9, 1917.

[37] Board Minutes, NAACP, March 11, 1918. James H. Dillard, "National Aid to Negro Education," *School and Society*, VII (June 8, 1918), 669–70, is an abstract of his paper submitted to the Atlantic City Meeting of the Department of Superintendents, March 1, 1918.

[38] Board Minutes, NAACP, March 11, 1918; Minutes, Annual Meeting, NAACP, January 6, 1919, in Board Minutes, NAACP.

to the means of promoting legislation for this purpose, the Board was divided. Mrs. Kelley believed in an aggressive campaign of promotion by the NAACP membership; Miss Ovington held that the NAACP should support such legislation indirectly and should advocate federal aid, not for the education of Negroes alone, but for the education of all. The latter tactic prevailed. Almost half a century later, however, no legislation had yet been passed which would equalize educational opportunities for Negroes in the manner visualized by the founders of the NAACP.[39]

In the meantime, the migration of Negroes to the North had resulted in the introduction of segregation into Northern public schools. In Hartford, Connecticut, an NAACP branch was founded as the direct result of efforts to oppose the segregation of children of Negro immigrants from the South. The Hartford branch initiated remedial classes for the children so that the school authorities would have no excuse for segregation. Other reports of school segregation in the North came from Indianapolis, Indiana, Carlisle, Pennsylvania, Dayton, Ohio, and Ypsilanti, Michigan. In Ypsilanti, the segregated school was closed by a court injunction obtained by the local branch.[40]

In Kansas, when a bill was introduced into the state legislature providing for separate schools for Negro children in second-class cities, the Kansas branches with the help of the national NAACP office brought about its defeat. The national office prepared a memorandum for the use of branches, and sent protests to the governor and the lieutenant governor. John R. Shillady mustered the support of state officials by persuading the lieutenant governor and the speaker of the state House of Representatives to appear at a statewide meeting in Topeka.[41]

Strong protests were made in Southern and Border cities such as Washington, Atlanta, Memphis, and Charleston, West Virginia. Here segregated schools already existed and the complaint was against unequal appropriations for white and colored schools. At Memphis the branch proposed to take the matter of unequal appropriations to the courts, and secured a $1,000 loan from the national office to be used as a retainer fee for legal counsel. After six months of investigation, the branch realized it could not win this legal battle and returned the money.[42]

In Atlanta, the Board of Education had some years earlier abolished the eighth grade in the colored grammar school without protest from colored citizens. In 1917, in order to make money available for a new white school, this same Board of Education proposed to eliminate the seventh grade from the colored schools.

[39] Board Minutes, NAACP, January 13, 1919.
[40] Minutes, Annual Meeting, January 3, 1916, in Board Minutes, NAACP; NAACP, *Ninth Annual Report 1918* (New York, 1919), pp. 63, 68
[41] Board Minutes, NAACP, March 10, 1919.
[42] Board Minutes, NAACP, June 9, 1919; September 9, 1919; October 13, 1919; *Washington Bee*, February 9, 1918; *New York Age*, March 29, 1917.

Learning of this proposal, James Weldon Johnson led the Atlanta NAACP branch in a successful protest which resulted in retention of the seventh grade and an admission from school board members that Negroes had been treated unfairly.[43]

A successful fight was made in 1919 by the Charleston, South Carolina, branch, assisted by the Columbia branch, for the right of trained Negroes to secure positions as teachers in the Negro public school of Charleston. Five years earlier J. C. Brinsmade had attempted without success to secure cooperation among organizations interested in Negro welfare in instituting a suit to test the legality of a Florida law prohibiting white instructors from teaching in Negro schools.[44]

To encourage Negro children to stay in school and to give status to those who successfully completed their work, James Weldon Johnson in 1917 organized a citizens' committee in New York which held a reception for all those who were graduated from the public schools. The national office contributed half the expense of this project, but the Board did not adopt Johnson's suggestion to make this an annual affair.[45]

Prior to the year 1913, two incidents concerning discrimination in Northern institutions of higher education appear in the records of the Association. The first was at Cornell University, where undergraduate women petitioned the faculty to remove two Negro girls from the women's dormitory. It was reported at the Boston conference in March, 1911. The *Transcript* asked, "Is it not enough to make Ezra Cornell turn in his grave?" Villard communicated with the president of the university, who assured him that Cornell would not countenance discrimination and that the girls would be housed in the regular dormitories.[46]

In the fall of 1913, Carrie Lee of New Bedford, Massachusetts, applied for admission to Smith College and was accepted. She did not mention her color, and when she arrived on the campus she was denied a room in the dormitories and could obtain quarters in college-approved boardinghouses only as a servant, not as a fellow student. As a servant she would have had to use the back entrance to the boardinghouse. According to Jessie Fauset, officials at Smith College maintained that, although Miss Lee was a native of Massachusetts, concession must nevertheless be made to Southern students.[47]

[43] *New York Age*, March 29, 1917.
[44] Board Minutes, NAACP, March 10, 1919; January 6, 1914; *Washington Bee*, March 1, 1919.
[45] Board Minutes, NAACP, October 8, 1917.
[46] *Boston Evening Transcript*, March 31, 1911; Minutes, Executive Committee, April 11, 1911, in Board Minutes, NAACP. The following year the Board discussed segregation at the summer school at Columbia University but took no action. Board Minutes, August 6, 1912. This problem was still unresolved in 1917. Board Minutes, NAACP, October 8, 1917.
[47] Jessie Fauset to Spingarn, October 9, 1913, J. E. Spingarn Papers (Howard). In the same letter Miss Fauset notes that she herself had matriculated at Bryn Mawr "amid rumors of prejudice" but that there was no difficulty.

The matter was handled by the Association without publicity. Joel Spingarn visited the college to discuss the incident with the administration. Jessie Fauset and May Nerney worked behind the scenes, while Storey protested vigorously to the president of Smith College, Marion LeRoy Burton. Unless the girl were admitted, he warned, the facts would receive wide publicity, and contributions would be withdrawn from institutions managed by "modern 'doughfaces.' "[48]

Some members of the Board of Trustees of Smith College wanted Miss Lee to postpone enrollment until the next term, or the following fall, but Mrs. William H. Baldwin, Jr., threatened to resign if the college took the position that colored women should not have equal opportunities at Smith. As a result of this pressure Miss Lee was admitted to the dormitory at the end of October. Four years later, at the time of her graduation, she wrote the NAACP, expressing her gratitude and her belief that color discrimination at Smith had been permanently ended.[49]

An episode at the time of the sixth annual conference involved The Johns Hopkins University and caused friction among officers of the NAACP. The last session of the conference was scheduled to be held in McCoy Hall of the university, but when delegates arrived they found the building locked, whereupon the group adjourned to the Bethel African Methodist Episcopal Church. It was a large meeting. Du Bois and others made a strong attack upon the university, and only with difficulty was Villard able to prevent the passage of a resolution of censure.[50]

His investigation revealed an apparent misunderstanding between university officials and the committee that arranged the meeting. Villard was willing to accept the explanation and apology of the president of the university's Board of Trustees, but Joel Spingarn, W. Ashbie Hawkins, and Bishop John Hurst, NAACP Board member and presiding officer at the meeting, were not satisfied. They believed that the registrar was the "chief culprit," and that there had been a "plot hatched in advance." Moreover, some students had been overheard boasting that a society that preached social equality would never be allowed to speak in a university building, and, later, that they had accomplished what they set out to do.[51]

---

[48] Ovington to Spingarn, October 23, 1913; Fauset to Spingarn, October 18, 1913; Charles Cranston Lee to Spingarn, October 26, 1913, in J. E. Spingarn Papers (Howard); Storey to Villard, October 14, 1913, Villard Papers.

[49] Ovington to Spingarn, October 23, 1913; Villard to Spingarn, October 23, 1913; Fauset to Spingarn, October 23, 1913; Lee to Spingarn, October 26, 1913. J. E. Spingarn Papers (Howard); Board Minutes, NAACP, June 11, 1917.

[50] Villard to Nerney, March 21, 1914; May 21, 1914; Villard to R. Brent Keyser, May 7, 1914; Ovington to [Spingarn], May 11, 1914; Villard to Spingarn, May 22, 1914; Spingarn to [Nerney], May 23, 1914, NAACP Files; Crisis, VIII (June, 1914), 80–81.

[51] John Hurst to Spingarn, May 11, 1914; W. Ashbie Hawkins to Spingarn, May 8, 1914, J. E. Spingarn Papers (Howard); Spingarn to Villard, May 14, 1914; May 21, 1914; Villard to Spingarn, May 20, 1914, NAACP Files.

That there was discrimination at Johns Hopkins became evident when Carl J. Murphy, a graduate of Harvard, was refused admission to the summer school in 1915 for the reason that no provision had been made for colored students. When the Association protested, President Goodenow replied that it was the educational policy of Maryland to provide separate schools. Since the university received a considerable appropriation from the state, he could not depart from the official policy.[52]

Discrimination was also practiced in graduate and professional schools and organizations. The plight of the Negro physician who sought postgraduate instruction in white hospitals was brought to light in 1912 when a colored doctor from North Carolina was accepted at the New York Post-Graduate Medical School and Hospital and later refused admission when the institution learned he was a Negro. The hospital claimed that because of the very limited number of colored patients applying at the clinics, they would be unable to supply him with the teaching he desired, especially since they were unable to compel other patients to accept treatment by a colored doctor. It was made clear that there was no official policy of refusing admission to colored physicians, and they hoped to be able to provide "proper material" for instruction in the future.[53]

Complaints also came to the legal committee from Cornell Medical College, Western Reserve University, and the Syracuse Hospital for Women and Children. The Syracuse Hospital had refused to accept as intern a graduate of the New York Medical School when it was discovered that she was a Negro. Since the hospital had signed her contract, the Association helped her institute a suit for damages. Arthur Spingarn later reported that a substantial offer of settlement had been secured. Nevertheless, legal action could seldom be taken in these cases, and the committee made plans to attempt to introduce into the State Legislature a bill to deny tax exemption to medical schools and colleges that refused to treat colored patients or to accept colored doctors as interns. In 1916, the Boston branch forced one tax-exempt hospital to abandon a policy of discrimination.[54]

Sometimes the doctors and interns themselves nullified the work of the Association in their behalf. Miss Ovington cited a case in which a branch of the Association intervened with the Board of Health of a Midwestern city to have a young Negro doctor reinstated. He had passed his examination and received the appointment but was removed because fourteen white interns went on strike when he reported for duty. Unable to face the hostility of the staff, the young

[52] *Crisis*, X (August, 1915), 200.
[53] G. G. Ward to Spingarn, October 2, 1912, J. E. Spingarn Papers (Howard).
[54] Board Minutes, NAACP, July 12, 1915; Minutes, Annual Meeting, January 3, 1916; Minutes, Annual Meeting, January 2, 1917, in Board Minutes, NAACP; Butler Wilson, "Boston, the Banner Branch," *Branch Bulletin*, I (March, 1917), 25–26.

man resigned without taking up residence in the hospital. It was not the first time, said Miss Ovington, that members of the Association had spent time and money, and subjected themselves to possible insult to secure justice for someone who lacked the firmness of purpose that would enable him to profit by the victory secured. The Association could not afford to take up cases without being assured of the staying powers of the person discriminated against. Some NAACP members, continued Miss Ovington, were satisfied simply to establish a legal principle. "They want to know that they can do a thing, though they may never exercise their right." She asked them not to bring such cases to the Association. To be an aggressive power, it was necessary to concentrate on specific fighting issues. Only in this way could the evil of race prejudice in the United States be overcome.[55]

Negro patients seeking hospital care found segregation and discrimination on every hand. When the Wisconsin State Tuberculosis Hospital announced the exclusion of Negroes on its application form, the Association protested to the superintendent. When the hospital failed to make an adjustment, the Association wrote to the governor and sent the story to twenty-two Wisconsin newspapers and to *Crisis* subscribers in Wisconsin, where there was no NAACP branch. The governor immediately ordered the State Board of Control, administrative authority for Wisconsin's charitable institutions, to remove any discriminatory practices in state institutions and ordered the superintendent of the sanitarium to admit Negro patients on the same basis as white. The Association was also able to enlist the interest of the National Tuberculosis Association, which initiated a survey of facilities for the care of Negro tuberculosis patients throughout the United States. The publicity and action in this case, and the response from *Crisis* subscribers, led to the calling of an organizational meeting for establishing a branch in Milwaukee.[56]

Publicity regarding protests and pressures was sometimes withheld for fear of intensifying prejudice. In 1913, the Harvard Club of Philadelphia wrote to class secretaries asking for the names of Negro graduates in each class in order to exclude them from invitations to the annual dinner. Storey was so incensed by this action that he drafted a letter of protest and enlisted a number of other Harvard graduates to sign it,[57] but he thought it would be unwise to publicize

[55] *Crisis*, XIV (October, 1917), 307.
[56] Board Minutes, NAACP, July 8, 1918; NAACP, *Ninth Annual Report 1918*, pp. 46–47.
[57] Richard Haugton to Charles Stratton, n.d. [February, 1913], copy in Villard Papers; Storey to Richard Haugton, February 27, 1913, copy in Villard Papers. The signers were Moorfield Storey '66, Vincent Bowditch '75, N. P. Hallowell '61, Robert Grant '73, John T. Morse, Jr. '60, Thomas S. Perry '66, William S. Hall '69, Edward S. Dodge '73, and James J. Myers '69. See also Mark A. De Wolfe Howe, *Portrait of an Independent, Moorfield Storey, 1845–1929* (Boston, 1932), pp. 258–60.

the letter, because this might strengthen the trend toward prejudice "by letting it be known that a Harvard Club is capable of such action."[58] Villard had been unsuccessful in an earlier attempt to take Harvard graduate Leslie Pinckney Hill, principal of the Manassas School, to the Harvard Club of New York as a guest speaker. Though Villard offered to compromise by arranging for Hill to leave before refreshments were served, the Board of Managers ruled that it would be improper to invite Hill to a social function in the Club.[59]

DISCRIMINATION IN PROFESSIONAL ORGANIZATIONS AND COMMERCIAL ESTABLISHMENTS

Color discrimination prevented the Negro from joining most professional organizations such as those for nurses, dentists, doctors, and lawyers. The result was that Negro professional men established their own national organizations while fighting to gain admission to the segregated groups. The NAACP's first attempt to open a professional organization to Negroes was aimed at the American Bar Association.

In 1911, three Negro lawyers were elected to this organization: William H. Lewis, Assistant Attorney General of the United States, Butler R. Wilson of Boston, and William R. Morris of Minneapolis. Southern members objected, although one Kentucky judge is reported to have said that "any man who is fit to be admitted to the bar is fit to be a member of the Bar Association." As a result of the controversy, the Bar Association's executive committee early in 1912 voted to rescind Lewis's election on the ground that all the information concerning him had not been available at the time of his election. United States Attorney General George W. Wickersham branded this action illegal. Moorfield Storey, a past president of the American Bar Association, was also greatly aroused. He wrote to NAACP members and to many of his friends who were lawyers, protesting Lewis's expulsion and threatening to resign if the Bar Association sustained the action of the executive committee.[60]

Meanwhile, the NAACP lodged protests with the president and prominent members of the Bar Association and with the press. The Boston branch was particularly active. A number of leading newspapers published editorials favor-

[58] Storey to Col. N. P. Hallowell, March 13, 1913, Storey Papers; Storey to Villard, March 13, 1913, Villard Papers.
[59] Villard to Langdon P. Marvin, December 28, 1909; Marvin to Villard, December 29, 1909; Villard to Marvin, December 30, 1909; Marvin to Villard, January 4, 1910; Marvin to Villard, January 8, 1910; Villard to Austin G. Fox, January 11, 1910; Villard to Marvin, January 11, 1910, in Villard Papers.
[60] Howe, *Portrait of an Independent: Moorfield Storey*, p. 260; *New York Age*, August 29, 1912; September 7, 1911. In the latter issue the paper boasts that Lewis's confirmation by the Senate was due to the Washington forces. Board Minutes, NAACP, March 5, 1912; Storey to Albert E. Pillsbury, March 4, 1912, Storey Papers.

able to the NAACP position, and William Wherry turned down an invitation to become a member of the Association because of its discriminatory action.[61]

Miss Nerney urged William H. Lewis to join the NAACP and assist in the struggle for Negro rights, but Lewis, a supporter of Booker T. Washington, evaded committing himself. William R. Morris, another of the three lawyers involved, resigned from the Bar Association as soon as he learned that it had drawn the color line.[62]

Unfortunately, Storey was ill at the time and unable to attend the 1912 annual meeting of the American Bar Association in Milwaukee. However, Albert Pillsbury and Judge Harvey H. Baker made the trip. They were joined by George W. Wickersham and, at the opening session of the meeting, won their fight to retain Lewis, Wilson, and Morris as members. A "compromise resolution" was also passed, which required local organizations to indicate the race of candidates for membership, and to Storey this resolution spelled defeat. The color line had been drawn, in spite of the fact (as he and Charles Bonaparte maintained) that there had been no intention to close the door to Negro applicants when the American Bar Association was founded.[63]

In order to bring public opinion to bear upon the Bar Association the NAACP Board authorized Du Bois to draft an appropriate resolution to be circulated in the name of the NAACP. Storey likewise drew up a letter for distribution to Bar Association members, signed by a majority of the local council for Massachusetts, attacking the action taken at the Milwaukee meeting. He advised Butler Wilson not to withdraw. Storey's statement was acclaimed by the *New York Age*, which omitted any reference to the NAACP or to the fact that Moorfield Storey was its national president.[64]

Albert E. Pillsbury took an independent course of action. He resigned from the Bar Association in July, 1913, proclaiming that the organization he belonged to no longer existed since it had acted in violation of its constitution.[65]

Storey continued his efforts within the framework of the organization, and at the 1914 meeting persuaded the delegates to rescind that part of the Milwaukee resolution which stated that admission of Negroes had never been contemplated. This was far from a total victory, for the Association unanimously voted that henceforth applications for membership should state both race and sex of the

[61] *Crisis*, IV (October, 1912), 299; Board Minutes, NAACP, March 5, 1912; June 4, 1912; September 3, 1912; William Wherry to Charles J. O'Connor, May 23, 1912, quoted in *Crisis*, IV (August, 1912), 179.
[62] William H. Lewis to Nerney, June 19, 1912; August 29, 1912, NAACP Files; *Crisis*, IV (October, 1912), 299.
[63] Storey to Villard, October 17, 1912, Storey Papers; *New York Age*, August 29, 1912.
[64] Storey to Villard, October 29, 1912; Storey to Du Bois, December 19, 1912, Storey Papers; Board Minutes, NAACP, November 12, 1912; *New York Age*, April 24, 1913.
[65] *New York Age*, July 17, 1913.

applicant. However, since the bar to Negro membership had been removed, Storey optimistically predicted that when a proper executive committee could be elected, qualified colored candidates would become members—though he admitted that this might not happen for some years.[66]

Discrimination was also practiced by life insurance companies and savings and commercial banks; the former charged higher rates for insuring colored persons, while the latter discriminated in issuing mortgages on property owned by Negroes. The NAACP sent questionnaires to all prominent insurance companies and banks in New York City in an attempt to determine the reasons for this discrimination. The legal committee conferred with the Urban League concerning practical remedies and tried to persuade the League to establish a mortgage company. Nothing came of this move and the problem persisted. Du Bois continued to urge the establishment of a building and loan association, but some Board members, especially Grimke, were opposed.[67]

The problem of breaking down discrimination by hotels and restaurants was one of the most difficult to solve. The Association turned its attention to this matter in 1913 when it was reported that the La Salle Hotel in Chicago had turned away a meeting of one thousand club women rather than admit Negro delegates to the dining room. Moorfield Storey reported to the legal committee that in New York a court decision had established that all persons, regardless of color, were entitled to accommodations. However, hotel managers evaded the issue by declaring that no rooms were available, throwing the burden of proof upon the applicant. It was Storey's opinion that in this instance Negroes had "ground to stand on" entirely independent of the Fourteenth Amendment.[68]

Attempts to secure remedial legislation on state and city levels in the form of civil rights bills and city ordinances found hard going. In California, the Los Angeles branch tried to get candidates for mayor and for city council to declare themselves on matters affecting Negroes of the city. In Pennsylvania, the Philadelphia, Pittsburgh, and Harrisburg branches cooperated in securing the passage of a civil rights bill, but it was so amended in passage through the two houses of the state legislature as to be practically worthless. Even so, it was vetoed by the governor.[69]

A great step forward was accomplished when an amendment to the New York State Civil Rights Law, drafted by the legal committee of the NAACP, was enacted into law on April 13, 1918. The Association now had a model law on

[66] Crisis, IX (December, 1914), 82.
[67] Board Minutes, NAACP, April 28, 1914; July 7, 1914; Nerney to Spingarn, January 5, 1916; Minutes, Annual Meeting, January 3, 1916, in Board Minutes, NAACP.
[68] Board Minutes, NAACP, April 1, 1913; Storey to Spingarn, July 7, 1913, J. E. Spingarn Papers (Howard).
[69] Board Minutes, NAACP, May 10, 1915; June 14, 1915; July 12, 1915; Minutes, Annual Meeting, January 3, 1916, in Board Minutes, NAACP.

the statute books which could be used in the struggle to secure civil rights legislation in other states. Similar bills were submitted to the legislatures of Connecticut, Pennsylvania, Ohio, New Mexico, Michigan, Rhode Island, and California.[70]

The most determined (although unsuccessful) effort to secure passage of the model bill was in Ohio. The national office asked the district organizer of the Great Lakes district, Robert Bagnall, to work for passage of the measure. He called a conference of all Ohio branches at Columbus to explain the significance of the bill and to stimulate support. The bill was sponsored by the former president of the Cincinnati branch, A. Lee Beaty, a Negro member of the Ohio House of Representatives. It passed the House by a large majority, but a sudden and unexpected motion to reconsider prevailed. Investigation revealed that immediately after passage of the measure, representatives of hotel, theater, food, and refreshment-vending interests had persuaded the Republican leadership to back down. The motion to reconsider was then introduced and passed. Moreover, many of the Ohio Conference committee members questioned whether Beaty had given the measure his wholehearted support. A state senator who had once been president of the Columbus NAACP branch indicated that he did not wholly believe in the principles of the bill. Disloyalty to the principles of the NAACP on the part of members echoed earlier warnings of Miss Nerney that many conservatives were infiltrating the Midwest branches.

In an effort to save the measure, several press stories were released in Columbus. Shillady met with the vice-chairman of the Republican State Advisory Committee and sent telegrams to the chairman, and to United States Senator Warren G. Harding. The NAACP national office and the Ohio Conference made it clear that they would hold the Republican Party responsible for the fate of the bill. In spite of these efforts the measure was killed.[71]

JIM CROW CARS IN INTERSTATE COMMERCE

Although the Association had early engaged in fighting segregated transportation, it was not until 1917 that it made an attack on Jim Crow railroad cars a part of its official program.[72] Progress was seriously hampered as in other aspects of the NAACP program, not only by public opinion and the attitude of the courts but by imperfect organization and lack of resources.

[70] Board Minutes, NAACP, April 8, 1918; February 10, 1919; April 14, 1919; March 10, 1919; NAACP, *Ninth Annual Report 1918*, p. 58. The bill had been introduced into the legislature by Assemblyman E. A. Johnson, New York's only Negro member.
[71] Board Minutes, NAACP, March 10, 1919; May 12, 1919.
[72] Nash to Mary Church Terrell, January 18, 1917, Mary Church Terrell Papers (Manuscript Division, Library of Congress) ; Board Minutes, NAACP, February 13, 1917.

One of the early Jim Crow car cases, *McCabe et al* v. *Atchison Topeka and Santa Fe Railway Company,* originated in Oklahoma. This case challenged an Oklahoma law which allowed railroads to provide dining and sleeping car accommodations only for whites. The case was in charge of William Harrison, a Negro attorney, and was lost in the United States Circuit Court of Appeals by a two to one decision.[73]

Storey examined the opinion of the court and the dissent of the oldest judge, Walter H. Sanborn. He thought the case should be argued in the Supreme Court of the United States even though in all probability it would be lost. It was his opinion that, if the Association responded to Harrison's request for help and cooperation by paying the cost of printing the record, the advance should be treated as a loan rather than an outright gift. He firmly believed that, whenever possible, the responsibility of protecting Negro rights should be assumed and paid for by the colored man. He wanted Negroes to be self-reliant, so that it would not be necessary to turn constantly to white men for help.[74]

When the record was printed and could be examined, however, Storey was not willing to plead the case, as it was not properly drawn and could not be supported. To plead this particular case, he wrote, would weaken his influence with the Court in other cases, and he was certain that there would be cases of greater importance to the colored race, in which he could be of assistance. Thereupon the NAACP withdrew, and Harrison argued the case before the Supreme Court and lost. That Storey and the Association were wise in the decision to withdraw is clear from the opinion of the Court delivered by Associate Justice Hughes, who claimed that the allegations were altogether too vague and indefinite to warrant the relief sought by the complaints.[75]

Du Bois commented that this sort of thing had happened time after time, in case after case. Negro lawyers appeared before the courts only half-prepared. The case might be just, and the lawyer might bring all his learning to bear on the case, but because the color line in the legal profession gave him little actual experience, the case might easily be lost. Harrison had been warned, but he chose to go it alone, and Du Bois complained that all the laborious work must now be done over again.[76]

[73] *Crisis,* IX (January, 1915), 133, 137; *The Federal Reporter: Cases Argued and Determined in the Circuit Courts of Appeal and District Courts of the United States,* Vol. 186 (June–July, 1911) (St. Paul, 1911), v, pp. 966–89. Circuit Court of Appeal, Eighth Circuit, February 10, 1911, No. 3,054. Suit by E. P. McCabe and others before circuit Judges Walter H. Sanborn of St. Paul, Minnesota; William C. Hook, of Leavenworth, Kansas; and Elmer B. Adams of St. Louis, Missouri. Adams gave the majority opinion; Sanborn dissented
[74] Storey to Nerney August 27, 1913, Storey Papers; Board Minutes, NAACP, October 7, 1913.
[75] Storey to [Brinsmade], November 19, 1913, quoted in *Crisis,* IX (January, 1915), 137; *McCabe* v. *Atchison Topeka and Santa Fe Railway Co.,* 235 U.S. 151 (1914).
[76] Du Bois, editorial, "Negro Lawyers," *Crisis,* IX (January, 1915), 133.

The "laborious work" was started almost at once. Joel Spingarn went to Oklahoma to encourage the branch to prepare the basis for legal action. W. Scott Brown of the Muskogee, Oklahoma, branch accompanied him. During the trip, Brown was twice discriminated against by the Atchison Topeka and Santa Fe Railway. The Association planned to bring two cases to test the Oklahoma law, both of which they hoped to carry to the United States Supreme Court.[77] The cases were still being made ready when the war preparedness campaign resulted in an increase in the size of the armed forces. This precipitated a struggle over the role of the Negro in the new army, which consumed all the time and energy of the Association. Spingarn left New York for officer training camp, and the railroads passed under government control and operation, which further complicated the situation. As a result the cases were never brought to trial.

At the local level, the Baltimore branch, through the efforts of W. Ashbie Hawkins, secured the quashing of an indictment against a Negro for violation of the separate car law, brought because of his refusal to take a Jim Crow seat on the Washington, Baltimore and Indianapolis Railroad. In 1918, the Baltimore branch won a most important Jim Crow case involving the suit of Julia B. Coleman, a doctor of medicine, against the same railroad for attempted segregation. This case was also tried by Hawkins, who won a judgment of one cent and damages and costs rendered. Upon appeal, the judge assessed the damages at twenty dollars. Hawkins wrote the national office that as a result of the suits, the company stopped enforcing the regulation—except with persons who could easily be intimidated.[78]

William Pickens gives a picture of the difficulties facing a Negro who wanted sleeping accommodations on a train:

> The berth cost me: a messenger's fee, thirteen hours of work, worry and strategy, my attendance at morning church services, part of my dinner, part of my time for evening address, the assistance of at least six other persons, three trips to the station—*and the regular fares.* And yet they say that jim-crowism is no burden to the black man.[79]

The Interstate Commerce Commission was the next target in the move to eliminate discrimination in transportation facilities. Florence Kelley sought the help of Louis Brandeis who was at that time counsel for the Consumer's League.[80] Brandeis advised the Association that the best approach was to petition the Commission for relief, citing definite cases in support of their conten-

---

[77] Board Minutes, NAACP, January 5, 1915; Minutes, Annual Meeting, February 12, 1915, in Board Minutes, NAACP.
[78] Board Minutes, NAACP, July 7, 1914; NAACP, *Ninth Annual Report 1918*, p. 65.
[79] William H. Pickens to Ovington, July 16, 1914, copy in J. E. Spingarn Papers (Howard).
[80] Goldmark, *Impatient Crusader*, p. 143.

tion. Thereupon the NAACP Board dispatched Montgomery Gregory of Howard University to collect evidence and take photographs of Jim Crow car conditions in the deep South. Gregory's investigation covered the lesser as well as major railroad lines, and the waiting room and dining facilities in a number of Southern cities. By the end of 1915, Arthur Spingarn and the legal committee had "almost perfected" the cases, which were to have been presented by Brandeis. Brandeis was appointed to the United States Supreme Court in January, 1916, however, and Albert Pillsbury agreed to make the presentation.[81]

As with the Oklahoma cases, the entry of the United States into the war prevented the continuation of the Interstate Commerce Commission cases, and the Association now had to deal with William G. McAdoo, Secretary of the Treasury, who was at the head of the unified railroad system operated by the federal government. Villard headed a special committee to determine what action the Association might take concerning the relation of the Jim Crow car question to government management. After James Weldon Johnson, the field secretary, conferred with Washington branch members, it was agreed that the only practical move was to give as much publicity as possible to the situation by means of an open letter of protest to President Wilson. Copies of the letter were sent to Northern and Southern editors, and the branches were urged to send in all the information they could gather concerning discrimination on the railroads.[82]

In June, 1919, Martin B. Madden of Illinois introduced a bill into Congress providing for equal accommodations on the railroads. Johnson conferred with Hays Baxter White of Kansas and William Green of Massachusetts in an attempt to rally support for the bill, but it got no further than the Interstate Commerce Committee. A similar fate befell a resolution introduced by Ernest Mason of Illinois, calling for a commission "to promote the well-being of the different races," a bill which was lost in the Committee on the Judiciary.[83]

DISFRANCHISEMENT

The second part of the NAACP national program in 1917 dealt with disfranchisement—the theme of the 1910 Conference. The first opportunity to strike an effective blow against disfranchisement came in the celebrated case of *Guinn v. United States*. This was the first time the NAACP played a decisive role in a case brought before the Supreme Court of the United States. The case

[81] Board Minutes, NAACP, August 4, 1914; October 6, 1914; August 9, 1915; September 13, 1915; February 13, 1917. A detailed report of Gregory's findings was published in three parts in *The Crisis*, XI (December, 1915), 87–89; (January, 1916), 137–38; (February, 1916), 195–98.
[82] Board Minutes, NAACP, January 14, 1918; February 11, 1918.
[83] Board Minutes, NAACP, April 14, 1919; October 13, 1919; *Congressional Record*, 66th Cong., 1st Sess. (H.R. 376), 20, 1006; (H.J.R. 192), 4883.

challenged the constitutionality of the "grandfather clause" of the state of Oklahoma. In 1913, John Milholland called the Board's attention to a decision of the Circuit Court of Maryland, which, for the first time, had rendered a decision in favor of those who opposed the Maryland grandfather clause. But it was in Oklahoma that the Association was successful in persuading the Solicitor General of the United States, John W. Davis, to challenge the constitutionality of a 1910 amendment to the state constitution providing for such exemptions from the requirements for voter registration.[84]

When the case came before the Supreme Court, Storey was given special permission to file a brief *amicus curiae* on behalf of the Association and to join in the argument. The NAACP was the only organization represented, and the Board was well aware of the prestige involved in having its brief filed by Moorfield Storey. In June, 1915, the decision read by Chief Justice Edward D. White of Louisiana held that the so-called grandfather clause was in violation of the Fifteenth Amendment to the Constitution of the United States and was therefore invalid.[85]

The Board in its resolution of gratitude to Storey for preparing and submitting his brief without cost to the Association recalled that the Solicitor General was in sympathy with Storey's position and declared that the favorable decision of the Court was undoubtedly influenced by his brief.[86]

The decision had little practical effect, but the spiritual effect was a moral victory for champions of the Negro. Joel Spingarn told NAACP members that the Supreme Court had, in this decision, affirmed the principle that evasion of the Constitution by legal chicanery could not deprive Negroes of the rights given them by the Thirteenth, Fourteenth, and Fifteenth Amendments.

From time to time the Board discussed the question of implementing Section Two of the Fourteenth Amendment, which called for reduction of representation in Congress to states that denied the franchise to any of its male citizens. At the NAACP annual meeting in 1916, Joel Spingarn again raised this problem in his address to the Association: It should not be the objective of the organization to curtail the political power of one section of the United States—or even merely to assist any fraction of the population, no matter how large that minority might be. The NAACP purpose, he thought, should be that a "common denominator" must determine the political power of every state. If one state should

[84] *Guinn* v. *United States*, 238 U.S. 347 (1915); Board Minutes, NAACP, June 3, 1913; Ovington, *The Walls Came Tumbling Down*, pp. 116–17; Walter White, *A Man Called White: The Autobiography of Walter White* (New York, 1948), pp. 84-85. See Chapter II for a discussion of disfranchisement including the "grandfather clause."
[85] Board Minutes, NAACP, October 7, 1913; July 12, 1915; Minutes, Annual Meeting, January 3, 1916, in Board Minutes, NAACP; *Guinn* v. *United States*, 238 U.S. 347 (1915).
[86] Board Minutes, NAACP, July 12, 1915.

refuse to accept the concept of democracy which animates the rest, it should, by this refusal, forfeit any favored treatment it received.

Spingarn believed that consideration of the reduction of representation should not be related solely to disfranchisement of the Negro, but should take into account disfranchisement for sex, color, property, or for any other reason. Storey advised the Association that enforcement of the Fourteenth Amendment was both legal and feasible, but Spingarn thought it possible that the NAACP might not be the best agent to work for enforcement, because of the animosity which might be created in many minds. He believed it would be necessary for the women of America to secure the vote by constitutional amendment, before the greater reform could be accomplished.[87]

The NAACP worked for the passage of the woman's suffrage amendment and attempted to cooperate with leaders of the movement, though there were occasional clashes between the two groups. In 1911, Du Bois wrote a pamphlet on disfranchisement for the National American Woman's Suffrage Association and on more than one occasion devoted an entire issue of *The Crisis* to the subject. He considered his address to the National Suffrage Convention in Philadelphia one of the most important lectures he had given during 1912.[88]

We have already seen that Villard and his family were interested in woman's suffrage. Other NAACP leaders who were active in the movement were Florence Kelley, Lillian Wald, Jane Addams, Inez Milholland, Martha Gruening, Mary White Ovington, Verina Morton-Jones, Addie W. Hunton, Adella Hunt Logan, Mary Church Terrell, and the Spingarns.

Woman's suffrage leaders, however, were sometimes hostile to the cause of the Negro. In 1911, Martha Gruening accused Anna Howard Shaw of refusing to allow a Negro delegate to the Louisville suffrage convention to introduce a resolution which condemned disfranchisement on grounds of both color and sex, and to which was appended a declaration of "sympathy with black men and women who are fighting the same battle." Mrs. Shaw denied that she had intentionally prevented the colored delegate from speaking, but Martha Gruening reported that Mrs. Shaw had written her that, in a Southern state, suffragists should not present any resolutions that might endanger the success of the convention.[89]

---

[87] Minutes, Annual Meeting, January 3, 1916, in Board Minutes, NAACP. A year later, through Milholland's efforts, legislation was introduced into Congress by Republican Senator Jacob H. Gallinger of New Hampshire, "looking toward the reduction of Southern representation." Board Minutes, NAACP, February 13, 1917.

[88] Du Bois, "Report of Department of Publicity and Research, September 1, 1910 to January 1, 1912"; "Annual Report of the Director of Publicity and Research for 1912," W. E. B. Du Bois Papers (now in the possession of Mrs. W. E. B. Du Bois, New York City); *Crisis*, IV (September, 1912); X (August, 1915).

[89] *Crisis*, III (March, 1912), 195–96; IV (June, 1912), 77.

At the height of the woman's suffrage battle in 1919, the Association clashed with Alice Paul, head of the National Woman's Party, who reportedly had said that all this talk of Negro women voting in South Carolina was nonsense, and that the Woman's Party was organizing white, not colored, women in that state. Attempts by the Association to get Miss Paul to retract or repudiate the statement were futile.[90]

The Board recorded its opposition to any alteration of the "Susan B. Anthony Amendment" which would have resulted in leaving its enforcement in the hands of the states. When the amendment was finally submitted to the states by Congress, *The Crisis* triumphantly predicted that colored women would now be able to vote.[91]

While the NAACP fought segregation and discrimination and sought the enfranchisement of women, it also moved against lynching and mob violence, the ugliest forms of extra-legal action used to intimidate and control Negroes.

[90] Board Minutes, NAACP, March 10, 1919.
[91] Board Minutes, NAACP, April 14, 1919; June 9, 1919; *Crisis*, XVIII (July, 1919), 131.

CHAPTER X

Lynching and Mob Violence

The NAACP was founded in response to an incident of mob violence. The crusade against similar horrors continued to be a motivating force behind the Association's work. The violence was a conspicuous manifestation of the degradation of the Negro brought about by various forms of discrimination, segregation, and Jim Crow. In the early days of the Association much energy was expended in the attempt to prevent the spread and increase of these extreme manifestations of racial conflict. Calling public attention to the shamefulness of mob violence in modern society was the foremost task of the NAACP. Sensationalism in the press distorted the role of the Negro and was in large measure responsible for many of the race riots and other forms of mob violence which took place with increasing frequency and savagery and reached a climax in 1919.[1]

The most hideous form of mob violence was lynching. *The Crisis* published the lynching toll annually, although accurate statistics were difficult to obtain. *The Crisis* claimed that at least one hundred persons were lynched in 1911, but the *Chicago Tribune* reported only sixty-three. In 1912, according to *The Crisis*, sixty-three persons were lynched and in 1913, seventy-nine. The *Chicago Tribune* reported fifty-four in 1914; Tuskegee Institute, which also collected lynching statistics, reported fifty-two, and *The Crisis*, seventy-five, including four Negro women and five white persons.[2]

[1] Minutes, Executive Committee, April 11, 1911; May 2, 1911, in "Minute Book of the Board of Directors of the National Association for the Advancement of Colored People" (now in the Manuscript Division, Library of Congress; hereafter referred to as Board Minutes, NAACP).

[2] NAACP, *Thirty Years of Lynching in the United States: 1889–1918* (New York, 1919), pp. 7, 10; Mary White Ovington, *The Walls Came Tumbling Down* (New York, 1947), p. 150; *Crisis*, III (November, 1911), 34; "First Annual Meeting of the Corporations" [First Annual Report, 1911], in *Crisis*, III (February, 1912), 157; *Crisis* III (March, 1912), 208.

209

Lynchings occurred in twelve Southern and Border states. The largest number took place in Mississippi (fifteen), Louisiana (thirteen), and Kentucky (eleven). Thirty persons were lynched for the alleged crime of murder; eight for rape, attempted rape, or presence in a woman's room; five for theft; two for arson; and one for resistance to search. Thirteen were killed by rioters and night riders. Mob violence often took the form of dynamitings and incendiary fires.[3]

A study of available records from 1889 to 1918, published by the NAACP, reveal that in this thirty-year period 3,224 persons, including 61 women, were lynched. Walter White some years later pointed out that each decade from 1900 through 1927 had shown a decline in lynching but that with the decline came greatly aggravated brutality, and the victims suffered almost unbelievable tortures. He held that fundamentalist religious sects in the South contributed to violence by releasing dangerous passions and contributing to the emotional instability which played a part in lynching.[4]

In the fight against lynching and mob violence, the Association tried to help the unjustly accused. They tried to see that lynchers were punished and attempted to prevent lynching by bringing about a change in public opinion. To accomplish this they did research for objective information, brought pressure to bear on national and state governments, and tried (but failed) to mobilize Southern white leadership. They fought for legislation to make lynching a crime punishable by the federal government, and in so doing achieved not the legislation, but the publicity they desired.

FIVE YEARS OF MOB VIOLENCE, 1911–15

The spring and summer of 1911 were marked by a series of especially brutal lynchings. In May a barbarous lynching in Livermore, Kentucky, galvanized the Association into action. Newspapers reported that a Negro charged with the murder of a white man was taken to the so-called opera house and tied on the stage. Regular admission fees were charged for those who wished to witness the lynching, the receipts going to the family of the murdered man. Those who purchased orchestra seats were allowed to empty their revolvers into the swaying body. Holders of gallery tickets were limited to a single shot.

[3] *Crisis*, IX (February, 1915), 196–98; (February, 1916), 198; Minutes, Executive Committee, December 12, 1911, in Board Minutes, NAACP; Board Minutes, NAACP, February 14, 1916; Minutes, Annual Meeting, January 2, 1917, in Board Minutes, NAACP.
[4] Walter White, *Rope and Faggot: A Biography of Judge Lynch* (New York, 1929), pp. 19, 304. White cites the frequency of lynching as follows:

1890–1900	1,665
1900–1910	921
1910–1920	840
1920–1927	304

The horrified NAACP Executive Committee appealed to government officials for action. A memorial, presented to the President of the United States, the Vice-President, the Speaker of the House, and the chairmen of the Judiciary Committees of the Senate and House, was released to the Associated Press and the newspapers. The resolution of protest implored the President to send a special message to Congress, asking for action against the "foul blot" and "intolerable conditions of Lynch Law."[5]

A committee of ten citizens of Washington, D.C., headed by Archibald Grimke, presented the resolution to President Taft, who replied that he was powerless to take any action, since this was a matter for the individual states. Oswald Garrison Villard, as chairman of the NAACP Executive Committee, wrote to the governor of Kentucky and spoke before the Ethical Culture Society in Philadelphia about the lynching and the unsuccessful attempt to move the President to action.[6]

Booker T. Washington worked quietly until his death in 1915, using his influence against extension of lynching. He was more outspoken on this subject than on problems of civil rights. Typically he saw the brighter side, emphasizing any gesture of a Southern white to punish crimes against Negroes. In May, 1911, he wrote to Villard, Robert R. Moton, and Lyman Abbott of *The Outlook*, calling their attention to a decision of the Supreme Court of Alabama, which resulted in the removal of a sheriff from office for permitting the lynching of a Negro committed to his custody. The action of the court brought unstinting praise from Washington. "Nothing could be better or braver," he wrote. Alabama Governor Emmett O'Neal, who later became associated with NAACP efforts to eliminate lynching, also received an accolade for dismissing the sheriff.[7] It was doubtless due to Washington's influence that *The Outlook* in 1911 published what Miss Ovington called a fine article regarding the lynching of six Negro men taken from the jail by a mob at Lake City, Florida.[8]

One approach of the NAACP to bring an end to mob violence was to put pressure on state officials and to give publicity to their activities. Villard wrote Governor Albert W. Gilchrist about the Lake City lynchings. He also communicated with seventy-five prominent members of the Association, urging them to write the governor as well as their local newspapers. He confirmed the facts

[5] Minutes, Executive Committee, May 2, 1911, in Board Minutes, NAACP.
[6] Minutes, Executive Committee, June 6, 1911, in Board Minutes, NAACP.
[7] Booker T. Washington to Oswald Garrison Villard, May 27, 1911; Washington to R. R. Moton, May 27, 1911; Washington to Lyman Abbott, May 27, 1911, Booker T. Washington Papers (Manuscript Division, Library of Congress).
[8] Ovington to J. E. Spingarn, June 9, 1911, Joel Elias Spingarn Papers (Moorland Foundation, Howard University); "Lynching and Southern Sentiment: From a Southern Correspondent," *Outlook*, XC (June 10, 1911), 289–91.

of the case from an instructor at Florida Institute at Tallahassee and sent an accurate account to forty newspapers throughout the country.[9]

Governor Gilchrist answered all who wrote to him with an identical letter, which appeared to lack hostility or antagonism. He explained that, although he had limited funds at his disposal, he would offer a reward and employ such detective force as he could with the money at hand. Miss Ovington was sure the governor was insincere since he did not have a good record for administering justice.[10]

A third case concerned the lynching of a mother and daughter by an Oklahoma mob. Protests sent to the governor of Oklahoma were ignored.[11]

In the summer of 1911, the terrorism spread to the North. Like the Springfield riot of 1908, the Coatesville, Pennsylvania, lynching shocked and aroused NAACP leaders even more than the lynchings in the Southern and Border states. Zach Walker, a Negro, was wounded in a fight with a Coatesville policeman, whom he killed. He pleaded self-defense. At a prearranged signal, on August 12, 1911, Walker was taken from the hospital by a mob, dragged through the streets of the town, and burned alive. The NAACP Executive Committee at once began a prolonged and costly investigation, for the first time making use of professional detectives in the hope of providing evidence for a conviction.[12]

The Association kept a close watch over the investigation and legal proceedings. One Board member, William Sinclair, who had followed the case daily, believed that the prosecuting attorney had done his duty.[13] Serious doubts were aroused among other Board members. Mrs. Maclean went to Coatesville to investigate. She reported as incorrect the impression that the prosecuting attorney had done everything in his power to bring the lynchers to justice. She found that the trial had not been completed, that important witnesses for the prosecution had never been called to testify, and that several suspects had not been brought to trial. She was convinced there was enough new evidence to reopen the case. As a result of her report, the NAACP Executive Committee voted to guarantee one-half of a lawyer's fee to reopen the case. The remaining portion

[9] Minutes, Executive Committee, June 6, 1911, in Board Minutes, NAACP.
[10] Albert W. Gilchrist to Spingarn, June 9, 1911; Ovington to J. E. Spingarn, June 9, 1911, J. E. Spingarn Papers (Howard).
[11] Minutes, Executive Committee, June 6, 1911, in Board Minutes, NAACP.
[12] Crisis, V (February, 1913), 192; Albert J. Nock, "What We All Stand for: The Significance of the Behavior of a Community toward Its Citizens Who Burned a Man Alive," American Magazine, LXXV (February, 1913), 53–57; Ovington, The Walls Came Tumbling Down, pp. 113–14.
[13] Minutes, Executive Committee, October 16, 1911, in Board Minutes, NAACP. Sinclair's father, a member of the South Carolina legislature during Reconstruction days, had been lynched. Ovington, The Walls Came Tumbling Down, p. 130.

of the fee was to be raised by citizens who had promised Mrs. Maclean cooperation.[14]

The Association employed the William J. Burns detective agency to secure
evidence against the lynchers, and agents were sent to Coatesville, where they
opened a restaurant as a screen for their activities. Villard assumed personal
liability for the initial fee. The Burns agency reported that the district attorney
had been in league with the lynchers from the beginning and that the state had
given up the prosecution of the case.[15]

In September, 1912, Wherry, the Association's attorney, Albert J. Nock of the
American Magazine, Villard, and William J. Burns traveled to Harrisburg to
present their findings to the governor of Pennsylvania, John K. Tener. The
governor was sincere and straightforward, according to Villard, and promised to
further the prosecution of the ringleaders.[16]

The trip to Harrisburg convinced Nock that the *American Magazine* should
print the Association's story, and he went to Coatesville to gather local color.
He made a public indictment of the community in his article, "What We All
Stand for: The Significance of the Behavior of a Community Toward Its Citizens Who Burned a Man Alive." Because of the conspiracy of silence, wrote
Nock, even the detectives failed to ferret out the ringleaders, and the verdict of
not guilty for the accused brought forth an ovation. To Nock both the lynching
and the attitudes condoning it were the result of a community life lacking elements of civilization. Like so many other industrial communities, Coatesville had
produced *"an upper class materialized, a middle class vulgarized, a lower class
brutalized."*[17]

Meanwhile, on the first anniversary of the lynching, John Jay Chapman, grandson of an abolitionist, and himself called a belated abolitionist, held a prayer
meeting of three in a vacant store in Coatesville. When Francis Garrison learned
that no resident of Coatesville had attended the prayer meeting, he wrote that
"the earth should yawn and swallow the whole community."[18]

---

[14] Minutes, Executive Committee, December 12, 1911, in Board Minutes, NAACP; Ovington,
The Walls Came Tumbling Down, p. 114.
[15] Villard to Francis Jackson Garrison, January 29, 1912; May 4, 1912, Oswald Garrison
Villard Papers (Houghton Library, Harvard University); Ovington, *The Walls Came
Tumbling Down*, p. 114.
[16] Villard to Garrison, September 26, 1912, Villard Papers; *Crisis*, V (February, 1913), 192.
[17] Villard to Garrison, September 26, 1912, Villard Papers; Nock, "What We All Stand for,"
pp. 54, 57.
[18] Villard to Garrison, September 26, 1912; Garrison to Villard, September 27, 1912, Villard
Papers. Chapman's address can be found in Jacques Barzun (ed.), *The Selected Writings of
John Jay Chapman* (New York, 1957), pp. 255–58. For events leading up to Chapman's
prayer meeting, see Barzun's introduction, pp. v–ix. See also John Jay Chapman, "Address
at a prayer meeting held in Coatesville, Pennsylvania," in *Harper's Weekly*, LVI (September
21, 1916), 6.

The Association held an anti-lynching rally in New York to raise money to continue the investigation and the prosecution of the lynchers. To link the old abolitionist movement with the new, Villard asked John Lovejoy Elliot to preside.[19]

Although it proved impossible to reopen the case, the NAACP scored a partial victory when Governor Tener recommended to the legislature that the charter of Coatesville be revoked, because the inhabitants had been "consorting with and shielding murderers."[20] Villard attributed the warmth of his message to NAACP activity in Coatesville.

The Philadelphia branch, assisted by friends of the Association in the Pennsylvania State Legislature, made energetic efforts to secure the adoption of a law similar to that of Ohio's, which made a county liable for damage inflicted by mob violence. Under the Ohio law a sheriff whose prisoner fell into the hands of a mob was immediately relieved of office. Similar legislation failed to pass in Pennsylvania. An anti-lynching bill was drawn up by J. C. Brinsmade at the national office, based on laws in force in Ohio, Illinois, Kansas, and Indiana. It also failed to pass.[21]

Publicity following investigation was the most frequently used weapon in the fight against lynching. Villard wrote editorials for publications such as *Century Illustrated Monthly Magazine*, and was instrumental in getting Albert J. Nock and John Jay Chapman to publicize the Coatesville crime. When Anne Bostwick, a Negro woman, was lynched at Cordele, Georgia, Villard gave publicity to the investigator's report in the *New York Evening Post*, and the story was sent to the Associated Press for national distribution.[22] Joel Spingarn was also active in calling attention to the wave of lynchings and the work the Association was doing in behalf of the Negro. He persuaded James Oppenheim to visit Bluefield, West Virginia, and to write an article on the lynching of Robert Johnson, which took place in that town in September, 1912.[23]

Sometimes publicity was denied. The state of Georgia was the scene of large-scale efforts in several counties to drive out Negroes and seize their property. In 1912 it was reported that in Forsyth and Dawson Counties the entire colored population was displaced. At the suggestion of William English Walling, Du

[19] Villard to Garrison, December 14, 1912, Villard Papers; *Crisis*, V (February, 1913), 192–93.

[20] *Crisis*, V (February, 1913), 192.

[21] Board Minutes, NAACP, February 4, 1913; April 1, 1913; October 6, 1914; May Childs Nerney to Spingarn, May 27, 1913, J. E. Spingarn Papers (Howard).

[22] Villard to Garrison, September 26, 1912, Villard Papers; Board Minutes, NAACP, July 2, 1912; "If Lincoln Could Return," unsigned editorial in *Century Illustrated Monthly Magazine*, LXXXV (November, 1912), 153–54.

[23] Nerney to Spingarn, October 15, 1912, J. E. Spingarn Papers (Howard); James Oppenheim, "The Lynching of Robert Johnson," *Independent*, LXXIII (October 10, 1912), 823–27, 864.

Bois investigated and discovered that white farmers throughout Cobb County had received anonymous letters demanding that their Negro tenants be dismissed. When a storekeeper ignored a threatening note, his store was burned to the ground. Although Joseph Pulitzer's *New York World* supported most major reform movements of the period, Miss Nerney reported that Pulitzer had informed her that a series of articles on conditions in northern Georgia would not be of sufficient news value to warrant space in his paper.[24]

In 1916, before he became the Association's secretary, Royal Nash, formerly a forester, was sent by Spingarn to investigate suspected acts of arson in Cherokee County, Georgia, said to be aimed at driving out Negroes. Assuming the role of a forester looking for timber, Nash was able to travel through the back country and talk to the natives without divulging his true purpose. In Forsyth County he found that a mob had lynched a Negro accused of rape and had then attacked Negroes throughout the county to drive them from the area. Nash concluded that the Forsyth County disturbances were based on competition between "crackers" and Negroes known to be industrious, law-abiding, and reliable. He claimed that, as a result of threatening letters, malicious burnings, and reprisals against employers, 2,100 Negroes out of a total population of 13,000 had fled the county, leaving the whites secure in their monopoly of the labor market. Many of these Negroes settled in adjacent counties, one of which was Cherokee County, where the fires of December, 1915, had started. There, unsettled conditions and the spreading of fear among the Negro population had an adverse effect on the economics of the county. Finding their chief labor supply affected and made more expensive, the white middle class appealed to the governor. The sheriff then took decisive action and within twenty-four hours the violence subsided.[25]

The lynching of a white man in the summer of 1915 called attention to a significant court decision which the Association was instrumental in eventually having overruled. Leo Frank was removed from the Georgia state prison and lynched by a mob following the commutation of his death sentence to life imprisonment by the governor. Frank, a Jew and a New Yorker, had been convicted of the rape-murder of a white girl who worked in his factory in Atlanta. He had been tried and condemned to death in a court intimidated by an armed mob in which anti-Semitic and anti-Northern prejudices were clearly evident. His case was appealed to the United States Supreme Court, which upheld the verdict on grounds that "as long as a state court observed the form of a trial the federal government had no right to go beyond the form and inquire into the

---

[24] Board Minutes, NAACP, January 7, 1913; February 4, 1913; February 14, 1916; *Crisis*, V (March, 1913), 247.
[25] Board Minutes, NAACP, February 14, 1916; Royal F. Nash to Spingarn, January 23, 1916, J. E. Spingarn Papers (Howard); Minutes, Annual Meeting, January 2, 1917, in Board Minutes, NAACP; Roy Nash, "The Cherokee Fires," *Crisis*, XI (March, 1916), 265–70.

spirit which animated the trial." The Court thus opened the door for what Walling called legal lynching.[26]

Shocked by Frank's murder, Villard wrote James Dillard that the report of this outrage was a summons to public duty and that the time had come for Southern men like Dillard to assume leadership of the struggle for law and order. Admitting that the North could be just as brutal as the South, Villard pointed out the difference: In the North people protested openly, organized, and tried for better things. He urged Dillard to lead and organize those in the South who did not care to act alone.[27]

NAACP leaders had tried at other times to persuade their liberal Southern friends to speak out. Attending a session of the Commission on the Negro in Athens, Georgia, in 1912, Joel Spingarn met J. D. Hammond, president of Paine College. This college, in Augusta, Georgia, was according to Mrs. Hammond one of few colleges for Negroes owned and operated by Southern whites. Following the meeting, at which problems of the South were openly discussed, Mrs. Hammond warned Spingarn that all that had been said had been said in confidence and that in public she spoke "differently" on the Negro question.[28]

Spingarn remarked that the Bleases and Vardamans were permitted to utter their thoughts freely, while those who represented the best thought of the South were forced to be silent, to which Mrs. Hammond replied that they were not cowards but would "speak out when the time comes—soon." Nevertheless, according to Villard, the Hammonds were driven out of Paine College by reason of their convictions.[29]

THE ANTI-LYNCHING CAMPAIGN

In February, 1916, Philip G. Peabody of Boston startled and electrified the Association by offering the NAACP $10,000, provided it could evolve an effective program to stamp out lynching. A committee of five was appointed to draw up a program for Peabody's consideration. Villard thought the money could be

---

[26] *Frank* v. *Mangum*, 237 U.S., 309 (1914); *Moore* v. *Dempsey*, 261 U.S., 86 (1923); *Crisis*, XXV (April, 1923), 258; Walter White, *A Man Called White: The Autobiography of Walter White*, New York, 1948), pp. 25–26.
[27] Villard to James H. Dillard, n.d. [August 18, 1915], Villard Papers.
[28] L. H. Hammond to Spingarn, December 26, 1912, J. E. Spingarn Papers (Howard). E. Clayton Calhoun to writer, April 26, 1966, confirms the statement as to the ownership of Paine College, as do James W. Lee, Naphtali Luccock, and James Main Dixon in *The Illustrated History of Methodism* (New York, 1900), pp. 660–61.
[29] Spingarn to L. H. Hammond, copy [December, 1912]; Hammond to Spingarn, January 4, 1913, J. E. Spingarn Papers (Howard); Villard to Dillard [August 18, 1915], Villard Papers. Hammond was president of Paine College from 1911 to 1915. Calhoun to writer, April 26, 1966.

LYNCHING AND MOB VIOLENCE

used as rewards for the apprehension and conviction of lynchers, but he later decided that this would instantly raise the cry of Northern interference.[30]

William English Walling, chairman of the Anti-Lynching Committee, reported the opinions of its members to the Board. Mrs. Kelley thought there would be little value in engaging Southerners to participate in anti-lynching work. She was in favor of continuing legal action, driving for federal anti-lynching legislation and reduction of Southern representation in Congress, and using the presidential campaign of 1916 to publicize the breakdown of democracy in the South.[31]

Du Bois proposed that the fund be used for a study of lynching, in which lynchings would be investigated as they occurred, public opinion in the South would be mobilized, and suits would be brought against negligent officials under existing laws. Dr. Owen M. Waller, however, felt that legal action had no chance of success anywhere in the South. He advocated that the Association seek to reach and mold the opinion of Southern student bodies.[32] Walling proposed enlisting the aid of the Southern Sociological Congress and similar organizations. Paul Kennaday agreed with Mrs. Kelley that neither persuasion nor an appeal to sentiment would in any way influence the South. He pressed for a program that would appeal to economic motives, arousing Chambers of Commerce to the costliness of lynching and to the hurt done to the labor market.[33]

Consensus of the meeting of the Anti-Lynching Committee was that the program should concern itself with three fields of activity: the gathering and compiling of facts; investigation of specific cases as they occurred; and, most important, organizing Southern business and political leaders who would speak out against lynching. The first step was to be the printing and distribution in the South of 50,000 copies of W. D. Weatherford's strong paper against lynching, prepared for the Southern Sociological Congress.[34]

Peabody, however, was not won over to the Association's program. Their study convinced him that $10,000 was too small a sum to accomplish the desired results. Because so-called outside interference in Southern affairs would not be tolerated, the NAACP would have to keep itself in the background of any work

[30] Board Minutes, NAACP, March 13, 1916; Villard to Dillard, February 29, 1916; May 18, 1916, Villard Papers.
[31] Board Minutes, NAACP, April 10, 1916.
[32] A Southerner, W. O. Scroggs, a professor at the University of Louisiana and member of the University Commission on Southern Race Questions, proposed that the Anti-Lynching Committee encourage Southern young people to think about the evils of lynching by offering prizes for "the best high school commencement orations and the best college essays on the subject." Board Minutes, NAACP, December 11, 1916.
[33] Board Minutes, NAACP, April 10, 1916.
[34] Board Minutes, NAACP, April 10, 1916; May 8, 1916. Weatherford was an official of the Southern YMCA. Villard called him one of the "fine young Southerners of the radical kind." Villard to Jane Addams, January 11, 1913, NAACP Files (Manuscript Division, Library of Congress).

that was undertaken, and Peabody did not like the idea of working in the dark. He wanted the Association to act in a direct open way, utilizing the Northern press to its fullest extent. He gave $1,000, promising that, if another $9,000 could be raised before August from people who were convinced he was wrong, he would then give another $1,000.

In spite of this setback, Storey urged the Association not to abandon the program, and promised an additional $1,000 when the NAACP had raised $8,000. Villard agreed to be chairman of a committee of three to raise the money. By the fifteenth of August, Peabody's deadline, they were still short of the goal. They asked for an extension of time and by October 7 had raised more than $10,000. Every group responded except the churches; both races contributed about equally.[35]

Three particularly savage lynchings in 1916 gave impetus to the campaign. The first was the case of Jesse Washington, a mentally retarded adolescent. Seized by a mob in a Waco, Texas, courtroom, where he had been found guilty and sentenced to death for murder of a white woman, he was taken to the public square, tortured, and burned alive before a crowd of 15,000 persons.[36]

To verify the facts, the committee called on Elizabeth Freeman, who was in Dallas on a speaking tour for the suffragists. She went immediately to Waco, where she spent ten days investigating the crime. Her report and photographs were used in an eight-page supplement to *The Crisis*. Entitled "The Waco Horror," this highly sensational supplement was used as the opening wedge in the drive for the Anti-Lynching Fund. It was distributed to 42,000 *Crisis* subscribers, to 700 white newspapers and fifty Negro weeklies, to all members of Congress, and to a list of 500 "moneyed men" in New York, who were asked to aid the campaign. Villard wrote personally to thirty prominent editors. To raise additional funds, the NAACP sent Miss Freeman on a lecture tour to report on what she had seen and heard at Waco.[37]

In the midst of the campaign, in August, 1916, a mass lynching took place near Gainesville, Florida. Five Negroes were murdered, two of them women. The trouble began with a quarrel between a Negro and a white man over a pig.

[35] Philip G. Peabody to Moorfield Storey, May 29, 1916, quoted in Board Minutes, NAACP, June 12, 1916; Storey to Nash, May 31, 1916, quoted in Board Minutes, NAACP, June 12, 1916; Board Minutes, NAACP, June 12, 1916; October 9, 1916; Minutes, Annual Meeting, January 2, 1917, in Board Minutes, NAACP.
[36] *New York Times*, May 16, 1916; Board Minutes, NAACP, June 12, 1916; "The Will to Lynch," editorial, *New Republic*, VIII (October 14, 1916), 261; Minutes, Annual Meeting, January 2, 1917, in Board Minutes, NAACP.
[37] Board Minutes, NAACP, June 12, 1916; July 10, 1916; Minutes, Annual Meeting, January 2, 1917, in Board Minutes, NAACP; *Washington Bee*, July 8, 1916. Other organizations circularized were the New York City Club (670 copies), the Indian Rights Association (600 copies), and the Intercollegiate Socialist Society (900 copies); copies were sent to 1,800 members of New York churches.

The local sheriff was called in, and the arrest took the form of a raid. The sheriff was shot. The mob then lynched the five Negroes, all of whom were innocent according to the editors of *The New Republic*, who called this atrocity to the attention of the Association and urged an investigation.[38]

In its editorial, *The New Republic* termed the psychological motive in lynching, a mere hunger for blood. In no sense was it the rough-and-ready justice of a frontier community, where courts of justice had not yet been established. It was rather a social orgy of cruelty, in which certain classes in the community expressed their hatred of a race they consider inferior, their contempt for the law, and their sense of Anglo-Saxon superiority. The editorial was good publicity for the NAACP's drive to marshal public opinion, not in a bitter or sectional spirit, but in a spirit of scientific investigation and diagnosis.[39]

Resentment of Negroes who acquired wealth and property was behind the lynching of Anthony Crawford at Abbeville, South Carolina, in November, 1916. Roy Nash investigated the case and found that Crawford, a well-to-do Negro farmer, had been jailed as a result of a dispute in which he had cursed a white man who had tried to defraud him. A mob broke into the jail and lynched Crawford. In this case, however, the "good citizens" of the town stepped in and prevented the lynching of the victim's family—nor was the family forced to abandon its property.[40]

Nash, in an article in *The Independent*, pointed out the significant aspects of the case: the fine character of Crawford (the "embodiment of the things that Booker T. Washington stood for"); the triviality of his offense; the fact that the Governor of South Carolina, Richard I. Manning, had demanded that the lynchers be tried; and the unanimous condemnation of the act by the South Carolina press. National attention was focused on the lynching and on the work of the Association when Nash's article was copied by Southern papers and received considerable editorial comment in the North. The lynchers never came to trial, however; the grand jury refused to indict them.[41]

Another technique used by the Association was to praise and reward those who averted lynching. At Lima, Ohio, the sheriff prevented a mob from seizing a Negro prisoner on September 30, 1916. In honor of his courage and devotion to duty, the Association arranged a mass meeting at Columbus, where the governor

[38] *New Republic*, VIII (October 14, 1916), 261; Minutes, Annual Meeting, January 2, 1917, in Board Minutes, NAACP.
[39] *New Republic*, VIII (October 14, 1916), 262.
[40] Board Minutes, NAACP, November 13, 1916; Ovington, *The Walls Came Tumbling Down*, pp. 150–51.
[41] Roy Nash, "The Lynching of Anthony Crawford," *Independent*, LXXXVIII (December 11, 1916), 456–62; Minutes, Annual Meeting, January 2, 1917, in Board Minutes, NAACP; Board Minutes, NAACP, March 12, 1917.

of Ohio on behalf of the NAACP presented a silver trophy to Sheriff Sherman Eley before an audience of 1,200 persons.[42]

At the end of 1916, the chairman of the NAACP Board said in his annual report that the injection of lynching into the public conscience as a national problem was the most striking achievement of the year.[43]

With the conclusion of the drive, a committee of five was appointed to draw up plans for administering the Anti-Lynching Fund. Storey took an active part in the work of this committee, stressing the importance of persuading Southerners to organize themselves to fight lynching. The experience of the Coatesville trial had proved that no criminal prosecution could successfully be brought if such outrages were upheld by the community. Storey hoped the committee could arouse those Southerners who were ashamed of their "barbarous communities." He thought a conference of Southerners and people from Border states, plus a fair infusion of Northerners, would be able to air the subject and form an organization against it.[44]

When the Anti-Lynching Committee met in October, 1916, they agreed to continue the work already started. In an attempt to inject the lynching issue into the presidential campaign, they drew up an anti-lynching pamphlet which was distributed throughout the branches. Milholland arranged for additional distribution through Republican state headquarters.[45]

Next, the committee decided to engage an agent to travel through the South to enlist friends of the Association, to determine their strength, and to sponsor a conference of Southern leaders. Mrs. J. D. Hammond agreed to visit the principal cities to learn how many leaders of Southern opinion could be persuaded to attend the Conference. James Dillard assured Walling that he would call the conference as soon as the preliminary conversations were completed.[46]

In February, 1917, the Anti-Lynching Committee reported to the Board that Mrs. Hammond's trip had yielded unexpectedly favorable results,[47] but in spite of this encouragement the hoped-for conference of Southern leaders did not materialize. The United States soon became involved in the World War, and it was two years before an anti-lynching conference could be held. By that time

[42] Board Minutes, NAACP, December 11, 1917; January 8, 1917; Minutes, Annual Meeting, January 2, 1917, in Board Minutes, NAACP.
[43] Minutes, Annual Meeting, January 2, 1917, in Board Minutes, NAACP.
[44] Board Minutes, NAACP, October 9, 1916; Moorfield Storey to Nash, October 6, 1916; October 9, 1916, Moorfield Storey Papers (in the possession of Mr. Charles Storey, Boston, Massachusetts).
[45] Board Minutes, NAACP, November 13, 1916.
[46] Board Minutes, NAACP, December 11, 1916; January 8, 1917; February 13, 1917; May 14, 1917; Villard to Dillard, February 29, 1916; May 18, 1916, Villard Papers.
[47] Board Minutes, NAACP, February 13, 1917.

the climate of opinion toward the Negro had worsened, and the conference, held in the North, was composed largely of Northerners.

THE EAST ST. LOUIS RIOT AND THE GREAT MIGRATIONS

On June 11, 1917, the Director of Publications and Research reported to the Board that he planned to go to East St. Louis, Illinois, to study conditions in a community typical of those which were attracting migration from the South. Before a month had passed, however, a riot occurred in that "typical" city, during which hundreds of Negroes were shot or burned alive in their homes. A large amount of property was destroyed, and nearly 6,000 were made homeless. Negroes were blamed for the outbreak, and a number were charged with inciting the riot and with murder.[48]

The exodus of Negroes from the South to Northern cities, accepted as the underlying cause of the riot and of unrest in other urban areas, was greatly accelerated by the outbreak of World War I. Increased demand for labor in the prospering war industries of the North and dissatisfaction with conditions in the South led to a migration of such magnitude that observers both North and South were concerned.[49]

Disasters in the South, such as the floods of 1915 and the devastation of the cotton fields by the boll weevil, were the principal economic causes. Added to these were the fact that the flow of European immigrant labor had been cut to a trickle with the coming of the war, and the agents of Northern industry were active in the South. The abuse and degradation of Negroes by Southern whites had made life intolerable for thousands, who readily responded to the enticements of better jobs, higher pay, and more satisfactory living conditions in the North.[50]

[48] Board Minutes, NAACP, June 11, 1917; James Weldon Johnson, *Along This Way* (New York, 1933), pp. 319–20. There were conflicting reports of the number of deaths. *The Crisis* said 125. *Crisis*, XV (April, 1918), 269. The report of the Congressional investigating committee said "at least thirty-nine Negroes and eight white people killed outright, and hundreds of Negroes were wounded and maimed." United States House of Representatives, 65th Cong., 2d Sess., Document No. 1231, *East St. Louis Riots*, pp. 1–24. One investigation conducted for the Association estimated that 175 had died. NAACP, *Ninth Annual Report 1918* (New York, 1919), p. 89.

[49] Although it was to be expected that the white South would take steps to limit the migration of its labor supply, it came as a surprise when the United States Railway Administration, under the direction of Georgia-born William G. McAdoo, Secretary of the Treasury, issued an order preventing anyone in the North from prepaying the transportation of a Southern Negro who wished to come North. Through the efforts of the Association and the intervention of Senator Warren G. Harding and Representative Henry I. Emerson of Ohio, the Railway Administration finally rescinded its "extraordinary" order. *Crisis*, XIX (March, 1920), 243.

[50] NAACP, *Ninth Annual Report 1918*, p. 61; *Crisis*, XIV (June, 1917), 63–66; U.S. Department of Labor, Division of Negro Economics, *Negro Migration in 1916–1917* (reports by R. H. Leavell *et al.*; Washington, 1919), p. 11; and *The Negro at Work During the War and*

Earlier, Booker T. Washington had tried to encourage Southern Negroes to stay in the country and on the farm. White Southern business was not alone in feeling the pinch caused by the migrations. Negro professional men and Negro businesses, such as insurance companies, were also hurt. But the advice of the conservative Negro preacher, teacher and professional man could not stop the flood, which neared its peak in 1916.[51]

The editor of *The New Republic* saw, however, that the dissemination of the Negro throughout the United States, by bringing him economic and political power, would serve as an antidote to his nearly defenseless position in the South. *The Crisis* took issue with colored leaders who were urging Negroes to stay in the South. Instead, mass exodus was encouraged as the only effective protest the Negro could make against lynching and disfranchisement in that "devilish country."[52]

Robert Moton echoed Booker T. Washington at a biracial conference on migration held at Tuskegee in January, 1917. Villard, on the other hand, criticized the conference for playing into the hands of the white South—the planters and employers of labor. He approved of the migration and regretted only the lack of organization behind it. Though he was aware that the migration would intensify the race problem in the North, he recognized the fact that the problem would eventually have to be faced in the North as well as in the South.[53]

In the same month the Urban League held a conference on migration in New York City, where all schools of thought were represented. Present at the conference were experts on migration and immigration, including the Commissioner of Immigration, and representatives of railroads and industries which were employing large numbers of Southern Negroes. Villard, Joel Spingarn, and Butler Wilson represented the NAACP.[54]

Hollis B. Frissell, spokesman for Hampton and Tuskegee, was convinced that the best place for the mass of Negroes was in the South. He acknowledged that some migrants would prosper in the North and that this would make the South realize the economic value of the colored man, but he feared that many would be subjected to competition in the labor market and exposed to the struggle of city life.

Dissension broke out on the floor of the conference when Butler Wilson proposed that Negroes should be encouraged to migrate "until the South shall accord

---

Reconstruction: Second Study on Negro Labor (Washington, 1921). See also Henderson H. Donald, "The Negro Migration, 1916–18," *Journal of Negro History*, VI (October, 1921), 383–498, an M.A. dissertation for Yale University.

[51] R. R. Moton to Allen Potts, April 26, 1913, Washington Papers; *Washington Bee*, August 4, 1917.

[52] *New Republic*, VII (July 1, 1916), 213–14; *Crisis*, XII (October, 1916), 270.

[53] *New York Age*, January 25, 1917; February 1, 1917; March 1, 1917.

[54] *New York Age*, February 1, 1917.

them their political rights . . . protect them from mob violence, open to them school advantages and protect their women and children from intolerable persecution." Realizing that a bitter floor fight between the conservative and radical wings of the Negro movement would threaten the newly established harmony and good will engendered by the Amenia Conference, Spingarn offered a substitute proposal which Wilson refused to accept. The conservatives, however, defeated the radical measures. The resolutions adopted protested the exploitation and abuse of migrant labor by industrial employers. It was proposed that organizations be formed in the South to improve conditions and to encourage a fair attitude toward Negro labor. Other organizations were proposed for instructing migrants in regard to the dress and habits of living necessary in a Northern climate, the demands of Northern employers, and the dangers and opportunities of city life.[55]

At the same time, in Wilmington, Delaware, a meeting was called by whites disturbed by the exodus. The Negroes were asked if better schools, churches, and other facilities would be sufficient inducement for them to stay in the South. When the Negroes indicated they wanted the vote, the meeting broke up in confusion, according to Miss Ovington, who was pleased that *The Crisis* and the NAACP had had something to do with this vigorous stand.[56]

The NAACP authorized an investigation of the facts concerning the migration. Du Bois visited six Southern states and secured additional information through agents in nearly all parts of the South. To the surprise of the Board, the data showed the movement to be much larger in scope than they had believed possible. Du Bois estimated that 250,000 colored workmen had gone northward, and declared that the United States was witnessing a social change of great moment among American Negroes.[57]

The problems of the Northern Negro were compounded by the migrations. Industry hired Negroes only when they could not obtain other labor. Frequently Negroes were brought in as strikebreakers, which earned them the enmity of white workers who feared competition. Moreover, the opportunities for employment nowhere equaled the number of migrants flooding the cities in search of economic and social betterment and greater freedom. This led to the concentration of masses of Negroes in slums, with all the attendant poverty, disintegration of family life, and delinquency that slum life entails. Some Negroes became

---

[55] *Ibid.*
[56] Ovington to Spingarn, February 15, 1917, J. E. Spingarn Papers (Howard).
[57] Board Minutes, NAACP, February 13, 1917; March 12, 1917; April 9, 1917; May 14, 1917; June 11, 1917; *Crisis*, XIV (June, 1917), 63–66. For reprints of newspaper comment and editorials on the migration, see *Crisis*, XIII (February, 1917), 179–82. For articles on the "exodus," see *Crisis*, XIII (March, 1917), 233–35; *Crisis*, XIII (April, 1917), 290–91. For an analysis of Du Bois's article, see *Survey*, XXXVIII (June 2, 1917), 226–27.

tools of corrupt politicians. All these factors led to increased prejudice and increased racial tension in the cities.[58]

Thus the violence that broke out in East St. Louis on July 2, 1917, was not entirely unexpected. The city was Southern in its racial attitudes. It was a center for heavy industry, a major railroad junction, and the site of stockyards and meatpacking plants. Workers lived in slums adjacent to the factories. During 1916 the industries waged war on unionization, using Negro labor to prevent the organization of labor. Public opinion was inflamed with stories, deliberately circulated, of Negro crime and with the claim of the local Democratic machine that the Republicans had imported Negroes to vote in the 1916 election. It was rumored that Dr. Le Roy Bundy, a dentist and Negro Republican leader, was organizing Negro migrants to vote both in East St. Louis and in Chicago. As Illinois was considered by the Wilson Administration to be a doubtful state in the coming election, the President himself, the Department of Justice, and the Office of the Attorney General warned of a conspiracy, predicting that fraudulent voting might result from the transportation of Negroes from the South to doubtful Midwestern states in order to secure a Republican victory.[59]

Martha Gruening and Du Bois went to East St. Louis to investigate the riot. Their reports brought to light the nature of the community where the riot took place, an area friendly to the criminal element of both races, where because of political corruption both could get protection.

When trouble started, city officials were ineffectual in coping with the situation and the militia was called in. There was evidence that some of the militia forced escaping Negroes into the hands of the mob.[60]

When news of the trouble reached the NAACP, the Board authorized Arthur Spingarn's legal committee to take appropriate action. The St. Louis branch cooperated by handling the investigation and the Chicago branch took charge of the legal action. At St. Louis, Du Bois organized a volunteer committee of twenty-five to take testimony. The NAACP took steps to bring suit against the city and county governments, and petitioned the governor of Illinois to remove the Sheriff of East St. Louis for failure to do his duty. Charles Nagel, former

[58] Gunnar Myrdal, *An American Dilemma: The Negro Problem and Modern Democracy* (New York, 1944), pp. 192–96; John Hope Franklin, *From Slavery to Freedom: A History of American Negroes* (2d ed.; New York, 1965), p. 429.
[59] Elliott M. Rudwick, *Race Riot at East St. Louis, July 2, 1917* (Carbondale, 1964), pp. 4–26. As early as 1912, Du Bois had pointed out in *The Crisis* that the Negro vote of Illinois, Indiana, Ohio, and New York could determine the presidential election. *Crisis*, IV (September, 1912), 236.
[60] Board Minutes, NAACP, September 17, 1917; *Crisis*, XIV (September, 1917), 219–38; Martha Gruening, "Democratic Massacres in East St. Louis," *Pearson's Magazine*, XXXVIII (September, 1917), 106–8; Oscar Leonard and Forrester B. Washington, "Welcoming Southern Negroes: East St. Louis and Detroit—A Contrast," *Survey*, XXXVIII (July 13, 1917), 331–35.

Secretary of Commerce under Taft, was engaged to supervise the defense of the ten Negroes indicted, but their trial led to their conviction for murder. Upon appeal, their conviction was upheld by the Supreme Court of Illinois.[61]

In the course of the testimony, Dr. Le Roy Bundy was implicated in the murders. He was then brought to trial. To the white community he was an aggressive type of Negro and an outspoken champion of the cause of equal rights. Moreover he had won the enmity of union leaders by criticizing the exclusion of Negroes from labor unions.[62]

Bundy alienated NAACP support when he refused to allow the national office to direct the conduct of his case. The Association became particularly concerned when Bundy, released on bail, went on tour, addressing Negro audiences and collecting funds for which he refused to give the NAACP adequate accounting. The Association therefore withdrew from the case. Bundy's trial resulted in his conviction, but upon appeal to the Illinois Supreme Court the judgment was reversed and the case was sent back to the lower court for a new trial. The state, recognizing the weakness of its case, never retried Bundy.[63]

To finance the defense and provide for Negroes in East St. Louis left destitute, the Association raised a special fund, and broadened the scope of the Anti-Lynching Fund, which now became the Anti-Lynching and Mob Violence Fund. Peabody agreed to a more liberal interpretation of the word lynching in connection with the fund, and as a result lynching was defined as "not only the illegal killing of an accused person, but also the killing of an accused person by mob violence."[64]

One significant reaction in the Negro world to the East St. Louis riot was the financial aid given to the NAACP for the first time by several of the great Negro secret and fraternal organizations, which had previously held aloof from the NAACP. Though the amounts were not large, contributions from these fraternal bodies later became an important element of support.[65]

[61] Board Minutes, NAACP, July 9, 1917; September 17, 1917; July 8, 1918; Ovington to Spingarn, September 29, 1917, J. E. Spingarn Papers (Howard); Johnson *Along This Way*, p. 320. In contrast most of the white rioters indicted were tried and let off with light sentences. Only four were convicted of murder. Rudwick, *Race Riot at East St. Louis*, pp. 94–98.

[62] *Washington Bee*, December 1, 1917; Board Minutes, NAACP, December 10, 1917; Rudwick, *Race Riot at East St. Louis*, pp. 111–21.

[63] Board Minutes, NAACP, June 10, 1918; July 8, 1918; September 9, 1918; October 14, 1918; *Crisis*, XVI (September, 1918), 224–25; XXV (November, 1922), 16–21; Rudwick, *Race Riot at East St. Louis*, p. 131.

[64] Board Minutes, NAACP, November 12, 1917; December 10, 1917; *New York Age*, November 29, 1917.

[65] Board Minutes, NAACP, October 8, 1917; September 17, 1917. The secret fraternal organizations pledging and giving aid were: the Knights of Pythias of Illinois, $100; the Knights of Pythias of Missouri, which levied an assessment of 25 cents on each member for a contribution to the Association; the Court of Calanthe of Ohio, women's division of the Knights of Pythias, which sent $50, indicating this was to become an annual contribution; and the Grand Lodge of Free and Accepted Masons of the State of Colorado, which sent $50.

In the early summer of 1917, a Negro named Ell Persons, suspected of being an "ax murderer," was burned alive in Memphis. James Weldon Johnson spent ten days in Memphis but found no direct evidence that Persons was guilty. Following the investigation, Johnson attended a meeting at St. Philip's Church in New York, called jointly by a number of organizations planning a public protest against the lynching.[66]

In the meantime, the East St. Louis riot erupted and the protest developed into a demonstration against the mass murders as well. Johnson credits Villard with the idea of a silent protest parade instead of a mass meeting.[67] The group accepted this idea and evolved as a nonpartisan citizens' movement—the "Silent Protest Parade." The NAACP claimed a good share of the credit for its success.[68] Between eight and ten thousand men, women, and children took part in the parade on Saturday, July 28, 1917. The march was accompanied only by the sound of muffled drums. Marchers carried banners and signs protesting lynching and mob violence. Circulars protesting discrimination, segregation, Jim Crow, and disfranchisement were distributed to the twenty thousand persons along the line of march.[69]

Because of Johnson's skill, tact, and diplomacy, the Silent Protest Parade organization did not adjourn when its work was done, but merged with the New York branch of the NAACP. Some prominent New York Negroes were thus drawn into the Association for the first time.[70]

Because of the widespread publicity given to the East St. Louis riots, Congress appointed an investigating committee which determined that interstate commerce and travel had been disrupted by the rioting. An inquiry into details of labor and race conflict was then authorized.[71] Congressman L. C. Dyer of Missouri was

---

[66] Board Minutes, NAACP, June 11, 1917; July 9, 1917; Johnson, *Along This Way*, p. 317.

[67] Minutes, Annual Meeting, January 7, 1918, in Board Minutes, NAACP. Johnson later said the meeting originated in a protest against the East St. Louis riot. Johnson, *Along This Way*, p. 320.

[68] Minutes, Annual Meeting, January 7, 1918, in Board Minutes, NAACP, September 17, 1917; *Washington Bee*, August 4, 1917. Four of the officers of the parade organization were prominent in the NAACP: The Reverend Hutchins C. Bishop, president, was a Board member; John E. Nail, Johnson's brother-in-law, was treasurer and also treasurer of the New York NAACP branch; Johnson was second vice-president, and an NAACP member; E. W. Daniel, was a member of the parade executive committee.

[69] *New York Times*, July 29, 1917; "Negroes March with Muffled Drums," *Survey*, XXXVIII (August 4, 1917), 405–6; Johnson, *Along This Way*, pp. 320–21.

[70] Board Minutes, NAACP, November 12, 1917; Ovington to Villard, October 5, 1917, Villard Papers.

[71] *Crisis*, XV (January, 1918), 116–21; *New York Times*, July 2, 1917; July 3, 1917; William Allen White, "Swing Low, Sweet Chariot," *Emporia Gazette*, July 3, 1917, reprinted in *La Follette's Magazine*, IX (August, 1917), 13, as "The Tragedy of the Colored Folk," and in *Washington Bee*, September 8, 1917.

helpful in preventing suppression of the report and told Spingarn that he intended to introduce a bill before Congress making lynching a Federal offense.[72]

PROTESTS AND LEGISLATION

John Shillady tried to bring lynchings to the attention of the federal government. When Jim McIllheron was tortured with red-hot irons and burned alive
on Lincoln's birthday in 1918 at Estill Springs, Tennessee, Shillady sent a telegram of protest to President Wilson. The President's secretary referred the
telegram to the Attorney General, who replied that the federal government had
no jurisdiction because the crime was in no way connected with the war effort.
Shillady again wrote Wilson, urging him to make a public statement condemning
lynching for the sake of the tremendously stimulating effect this would have on
the morale of colored people.[73]

In spite of Shillady's messages, Wilson did not hear of the Estill Springs affair
until James Weldon Johnson mentioned it at a White House interview. The
Association had already tried to persuade Wilson to mention lynching in his
second inaugural address, but without success. Johnson again pressed this point
and after much urging Wilson finally promised that he would "seek an opportunity" to say something on the subject.[74]

To increase the pressure on the President, Shillady sent letters and telegrams
to forty-four of the most active NAACP branches, urging members to write or
telegraph Wilson, asking that he condemn lynching in his Fourth of July address
to the nation. In West Virginia, Mordecai W. Johnson, head of the Charleston
branch of the NAACP and later president of Howard University, succeeded in
persuading the governor and two judges of the West Virginia Supreme Court
and other influential white and colored citizens to send telegrams. Again the
President ignored the pleas.[75]

Wilson finally made a public statement on July 26, 1918, asking the governors
of all states, law officers, and, above all, the men and women of every community
to cooperate "not passively merely, but actively and watchfully" to bring an end

[72] Board Minutes, NAACP, March 11, 1918; *Congressional Record*, 65th Cong., 2d Sess.,
LVI, Part 2, 1653–55; *Washington Bee*, March 16, 1918. Representative Benjamin Johnson
tried to keep the "full testimony" of the hearings from being published. He said about "fifty
corpses had been viewed." Dyer and others wanted the full testimony published and insisted
that several hundred had died in the riot. *Congressional Record*, LVI, Part 2, 1653–55. The
report, without pictures, was ordered to be printed July 15, 1918. U.S., House, 65th Cong.,
2d Sess., Document No. 1231, *East St. Louis Riots*.
[73] Johnson, *Along This Way*, p. 329; Ovington, *The Walls Came Tumbling Down*, pp. 145–59;
Crisis, XV (April, 1918), 281.
[74] Board Minutes, NAACP, January 8, 1917; February 13, 1917; Johnson, *Along This Way*,
pp. 323–34.
[75] Board Minutes, NAACP, July 8, 1918.

to lynching, which could not "live where the community does not countenance it." The Board rejoiced in the President's message, and ordered 50,000 copies to be printed and distributed.[76]

In a letter written by Du Bois, the Association also sought to bring pressure to bear on the Attorney General of the United States, Thomas W. Gregory, calling his attention to the relationship between the number of lynchings that had taken place since he assumed office and his attitude that the federal government had no jurisdiction in cases of lynching. Why, Du Bois asked, was the federal government able to take action when a German, Robert Prager, was lynched on April 4, 1918, in Collinsville, Illinois, but unable to intervene in the case of colored American citizens? Gregory's only response came in an address to the Executive Committee of the American Bar Association in May, 1918, recommending an educational campaign against lynching and mob violence.[77]

A month later lynching and mob violence was once more forcefully brought to the attention of the legal profession by Moorfield Storey in an address to the Wisconsin Bar Association entitled "The Negro Question." Referring to the conspiracy of silence, he asked: "What college president, what orator at Commencement, takes the evil of lynching as his subject?" In response to Storey's eloquence, the Wisconsin Bar Association passed a resolution expressing unqualified condemnation of mob violence toward the colored race and calling upon the profession to invoke the law and suppress the rule of the mob.[78]

Shillady also took strenuous action to bring lynching before state officials. The Estill Springs atrocity was only one of three burnings in Tennessee within a nine-month period. Shillady not only sent Governor Tom C. Rye a telegram of protest but wrote him that the Association could, if necessary, make funds available to the state for an investigation at Estill Springs. This was followed by telegrams to the two United States Senators from Tennessee, to the Representative of the Third District, and to six Chambers of Commerce in Tennessee cities. After inquiring what Tennessee proposed to do to vindicate her law and clear her name in regard to the torturing and burning at Estill Springs, Shillady asked bluntly, "Do you stand for law, or do you approve mob violence?" The governor responded, deploring the murder; the Chamber of Commerce of Chattanooga answered with a resolution censuring mob violence; and the *Nashville Banner* printed an editorial condemning the burning.[79]

[76] NAACP, *Ninth Annual Report 1918*, p. 25; John R. Shillady to Spingarn, July 30, 1918, J. E. Spingarn Papers (Howard); *Crisis*, XVI (September, 1918), 227–28. Text of the "open letter" is in *Independent*, LCV (August 10, 1918), 172.
[77] Board Minutes, NAACP, May 13, 1918; *Washington Bee*, May 25, 1918.
[78] Storey, *The Negro Question: An Address Delivered before the Wisconsin Bar Association, June 27, 1918* (New York, n.d.), pp. 1–2, 25. This same complaint "he was fond of urging also against the clergy." Howe, *Portrait of an Independent, Moorfield Storey, 1845–1929*, p. 269.
[79] Johnson, *Along This Way*, p. 324; *Washington Bee*, March 2, 1918; *Nashville Banner*, February 18, 1918, quoted in *Crisis*, XV (April, 1918), 281.

In addition, a citizens' group organized the Tennessee Law and Order League to suppress lynching and encourage similar movements in all Southern states. Here, finally, was a manifestation of the Anti-Lynching Committee's constructive publicity program, which had envisaged the use of Southern agencies to fight lynching without involving the NAACP by name.[80]

The harsh glare of publicity was focused upon Governor Hugh M. Dorsey and the state of Georgia following a five-day "orgy" in Brooks and Lowndes Counties which resulted in the lynching of eight Negroes. The reign of terror began with the fatal shooting of a white landlord and the wounding of his wife by a Negro they had held in peonage. Mob vengeance resulted in the deaths of several innocent Negroes, one of whom was Haynes Turner. Mary White Ovington described the scene:

His wife Mary, after her husband's death, mourned and loudly proclaimed his innocence. For this she was slowly burned to death, watched by a crowd of men and women. She was pregnant, and as she burned, the infant fell to the ground and was trampled under a white man's heel.[81]

Walter White and James Weldon Johnson carried out separate investigations for the Association. John Shillady sent the findings to Governor Dorsey, naming the two ringleaders and fifteen participants in the murders.[82] Dorsey had risen to the governorship of Georgia as the result of his prosecution of Leo Frank, whose trial had been dominated by an armed mob.[83] His answer to Shillady, stating that no definite results had been obtained in efforts to apprehend the guilty parties, bore a rubber-stamp signature.[84]

Shortly after Governor Dorsey's letter was dispatched, a seventeen-year-old Negro, Sandy Reeves, was taken from peace officers and lynched near Blackshear, Georgia. He had been accused of assaulting a three-year-old child. The Waycross, Georgia, branch investigated and claimed that no assault had been committed or attempted. The child, a daughter of Reeves's employer, had been

[80] Board Minutes, NAACP, March 11, 1918; NAACP, *Ninth Annual Report 1918*, p. 36; "Tennessee Mobilizing for Law and Order," *Survey*, XXXIX (March 23, 1918), 690–91. This article tells of a meeting of 300 leading white citizens who organized to protest atrocities and form other leagues throughout the South. At the same time a group of 400 colored citizens led by J. C. Napier of Nashville sent a protest to Governor Rye and arranged to meet and cooperate with the Tennessee Law and Order League.
[81] Board Minutes, NAACP, December 9, 1918; NAACP, *Ninth Annual Report 1918*, p. 30; *Washington Bee*, August 10, 1918; Ovington, *The Walls Came Tumbling Down*, p. 152. Moorfield Storey related the incident in his address to the Wisconsin Bar Association. Storey, *The Negro Question*.
[82] Board Minutes, NAACP, December 9, 1918; *Washington Bee*, August 10, 1918. One witness to the lynching of Mary Turner was unwilling to appear before the Senate Investigating Committee because he believed that testifying would endanger the lives of his family. He also owned property and ran a small business. Board Minutes, NAACP, December 9, 1918.
[83] White, *A Man Called White*, pp. 25–26.
[84] *Washington Bee*, September 21, 1918.

playing near Reeves while he was picking grapes. A five-cent piece dropped from his pocket and she picked it up. When he tried to take the coin from her, she made a scene and an outcry. For this Reeves was lynched.[85]

There were nineteen verified and twelve probable lynchings in Georgia in 1918. The only effect of Wilson's public statement against such violence was an apparently concerted agreement between the press and the authorities to keep all news regarding lynchings out of the Georgia press. No account of the NAACP investigation of the Brooks and Lowndes County massacres appeared in the Georgia papers, although the governor knew the names of the leaders of the mob and there was considerable comment in the press of other states.[86]

The administration of Governor William P. Hobby of Texas was also subject to criticism and unfavorable publicity by the NAACP. Shillady made public a telegram sent to the governor protesting the lynching of Mrs. Sarah Cabiness and her five sons at Huntsville, Texas, on June 1, 1918. There were three more lynchings in Texas that year.[87] NAACP branches united to press for a state anti-lynching bill. They urged Governor Hobby to back appropriate legislation and offered to engage a prominent white lawyer to draft a bill. They proposed that all lynching trials should be held in the state capital, that the attorney general should prosecute all such cases, that the state should offer rewards for information leading to arrest and conviction in lynchings, that an indemnity should be paid to dependents of persons lynched, and that the crime of lynching should be legally defined, so as to include cases where three or more persons take the life of another without due process of law.[88]

In spite of all the discouraging news from the South there were some efforts to curb mob violence. A few incidents occurred in which state executives, local officials, and newspapers were willing to take a stand for law and order. Tennessee's governor and attorney general asked John Shillady for assistance in drafting a state anti-lynching bill.[89]

Governor Thomas W. Bickett of North Carolina requested federal authorities to assist the mayor and the home guard of Winston-Salem to prevent a mob from breaking into the jail and lynching a Negro prisoner. The local officials were given the support of a tank corps of 250 federal soldiers. The prisoner was successfully protected, "at the cost of the lives of some of the 'Home Guards.' " The Association publicly commended the governor and mayor for their stand. Fifteen persons were convicted and sentenced to terms ranging from fourteen months to six years.[90]

---

[85] Board Minutes, NAACP, October 14, 1918.

[86] NAACP, *Ninth Annual Report 1918*, pp. 27–28.

[87] *Washington Bee*, June 8, 1918; August 10, 1918; December 28, 1918; Board Minutes, NAACP, October 14, 1918.

[88] Board Minutes, NAACP, January 13, 1919; NAACP, *Ninth Annual Report 1918*, p. 64.

[89] Board Minutes, NAACP, January 13, 1919.

[90] NAACP, *Ninth Annual Report 1918*, pp. 31–32; Board Minutes, NAACP, March 10, 1919.

Governor Stanley of Kentucky personally defied a mob at Murray, Kentucky, and saved from lynching a Negro who was later legally tried and condemned to death. The Anti-Lynching Committee engaged a writer from the *Louisville Courier-Journal* to secure complete details for a story about the incident, which was published in *The Independent*. The Constitution of Kentucky was later amended to permit the removal from office of any sheriff, jailer, constable or peace officer for neglect of duty.[91]

The South was not the sole target of NAACP protests. In Wyoming, the lynching of Edward Woodson at Green River in December, 1918, brought publicized protests to the governor of that state against the lynchings and the driving from their homes of Negro residents of the community. In 1919, Wyoming enacted a law against mob violence.[92]

By mid-1918, the Association was sending out press stories to nearly four hundred newspapers. Some responded by giving editorial support to the anti-lynching campaign. In Texas, the *San Antonio Express* offered a $500 reward for the conviction and punishment of lynchers of a white person—$1,000 if the victim were a Negro. Although no one came forward to claim the reward, the offer served to call attention to the spread of mob violence in the South.[93] Nevertheless, it was usually difficult to get Southern newspapers to print NAACP press releases, and response from state officials and civic groups was discouraging. Upon receiving a letter of protest from the NAACP, signed by Shillady, following the lynching of four Negroes at Shubata, Mississippi, Governor Theodore G. Bilbo was reported by the *Washington Bee* to have given a state official "Advance information to the effect that I will tell them, in effect, to go to h—."[94]

Efforts to introduce and secure passage of legislation providing penalties against participants in lynchings became a major project of the Association on the national as well as the state level. Two anti-lynching bills were introduced in Congress in 1918, one by Dyer of Missouri and the other by Merrill Moore of Indiana. Neither of these seemed to fulfill the requirements of the NAACP, however, and the Anti-Lynching Committee attempted to have another bill introduced. At the same time they decided to participate in the hearing on Dyer's bill for publicity purposes. Joel Spingarn, then in the intelligence service of the army, enlisted the help of a fellow officer, a lawyer, Captain George S. Horn-

---

[91] Board Minutes, NAACP, February 13, 1917; March 12, 1917; December 8, 1919; *Crisis,* XIX (March, 1920), 243; *Independent,* LXXXIX (January 22, 1917), 140.

[92] *Washington Bee,* December 28, 1918; *Crisis,* XIX (March, 1920), 243.

[93] Shillady to Hon. L. C. Dyer, August 5, 1918, J. E. Spingarn Papers (Howard); NAACP, *Ninth Annual Report 1918,* p. 34.

[94] *Washington Bee,* January 4, 1919. In twelve states (one Western and eleven Southern) where lynchings occurred, thirty-two "telegrams and letters of inquiry, protest and condemnation" were sent to the governors and nine responses were received. NAACP, *Ninth Annual Report 1918,* p. 33.

blower, who drew up a third bill. On June 6, 1918, it was introduced by Warren Gard of Ohio at the hearing before the House Committee on the Judiciary as a substitute for Dyer's bill.[95]

Storey examined the three bills. He held the Dyer bill to be unconstitutional because it assumed that an *individual* could be punished for depriving United States citizens of the privileges or immunities granted them under the Fourteenth Amendment. This intrepretation had already been invalidated by the Supreme Court which held that the Fourteenth Amendment was concerned only with "encroachment by the states" against the rights of citizens. The Moore bill proposed to give the right to appeal directly to a federal court to every citizen who felt he was likely to be denied equal protection of the laws. This Storey also held to be unconstitutional. He did not believe the bills could be rewritten and declined to appear before the House Judiciary Committee on behalf of either the Dyer or the Moore bill.

He thought the Gard bill, with some modification, would pass the test of constitutionality. It was aimed primarily at protecting persons of draft age for the duration of the war. Two factors would aid its passage, said Storey—first, it had been prepared and introduced by army officers with the approval of the War Department; second, there was no indication that it was especially designed to protect Negroes. Storey strongly advised the Association not to play a prominent role in pressing for the bill, so as not to arouse undue opposition by Congress.[96] The ending of the war in November, 1918, made the Gard bill obsolete. Dyer continued to reintroduce his own bill, however, and Storey eventually changed his mind and supported Dyer.

THE ANTI-LYNCHING CONFERENCE

Efforts of the Anti-Lynching Committee to organize a conference of Southern leaders failed in spite of the early encouraging reports. At the end of 1918 the Committee decided to work for a national conference, calling on "the most substantial and influential leaders of public opinion" to endorse it. They even hoped to persuade a number of state governors, particularly of the Southern states, to attend the conference. The increasing number of incidents of mob violence against the Negro was clearly evident. During the year, sixty-four Negroes (five of them women) and four white men were lynched. These figures did not include the victims of the East St. Louis riots in July nor the Chester, Pennsylvania, riot in September. In eight Southern states thirteen victims were taken

[95] Board Minutes, NAACP, May 13, 1918; Brief of Captain George S. Hornblower, *To Protect Citizens Against Lynching*, July 12, 1918. Hearing before the House Committee on the Judiciary, 65th Cong., 2d Sess., on H.R. 11279, Serial 66, Part 2 (Washington, D. C., 1918), in J. E. Spingarn Papers (Howard).
[96] Storey to Walter F. White, July 11, 1918, copy, in J. E. Spingarn Papers (Howard).

from jails or from the custody of law enforcement officers. In Dewey, Oklahoma, when a mob was frustrated in its efforts to lynch a Negro, it retaliated by burning the town. A discouraging sign was that in the stress of wartime, mob violence began to menace communities heretofore relatively immune. There were lynchings in California, Wyoming, and Illinois, and race riots in Brooklyn, New York, Philadelphia, and New Jersey.[97]

During the first four months of 1919, nine known lynchings took place in five Southern states. In each case the victims were taken from jails or seized from officers of the law. The Hillsboro, Texas, lynching was reminiscent of the Waco atrocity where the victim was burned alive in the public square. An NAACP wire of protest to Governor Hobby was met with silence, as were those sent to the Chambers of Commerce in Dallas, Galveston, and Fort Worth. The Austin Chamber of Commerce sent a token reply: The situation was being investigated.[98]

At this time the NAACP was frequently referred to in the South as the Advancement Association, or Negro Advancement Society. In response to an inquiry by the Association concerning the lynching of Eugene Green at Belzoni, Mississippi, Governor Bilbo was said to have answered with an ironic play on words, "He was 'advanced' all right from the end of a rope, and in order to save burial expenses his body was thrown into the Yazoo River."[99] In spite of Bilbo's attitude, the sheriff from whom Green was taken was arraigned for neglect of duty, and an NAACP member in Mississippi reported that the judge had made a sincere effort to have the lynchers punished.[100]

The governor of Florida, in answer to a protest, replied that the NAACP was upholding lawlessness among Florida's Negroes and advised the Association to concentrate its efforts on educating and otherwise uplifting the colored people.[101]

The NAACP Anti-Lynching conference was held the first week in May, 1919. About 120 signatures were on the "call" which went out in April, including such notables as Attorney General A. Mitchell Palmer, former Secretary of State Elihu Root, Henry Van Dyke, Minister to the Netherlands, Charles Evans Hughes, and the president of the American Bar Association. Also included were four governors, three former governors (among whom was ex-governor O'Neal of Alabama), and seventeen signers from Southern states. To insure that the appeal would be biracial, representative colored men and women were among the signers.

[97] Board Minutes, NAACP, September 9, 1918; October 14, 1918; December 9, 1918; *Crisis,* XVII (February, 1919), 180–81; XIX (March, 1920), 243; *New York Age,* January 18, 1919; NAACP, *Ninth Annual Report 1918,* pp. 25–33.
[98] Board Minutes, NAACP, February 10, 1919; March 10, 1919; April 14, 1919.
[99] *Mississippi Daily News,* March 9, 1919, quoted in *Washington Bee,* March 22, 1919.
[100] *New York Globe,* April 2, 1919, quoted in Board Minutes, NAACP, April 14, 1919.
[101] Board Minutes, NAACP, April 14, 1919.

Some who were asked declined to endorse the call. Robert R. Moton was unwilling to discuss lynching in the North. Emmett Scott agreed with Moton. Among the friends of the Negro of the so-called philanthropic wing who refused to sign was George Foster Peabody, whose reason for declining was that attempts by the NAACP to arouse public opinion against lynching would inflame the South and result in more lynchings. He believed the only true policy was that of gradually educating Southerners until they recognized their duties as civilized people. In a letter to Peabody, Storey pointed out that, though lynching had been the practice for many years, in very few cases had anyone been punished, and no substantial movement to put an end to lynching had ever originated in the South; toleration of lynching was itself an educational force.[102]

The Anti-Lynching Conference opened at Carnegie Hall with an attendance of 2,500. Charles Evans Hughes, Governor Emmet O'Neal, Anna Howard Shaw of the woman's suffrage movement, Brigadier General John H. Sherburne of the 92nd (Negro) Division, and James Weldon Johnson were speakers. Walter White in his autobiography described the looks of astonishment that crossed the faces of the liberal-minded whites seated on the platform when Johnson gave voice to his conviction that the race problem was not only one of saving black men's bodies but of saving white men's souls.[103]

Three resolutions were adopted by the conference: that efforts should be made to secure legislation making lynching a federal crime; that the NAACP should organize state committees to create a climate of favorable public opinion and work for legislation at the state level; and that the Anti-Lynching Committee should carry on a systematic fund-raising and advertising campaign against lynching.[104]

The New York City Bar Association adopted resolutions calling for a congressional investigation of lynching and federal legislation for its prevention. NAACP members were disappointed that so few New York lawyers attended the session conducted by Storey on the legal aspect of lynching.[105]

Following the Anti-Lynching Conference, Shillady and the Anti-Lynching Committee drew up "An Address to the Nation on Lynching," signed by 130 prominent citizens including those who had signed the call and several important new sponsors—former President William Howard Taft, William Dean Howells, President John Grier Hibben of Princeton, Theodore D. Bratton, Episcopal

---

[102] Board Minutes, NAACP, March 10, 1919; April 14, 1919; *Crisis*, XVIII (May, 1919), 23–24; Storey to George Foster Peabody, June 26, 1919, Storey Papers.
[103] White, *A Man Called White*, p. 34; *New York Age*, May 10, 1919. Charles Edward Russell had expressed the same idea earlier, but the catchy phrase was Johnson's. See Russell's pamphlet, *Leaving It to the South* (New York, 1912), p. 3.
[104] *Crisis*, XVIII (June, 1919), 92.
[105] Board Minutes, NAACP, April 14, 1919; Ovington, *The Walls Came Tumbling Down*, p. 153; *New York Age*, May 10, 1919.

Bishop of Mississippi, and the governor of Tennessee. This manifesto was used for further publicity, and exerted additional pressure for a congressional investigation.[106]

RED SUMMER

In 1919, the NAACP sent Herbert Seligmann on a trip to Tennessee and Mississippi to investigate increased racial tension. From his talks with leading Negroes and whites, Seligmann learned that the shortage of cheap labor in rural regions of the South was deeply resented by plantation owners. Southerners complained that the drafting of Negroes for the army tended to put them on an equal footing with white men. An additional cause of antagonism was the widespread belief that Negro soldiers were "recognized on equal terms by white women in France." These indications that Negroes were gaining status as citizens gave rise to what Du Bois called "the sex motive, the brutal sadism into which race hate always falls." Colored soldiers were lynched in Georgia and Mississippi for having appeared on the streets in uniform.[107]

Seligmann found that Southern whites universally condemned what they termed a campaign or agitation from outsiders for equal rights for Negroes. Most considered the Negro inherently inferior, forever unsuited to political, economic, and social equality. Finally, white and Negro intellectuals alike recognized that tensions were heightened by the press and by politicians such as Vardaman, who, in his weekly political paper, the *Issue*, promoted race hatred in default of other issues. One politician, candidate for the Louisiana State Legislature, told Seligmann that lynching was necessary, and that no Negro should ever be allowed to vote or acquire an education—because education made confidence men of the males and prostitutes of the females. Some professional and business people deplored lynching, but only in a half-hearted fashion, and predicted the resurrection of the Ku Klux Klan among "the best people" of the South.

Seligmann reported that practically all intelligent Southerners believed that federal legislation was the only way to stop lynching, but extremists claimed they would punish offenders against Southern womanhood, regardless of the consequences. A leading Negro of Memphis, Robert Church, told Seligmann that antagonism between races in the South was mounting, that Negroes were arming, and that federal action was the only hope of averting serious conflict.[108]

[106] Board Minutes, NAACP, July 11, 1919; *New York Age*, August 2, 1919.
[107] Board Minutes, NAACP, April 14, 1919; June 9, 1919; NAACP, *Ninth Annual Report 1918*, p. 47; W. E. B. Du Bois, *Dusk of Dawn: An Essay toward an Autobiography of a Race Concept* (New York, 1940), p. 264; Johnson, *Along This Way*, p. 341.
[108] Board Minutes, NAACP, June 9, 1919.

In mid-summer, 1919, in the midst of violence, restlessness, tension, and crisis, the NAACP resumed the pattern of holding its annual conference. In 1915 there had been no conference because of the financial condition of the Association. In 1916, Booker T. Washington's death had led to the Amenia Conference rather than an all-NAACP conference. In 1917 and 1918 there were no regular conferences because of wartime restrictions on travel.

The 1919 conference, held in Cleveland, was different from any of the previous annual meetings. It was the largest and the longest. The dramatically expanded membership was represented by delegates from thirty-four states. Also notable was the absence of white leadership, which had been so obvious a feature of the earlier conferences. The Association, organized by whites ten years before, was now being organized all over the United States by Negroes.

Bishop John Hurst set the tone of the conference in his address to the delegates. Negroes, he told them, had been lulled to sleep under the delusion that if they quit crying out so loudly for their rights and kept on working, justice would eventually be meted out to them. But the South renewed its assaults upon the black man with every forward step, and he called on the delegates to die if need be in the fight for their rights.[109]

The race riots of the summer and fall of 1919 were violent and bloody. As if in response to the new note of defiance sounded at the conference, the Negro fought back. The fighting spirit of the new abolitionism, the fighting words of *The Crisis*, the yearning for better economic and citizenship status, and the Negro's wartime experiences—all were reflected in the incidents that took place in Washington, Chicago, Omaha, Knoxville, and Indianapolis, and in Phillips County, Arkansas, where the worst of the many riots of that year occurred.

The curtain raiser was the riot at Longview, Texas, in June, 1919, between whites and returning Negro soldiers, in which a number of both races lost their lives.[110] The clash, typical of the lawlessness stalking restlessly through the nation, showed that Negroes were ready to resist. "Negroes are not planning anything," stated an Associated Press report in a Longview newspaper, "but will defend themselves if attacked."[111]

In Washington, D.C., the rioting lasted three days; as in Longview, the Negro fought back. Investigating the riots, James Weldon Johnson observed a new spirit of determination among Negroes, a resolve "not to run, but to fight—fight in defense of their lives and their homes." He blamed the press of Washington for carrying on mob violence propaganda in the form of daily stories of attacks on white women. He claimed that this propaganda was in fact an attempt to dis-

[109] Ovington, *The Walls Came Tumbling Down*, pp. 167–68, 171.
[110] Board Minutes, NAACP, September 8, 1919; *Crisis*, XVIII (October, 1919), 297.
[111] Quoted in *Crisis*, XVIII (October, 1919), 298.

credit the Washington police department and to convince the public that crime in Washingon had increased with the advent of Prohibition.[112]

Johnson conferred with the District Commissioners, the chief of police, the editors of the *Post*, the *Times*, and the *Evening Star*, giving them NAACP literature on lynching and discussing with them the responsibility of the press for the riots. The *Evening Star* printed three editorials which the editor claimed had been influenced by the interview. In one editorial, the *Star* called for a congressional investigation, commenting that "every time the white mob runs amuck against the Negroes, the latter grow more bitter and defensive in their retaliatory measures." [113]

Johnson interviewed a number of Senators, and the NAACP launched a campaign for an investigation. As a result of this pressure, Charles Curtis of Kansas introduced a resolution in the Senate on September 22, 1919, calling for an inquiry into the causes of the race riots in Washington and other cities and an investigation of the wave of lynchings throughout the country. The resolution was referred to the Senate Committee on the Judiciary.[114] Curtis asked the Association to send him a brief to present to the committee, setting forth reasons why there should be an investigation, what might be revealed by such an inquiry, and what remedies could be recommended. Curtis also urged the Association to have persons of influence write the chairman of the Judiciary Committee, endorsing the resolution and urging its adoption. Dyer introduced a similar resolution in the House, but both resolutions died in committee.[115]

The violence continued. Sixteen lynchings, including two burnings, took place in September. There were two whippings and two incidents in which mobs seized prisoners from peace officers; the victims were presumed dead. With the end of the war, unemployment and an unprecedented number of strikes accompanied by violence swept the country, further aggravating race relations. Political radicals and members of other ethnic groups were also victims in the postwar reaction against Wilsonian idealism and internationalism. Two Mexicans were lynched in Colorado. A member of the Industrial Workers of the World was

[112] *Crisis*, XVIII (September, 1919), 243; *Washington Post*, July 23, 1919; *New York Age*, August 2, 1919. An investigation of the police department was started by the House Committee on the District of Columbia but was dropped after "three days of hearings before the sub-committee." *Washington Evening Star*, September 26, 1919.
[113] Board Minutes, NAACP, September 8, 1919; *Washington Evening Star*, July 30, 1919; July 28, 1919; July 29, 1919.
[114] Board Minutes, NAACP, September 8, 1919; *Congressional Record*, 66th Cong., 1st Sess. (S.R. 189), p. 5673.
[115] Board Minutes, NAACP, October 13, 1919; November 10, 1919; *Congressional Record*, 66th Cong., 1st Sess., (H. R. 319), p. 6312. Earlier, at the time of the Washington riots, Representative Henry I. Emerson of Ohio had also introduced a resolution calling for an investigation of the rioting. It had died in the Committee on Appropriations. *Congressional Record*, 66th Cong., 1st Sess., (H.J.R. 160), p. 317.

taken from the jail and lynched at Centralia, Washington. In Stafford, Kansas, a member of the Non-Partisan League was lynched; the fate of two other members of the League seized by the mob was unknown.[116]

In spite of the violence of the summer, Robert Moton, following in the steps of Booker T. Washington, whom he had succeeded at Tuskegee, wrote optimistically that lynching was on the wane. Incensed, Villard objected to the glaring untruth and the positive harm done by the reports from Tuskegee, which "lull people's consciences to sleep." In *The Crisis*, Du Bois urged Negroes to prepare for attack with bricks, clubs, and guns, yet he cautioned against angry retaliation or seeking reform by violence; in the same issue Johnson wrote that the riots in Washington and Chicago marked a turning point in the psychology of the nation regarding the Negro problem.[117]

The Chicago riots followed closely on the violence in Washington. Twenty-three Negroes and fifteen whites were killed, and many Negroes were arrested, indicted, and tried for participating and inciting to riot. Walter White, John Shillady, and Herbert Seligmann went to Chicago to investigate for the NAACP and reported that again the newspapers were to blame for the eruption of violence because of their distorted reports of Negro crime. White listed other factors playing a part in the Chicago outbreak—racial prejudice, economic rivalry, political corruption and exploitation of Negro voters, police inefficiency (leading to many unpublished crimes against Negroes), the problem of Negro housing, and the moral letdown that follows every war.[118]

Joel Spingarn conferred with the Chicago branch, and as a result of the deliberations, a delegation called on Mayor William Hale Thompson and Governor Frank O. Lowden of Illinois. The mayor took no action, but the governor, who had refused to call out the state militia, appointed a commission to study the riots and prepare a plan for preventing them in the future. The NAACP Board made $5,000 immediately available for the legal defense of the victims of the Chicago riots, and Arthur Spingarn went to Chicago to confer with the legal committee of the branch concerning their defense.[119]

[116] Board Minutes, NAACP, November 10, 1919; December 8, 1919. For the story of an earlier lynching of an IWW official, see *Emporia Gazette*, August 1, 1917.

[117] Robert R. Moton, "The South and the Lynching Evil," *South Atlantic Quarterly*, XVII (July, 1919), 191–96; Villard to Moton, October 14, 1919, Villard Papers; *Crisis*, XVIII (September, 1919), 231, 243.

[118] Board Minutes, NAACP, November 10, 1919; *Crisis*, XVIII (September, 1919), 244; *Crisis*, XVIII (October, 1919), 293–97.

[119] Board Minutes, NAACP, September 8, 1919; adjourned meeting, September 9, 1919. Members of the commission were Edgar A. Bancroft, Julius Rosenwald, Victor F. Lawson, Harry Eugene Kelly, William Scott Bond, Edward Osgood Brown, president of the Chicago NAACP branch. "Those representing the Negro" were Dr. George C. Hall, director of the Urban League; Edward H. Morris, former state representative; Robert S. Abbott, editor of the *Chicago Defender;* Adelbert H. Roberts, state representative; George H. Jackson, merchant; and the Reverend Dr. L. K. Williams, pastor of the Olivet Church.

The race riots in the North had repercussions in the South. Two lynchings in Georgia were the result of fear of a Negro uprising aimed at wiping out the white population. In Georgia a man was lynched because he was supposed to have said that the Negroes of Georgia were going to do what Negroes had done in Chicago. In Mississippi a Negro was lynched for "expressing his views too freely concerning another lynching in that state."[120]

The NAACP investigations and the new fighting spirit among Negroes led to efforts to curtail activities of the Association. Early in August, 1919, the Austin, Texas, branch informed the national office that the state attorney general had subpoenaed the branch president to bring all NAACP books, papers, and correspondence to court. Texas seemed determined to close down all branches operating in the state on the grounds that the Association was not chartered to do business in Texas. The national office advised the Austin branch that the NAACP was not a business but a membership corporation, whose purposes were civic and educational. If Texas could stop the operation of the NAACP within its borders, other Southern states might follow suit. At that time there were 31 branches and 7,046 members in Texas. According to Miss Ovington, the subpoena had been issued because copies of *The Crisis*, containing resolutions adopted at the 1919 annual conference urging the end of segregation in public transportation, had come into the hands of Texas officials.[121]

In response to this situation, John Shillady wired Governor Hobby and the Texas attorney general asking for an opportunity to explain the aims and purposes of the Association and immediately left for Texas. In Austin, he was unable to meet either the governor or the attorney general but talked with the acting attorney general and tried to explain that the NAACP was not engaged in organizing Negro uprisings against whites. When Shillady left the attorney general's office, he was haled before a secret session of what purported to be a court of inquiry, where the county attorney asked legitimate as well as insultingly personal questions. The following morning Shillady was set upon and beaten unconscious by a group of men who had been seen loitering about the building the night before. Six or eight men took part in the assault, while "an auto full of tough-looking men" stood by. Among the assailants were a judge and a constable, both of whom frankly admitted their part in the attack, claiming that Shillady was inciting Negroes against whites and had been warned to leave Austin.[122]

Upon receiving news of the attack on Shillady through an Associated Press dispatch, the national office telegraphed Governor Hobby demanding that the as-

[120] Board Minutes, NAACP, September 8, 1919; *Washington Bee*, August 16, 1919.
[121] *New York Age*, August 30, 1919; Johnson, *Along This Way*, pp. 342–43; Ovington, *The Walls Came Tumbling Down*, pp. 172–73; White, *A Man Called White*, p. 46.
[122] Shillady, signed article, *New York Age*, August 30, 1919; September 6, 1919; Ovington, *The Walls Came Tumbling Down*, p. 173.

sailants be punished. Hobby replied that Shillady was the only offender and that he had already been punished.[123] When Miss Ovington wrote to police officials at Austin, the deputy sheriff answered that Shillady had been "received by red-blooded white men," who did not want "Negro-loving white men" in Texas. They had sent him back home with the admonition: "We attend to our own affairs down here, and suggest that you do the same up there."[124]

James Weldon Johnson was able to verify the rumor that a prominent Negro clergyman of Austin had brought about the attack on Shillady by informing a Texas Ranger that the NAACP was banding together to excite sedition and race riots. Johnson exposed the clergyman in the Negro press and urged the severest, most complete ostracism for such Negroes. At about the same time Richard Carroll, the Negro lecturer from Columbia, South Carolina, who had helped the NAACP with the Pink Franklin case, wrote in the *New York Age* that "fully half the outrages and lynchings and brutality were caused by 'Judas Iscariots' among Negroes."[125]

At a special meeting of the Board, an appeal was sent to President Wilson asking him to appoint a "responsible commission" to investigate and report on the Shillady attack. Resolutions were drafted, calling for congressional investigation on the grounds that the governor of Texas had approved and condoned a criminal assault by public officials. The Board requested Governor Hobby to remove from office the judge who took part in the assault, and the governor of New York was urged to demand protection for citizens of New York visiting Texas. Mass meetings throughout the country and in New York protested the attack on Shillady.[126]

A committee of lawyers, Moorfield Storey, Arthur B. Spingarn, Charles Studin, George Crawford, and Butler Wilson, was appointed to investigate the legal aspects of the case. They determined to secure only counsel of high standing, the inference being that if such counsel proved unavailable, the publication of this fact would itself constitute a severe indictment of the Texas authorities. The committee agreed that if Shillady returned to Austin to testify, he must first be given guarantees of protection from physical violence.[127]

Shillady's experience in Austin was not without grave physical and psychological after effects. Years later, Johnson wrote that Shillady never fully recovered spiritually from the experience. A. B. Spingarn was more harsh in his judgment, claiming that the secretary had shown the white feather and quit the

---

[123] *New York Age*, August 30, 1919.
[124] Gene Barbish to Ovington, quoted in *New York Age*, September 6, 1919.
[125] *New York Age*, August 30, 1919; September 13, 1919.
[126] Board Minutes, NAACP, August 26, 1919; October 13, 1919; *New York Age*, September 6, 1919.
[127] Board Minutes, NAACP, September 8, 1919.

Association out of fear of returning to Austin. Walter White was more sympathetic. Miss Ovington compared Shillady to a shell-shocked soldier. By November the secretary's health was so obviously failing that he was given a vacation on full pay for six weeks to recuperate. The Board agreed to reimburse him for medical and other expenses resulting from the ordeal. Shillady returned to his duties as executive officer of the Association for a time, but resigned in August, 1920.[128] His resignation brought an end to the possibility of a trial in Austin. It is doubtful that it would ever have been held, for the NAACP was unable to secure a local lawyer willing to argue the case.[129]

In his letter of resignation, Shillady expressed his disillusionment. "I am less confident than heretofore of the speedy success of the Association's full program, and of the probability of overcoming, within a reasonable period, the forces opposed to Negro equality by the means and methods which are within the Association's power to employ."[130]

To Du Bois, Shillady's conclusion was not news. The American Negro knew that his problem could not be solved quickly, that there were strong forces opposed to equality, and that the methods of combating these forces were limited. But white people, warned Du Bois, especially white social workers, must learn that the problem could not be avoided. The 90,000 members of the Association had banded together in an attempt to solve it. Shillady had tried to talk quietly and reasonably to Texans but "the haters of black folk beat him and maltreated him and scarred him like a dog." If peaceful, legal, reasonable methods were not adequate, what else, asked Du Bois, did America propose, and what were white men going to do about it?[131]

THE PHILLIPS COUNTY CASE

Neither the President's pronouncement against lynching nor the introduction of the Curtis resolution had any immediate effect on the race conflict and rioting, which continued into the fall. On September 29 in Omaha, Nebraska, a mob burned the county court house and seized a Negro who had been jailed on charges of attacking a white woman. The prisoner was lynched in the heart of the business district.[132]

[128] Johnson, *Along This Way*, p. 343; Interview with Arthur B. Spingarn, New York City, July 27, 1956; White, *A Man Called White*, pp. 46–47; Ovington, *The Walls Came Tumbling Down*, p. 175; Board Minutes, NAACP, November 10, 1919; June 14, 1920.
[129] *Crisis*, XXIV (July, 1922), 107; Board Minutes, NAACP, September 8, 1919; October 13, 1919; November 10, 1919; February 9, 1920; March 8, 1920.
[130] *Crisis*, XX (June, 1920), 72.
[131] *Crisis*, XX (August, 1920), 165–66.
[132] *Crisis*, XIX (December, 1919), 56–62; Board Minutes, NAACP, October 13, 1919; *Washington Bee*, October 4, 1919.

The climax of the "Red Summer" came, however, with the riots which broke out in October in Phillips County, Arkansas. Stories in the press had made it appear that the Negroes of the county were organizing to massacre whites, seize their property, and assume control of local and state government. The truth was that the Negroes of Phillips County were held in a state of peonage under the sharecropping system and were organizing themselves under the banner of the Progressive Farmers and Household Union in an attempt to end economic exploitation. Negroes in the Union were asking that landlords put an end to the deliberate misrepresentation of their efforts to secure redress. Violence broke out on the night of October 2 at a Negro church in Hoop Spur, Arkansas, where the Farmers Union was meeting to raise funds to retain the legal services of U. S. Bratton, a prominent white attorney of Little Rock. White citizens of the area fired into the meeting, and in the course of the disturbance both Negroes and whites were killed. For a number of days afterwards armed bandits of whites roamed the countryside, hunting down and killing Negroes on sight. It was estimated that over 200 lost their lives during the outbreak.[133]

Seventy-nine Negroes were indicted and brought to trial at Elaine, Phillips County, Arkansas, on charges of murder and insurrection, The trials were held in the presence of an armed mob, and the jury quickly brought in verdicts condemning twelve to death and sixty-seven to prison terms ranging from twenty years to life. On October 8 the NAACP sent Walter White to Arkansas to investigate. Pretending to be a reporter from a Northern newspaper, he interviewed Governor Charles H. Brough. He was unable to talk with the prisoners, who were being held in Helena, and left that town when it was rumored that his identity had become known and that plans were being made to lynch him.[134]

White and attorney Bratton prevailed upon Congressman Dyer, Senator Curtis, and officials of the Justice Department to initiate an investigation. The investigation revealed no evidence that a massacre of whites had been planned. Moreover, it was clear that the Progressive Farmers and Household Union of America had merely sought, through legal means, to test the methods by which landowners, their agents, and merchants exploited Negro sharecroppers and farmers.[135]

The national office appealed for funds to defend the condemned men. The case came at a time when the drive against lynching had lost its initial appeal,

---

[133] Board Minutes, NAACP, October 13, 1919; November 10, 1919; January 12, 1920; March 8, 1920; *Crisis*, XXIX (April, 1925), 272–73; *New York Age*, October 18, 1919; Johnson, *Along This Way*, p. 342; White, *A Man Called White*, pp. 47–49; Ovington, *The Walls Came Tumbling Down*, pp. 157–58; *Crisis*, XXV (November, 1922), 10–11.
[134] Board Minutes, NAACP, October 13, 1919; November 10, 1919; *Crisis*, XXI (December, 1920), 65-66; White, *A Man Called White*, pp. 49–51.
[135] Board Minutes, NAACP, November 10, 1919.

but the story of "lynching by law" of men whose only crime was an effort to better their economic lot evoked wide sympathy. Conditions of Negro peonage in the South were just becoming known, and public attention was focused on the Arkansas cases because of the labor slant. Before the cases were closed, more than $50,000 had been raised and expended by the national office and the Negroes of Arkansas.[136]

Difficulties beset the conduct of the cases. The Bratton family found it expedient to leave Arkansas and settle in the North.[137] Colonel G. W. Murphy, an elderly and highly respected attorney of Little Rock, agreed to represent all the defendants, but he died before the case was settled. His law firm then demanded exorbitant fees and resigned from the case when the NAACP refused to meet the terms. The Little Rock branch of the NAACP then retained Negro attorney Scipio Africanus Jones, and he bore the burden of the cases, which he conducted in what the Board considered a masterly manner.[138]

In Arkansas the press and various white civic organizations, such as the Rotary Club and the American Legion, clamored for the execution of the defendants. The NAACP telegraphed the national commander of the Legion, inquiring if the policy of the Legion was "not only to exclude colored veterans of the World War from membership but to publicly urge the execution of colored men whose cases are before the courts." Governor Brough of Arkansas joined the demand for the executions. According to *The Crisis*, he made every effort to see that the men were hanged, even to the point of attempting to influence the court by newspaper articles, in which he cited the various state organizations which were demanding the death penalty.[139]

Of the twelve men sentenced to death, the convictions of six were upheld by the Arkansas Supreme Court. The convictions of the other six were twice reversed by that court and remanded for retrial. On each occasion when the case was set for trial, the state pleaded unreadiness and secured a postponement over the objection of the defense counsel. After two years had passed, attorneys for the

---

[136] Board Minutes, NAACP, special meeting, November 24, 1919; Ovington, *The Walls Came Tumbling Down*, pp. 157–58; *Crisis*, XXV (November, 1922), 10–11.

[137] The law firm of Bratton and Bratton of Little Rock had been retained by the Farmers Union group because it was known that they would fight to the end a legal case for Negroes. The younger Bratton was at the meeting at Hoop Spur and was arrested along with the Farmers Union group and charged with "inciting Negroes to riot." He was held without bond for thirty-one days. *Crisis*, XIX (December, 1919), 59.

[138] *Crisis*, XXI (December, 1920), 65–66; Board Minutes, NAACP, March 14, 1921; September 12, 1921; October 10, 1921; Ovington, *The Walls Came Tumbling Down*, p. 159. The Little Rock branch president, J. H. McConico, organized a Citizens Defense Fund Commission to help the branch fight the case and to raise money. "Confidential Report of the Citizens Defense Fund Commission," April 7, 1920, in Board Minutes, NAACP, May 10, 1920.

[139] Ovington, *The Walls Came Tumbling Down*, p. 160; Board Minutes, NAACP, December 13, 1920; *Crisis*, XXI (January, 1921), 118–19.

Association secured a dismissal of all six cases, based on the statute of limitations.[140]

Meanwhile, to prevent the execution of the six who had been condemned, NAACP attorneys filed an appeal to the Supreme Court of the United States. Moorfield Storey argued the case. On February 19, 1923, a decision in favor of the "Arkansas peons" reversed the convictions of the six men and ordered the federal district court to ascertain if they had received a fair trial in the state courts of Arkansas. The majority opinon, written by Justice Holmes, who had written the dissent in the Frank case, ruled that a trial in a mob-dominated court resulting in a miscarriage of justice constitutes a failure to provide due process of law.[141]

In April, 1923, Scipio Jones warned the national office that there was a possibility of an adverse decision in the federal district court. He suggested disposing of the cases through a compromise, which would entail pleading guilty to a charge of second degree murder or some other crime in return for short prison sentences. Storey was vehemently opposed to such a move. He felt that the six men had better lie in jail without plea for a year or two than incur certain imprisonment and discredit all attempts to save them by pleading guilty. Storey's view prevailed.[142]

In the autumn of 1923 the sentences of the six were commuted by Governor McRae to short prison terms. This was made possible by a group of white citizens of Phillips County who had smoothed the way by petitioning state authorities for clemency.[143]

Moorfield Storey gave full credit to Walter White, and James Weldon Johnson commented on the intelligence and skill with which White had conducted the original investigations and the subsequent work on the cases at the national office. The reputation White acquired in these years undoubtedly led to his selection as Johnson's successor as secretary of the Association.[144]

On January 14, 1925, Scipio Jones wired the national office that the six-year fight to save the lives of the twelve men condemned to death and to shorten the sentences of the sixty-seven Negroes serving life imprisonment or very long prison

[140] *Crisis*, XXVI (August, 1923), 163–64.
[141] *Crisis*, XXIII (December, 1921), 72; Board Minutes, NAACP, February 7, 1923; *Moore v. Dempsey*, 261 U.S. 86 (1923). The majority opinion was concurred in by Chief Justice Taft and Associate Justices Brandeis, Butler, Van Devanter, and McKenna. The dissenting opinion was written by Justice McReynolds and was concurred in by Justice Sutherland. *Crisis*, XXV (April, 1923), 258–61; *Frank* v. *Mangum*, 237 U.S. 345 (1914).
[142] Board Minutes, April 9, 1923; May 9, 1923; Storey to White, May 7, 1923, quoted in Board Minutes, NAACP, May 9, 1923.
[143] Board Minutes, NAACP, November 12, 1923; *Crisis*, XXVII (January, 1924), 124–25.
[144] Storey to White, n.d., quoted in Board Minutes, NAACP, November 12, 1923; Board Minutes, NAACP, July 9, 1923.

terms had come to an end with the release of the last of the prisoners. The Association proudly asserted that the victory was the greatest of its kind ever won.[145]

The significance of the Arkansas cases lay not only in the freeing of seventy-nine men unjustly accused of murder and other crimes but also in the fact that the riot was a carefully manufactured plot designed to give credence to the story that the Negro farmers planned to massacre the whites and seize their land. If mob violence directed against the Negro peon in Arkansas had gone unchallenged, more Negroes would have been murdered throughout the South, with the justification that they were organizing to massacre whites and appropriate land. The Phillips County case exposed to the American public the practice of peonage and economic exploitation of Negro and white sharecroppers and tenant farmers in the South. It also revealed that the planters of Phillips County used violence and the courts to keep the Negro in a position where he was economically exploitable.

The Supreme Court in its decision held that if a trial is dominated by a mob to the extent that justice is interfered with, then the principle of due process has been violated. This was a reversal of the Court's stand in the Leo Frank case, in which it ruled that so long as a court went through the form of a trial, there could be no interference from the federal government, even though the trial had been dominated by a mob. This decision meant that protection was now assured for all Americans, both white and black, who might at some future time be tried and convicted in courts influenced by mobs.[146]

Another outcome of these trials was the enrollment of Louis Marshall in the work of the NAACP. Marshall, the distinguished lawyer who had been counsel for Leo Frank, sent a generous contribution and called the Supreme Court's decision a great achievement in constitutional law. He became an active member of the Association's legal committee and continued to serve the NAACP in this capacity until his death in 1929.[147]

THE ATLANTA CONFERENCE

Throughout the fall and winter of 1919, the question of whether to hold the 1920 annual conference in Atlanta or in a Northern city divided both membership and Board. In the light of a campaign designed to intimidate members and stamp out the organization in Southern communities, there was justifiable

[145] Board Minutes, NAACP, February 5, 1925; NAACP, *Fifteenth Annual Report 1924* (New York, 1925), p. 68.
[146] *Frank* v. *Mangum*, 237 U.S. 309 (1914); *Crisis*, XXV (April, 1923), 261; XXVII (January, 1924), 124–25; XXIX (April, 1925), 272–73.
[147] Board Minutes, NAACP, September 30, 1929; October 14, 1929; November 7, 1929; Ovington, *The Walls Came Tumbling Down*, p. 162.

fear that the Atlanta riots of 1906 might be repeated. In the attack on Shillady, Texas had shown the attitude of the South toward the NAACP and all "outsiders." Would Atlanta do the same? These fears were allayed, however, when invitations came from the Mayor of Atlanta, the Chamber of Commerce, and even from Governor Dorsey, indicating that the Association's convention would be welcome.[148]

It was a shorter conference than the 1919 meeting at Cleveland, lasting only four days, and there were fewer participants, but the Atlanta conference marked another epoch. The Association was at last able to meet openly in the deep South and to express freely and frankly its radical aims. To Du Bois this was an announcement to the whole country that there was "no difference of aim and desire" between Negroes of the South and those of the North. James Weldon Johnson was moved to observe more than the wonted public courtesy in the city of Atlanta and a noticeable elasticity in the traditional racial bounds. So encouraged were the Board members by the Atlanta meeting that the following year they invited Governor Dorsey of Georgia to speak at the Detroit conference.[149]

Racial violence was now a national problem. The protests and the publicity had focused public attention on the evil. Efforts to obtain passage of a federal anti-lynching law had been unsuccessful, but fear of federal interference and public awareness of the economic effects of the ill-treatment of Negroes in the South eventually brought about a decrease in the number of lynchings and a lessening of mob violence. Negroes had responded to the tension of the war years and their aftermath by aligning themselves with the NAACP and by subscribing to *The Crisis* as never before in the history of the organization.

[148] Board Minutes, NAACP, October 13, 1919; November 10, 1919; December 8, 1919; January 12, 1920; Johnson, *Along This Way*, p. 356.
[149] *Crisis*, XX (July, 1920), 117, 132; Johnson, *Along This Way*, p. 367; Board Minutes, NAACP, April 12, 1920; May 9, 1921. There is no evidence that Dorsey appeared.

CHAPTER XI

The NAACP and the Great War

A year and a half before World War I broke out, disquieting rumors were prevalent that Negroes were to be eliminated from the United States Army. The *Washington Post* carried a story to the effect that this move was to be considered at a conference of high ranking officers in Washington on January 8, 1913. The alleged resentment of the Filipinos and the dissatisfaction of the people of Hawaii at the introducton of Negroes as garrison troops were given as reasons. It was also reported that friends of the Negro would make a strenuous fight against this move.[1]

There had been four colored regiments in the army since 1870, two cavalry and two infantry. There were no Negro artillery regiments, though Booker T. Washington had tried to convince Elihu Root in 1901, and Theodore Roosevelt in 1907, that colored soldiers should be recruited when new artillery units were added. Washington claimed credit for the appointment of colored bandmasters in Negro regiments in 1907.[2]

In the *New York Age*, Booker T. Washington maintained that Negro soldiers had "the stuff that counts." Captain Marchand, leader of the French expedition to Fashoda in the Sudan in 1898, was a Negro; a Negro general was presently in command of one of the French Army Corps; and in a clash between the Prussian Guard and French Senegalese Riflemen the Germans had suffered heavily. Washington asserted that the United States owed its victory over Spain in Cuba to Negro troops and suggested that France, in the war with Germany,

---

[1] *Washington Post*, December 24, 1912, clipping in Joel Elias Spingarn Papers (Moorland Foundation, Howard University).

[2] *Crisis*, XII (May, 1916), 40; Emmett J. Scott to Theodore Roosevelt, March 8, 1907, Booker T. Washington Papers (Manuscript Division, Library of Congress); Oswald Garrison Villard to Booker T. Washington, May 20, 1907; Scott to Villard, May 31, 1907, Oswald Garrison Villard Papers (Houghton Library, Harvard University).

might likewise owe its continued existence as a nation to black soldiers from Senegal.[3]

The National Defense Act of June, 1916, was still pending, when the NAACP urged the House and Senate Committees on Military Affairs to permit Negroes to enlist in the artillery and infantry regiments being created by Congress. Oswald Garrison Villard wrote to Secretary of War Newton D. Baker, advocating that some of the new units be colored regiments. Baker at first intimated that something could be done to implement Villard's suggestion, but he later reverted to a narrow interpretation of the 1866 law (which specified that two regiments of cavalry and two of infantry be composed of Negroes), claiming that the War Department could make no distinction as to race or color between qualified citizens of the United States unless required to do so by Congress.[4]

Villard pointed out to the Secretary of War that the lag in recruitment could be overcome by using more Negro soldiers. Negroes were "magnificent military material," he wrote, and enlisted more readily than white men because of the limited economic opportunities open to them. If the War Department refused to take Negro soldiers after the four authorized regiments reached their complement, then the Department was guilty of discriminating against qualified citizens. Baker responded that the explicit designation of certain units as colored always caused unhappiness and resentment and denied that his Department had refused to accept additional Negro recruits.[5]

The navy, which accepted Negroes only as mess corpsmen, was even harder to open to Negro enlistments. The NAACP Board decided that the best approach to the problem at this time was to publicize conditions in the navy.[6]

In 1916 there was a move to keep Negroes from advancing in the service. A bill was introduced by Southern Congressmen attempting to make it unlawful for Negroes to be appointed as commissioned or noncommissioned officers in either army or navy. Another bill was aimed at preventing enlistment of Negroes in all branches of the service.[7]

When Congress declared war on the German Empire in April, 1917, George Crawford warned Joel Spingarn that the Board should refrain from taking any

[3] "Editorial for the *New York Age* to appear under the date of August 29, 1914," in Washington Papers; *New York Age*, September 3, 1914.
[4] *Washington Bee*, April 1, 1916; Newton D. Baker to Villard, April 13, 1916; April 14, 1916, Villard Papers.
[5] Villard to Baker, April 17, 1916; Baker to Villard, April 19, 1916, Villard Papers.
[6] Board Minutes, September 13, 1915, in "Minute Book of the Board of Directors of the National Association for the Advancement of Colored People" (now in the Manuscript Division, Library of Congress; hereafter referred to as Board Minutes, NAACP).
[7] Minutes, Annual Meeting, January 2, 1917, in Board Minutes, NAACP; *The Negro as a Soldier and a Sailor*, reprint of remarks of the Hon. Murray Hulbert of New York, in the House of Representatives, Wednesday, September 6, 1916, printed by the Republican Party, n.d., n.p. (refers to bill H.R. 17183), J. E. Spingarn Papers (Howard).

official action concerning the war because of the strong pacifist opinions of important Board members and their "violent adherence to peace." He feared that bitter dissension would divide the Board.[8] Among the influential Board members who were very decidedly against American participation in the war were Villard, Lillian Wald, Jane Addams, John Haynes Holmes, and Mary White Ovington.

Villard's antiwar position was a result of America's conquest of Cuba and the Philippines, with its "needless waste of life and shocking cruelties." He had founded the League to Limit Armaments, later called the American Union Against Militarism, of which Lillian Wald became president, and he belonged to no fewer than seven peace organizations.[9]

Villard, Jane Addams and Lillian Wald were listed by military intelligence as active members of organizations opposing the war effort. Other Board members and supporters of the NAACP who belonged to what Villard called his Peace League were Hamilton Holt, George Foster Peabody, Mary White Ovington, Charles T. Hallinan, and John Haynes Holmes. Holmes was one of a small company of clergymen who withstood the mounting pressure of public opinion in favor of war. With this group of ardent pacifists on the Board, headed by the redoubtable Villard, Crawford's warning to Spingarn takes on added significance.[10]

Joel Spingarn, his brother Arthur, and Roy Nash, on the other hand, had all volunteered and were eventually commissioned as officers in the army. Mary White Ovington was no believer in nonresistance, but she hated the loss of freedom inherent in militarism. She chided Joel Spingarn and Nash, comparing them to men who had retired into monasteries where freedom of speech and thought were suppressed, and authority alone ruled. She regretted that Spingarn's new duties would compel him to teach obedience of the emptiest kind, for he had the "rare gift of teaching audacity and disobedience to forms."[11]

---

[8] Crawford to Spingarn, April 7, 1917, J. E. Spingarn Papers (Howard).

[9] Villard, *Fighting Years: Memoirs of a Liberal Editor* (New York, 1939), pp. 100, 248, 323; D. Joy Humes, *Oswald Garrison Villard: Liberal of the 1920's* (Binghamton, 1960), p. 195; Robert Luther Duffus, *Lillian Wald: Neighbor and Crusader* (New York, 1938), p. 151.

[10] Ray H. Abrams, *Preachers Present Arms: A Study of Wartime Attitudes and Activities of the Churches and Clergy in the United States 1914–1918* (New York, 1933), pp. 32, 199–200; *New York Tribune*, April 2, 1917; Beryl Williams Epstein, *Lillian Wald: Angel of Henry Street* (New York, 1948), p. 181; Spingarn to Board of Directors NAACP, May 1, 1917; May 14, 1917; Minutes of Annual Meeting, May 6, 1919, in Board Minutes, NAACP; Royal F. Nash to Spingarn, August 18, 1917; *Louisville Courier-Journal*, May 6, 1918, clipping, in J. E. Spingarn Papers (Howard). Johnson, before becoming field secretary, had criticized Holmes's position as hurtful to the cause of international peace. James Weldon Johnson, "Hurting Helpfulness," in *New York Age*, July 15, 1915.

[11] Mary White Ovington, *The Walls Came Tumbling Down* (New York, 1947), pp. 133–34; Ovington to Spingarn, July 5, 1917; August 15 [1917], J. E. Spingarn Papers (Howard).

Following the declaration of war in April, 1917, the Board demanded that additional units be opened to enlistment of Negroes, and made it known that the NAACP would take every feasible step to prevent discrimination in the services. Although Miss Ovington was opposed to war and compulsory military service, she believed that every member of the Association and every branch should fight against any attempt to put the Negro in a position below that of other citizens. Aware that the South would try to prevent the Negro from wearing the uniform of a federal soldier, she and Miss Wald insisted that the Negro demand this prima facie evidence of citizenship on the same terms as other Americans. The vote for this policy was unanimous, but Villard asked that it be recorded that his vote in favor of the motion in no way indicated support of conscription or of any form of militarism. The Board also agreed that the NAACP would oppose the exclusion of Negroes from military service by use of the subterfuge of exemption of agricultural labor.[12]

THE ISSUE OF SEPARATE TRAINING CAMPS

Because of the increasing number of requests for a declaration of policy on questions of particular importance to Negroes growing out of the wartime emergency, the Board decided that it was time for a general Negro conference to take counsel as to the best course of action. This two-day conference was held in Washington in mid-May, and the NAACP invited not only the branches, but delegates from other Negro organizations. The seven hundred present adopted resolutions which attributed the cause of the war "to the despising of the darker races by the dominant groups of men, and the consequent fierce rivalry among European nations in their effort to use darker and backward people for purposes of selfish gain." Nevertheless, the conference was united in calling on Negroes to enlist in the army and to join in the war effort in spite of continued insult and discrimination. The conference also demanded the right of Negroes to serve on the battlefield, to lead troops of their own race in battle, and to receive training in preparation for this service and leadership.[13]

Joel Spingarn proceeded independently to work for a separate officers' training camp for Negroes. He had already begun to sound out various individuals con-

[12] Board Minutes, NAACP, April 9, 1917.
[13] Board Minutes, NAACP, April 9, 1917; May 14, 1917; Crisis, XIV (May, 1917), 7; XIV (June, 1917), 59-60; XIV (July, 1917), 131. Du Bois took a leading part in drafting the resolutions; Arthur Spingarn, Miss Ovington and Washington members Archibald Grimke, Professor George W. Cook of Howard University, and Charles E. Russell made the plans and arrangements for the conference. Washington Bee, May 12, 1917; May 26, 1917; New York Age, May 17, 1917.

cerning this idea and had been advised that the scheme should be a matter of personal effort, not officially sponsored by the NAACP.[14]

Three months before America entered the war, Spingarn learned from General Leonard Wood, the Commander of the Eastern Department of the Army, that if 200 Negroes applied for admission, the army would set up a four-week military training camp for Negroes, who would then be ready to volunteer their services in case of war. Spingarn immediately broadcast this news in an open letter to "Educated Colored Men" urging that all eligible Negroes send him applications and endeavor to influence their friends in support of the program. It was necessary to convince General Wood that more than 200 would join immediately or the opportunity for training young colored men for positions of leadership would be lost. When Spingarn provided Wood with a list of applicants, however, the General increased the minimum requirement for the camp to 250.[15]

Since it seemed likely that those who were accepted would have as their only expense the cost of uniforms, Spingarn sought to lighten the burden by offering to pay for the uniforms of 100 Howard University students who applied. This generosity was without doubt a considerable factor in securing more than the 250 applicants demanded by the army.[16]

When war was declared on April 6, Spingarn sought advice from Edmund Platt, Representative of New York's Twenty-sixth Congressional District, regarding Wood's promises. At this time he had in hand 280 applications of young men, most of whom had been graduated from college or normal school, a few with previous military training. He pointed out that they were making a great concession in agreeing to segregated training because of a patriotic desire to serve their country. More radical Negro leaders, however, opposed the segregated camp and would not compromise. Platt, who had promised to help, commented: "It is a pity we have to go into this war with the South in the saddle and a lot of hampering prejudices that will interfere with the proper conduct of affairs."[17]

By the middle of April Spingarn had 350 applicants, though plans for the camp were still in doubt. Two thirds of the applicants were graduates or under-

[14] George W. Crawford to Spingarn, April 7, 1917, J. E. Spingarn Papers (Howard).
[15] "An Open Letter from Dr. J. E. Spingarn to the Educated Colored Men of the United States," February 15, 1917; Leonard Wood to Spingarn, January 9, 1917; March 8, 1917, J. E. Spingarn Papers (Howard).
[16] George E. Brice to Spingarn, March 14, 1917, J. E. Spingarn Papers (Howard).
[17] Spingarn to Edmund Platt, April 7, 1917; Platt to Spingarn, April 9, 1917, J. E. Spingarn Papers (Howard). Moderates such as President Stephen M. Newman and Professor George W. Cook of Howard University supported Spingarn and formed a committee of faculty, students, and prominent Negroes of Washington, who worked for the camp and interviewed government officials. Charles H. Williams, *Sidelights on Negro Soldiers* (Boston, 1923), p. 38.

graduates of colleges or universities, and most of the remainder had a high school education. Among the applicants there were two college presidents, twenty-three college professors, twenty physicians, ten lawyers, ten clergymen, three newspaper editors, five dentists, and twenty government clerks or officials.[18]

Later in April, when Spingarn received notice from the War Department that there would be a training program for Negro officers, he urged Howard University students to take advantage of the opportunity, predicting that the training camps would be historic and attendance at them a proud heritage to pass down to one's children's children.[19]

In the meantime, Nash, who had been conferring with members of Congress, learned that Southern members of the House Military Affairs Committee had attempted to eliminate Negroes from the draft, but had been opposed by the Secretary of War. Congressman Martin B. Madden of Chicago tried without success to persuade Republican members of the Committee to draft a bill specifically providing for the inclusion of Negro soldiers, but they objected on the ground that any mention of race was needless discrimination. As a result of his conferences, Nash and his committee decided that the best procedure was to refrain from lobbying unless the race issue came up in debate on the floor of Congress.

The next step was an attempt to put the War Department on record as to the administration of the bill providing for selective service. Nash drafted a letter for Congressmen Madden to send to Secretary of War Baker inquiring whether any distinction would be made as to Negroes in the administration of the law and whether they would be accepted at officers' training camps. Baker's answer was so evasive that no portion of it could be read into the record during the debate on the bill. Madden, however, secured an amendment to the bill which provided that each state must send a quota of men based on its total population, regardless of exemptions. Thus, if a Southern state excluded Negroes from the draft, it would have to draft a larger proportion of white men than other states.[20]

At the end of April a biracial delegation of NAACP members headed by Moorfield Storey, with Spingarn as spokesman, conferred with the Secretary of War and urged him to authorize the admission of 300 Negro applicants to the camp at Plattsburgh, New York, or any of the other regular training camps which had been established. The Secretary replied that he had the matter under con-

---

[18] Spingarn to R. B. Thompson, April 17, 1917; Spingarn to William H. Pickens, April 17, 1917; Spingarn to Major Allen Washington, April 17, 1917; Spingarn to Robert R. Moton, April 20, 1917; Spingarn to Major Halstead Dorey, April 20, 1917, J. E. Spingarn Papers (Howard).

[19] Spingarn to George W. Cook, April 24, 1917, J. E. Spingarn Papers (Howard).

[20] Board Minutes, NAACP, May 14, 1917; *Congressional Record*, 65th Cong., 1st Sess., pp. 2421, 2429.

sideration; he was committed to the plan for training colored officers for colored regiments but still had not come to a decision about a separate camp. He claimed he wanted to do whatever was least offensive to the colored people.[21] The delegation left the interview convinced that they could do nothing further to insure fair treatment for Negroes in the new army. Within a few days the NAACP was notified that a training camp for Negro officers would open on June 17, 1917, at Des Moines, Iowa.[22]

Violent opposition to Spingarn's plan had broken out among Negroes following the publication of his open letter in February. Butler Wilson spoke of the proposed camp as the rankest kind of segregation. He completely opposed countenancing segregation by accepting its benefits, which were, he said, in the long run always more expensive than beneficial. Another Board member, George Crawford, had serious doubts as to the wisdom of Spingarn's plan. He thought that a request for separate camps would be construed as tacit approval of segregation in the army, and that the harmful effects would far outweigh the advantages. George Kelley, secretary of the Afro-American League, was concerned lest Spingarn's plan should prevent the opening of all branches of the army to Negroes. Spingarn assured him that the NAACP objective was to have Negro units in every branch of the service.[23]

The problem of separating the personal activities of the Board chairman from official NAACP policy was difficult to solve. Because Spingarn's own beliefs and actions might endanger the Association's prestige and usefulness, he offered to resign as chairman. Archibald Grimke, who took issue with Spingarn over the camp question, insisted that the Board should not for one moment consider Spingarn's resignation. A showdown with the Board was averted when Spingarn left to enter Reserve Officers Training Camp, and Miss Ovington became acting chairman. Grimke later changed his mind and supported Spingarn's position, but some NAACP members refused to dissociate his camp project from official NAACP policy.[24]

[21] Spingarn, news release [April 28, 1917], in J. E. Spingarn Papers (Howard). Others in the delegation were Archibald Grimke, George Cook, Montgomery Gregory, James W. Robinson, James A. Cobb, Kelly Miller, Whitfield McKinley, and Royal Nash.
[22] Board Minutes, NAACP, May 14, 1917; Grenville Clark, Adjutant General, to James Weldon Johnson, May 25, 1917, copy, in J. E. Spingarn Papers (Howard).
[23] Butler Wilson to Richetta Randolph, September 28, 1916; Crawford to Spingarn, March 3, 1917; Spingarn to George B. Kelley, April 13, 1917, J. E. Spingarn Papers (Howard).
[24] Spingarn to Grimke, April 3, 1917; Grimke to Spingarn, April 4, 1917; Spingarn to Mrs. M. C. Simpson, April 25, 1917; Nash and Grimke to Baker, April 19, 1917, copy, J. E. Spingarn Papers (Howard); Board Minutes, NAACP, May 14, 1917; Spingarn to Nash, April 30, 1917, quoted in Board Minutes, NAACP, May 14, 1917. The separate training camp became an actuality on June 18, 1917. *New York Times*, June 19, 1917.

The Negro press as a whole bitterly condemned the proposal. Criticism of Joel Spingarn became so sharp and so general that he found it advisable to make a public defense of his proposal in speeches, in newspapers, and in the Association's *Branch Bulletin*. His argument was that the army wished the segregated camp to fail so that it would be in a position to say that Negroes had had their chance but refused to take it. He was sure that only after a number of Negro officers had been trained would it be feasible to press for a wide-open army; the segregated camp was a temporary expedient forced on the race by circumstances but capable of changing the role of the Negro in the war. He reminded his readers and listeners that the South, frightened at the thought of black millions, disciplined, organized, and dangerously effective, did not want Negroes to receive any military training at all, and that with conscription Negroes would have the opportunity of becoming leaders and officers rather than mere followers and privates.[25]

To Du Bois the segregated camp was a perpetual dilemma. He considered the arguments academic because they assumed that the choice was between volunteering and not volunteering, whereas the real choice was between conscription and rebellion. He saw the horns of the dilemma as, on the one hand, the affront of being put in a segregated camp and, on the other hand, the irreparable injury that might be done if Negroes were to be denied positions of military authority because of the lack of a separate camp for officers' training.[26]

William Pickens, an NAACP member who was then Dean of Morgan College for Negroes in Baltimore, defended Spingarn, as did Colonel Charles Young, a Negro graduate of West Point and an officer in the regular army. To Pickens the formation of a separate camp was logical because separate units already existed within the army and the separate camp would provide more opportunities for promotion of Negroes than a predominantly white training camp.[27] Colonel Young, who as a brevet major had commanded the Negro Ninth Ohio Infantry in the Spanish American War, spoke out in behalf of Spingarn's plan. He believed Spingarn to be as right in practice as the objectors were in theory.[28]

[25] The *New York Age*, the *Boston Guardian*, the *Afro-American* (Baltimore), and the *Chicago Defender* were all opposed to the camp, according to W. E. B. Du Bois, *Dusk of Dawn: An Essay toward an Autobiography of a Race Concept* (New York, 1940), p. 25. *New York News*, February 22, 1917; *New York Age*, March 1, 1917; *Cleveland Gazette*, March 10, 1917; *Amsterdam News* (New York), May 3, 1917, clippings; J. Q. Adams (editor of *St. Paul-Minneapolis Appeal*) to Spingarn [May, 1917], J. E. Spingarn Papers (Howard); *Branch Bulletin*, I (March, 1917), 30–31; *Washington Bee*, letter, March 24, 1917.
[26] *Crisis*, XIII (April, 1917), 270–71; *Branch Bulletin*, I (March, 1917), 31.
[27] Pickens to Spingarn, February 27, 1917. This letter was printed in the *Maryland Voice*, VI (March 10, 1917), 1, official organ of the Maryland Baptist churches, clipping in J. E. Spingarn Papers (Howard).
[28] John Hope Franklin, *From Slavery to Freedom: A History of American Negroes* (2d ed.; New York, 1965), p. 413; Charles Young to Harry C. Smith, March 23, 1917, copy, in J. E. Spingarn Papers (Howard).

Spingarn sent Young's statement to the Negro press in order to take advantage of Young's prestige. The *New York Age* commented bluntly that Negroes had no business segregating themselves until the government had made it clear that it intended to segregate them.[29]

Some NAACP branches supported the idea of a separate camp, but it was inevitable that there would be confusion and uncertainty among the branches. The president of the Cleveland branch asked Spingarn to reassure members because one newspaper editor had cast doubt on Spingarn's sincerity and had hinted that they were being double-crossed.[30]

Spingarn volunteered for service and left for the Reserve Officers Training Camp at Madison Barracks, New York, before the Des Moines camp issue was settled. He wanted the NAACP to commit itself to training for Negro officers, preferably in unsegregated camps, but he warned that results should override every other consideration.[31] This caused lengthy debate among Board members. The resolution finally adopted by the Board stated that "while thoroughly opposed to segregation in case of officers training camps as well as in all other cases, yet rather than have no officers training camp for colored men who under the new draft law are to be placed in separate regiments, this Association favors separate training camps for colored officers." Joseph Loud of Boston and Dr. Owen Waller of Brooklyn asked that their opposition to the resolution be recorded.[32]

Thus the Association put itself on record in favor of separate camps. Little or no publicity was given to this decision, but when the Des Moines camp was announced, *The Crisis* jubilantly proclaimed: "We have won! The camp is granted; we shall have 1,000 Negro officers in the United States Army! Write us for information."[33]

Spingarn considered that he had waged the battle alone, except for the help of two or three men like Dean William Pickens and Professor George Cook. He later refuted James Weldon Johnson's statement that it was the NAACP (under Spingarn's leadership) that undertook to see that provision was made for the training of colored men to be officers in the army. Spingarn claimed that the NAACP never took organized action in the matter, regardless of what its officials may have done as individuals. He further asserted that the NAACP never recorded in its minutes or official publications any action for or against the

[29] J. H. Anderson to Spingarn, March 29, 1917; Spingarn to Fred R. Moore, April 3, 1917, in J. H. Spingarn Papers (Howard); *New York Age*, March 29, 1917; *Washington Bee*, March 31, 1917.
[30] Spingarn to Mrs. J. E. McClain, secretary, Des Moines, Iowa, branch, April 12, 1917; Francis E. Young to Spingarn, August 5, 1918, J. E. Spingarn Papers (Howard).
[31] Spingarn to Nash, April 30, 1917, in Board Minutes, NAACP, May 14, 1917.
[32] Board Minutes, NAACP, May 14, 1917.
[33] Platt to Spingarn, May 21, 1917, J. E. Spingarn Papers (Howard); *Crisis*, XIV (June, 1917), 60.

project.[34] In this he was mistaken, but it is true that the Board did not take action favoring the separate camp until a few days before the announcement of the official decision to institute the camp was issued. Therefore full credit for the effort should go to Spingarn.[35]

While in the army both Joel Spingarn and Roy Nash tried to combine soldiering with working for Negro advancement. Nash felt guilty at leaving the Association. Referring to the East St. Louis riots, he wrote, "With St. Louis and all the rest that colored people have had to endure this summer, it seems pretty hard to be laying down the work, but the bigger job must be finished before the lesser." Spingarn, through his connections with Henry Morgenthau, Democratic national committeeman from New York City, asked to be transferred from Madison Barracks to Des Moines to assist in organizing the camp. He was refused on the ground that no exception could be made while he was still in training. Nash, who became a Captain in the Field Artillery also tried to be transferred to a Negro division and later succeeded in being sent to the 167th Field Artillery Brigade, which was composed of Negro troops.[36]

Lack of a fixed policy by the War Department caused some trouble at the Des Moines camp. When the training term was extended to four months a number of the men became restive and threatened to return home as there was some indication that the Army might not commission them at the end of the extended term. Telegrams were dispatched from the national office of the NAACP to the men and to their commanding officer and every effort was made to persuade them to complete the course. James Weldon Johnson conferred in Washington with the Senate Military Affairs Committee on the commissioning of the trainees. He learned that the Southern ring in power in Washington was causing the senators on the Committee to have doubts as to the wisdom of granting commissions to Negroes. Because of Johnson's prodding the Committee finally conferred with Secretary Baker and reported that the men would be commissioned.[37]

JIM CROW IN WARTIME

In the fall of 1917 the NAACP sent Du Bois to Secretary Baker with a lengthy memorandum calling his attention to a number of conditions which the

[34] Spingarn, news release [April 28, 1917], J. E. Spingarn Papers (Howard); James Weldon Johnson, *Along This Way* (New York, 1933), p. 318; Johnson to Spingarn, October 24 [1933]; Spingarn to Johnson, October 27, 1933, Joel Elias Spingarn Papers (James Weldon Johnson Collection, Yale University; hereafter referred to as the Johnson Collection).
[35] Du Bois to Spingarn, October 22, 1917, Johnson Collection.
[36] Nash to Spingarn, August 18, 1917; Grenville Clark to Henry Morgenthau, June 18, 1917; Spingarn to Nash, October 31, 1917, J. E. Spingarn Papers (Howard); Board Minutes, NAACP, September 9, 1918.
[37] Board Minutes, September 17, 1917; October 8, 1917; Du Bois to Spingarn, September 25, 1917, Johnson Collection.

NAACP maintained were having an unfortunate effect upon the morale of twelve million citizens. Among the items to which the NAACP objected were: identification by race on draft registration papers; refusal to accept Negroes as volunteers in proportion to the population; exclusion of Negroes from various branches of the armed forces such as the artillery,[38] air corps, and navy; allegations that the government planned to draft Negroes for labor and menial service, rather than all-around military duty; refusal to allow Negroes to enter training camps on the same terms as whites; the long delay in establishing the camp at Des Moines; refusal to open a second camp for Negro officers; the unexplained delay in granting commissions to the Negro trainees at Des Moines; the retirement of Colonel Young from active service; indecision in determining the future of Negro units of the National Guard; the delay in calling up Negroes in the draft; and treatment of colored recruits. To meet Baker's reiterated protest that it was not his business as Secretary of War to settle the Negro problem, the NAACP countered that the best way to raise an army was to settle that portion of the problem that interfered with the effective training and use of Negro troops.[39] Baker, however, did give official confirmation to the report that the officer candidates at the Des Moines camp would receive their commissions, and he also assured the NAACP that he would see to it that Negro soldiers were justly treated. In October, 1917, more than 600 men at Des Moines were commissioned as officers, a result which the *New York Age* at last admitted could have been achieved in no other way.[40]

One of the Association's complaints to Secretary Baker had been the early retirement on grounds of physical disability of Colonel Charles Young, one of the few high-ranking Negro officers. Storey advised the Board not to take a stand without ascertaining whether Young (who had announced that he was in excellent physical condition) was really disabled. After investigating, the Board was convinced that Young had lost the rank due him because of his color. Du Bois tried in vain to see Baker on Young's behalf, and the national office sought to bring influence to bear on the War Department through Villard, Florence Kelley, Walter Lippmann, and Governor Samuel W. McCall, of Massachusetts.[41]

[38] A year later the artillery was opened to Negroes and the commanding general of the 167th Field Artillery, A.E.F., John H. Sherburn, together with Nash, asked for the help of the NAACP in recruiting the Brigade to full strength by securing certain specialists. Board Minutes, NAACP, September 9, 1918.
[39] Board Minutes, NAACP October 8, 1917. Shillady speaks of Baker's "well known attitude." Board Minutes, NAACP, March 11, 1918.
[40] Board Minutes, NAACP, November 12, 1917; *New York Age*, October 18, 1917. The new officers, to show their appreciation for what the NAACP had done for them, held a concert at the camp and turned over the proceeds of $272.05 to the treasury of the Association.
[41] Moorfield Storey to Du Bois, August 3, 1917; August 29, 1917, Moorfield Storey Papers (in the possession of Mr. Charles Storey, Boston, Massachusetts); Board Minutes, NAACP, September 17, 1917; March 11, 1918.

Colonel Young, according to Miss Ovington, was not a man with a grudge. He did not wish to antagonize or challenge the army physicians in his case, but he had hoped to be given command of a regiment of Negro conscripts. This the Association was able to accomplish and Young was temporarily assigned to active service in November, 1918, as commander of Negro troops at Camp Grant at Rockford, Illinois.[42]

The NAACP memorandum which Du Bois had presented to the Secretary of War had commended the army's decision to accept Negro physicians as medical officers. When it was revealed that they could serve only in colored regiments, which were limited in number, Johnson took the matter up with Emmett J. Scott but without success. Scott had risen to eminence as Booker T. Washington's lieutenant and confidant and had been appointed Special Assistant to the Secretary of War. Scott's job was to advise Baker in all matters affecting the Negro and the prosecution of the war.[43]

It soon became obvious that the government was taking no steps to utilize Negro nurses, either at home or abroad, and had, in fact, ruled that Negroes were not eligible to become Red Cross nurses. The Association at once challenged this ruling, and the result was a long drawn out controversy. The chief stumbling block to a solution was the hostility of the Surgeon General of the United States, William Crawford Gorgas. The problem had been only partially solved at the time of the Armistice, in November, 1911. A few Negro nurses had been assigned to army installations in the United States, but none had been assigned to duty overseas because of the lack of segregated facilities.[44]

Throughout the war, civilian agencies serving the army continued to discriminate against Negroes in a variety of ways. The YMCA, particularly in the South and in such Northern industrial centers as Detroit, showed marked discrimination against colored soldiers. This condition was revealed in complaints to the NAACP and in the reports of the Committee on the Welfare of Negro Troops, which had been set up under the joint auspices of the Federal Council

---

[42] Ovington to Spingarn, July 5, 1917, J. E. Spingarn Papers (Howard); Board Minutes, NAACP, April 8, 1918; NAACP, *Ninth Annual Report 1918* (New York, 1919), pp. 39–40. At the close of the war Colonel Young was reinstated in the army and sent on a mission to Liberia, where he died. Ovington, *The Walls Came Tumbling Down,* p. 135; Johnson, *Along This Way,* p. 345, n. 1.
[43] Board Minutes, NAACP, October 8, 1917; January 14, 1918; Du Bois, *Dusk of Dawn,* p. 248. Scott was appointed on October 5, 1917, in a move to counteract "mounting race friction . . . continued lynching . . . and the German propaganda." Franklin, *From Slavery to Freedom,* p. 449.
[44] Board Minutes, NAACP, May 13, 1917; July 8, 1918; NAACP, *Ninth Annual Report 1918,* pp. 40–41.

of Churches of Christ in America and the Phelps-Stokes Fund with former Howard University president W. P. Thirkield as chairman.[45] Officials of the YMCA, disturbed at the publicity, disavowed the charges and promised to look into the matter, but discrimination continued.[46]

The War Camp Community Service was another civilian agency serving the army which practiced discrimination against Negro troops. This group was in charge of civilian activities concerned with the general welfare and entertainment of the soldiers in training camps. John Shillady offered the organization the cooperation of the NAACP, proposing a program that would utilize *The Crisis* and NAACP branches near the camps to mobilize colored people to contribute more effective services to Negro troops. He suggested that a representative of the NAACP be appointed to the national body of the War Camp Community Service and offered the Association's aid in raising money for this program. The Service, however, refused the offer, claiming that there was no committee structure to carry out Shillady's proposals and that the Service could not be used for propaganda of any kind, thus purposely distorting the reason for the NAACP offer. The Association, however, was able to cooperate with the National Association of Colored Women and with colored YMCA and YWCA workers in an attempt to get the War Camp Community Service to make better provisions for Negro soldiers.[47]

Recreational facilities at army camps were often limited. Negro soldiers at Camp Upton, New York, complained that they were restricted to the use of a single inadequate "hostess house" in which to entertain their guests. The NAACP sent protests to the War Department and gave news stories to the Negro and the friendly white press—as a result of which the director of training camp activities offered the following explanation: The purpose of the order had not been to exclude Negro troops from any particular hostess house but rather to call attention to the one that had been built solely for the use of colored troops. This was far from a satisfactory explanation but Board members were unable to achieve any further recognition of the situation. They met this type of frustration again in an incident which took place at Camp Funston, Kansas. A dispute broke out because a local moving picture house relegated Negro troops to the balcony. Major General C. C. Ballou, commander of the

---

[45] Thirkield was early connected with the NAACP as a member of the Committee of One Hundred. Minutes, Executive Committee, June 7, 1910, in Board Minutes, NAACP.
[46] *Crisis*, XVII (November, 1918), 8; Board Minutes, NAACP, March 10, 1919; April 14, 1919; Williams, *Sidelights on Negro Soldiers*, p. 11.
[47] Board Minutes, NAACP, July 8, 1918; May 12, 1919; NAACP, *Ninth Annual Report 1918*, pp. 70–71. In addition, there was some discussion of the NAACP "taking over" the Circle of Negro War Relief, but this did not occur. Board Minutes, NAACP, June 10, 1918.

92nd Division of Negro Troops, had secured the right of the soldiers to sit where they chose, but he nevertheless issued his famous Bulletin No. 35, advising officers and men to refrain from going where they were not wanted, regardless of their legal rights. Any action on their part that would cause the color question to be raised would be "prejudicial to the good of the service."[48]

Discrimination was also attempted in certain areas by officials of the Student Army Training Corps. Students of Oberlin College, Western Reserve, and Ohio State University were denied admission to the Corps by the regional director, who based his decision on a War Department regulation that colored and white students must be housed in separate barracks. The students, with the help of the Cleveland, Columbus, Cincinnati, and Oberlin NAACP branches, appealed to the national office. Shillady notified Emmett Scott, who informed him that the War Department had not issued such orders and that any student who qualified mentally and physically was eligible for admission to the Student Army Training Corps. A similar situation was uncovered in Nebraska, and the Association took steps to inform Negro students of their rights.[49]

There were numerous complaints of discrimination by draft boards, especially in the South. A common practice was to induct Negroes who were physically unfit and those who were above and below the draft age. Negroes were seldom granted exemption from the draft because of dependents.[50]

Numerous cases of personal abuse by superior officers were reported to the Association. One of these was taken up by the Boston branch and resulted in a general order prohibiting the use of epithets and abusive language. Other insults involved the refusal of white soldiers to salute Negro officers. An officer at Camp Pike, Arkansas, who refused to assemble his men beside Negro troops was court-martialed and dismissed from the army.

Since there were frequent cases of police brutality against Negroes in civilian life, it was not surprising that the military police indulged in the same practices. The legal department of the District of Columbia branch took up the shooting of a colored girl by a marine. A member of the District Attorney's office had been at the scene and believed that the marine, in anger, had intentionally shot the girl; the marine was exonerated by the Navy Department over the protests of the NAACP branch.[51]

The brutality of civilian police toward Negro soldiers and civilians was largely responsible for the Houston, Texas, race riot. The riot took place on the night of August 23, 1917, and involved a battalion of the Twenty-fourth Infantry, a

---

[48] *Washington Bee*, April 27, 1918; Board Minutes, NAACP, May 13, 1918; March 10, 1919; NAACP, *Ninth Annual Report 1918*, pp. 38–39; Ovington, *The Walls Came Tumbling Down*, pp. 135–36.
[49] Board Minutes, NAACP, October 14, 1918; NAACP, *Ninth Annual Report 1918*, p. 39.
[50] Board Minutes, NAACP, September 9, 1918.
[51] Board Minutes, NAACP, July 8, 1918; NAACP, *Ninth Annual Report 1918*, pp. 67–68.

Negro regiment of the regular army stationed at Camp Logan, Houston, Texas. Seventeen white persons and two Negroes were killed. City officials blamed the soldiers for the incident, but an investigation conducted by Martha Gruening for the NAACP put the underlying blame for the riot on the habitual brutality of the white police officers in their treatment of Negro residents. She claimed that contributing causes were the disarming of the Negro military police upon the insistence of the local authorities and the lax discipline at the camp which permitted promiscuous visiting, drinking, and immorality among the soldiers.[52]

The Association engaged a local white attorney, A. J. Houston, a son of Sam Houston, to aid in the soldiers' defense. Great pressure was exerted to have the soldiers tried in the civilian courts of Texas, but the army maintained control. Sixty-three men were court-martialed, thirteen of whom were in December, 1917, summarily hanged without the right of appeal under a law which, according to the NAACP attorney, applied only to troops in action. Forty-one men were sentenced to life imprisonment, four were given long prison terms, and five others condemned to death. In a second court-martial, eleven more men received the death sentence. The Crisis noted bitterly that none of the white policemen whom it blamed for causing the riot were indicted, nor were any of the white officers in charge of the camp brought to trial.[53]

During the more than fifty years that Negro regiments had served in the regular army there had been only one other occasion where serious trouble had broken out between colored troops and the civilian population. This, too, had occurred in Texas, at Brownsville, in 1906. Like the Houston incident, it had been brought about as a result of the attitude of the South toward Negro troops, but President Theodore Roosevelt had dismissed the entire battalion "without honor."[54]

In an effort to save the lives of the sixteen men condemned at Houston, James Weldon Johnson conferred with Scott at the War Department, and in February, 1918, at the head of a committee, presented a petition with nearly 12,000 names to the President, asking clemency for the condemned men and for those sen-

<hr/>

[52] Board Minutes, NAACP, September 17, 1917; Crisis, XV (November, 1917), 14–19; Crisis XV (April, 1918), 269. Johnson claimed that the Houston officials "insisted" on policing the soldiers, that white police were habitually "insulting and brutal" and the day before the riot had "cruelly" and "without need" used their nightsticks on a number of soldiers. Johnson, Along This Way, pp. 321–22. Police brutality and the shooting of Negro soldiers was not limited to the South. Board Minutes, NAACP, October 14, 1918.
[53] Board Minutes, NAACP, December 10, 1917; Minutes, Annual Meeting, January 7, 1918; Johnson, Along This Way, p. 322; Crisis, XV (April, 1918), 269.
[54] Garrison to Villard, November 8, 1906, Villard Papers. The Constitution League led the fight to clear the soldiers. New York Age, April 4, 1907; Preliminary Report of the Commission of the Constitution League of the United States on Affray at Brownsville, Texas, August 13 and 14, 1906, Senate Document No. 107, 59th Cong., 2d Sess. (Washington, 1906), pp. 1–32; Voice of the Negro, IV (May, 1907), 160–61; Washington to George B. Cortelyou, January 28, 1907, Washington Papers.

tenced to life imprisonment. Wilson agreed to have the records reviewed. As a result of the review, ten of the death sentences were commuted to life imprisonment. Six death sentences were affirmed and the men subsequently hanged. A report was current that Wilson had ordered the reprieve of the ten because of pleas from clergymen and Negro organizations, but the NAACP Board, although disappointed in the outcome of the appeal, claimed that the clemency was the result of the work of the Association and Johnson's committee. The Association continued to agitate and to work actively for the release of the remaining prisoners. In 1921, a petition containing 50,000 signatures was handed to President Harding. As a result several of the prisoners were released and a number of the life sentences reduced. In another campaign, November 11, 1923, was designated as "Houston Martyrs Day," and early in 1924, a third petition containing more than 124,000 signatures was presented to President Coolidge. Countermeasures were taken by Texans to prevent any extension of clemency. The NAACP continued its efforts, however, until the last prisoner was finally released on July 20, 1938, by order of President Franklin D. Roosevelt.[55]

The NAACP attacked other forms of discrimination in the army with little success. A disproportionate number of Negro draftees were assigned to noncombatant forms of service in industrial and stevedore battalions. Skilled workers and professional men, especially physicians and dentists, were not assigned to work for which they were trained, even though there was a need for technicians and medical personnel.

The question of the segregation of troops on the railroads, which had been placed under direct control of the government, was never satisfactorily settled. Appeals to McAdoo, the Director General of the Railroads, brought the excuse that he had no authority over Jim Crow cars, that state laws had not been suspended, and that only Congress could remedy the situation.[56]

Villard and Crawford brought the attention of the Board to the case of a Negro lieutenant, a graduate of Yale's Sheffield Scientific School, who was taken from a Pullman car at Chickasha, Oklahoma, fined, and jailed for refusing to enter the Jim Crow day coach. Again, the answer to protests from the NAACP was that state law prevailed. A similar case involved a private, a dentist in civilian life, who had been ordered out of a Pullman car at Texarkana. The Secretary of War was asked for a specific ruling as to whether the War Department would insist that army personnel traveling under government orders be

---

[55] Board Minutes, NAACP, January 14, 1918; February 11, 1918; March 11, 1918; October 10, 1921; December 6, 1923; May 8, 1924; *Washington Bee*, February 23, 1918; NAACP, *Ninth Annual Report 1918*, p. 37; *Fourteenth Annual Report 1923*, pp. 35–37; *Twenty-ninth Annual Report 1938*, p. 18; *Crisis*, XXIII (November, 1921), 21; XXVII (December, 1923), 72–73; XXVII (April, 1924), 269; XXVIII (June, 1924), 70; Johnson, *Along This Way*, p. 325.
[56] Board Minutes, NAACP, November 12, 1917; March 11, 1918.

given the type of service authorized by the government without discrimination. The War Department made no attempt to clarify the issue and instead passed the question on to the Attorney General and the Adjutant General.[57]

James A. Cobb, a lawyer on the legal committee of the Washington NAACP branch, made a compilation of decisions affecting interstate and intrastate passengers. The Supreme Court had held that a state could not interfere with interstate passengers. Moreover, in all the decisions affirming the constitutionality of the "separate coach laws," the separation of whites and Negroes was held not to be a denial of rights guaranteed by the Fourteenth Amendment, provided there was equality in accommodation. In 1918, however, no amount of pressure on the part of the Association could make Pullman accommodations available to Negro officers and men. The excuse given was that state laws must be observed.[58]

Attempts were also made to safeguard the Negro soldier's right to vote and to make sure his vote would be counted, especially after Wilson's appeal to the country for a Democratic Congress in the fall of 1918. Shillady and Grimke went to the War Department to find out what procedures for voting were to be set up in the training camps. They suggested that the Secretary of War issue a general order requiring camp commandants to report which State Commissions came to the camps to canvass votes, to make public the dates of voting, and to identify the units that would be voting. The Secretary of War rejected these suggestions but said he would welcome any complaints brought to his attention "after the event." Shillady then wrote to President Wilson, as head of the Democratic party, that the NAACP was apprehensive that Negro soldiers of some states would be deprived of their right to vote. Wilson ignored the appeal.[59]

In November, 1918, John Shillady and James Weldon Johnson represented the NAACP at a conference on Demobilization and the Responsibilities of Organized Social Agencies. The conference framed a resolution, urging that every program for national and community reconstruction should adequately and consciously make provision for Negro citizens and for their cooperation in setting up the programs.[60]

After the Armistice, the Association protested in vain against an order that required units to be demobilized at their point of origin, an order that forced many Negroes to return to the South against their will. The Association also tried to help Negro officers who wished to make the army a career. The NAACP field secretary visited the camps and compiled lists of officers who had sub-

[57] Board Minutes, NAACP, July 8, 1918.
[58] NAACP, *Ninth Annual Report 1918*, pp. 37–38; Board Minutes, NAACP, July 8, 1918.
[59] Board Minutes, NAACP, October 14, 1918; November 11, 1918; NAACP, *Ninth Annual Report 1918*, pp. 42–43.
[60] Board Minutes, NAACP, December 9, 1918.

mitted applications to be retained in the service. He turned the applications over to Scott's office, and in addition secured assurance from the adjutant general's office that Negro officers would be given the same opportunity to qualify as white officers. He tried to bring political pressure to bear by visiting Congressman Fiorello La Guardia of New York and several senators, including the ranking Republican on the Senate Military Affairs Committee, Senator Warren of Wyoming, who was General Pershing's father-in-law.[61]

Shillady was called upon to investigate conditions among Negro soldiers in camps from Massachusetts to Georgia, and to bring legitimate grievances to the attention of the War Department. The NAACP was also active in seeking to secure vocational education for Negro soldiers returning to civilian life, working through the office of George E. Haynes, director of the Division of Negro Economics in the Department of Labor.[62]

The returning soldier was the object of vicious attacks, especially in the South, where reaction to the social changes that came with the end of the war were even more hysterical than in the North. During the war, Negroes had experienced the full force of wartime propaganda stressing democracy and were anxious to share in its blessings. In the years since the NAACP was founded, Negroes had made increased use of educational opportunities. The annual education issues of *The Crisis* during these years showed a steady growth in the number of Negroes graduating from college and going on to professional schools. These graduates provided a new and militant leadership. Moreover the Negro soldier who had been in France had experienced an acceptance and recognition he had not known in America. Neither the returning soldier nor the new Negro leadership was willing to accept prewar conditions. Instead they looked forward to an extension of democracy. In a speech before the Washington branch, John R. Hawkins, executive secretary of the National Race Congress, set forth fourteen objectives the Negro had for postwar America, in imitation of Wilson's Fourteen Points.[63] But Southern whites were a power in the Wilson Administration and they were determined that democracy should not include the Negro. How, Miss Ovington asked, was the Negro to secure these objectives when the "last place to which the returning soldier can look for justice is Washington, the very fountainhead of the government he has so faithfully served . . . a government in the hands of men inimical to his claims for citizenship?"[64]

[61] Board Minutes, NAACP, January 13, 1919; April 14, 1919.
[62] Board Minutes, NAACP, April 14, 1919.
[63] Hawkins was a member of Bishop Thirkield's Committee on the Welfare of Negro Troops together with Robert Moton and James Dillard. He was a Baltimore high school teacher and financial secretary of the African Methodist Episcopal Church. *New York Age*, December 14, 1918; *Washington Bee*, October 11, 1919; October 18, 1919; Franklin, *From Slavery to Freedom*, p. 451.
[64] Ovington, "Reconstruction and the Negro," *Crisis*, XVII (February, 1919), 169–73.

The returning Negro soldier found himself discriminated against by the largest and most effective organization of veterans, the American Legion. Joel Spingarn was active in the Legion and had organized a post at Amenia, New York. He was a delegate to the first convention in Minneapolis, in November, 1919, where he attempted to prevent the exclusion of Negro posts in the South. He proposed that the constitution of the Legion permit appeals to the national body from groups to whom charters had been refused by state committees. Southern delegates defeated this move and retained the word "Caucasian" in the definition of eligibility for membership. In the meantime three organizations of Negro veterans were formed, the Grand Order of Americans, the League for Democracy, and the American Alliance, but they lacked wide appeal.[65]

On the home front Negro civilians also met with frequent discrimination and insult.[66] In the South the arbitrary tactics of the War Savings Stamps and Liberty Loan Committees evoked a series of protests and actions by the NAACP. When a Louisiana newspaper carried an article headlined "Adopt Force to Get Negroes to Buy War Savings Stamps,"[67] Shillady protested to the Secretary of the Treasury that such measures were an abuse of the prestige given by the government to the chairman of the War Savings Campaign Committees and were an affront to loyal Negroes who cooperated in the drives. The Treasury promised to investigate and to request local committees to avoid this type of pressure in the future.[68]

At Vicksburg, Mississippi, a Negro physician, a graduate of the University of Michigan, was ordered by the War Savings Committee to buy $1,000 worth of stamps. Upon his refusal to buy the full amount he was tarred and feathered, and his home was broken into and looted. Police, city officials, and leading citizens participated. The Committee and the mayor then ordered the physician to leave Vicksburg.

Two other Negroes were driven from Vicksburg, allegedly for refusing to cooperate with the War Savings Committee. The refugees claimed that the real reason was that they had tried to protect Negro soldiers who appeared on the streets of the city in uniform and were in danger of having their clothes torn from their backs. They had also tried to arouse the Negro community to resist the appointment as teachers in the Negro schools of two notorious Negro women, known to be the mistresses of politicians. One of the two men compelled to leave

[65] *Crisis*, XIX (December, 1919), 66; Board Minutes, NAACP, April 14, 1919; December 8, 1919; NAACP, *Tenth Annual Report 1919*, p. 43.
[66] A popular song was written and published under the title, "Nigger War Brides." When Shillady protested to the publishers, the title was changed. Board Minutes, NAACP, November 11, 1918.
[67] *Shreveport Times*, June 12, 1918, quoted in Board Minutes, NAACP, July 8, 1918.
[68] Board Minutes, NAACP, July 8, 1918.

Vicksburg was a druggist. He was forced to dispose of his property at about one-quarter of its value. The local draft board thereupon reassigned him from Class Four to Class One and he was inducted into the army. Appeals to the Departments of War, Treasury, and Justice were answered with the reply that the registrant's troubles with a few people in Vicksburg had no bearing upon the case so far as selective service officials were concerned. The Association could go no further with the case because of the signing of the armistice.[69]

In spite of the arbitrary actions against Negroes of Southern War Stamp and Liberty Loan Committees, the NAACP cooperated with the Fourth Liberty Loan Drive and joined with the National Association of Colored Women to push the drive among Southern Negroes. Although some state chairmen of the women's Liberty Loan committees refused to let colored women participate in the drive, good results among Negro citizens were reported.[70]

NEGRO LABOR AND THE WAR

The economic status of the Negro and his opportunities for employment were the primary concern of the Urban League, but from time to time there were complaints that the NAACP was evading its responsibilities by staying out of the economic field. Negro newspapers put pressure on the Association during 1916 and 1917, in the midst of the mounting crisis caused by migration and labor problems. They called upon the Association to enlarge its scope of usefulness and to deal with problems of poverty, jobs, and physical needs. The *Washington Bee* queried: "What are rights without bread to eat, houses to live in, clothes to wear and some simple luxuries? Let us have our political rights, but also the rational means to enjoy them."[71]

By 1918, the Negro had entered into the industrial life of the nation in competition with white workers. John Shillady was the first to work out a practical basis of cooperation between the NAACP and the Urban League in opening up new job opportunities for Negroes and gaining them admission to the ranks of organized labor. Shortly after his appointment as NAACP secretary, Shillady addressed the annual conference of the Urban League, stressing the need for Negro workmen to affiliate with the American Federation of Labor.[72]

The Urban League invited him to join their delegation as the representative of the NAACP at a Department of Labor conference, and later at a conference with

[69] Board Minutes, NAACP, September 9, 1918; October 14, 1918; NAACP, *Ninth Annual Report 1918*, pp. 47–48.
[70] Board Minutes, NAACP, October 14, 1918; November 11, 1918.
[71] *Washington Bee*, September 1, 1917.
[72] *New York Age*, February 9, 1918.

the executive committee of the American Federation of Labor.[73] The meetings at the Department of Labor were concerned with Negro representation in the new bureaus being set up in that department for organizing the nation's labor supply under the National Emergency Labor Program. The NAACP and the Urban League also requested that a Negro be appointed to the Advisory Council of the Secretary of Labor, or to any other policy-making group that might be evolved. They were interested in having a bureau created within the Department of Labor concerned with Negro labor problems, which would be headed by a Negro and would have charge of all matters concerning Negro workers.[74]

The Secretary of Labor at first ruled that such a bureau could not be established without specific authorization from Congress, but when other organizations applied further pressure, he established a Division of Negro Economics, and appointed as its director George Haynes, education secretary of the Urban League.[75]

The Division of Negro Economics launched a program to create better relations between Negro and white workers and to secure public understanding of, and cooperation with, the war plans of the Department. The Division also studied Negro migration,[76] and reported on Negro labor in Chicago and in a number of Northern and Southern states. Under its sponsorship, a national biracial conference was held in Washington in February, 1919, at which representatives of Northern and Southern welfare and social service organizations, including the NAACP and the Urban League, discussed the improvement of race relations, working conditions of Negroes, racial tolerance among workers, aid to Negro tenants and farm workers, the education of Negro laborers, and problems of women in industry. As a result of this conference, a national program was adopted and approved by the Secretary of Labor.[77]

The NAACP was interested in achieving the benefits of organized labor for Negro workers. Because Negroes were often used as strikebreakers, the American Federation of Labor invited the Urban League, the NAACP, and other interested organizations to a conference in February, 1918, for the purpose of

[73] Board Minutes, NAACP, February 11, 1918. The other delegates were E. J. Scott, R. R. Moton, Fred R. Moore, E. K. Jones, J. H. Dillard, and T. J. Jones. *New York Age*, February 16, 1918.
[74] Board Minutes, NAACP, March 11, 1918; NAACP, *Ninth Annual Report 1918*, p. 70.
[75] Board Minutes, NAACP, April 8, 1918; May 13, 1918; NAACP, *Ninth Annual Report 1918*, pp. 69–70. At this time the press reported that T. Thomas Fortune had been named, at the state level, executive secretary of the Migrant Bureau of the Department of Labor of New Jersey. *New York Age*, April 27, 1918.
[76] For the report of this study see U.S. Department of Labor, Division of Negro Economics, *Negro Migration in 1916–1917* (reports by R. H. Leavell et al.; Washington, 1919).
[77] U.S. Department of Labor, Division of Negro Economics, *The Negro at Work During the War and Reconstruction: Second Study on Negro Labor* (Washington, 1921), pp. 1–18.

organizing a united labor front.[78] The results were not very tangible, but Shillady reported optimistically to the NAACP Board that the forthcoming AFL convention would act to help Negro workmen.[79]

The NAACP wanted to open existing unions to colored workmen. The unions, however, proposed separate and segregated organizations. The Brotherhood of Locomotive Firemen, for example, claimed that the railroads were bringing in Negro labor to depress conditions of white workmen and suggested that the NAACP should help Negro firemen to form a union of their own. In spite of this, the NAACP tried to secure approval of the AFL for an International Union of railroad employees with full recognition of the rights of Negroes. Officers of the Association signed a petition of the Railroad Men's Benevolent Industrial Association, composed of colored railroad workers, asking for wider acceptance of Negro workers into unions affiliated with the AFL without discrimination. The petition also suggested that capable Negro organizers be assigned to the work. Although these objectives were not achieved, Shillady was sure that some progress had been made at the 1918 AFL convention and that the delegates were now more willing to welcome Negroes into their organizations.[80]

At the 1919 AFL convention, according to *The Crisis*, extraordinary interest and even enthusiasm was shown for the Negro worker. There were nearly four times the number of Negro delegates as in 1918, six Negro unions were represented, and a resolution was passed, calling on the AFL to give special attention to the organizing of Negro workers and to the use of Negroes as organizers. The resolution also proposed that when individual unions refused to admit Negro workers, the AFL should organize Negroes in separate unions. The passage of this resolution, reported *The Crisis*, was accompanied by a demonstration of such magnitude that the onlookers believed that the Negro had at last come into his own in the world of labor. As a demonstration of solidarity, forty heads of International Unions rose to their feet and welcomed black men into their ranks. Du Bois considered this the beginning of a "square deal" from labor,[81] but in spite of this optimistic pronouncement, organized labor remained virtually closed to Negroes.

[78] Board Minutes, NAACP, March 11, 1918; Franklin, *From Slavery to Freedom*, p. 466.
[79] Board Minutes, NAACP, May 13, 1918; April 8, 1918. The unions represented at the conference were the United Association of Plumbers and Steamfitters, the Metal Trades Department and the Building Trades Department of the AFL and the Central Labor Union. *Crisis*, XVIII (September, 1919), 240.
[80] Board Minutes, NAACP, February 11, 1918; March 11, 1918; July 8, 1918; NAACP, *Ninth Annual Report 1918*, pp. 69–70; *Crisis*, XVIII (September, 1919), 240.
[81] Du Bois, "The Negro and the Labor Union," editorial, *Crisis*, XVIII (September, 1919), 239–41.

Shillady knew that it was necessary to attack the problem of discrimination in employment at both state and local levels. He planned and cooperated with the Urban League in a successful effort to secure legislation, setting up a state employment bureau in Harlem to facilitate the placement of Negro workers.[82]

The NAACP fought against discriminatory labor practices in plants holding war contracts from the government. Complaints of discrimination in a shipyard and at an airplane factory were referred to the Aircraft Board, which answered that the government had no jurisdiction over the labor policy of an independent corporation. The Association then turned the matter over to the Director of Negro Economics in the Department of Labor, and the complaints were satisfactorily adjusted.[83]

NAACP protests were of no avail in the South. The Cleveland branch notified the national office that five Negro union bricklayers, hired through the United States Employment Bureau at Cleveland for work in Sheffield, Alabama, were discharged because local white unionists refused to work side by side with Negroes. The NAACP protested vigorously to the employers and to the International Union through the executive council of the AFL but without success.[84]

The NAACP also fought the discriminatory labor practices of the federal government. In August, 1918, the Navy Department advertised that it needed women high school graduates but refused to process the applications of Negroes. Shillady wrote to Secretary of the Navy Josephus Daniels, but his letter was not acknowledged.[85] More encouraging was an incident in which the Chicago branch reported that the regional director of the Western railroads had ordered that Negroes were not to take the places of white men or to be employed as firemen, hostlers, switchmen, or brakemen, or at any job not previously open to them. Shillady telegraphed strong protests to McAdoo and President Wilson, and the order was promptly withdrawn.[86]

Local branches of the NAACP sometimes tackled the wartime employment problem on their own with success. When the Navy Yard at Charleston, South Carolina, sought to employ only white females, the Charleston branch, with the help of the Washington branch, secured about 250 positions for Negro women. The San Antonio, Texas, branch was able to obtain employment for 300 colored women at the local Reclamation Station, and the Memphis and Louisville branches brought about the reassignment of Negro women who, under

[82] Board Minutes, NAACP, April 8, 1918; May 13, 1918; NAACP, *Ninth Annual Report 1918*, p. 70.
[83] Board Minutes, NAACP, May 13, 1918; June 10, 1918; July 8, 1918; October 14, 1918; NAACP, *Ninth Annual Report 1918*, p. 45; *Washington Bee*, November 2, 1918.
[84] NAACP, *Ninth Annual Report 1918*, p. 45.
[85] Board Minutes, NAACP, September 9, 1918.
[86] Board Minutes, NAACP, December 9, 1918.

the South's Compulsory Work Laws, had been employed at "over-rough or disgusting tasks."[87]

Wartime labor shortages in the South led to numerous abuses of the so-called work-or-fight laws, which were frequently made to apply to anyone an employer wanted to retain or hire at a low wage. Local NAACP branches were successful in a number of Southern towns in protecting the rights of Negro women who were subject to police action because they refused to work at the local wage level. The Little Rock, Arkansas, branch appealed to the national office for help in fighting plantation owners who were forcing Negro women to work at low wages as cotton pickers. This practice ended when the NAACP protested against this type of peonage to the governor of Arkansas, the President, the Assistant Secretary of Labor, the Solicitor General, and the Director of Negro Economics.[88]

John Shillady used the emergency created by wartime labor needs as an opportunity to present the problems of Negroes to Southern businessmen. He was invited to address the Committee on Cooperation with Negroes of the Memphis Chamber of Commerce on the subject, "Negro Workmen Leaving the South." He only incidentally referred to lynching, Jim Crow, and the assumption of a superior status by the whites. Instead, he approached the subject of migration from the point of view of national unity and efficiency as they were affected by illiteracy, education, wages, the organization of labor, and adverse health factors. The talk caused great excitement among some of the businessmen present, who were afraid that if Shillady's speech were heard by the Negroes of the community, dissatisfaction and unrest would be accentuated and migration stimulated. Some, in fact, did not want Shillady to meet with the local NAACP branch. They brought in the United States District Attorney and an agent of the Department of Labor to emphasize to him the seriousness of the local labor situation. Nevertheless, Shillady gave the same address on the following day without incident to about 2,000 friends and members of the Memphis branch of the NAACP.[89]

Because the scope of peonage in the South was being extended under the guise of patriotism, Walter White was sent on a nine-week trip to investigate the general labor situation, compulsory work laws, and lynching. He found conditions at their worst in small towns and rural areas. Here the Negro dared not complain or reveal true conditions for fear of reprisals or lynching. In cities

[87] NAACP, *Ninth Annual Report 1918*, p. 61.
[88] NAACP, *Ninth Annual Report 1918*, p. 63; Board Minutes, NAACP, October 14, 1918; November 11, 1918; *Washington Bee*, October 5, 1918. Although cotton was bringing thirty-five cents a pound, plantation owners were offering the same wage as when it brought ten cents a pound. Board Minutes, NAACP, October 14, 1918.
[89] Board Minutes, NAACP, May 13, 1918; *Crisis*, XVI (August, 1918), 174.

and larger towns, Negroes themselves had often been successful in checking the worst abuses.[90]

At the end of the war, when the President's Industrial Conference Committee was established in an attempt to arrive at a new relationship between capital and labor, the NAACP requested President Wilson to appoint a Negro to the Committee. Shillady called attention to the fact that about 17 per cent of the labor supply was Negro, and to the role played by Negro labor in winning the war, but no action was taken to implement the request, and the President's illness prevented any further communication with him on the subject.[91]

At the 1910 NAACP conference, suggestions to include the relationship of the Negro to the labor movement had been abandoned because labor leaders would not discuss the possibility of Negroes belonging to unions. By 1919 the AFL was seeking the Association's help in working out labor problems involving Negroes. At the Cleveland NAACP conference in 1919, one full day and an evening were devoted to the discussion of topics relating to the Negro and Labor: migration, scarcity of Southern labor, problems in rural districts and in war industries, Negroes in government positions, and the Division of Negro Economics of the Department of Labor. It was the first time the labor problem had been seriously considered at an annual NAACP conference.[92]

A COMMISSION FOR DU BOIS

Wartime hysteria and the passion for conformity led to loss of civil rights for such groups as the Non-Partisan League, the Industrial Workers of the World, German-Americans, socialists, pacifists, aliens, and Negroes. Under the espionage acts, the Department of Justice attempted to rid the United States of traitors and subversives.[93] It was in this disquieting atmosphere that rumors spread that there was "widespread sedition" among Negroes. The *New York Tribune* reported that German agents were said to be urging Negroes to go to Mexico to join the Germans in an attack on the United States. The NAACP protested to the managing editor of the *Tribune*, and urged Negro editors to challenge publicly all similar rumors.[94]

The Crisis came under the scrutiny of the Department of Justice, which· objected to the "tone" of some of the articles. When passage of the Sedition Act appeared inevitable, Du Bois informed the Board that care in discussing the war

[90] Board Minutes, NAACP, October 14, 1918; November 11, 1918; Walter White, " 'Work or Fight' in the South," *New Republic*, XVIII (March 1, 1919), 144–46.
[91] Board Minutes, NAACP, November 10, 1919; *New York Age*, September 27, 1919.
[92] *Crisis*, XVIII (June, 1919), 89.
[93] Zechariah Chafee, Jr., *Free Speech in the United States* (Cambridge, Massachusetts, 1941), pp. 36–42, 99–102, 173–74, 269–82.
[94] Board Minutes, NAACP, April 9, 1917; *New York Tribune*, April 8, 1917.

would be necessary. The Board appointed Charles Studin to the *Crisis* committee so that he could make a legal judgment on all *Crisis* material before publication, and the committee agreed to confine *The Crisis* to facts and constructive criticism for the duration of the war.[95]

Not long after this, a conference of Negro editors was called by the War Department to consider how the Negro could best aid in winning the war. Du Bois, representing *The Crisis*, took a leading part in drafting resolutions which were adopted unanimously by the thirty-one editors present. Though the resolutions stressed such grievances as lynching, mob violence, the case of Colonel Young, the refusal to use Negroes as Red Cross nurses, and the failure to assign Negroes as war correspondents, the conference proved successful in uniting the Negro press in support of the war effort.[96] Du Bois advocated prosecution of the war in an editorial in the July *Crisis*, urging the Negro to forget his special grievances and "close ranks" with his white fellow citizens and the nation's allies in the fight for democracy.[97]

In May, 1918, Joel Spingarn was transferred to the Intelligence Bureau of the General Staff of the Army in Washington. He persuaded his superiors to offer Du Bois a captaincy in the Intelligence Bureau as his assistant, whose function would be, according to Du Bois, the implementation of Spingarn's plan of "far-reaching constructive effort to satisfy the pressing grievances of colored Americans."[98]

Du Bois consulted the NAACP Board, requesting that he be allowed to retain "general oversight of *The Crisis*," as well as his salary as editor. The Board, however, voted that it was not advisable for him to combine his duties as Director of Publication and Research with those of an intelligence officer in the army.[99]

Spingarn urged Du Bois to accept the commission, but Du Bois was unwilling to turn *The Crisis* over to James Weldon Johnson. He complained that the Board meeting that had decided against him had been poorly attended and strongly pacifist. Shillady, maintaining that Du Bois had misinterpreted the Board's action, wrote Spingarn that nothing had taken place which would warrant the inference that the Board regarded military service as work unworthy of its members and that the deliberations had not hinged on a division between pacifists and nonpacifists.[100]

[95] Board Minutes, NAACP, May 13, 1918; June 10, 1918.

[96] *Washington Bee*, July 6, 1918; July 13, 1918; August 3, 1918; August 10, 1918; *Crisis*, XVII (November, 1918), 8; Franklin, *From Slavery to Freedom*, p. 467.

[97] *Crisis*, XVI (July, 1918), 111.

[98] *Washington Bee*, June 1, 1918; July 6, 1918; Du Bois, "A Momentous Proposal," editorial, *Crisis*, XVI (September, 1918), 125.

[99] *Crisis*, XVI (September, 1918), 125; Board Minutes, NAACP, July 8, 1918.

[100] Du Bois to Spingarn, July 9, 1918; July 19, 1918, Johnson Collection; John Shillady to Spingarn, July 30, 1918, J. E. Spingarn Papers (Howard).

When it became known early in July that Du Bois wanted to accept the captaincy[101] without relinquishing control of *The Crisis,* there was an uproar. The Washington branch was reported to have had its stormiest meeting. Du Bois was censured for his "selfish" desire to hold two positions, and the meeting went on record as supporting the decision of the Board.[102]

The Negro press was hostile to Du Bois. The issue of segregated officers' training camps, which Du Bois had supported, still rankled, and the "Close Ranks" editorial in the July *Crisis* was now interpreted as payment of a bribe in return for the captaincy. The *New York News* accused Spingarn and Du Bois of striving valiantly to temporize and surrender and advised them to withdraw from the NAACP, which stood foremost for race rights without let, hindrance or compromise. The *News* claimed that by retaining these men the NAACP was surrendering to those interested in the degradation of colored people. It was "Tuskegee . . . out-Tuskegeed."[103]

Neval H. Thomas, a leader in the Washington branch, now regarded both Du Bois and Spingarn as enemies and planned to "start after" Spingarn at the next meeting. He insisted that the largest of all NAACP branches should have a voice in the choice of an editor for *The Crisis.*[104]

The *Washington Bee* held that Du Bois had lost the confidence of his followers and should resign from *The Crisis.* Another Washington paper, the *Eagle,* mourned that "the once towering column of influence and power among colored American radicals as they are gathered together in the Association for the Advancement of Colored People is broken and fallen down."[105]

Du Bois stated in the September *Crisis,* that although some saw in his "Close Ranks" editorial evidence that he was a traitor to the cause of the Negro and that the government had indulged in bribery, his editorial had nevertheless been in exact accord with, and almost in the very words of, the resolution passed by the conference of Negro editors. He and the Association, he said, still stood for full citizenship for Negro Americans.[106]

The offer of a captaincy was finally withdrawn (according to Du Bois) because it was feared that the work contemplated would "lead beyond the proper

---

[101] Neval H. Thomas (a teacher in the Dunbar High School in Washington, D. C., who later succeeded Grimke on the NAACP Board) wrote to Villard: "We down here knew it in May." Thomas to Villard, September 13, 1918, Villard Papers.

[102] *Washington Bee,* July 6, 1918; July 20, 1918; *New York Age,* July 13, 1918; July 20, 1918; *New York News,* July 18, 1918.

[103] Thomas to Villard, September 13, 1918, Villard Papers; *Crisis,* XVI (September, 1918), 125; *New York News,* July 18, 1918.

[104] Thomas to Villard, September 13, 1918, Villard Papers.

[105] *Washington Bee,* July 27, 1918; *Washington Eagle,* July 27, 1918, clipping in Johnson Collection.

[106] *Crisis,* XVI (September, 1918), 125, 216.

limits of military activities." Du Bois blamed his failure to receive the appointment on reaction and suspicion against Spingarn in the War Department, on opposition from Negroes, and on the influence of white Southerners who got their information from Negro sources. A somewhat different reason was later given by Emmett Scott: As soon as it became evident that the proposed Du Bois appointment was being widely criticized and vigorously opposed by prominent individuals and by Negro newspapers all over the country, the offer was withdrawn because it was dividing rather than uniting Negro opinion.[107]

POSTWAR CONTROVERSIES

The prejudiced treatment accorded Negro soldiers in America followed them overseas. In France, there were efforts to discredit the troops by charges of rape and other crimes, and Negro officers were alleged to be incompetent. Reports of unfair treatment and of discrimination against Negro soldiers by the army in France lowered morale and led to widespread dissatisfaction among colored people on the home front.

At the insistence of Butler Wilson and Joseph Loud, the NAACP Board adopted a resolution calling for a congressional investigation of the treatment of Negro soldiers both at home and in France. In an effort to resolve the controversy centering around the Negro troops, the Thirkield Committee, early in 1919, sent one of its field secretaries, Charles H. Williams of Hampton Institute, to France to investigate; the government dispatched Robert R. Moton, who sailed on the *Orizaba*, which carried representatives of the press to Europe to report the Peace Conference. Du Bois was also on board, bound for France to collect material for a projected NAACP history of Negro soldiers in the war.[108]

It was alleged that Moton, during his visits to Negro troops, advised them against pressing for an extension of freedom upon their return home, and that he urged them to do nothing that would reflect on their war record. Du Bois, filled with indignation and anger at the army's treatment of the Negro soldier, had nothing but contempt for Moton's attempt to minimize the extent of the discrimination and mistreatment. On his return to America Du Bois immediately began a series of violently critical articles in *The Crisis*, accusing Moton and Emmett J. Scott with dereliction of duty.[109]

The chief charges made against Moton were that he had not taken time to investigate the situation adequately and that he had not given the officers and

---

[107] Du Bois, *Dusk of Dawn*, pp. 257–58; Scott to Moore in *New York Age*, July 26, 1919.
[108] Board Minutes, NAACP, March 10, 1919; April 14, 1919; Ovington, *The Walls Came Tumbling Down*, pp. 138–46; Williams, *Side Lights on Negro Soldiers*, p. 11; Du Bois, *Dusk of Dawn*, p. 261; *Crisis*, XVIII (May, 1919), 9.
[109] Franklin, *From Slavery to Freedom*, pp. 461–62; Du Bois, "Robert R. Moton," editorial, *Crisis*, XVIII (May, 1919), 9–10; XVIII (July, 1919), 63–87, 127–30.

troops any real opportunity to inform him about conditions. Moreover, Moton had failed to avail himself of an opportunity to address the Peace Conference and had failed to keep an appointment with Lloyd George in London, even though, according to Du Bois, the destiny of the Negro race was in British hands. Instead of meeting with the Prime Minister, Moton had hurried home to attend a Tuskegee conference. He had failed his race, charged Du Bois, and his actions were a bitter disappointment to friends and enemies alike.[110]

As for Emmett Scott, Du Bois pointed out that the NAACP and *The Crisis* had accorded him loyal support and cooperation when he was Special Assistant to the Secretary of War. They had believed that Scott, though working under a great handicap, was doing everything possible for Negro soldiers, but Du Bois's investigations had brought to light astounding conditions in France. In *The Crisis* he publicly asked Scott if he had known of the conditions, and what steps he had taken to deal with the problem.[111]

At once controversy raged in the Negro press, and the *New York Age* tried to refute the *Crisis* charges. Fred Moore, editor of the *Age*, gave a banquet for Moton, who told the gathering that false rumors had been circulated as to his advice to the troops and that it was all part of a plot to misrepresent and vilify him.[112]

Meanwhile, *The Crisis* editor, in meetings in Washington and Richmond, had challenged Scott concerning alleged conditions among the troops in France, making what the *Washington Bee* called veiled insinuations against Scott's effectiveness in looking after the welfare of Negro soldiers. Scott, who by this time was secretary-treasurer and business manager of Howard University, wrote an open letter to Moore for publication in the *Age*, defending his record and citing his cooperation with Du Bois in joint efforts to further the interests of the Negro during the war. He deplored what he called Du Bois's tendency to give credit to white people, but always to discredit Negroes in official positions. He questioned the existence of the flagrant cases of injustice reported by Du Bois and challenged him to cite a single case.[113]

Bitter disillusionment with the war and its aftermath, however, was not confined to Du Bois and a few radical Negro intellectuals but filtered down to the masses, who became increasingly aware that the democracy for which they had fought was destined to elude them in postwar America.

---

[110] *Crisis*, XVIII (May, 1919), 9–10.
[111] *Crisis*, XVIII (May, 1919), 10; *Crisis*, XVIII (July, 1919), 127–30.
[112] *New York Age*, May 10, 1919; May 17, 1919; July 5, 1919; July 26, 1919; *Washington Bee*, May 24, 1919; July 5, 1919; July 12, 1919; September 6, 1919.
[113] *Washington Bee*, May 24, 1919; Scott to Moore, in *New York Age*, July 26, 1919.

CHAPTER XII

Internationalism, Bolshevism, and the NAACP

The Second Universal Races Congress, scheduled to meet in Paris in 1915, was canceled because of the war. The NAACP had sent four delegates to the first Congress held in London in 1911, because its purpose was to further understanding among races and peoples of the world. When war broke out in Europe, Du Bois attempted without success to have the second meeting held in New York rather than to let it go by default.[1]

Toward the end of the war, the League of Small and Subject Nationalities requested the NAACP to take a seat on its council and become one of its constituent members to represent Africa and the Negro race. Du Bois strongly advised that the NAACP Board align itself with the League and contribute toward its expenses. In spite of the fact that the question was tabled on Villard's insistence, Du Bois announced two months later that he had been sitting on the League's council as the representative of the NAACP. At this time it was the consensus of the Board that it would be unwise for the NAACP to become affiliated with other organizations. They did, however, agree that with Board approval staff members could accept appointments or take part in other movements in an individual and personal capacity.[2] Du Bois refused to let the matter rest there, however, and in September, 1918, he told the Board that the NAACP should at once take action concerning the future of Africa. He himself was seeking ways

[1] Board Minutes, October 6, 1914 in "Minute Book of the Board of Directors of the National Association for the Advancement of Colored People" (now in the Manuscript Division, Library of Congress; hereafter referred to as Board Minutes, NAACP); *Crisis*, II (September, 1911), 200–02.

[2] Board Minutes, NAACP, January 14, 1918; March 11, 1918. The Association had, however, prior to incorporation, voted to "accept affiliation with the Subject Races International Committee." Minutes, Executive Committee, June 6, 1911, in Board Minutes, NAACP.

to influence the United States government so that the rights of Negroes in Africa would be recognized at the coming Peace Conference.[3]

Representatives of other Negro protest organizations had announced plans to intercede and to lobby at the Peace Conference. Several rival organizations had emerged in competition to the NAACP, in response to the problems of Negroes attendant upon the war and the migrations to the North. W. H. Jernagin of Washington planned to lobby for the National Race Congress, the largest of the new organizations, and William Monroe Trotter planned to represent the older National Equal Rights League. Their purpose was to promote the interests of the colored races of the world, especially the Negroes of the United States. These moves and pronouncements by rival leaders and organizations spurred Du Bois in his determination to get to France so that he could personally appeal to the Peace Conference on behalf of the subject peoples of Africa.[4]

His opportunity came when the Board approved Villard's recommendation that the NAACP at once take steps to compile a history of the Negro soldier in the war. Du Bois was authorized to undertake the research and the Board appropriated $2,000 for the project, $1,500 of which was advanced to him by Miss Ovington as acting chairman of the Board. When the official press ship, *Orizaba*, sailed for the Peace Conference, Du Bois was on it.[5]

Although the Board approved Miss Ovington's action in sending Du Bois, there was much debate about the expenses involved, and the editorial and management policy of *The Crisis* during the editor's absence. It was finally agreed that half of the expenses incurred in Europe in gathering data for the war history should be paid by the Association. Since Du Bois was also acting as a press representative for *The Crisis* at the Peace Conference, the other half of his expenses should be paid from *Crisis* funds.[6]

[3] Board Minutes, NAACP, September 9, 1918.
[4] *Washington Bee*, October 12, 1918; *New York Age*, December 14, 1918. W. H. Jernagin was pastor of the Mt. Carmel Baptist Church of Washington. The National Race Congress was founded in 1915. Some indication of its strength can be seen by the report that 600 delegates attended the third annual meeting in Washington in October, 1918; 500 attended the 1919 meeting, when a delegation was sent to the White House to protest the status of the Negro. J. Milton Waldron was a member. John R. Hawkins was executive secretary. *Washington Bee*, September 23, 1916; October 5, 1918; October 11, 1919; *New York Age*, November 30, 1918; December 14, 1918. Other new protest organizations were the National Liberty League, headed by W. Calvin Chase, editor of the *Washington Bee*, and the National Association for the Consolidation of the Colored Race, of which Edmund H. Armstrong was president. *Washington Bee*, November 2, 1918; March 15, 1919; March 29, 1919.
[5] Board Minutes, NAACP, October 14, 1918; December 9, 1918.
[6] Board Minutes, December 9, 1918. Du Bois left his new literary editor, Jessie Fauset, in charge of *The Crisis*, under Miss Ovington's "general oversight." The Board assigned the secretary and the field secretary as permanent members of the *Crisis* committee. Miss Fauset was a graduate of Cornell University with Phi Beta Kappa honors. She took an M.A. degree at the University of Pennsylvania and for a time taught Latin and French at Dunbar High School in Washington. *Crisis*, XIX (November, 1918), 341.

THE PAN-AFRICAN MOVEMENT

At the December, 1918, meeting of the Board, Miss Ovington explained to the other members that, although Du Bois's primary activity would be to collect material for a history of the Negro soldier in the war, he would also take part in a Pan-African Congress in Paris to be called for the purpose of securing the internationalization of Africa and obtaining partial self-determination for the former German colonies.[7]

Du Bois's prior interest in and growing preoccupation with a Pan-African Congress soon pushed the announced purpose of his trip into the background. The indirectness with which he presented the Congress idea to the Board for approval doubtless led him to write many years later that the Association "did not adopt the Pan-African movement on its official program, but it allowed me on my own initiative to promote the effort." However, the NAACP Annual Report for 1918, published shortly after that meeting, states that Du Bois was sent to France in a three-fold capacity—as special representative of *The Crisis* to report the Peace Conference; as historian, to collect material for a history of the Negro's part in the war; and "as representative of the NAACP to summon a Pan-African Congress."[8]

The idea of a Pan-African Congress had its origins at the beginning of the century. H. Sylvester-Williams, a young Negro barrister from the West Indies practicing in London, is generally credited with originating the movement. In 1906, when Booker T. Washington suggested that it was time to hold a conference on Africa, T. Thomas Fortune claimed that a decade earlier he had suggested holding such a meeting. According to Fortune, Williams had taken his idea and issued the call for the first Pan-African Congress, held in Westminster Hall, London, in July, 1900, to coincide with the Methodist Ecumenical Congress and the Paris Exposition.[9] About thirty delegates had attended, including Du Bois, who had been elected a vice-president of the permanent organization.[10]

Du Bois's later assertion that the movement and the idea died for a generation, is not completely accurate, for in 1906 the Pan-African Association was still

[7] Board Minutes, NAACP, December 9, 1918.
[8] Du Bois, "The Pan-African Movement," in George Padmore, ed., *History of the Pan-African Congress* (Manchester, England, 1945), p. 13; NAACP, *Ninth Annual Report 1918* (New York, 1919), p. 57.
[9] Alexander Walters, *My Life and Work* (New York, 1917), p. 253; Du Bois, "The Pan-African Movement," p. 13; T. Thomas Fortune, "A Pan-African Congress," editorial, *New York Age*, March 22, 1906.
[10] Walters, *My Life and Work*, p. 253; *Crisis*, XXI (March, 1921), 198; Du Bois, "The Pan-African Movement," p. 13; Walters, "The Pan-African Congress," *A.M.E. Zion Quarterly Review*, XI (1901), 164–65. Actually Negro Americans with ten delegates present comprised the largest group. Britain came next with nine. The West Indies had seven delegates, while four African countries each sent one representative. Walters, *My Life and Work*, p. 253.

in existence with Bishop Alexander Walters as its president. Moreover, J. Max Barber, who was head of the Pan-African League Department of Du Bois's own Niagara Movement, was in touch with at least one prominent African, A. K. Soga, concerning the Pan-African movement.[11]

Booker T. Washington had held an International Conference on the Negro, in April, 1912, at Tuskegee Institute—a far larger and more representative gathering than the 1919 Pan-African Congress.[12] The Tuskegee conferees studied to what extent the methods employed by Tuskegee and Hampton might be applied to conditions in Africa, the West Indies, and South America. It was claimed that the conference for the first time brought together Negro representatives from all parts of the world and that it gave new impetus to sentiment in favor of an African nationality. It was decided that the conference should become a triennial affair and that Booker T. Washington should go to South Africa to try to reconcile the white population there to the just aspirations of the Negro. Before a second conference could be held World War I erupted, and a year later Washington died. In the light of these events, Du Bois's claim that he was the founder and convener of the First Pan-African Congress is something of an exaggeration.[13]

The cause of the African peoples was very much in the minds of NAACP members, and in January, 1919, John Shillady proposed that the theme of the annual meeting should be "Africa in the World Democracy." Archibald Grimke, for one, was concerned lest the Association's efforts be diverted from the problems in America. Walling and Miss Ovington assured him that, while no disproportionate amount of time would be given to Africa, the African question was a live topic and its inclusion on the agenda would result in much valuable publicity for the NAACP, which in turn would help to promote the general cause.[14]

A mass meeting accordingly was held on the evening of the annual meeting, January 6, 1919, and the theme of the speakers was that Africa ultimately must

[11] Du Bois, "The Pan-African Movement," p. 13; *New York Age*, March 22, 1906; A. K. Soga to J. E. Bruce, March 25, 1907, John E. Bruce Papers (Schomburg Collection, New York Public Library, New York).

[12] *New York Age*, April 18, 1912, states that the conference was composed of delegates of thirty-six missionary societies, representing sixteen religious denominations, and the official or unofficial representatives of twenty-one "foreign countries or colonies of foreign countries." Robert M. Park says that representatives of eighteen foreign countries or colonies were present and that there were twenty-five different missionary societies representing twelve religious bodies. Park had been secretary of the Congo Reform Association in America. Robert M. Park, "Tuskegee International Conference on the Negro," *Journal of Race Development*, III (July, 1912), 117–20.

[13] *Washington Bee*, April 1, 1911; April 20, 1912; Park, "Tuskegee International Conference on the Negro," pp. 117–20; *Crisis*, XVII (April, 1919), 270; Du Bois, "Pan-Africanism: A Mission in My Life," *United Asia* (April, 1955), p. 65.

[14] Board Minutes, NAACP, November 11, 1918; December 9, 1918.

be turned over to Africans. Charles Edward Russell, who had just returned from Russia, where he had been a member of Elihu Root's diplomatic mission,[15] and James Weldon Johnson, the NAACP field secretary, were among those who addressed the meeting. Johnson related the problem of Africa to the bitter race hatred and the national apathy and indifference at home. Africa, he claimed, was "at the bottom of the war" and consequently an international question which would have to be settled if peace were to be maintained. The NAACP, he stressed, was concerned with the fate of the Negro, not only in the United States, but everywhere in the world.[16] The meeting endorsed the formation of a League of Nations that would have as one of its chief duties the care and protection of the peoples of Middle Africa. This resolution was sent to the Senate and to President Wilson in Paris.[17]

Du Bois soon found that his projects were costing more than he had been allowed by the Board. From Paris he reported his plans for gathering materials for the history. These plans included interviews with Negro troops, visits to various parts of France, and short trips to England, Belgium, Germany, and Algeria. He planned to return to America by way of Haiti in March, estimating that it would now cost between $2,000 and $2,500 to complete his work. Concerning the history of the Negro soldier he proposed a grandiose scheme for a three-volume *History of the Black Man in the Revolution of 1914–1918*, including two volumes of documents. To meet the cost of publication, he estimated that the NAACP would have to raise between five and ten thousand dollars.[18]

In January, Du Bois asked the NAACP for funds to meet the expenses of the Pan-African Congress. Miss Ovington complied, but again a heated debate over

---

[15] William English Walling had declined Wilson's invitation to serve as a member of the mission. David A. Shannon, "William English Walling," in Robert Livingston Schuyler and Edward T. James (eds.), *Dictionary of American Biography: Supplement Two* (New York, 1958), XXII, 689–90.

[16] *Crisis*, XVII (February, 1919), 173–76. Others who spoke were John Shillady, Dr. William H. Sheppard of Louisville, Kentucky, and the pluralist philosopher, Horace Meyer Kallen, who was working with Norman Angell for the establishment of a League of Nations. Board Minutes, NAACP, January 13, 1919; February 10, 1919.

[17] *Crisis*, XVII (February, 1919), 173–76.

[18] Du Bois to Board of Directors, December 24, 1918, in Board Minutes, NAACP, February 10, 1919. Upon his return, Du Bois continued to insist that the NAACP publish a multi-volume work. The Board, however, was unwilling to incur further expense. It also believed a one-volume history would meet the "immediate need" for a publication narrating the "accomplishments of the Negro soldiers." The history was never published, partly because Du Bois lost interest, since the material he had gathered had already served its purpose in the pages of *The Crisis*. Du Bois to Board of Directors, December 24, 1918, in Board Minutes, NAACP, February 10, 1919; "Report of the Director of Publication and Research, April 8, 1919," appended to Board Minutes, NAACP, April 14, 1919; Board Minutes, NAACP, May 12, 1919; Du Bois to Board of Directors, memorandum, May 12, 1931, Arthur B. Spingarn Papers (now in the Manuscript Division, Library of Congress).

his program and its cost took place at the Board meeting. The Board authorized an additional expenditure of $500 but cabled that they were opposed to his going to Algeria and Haiti. Grimke was so angered at Du Bois's request that he withdrew from the meeting—an act which caused grave concern lest the Association lose the support of the powerful Washington branch.[19]

Great difficulties stood in the way of a Pan-African Congress. After lengthy negotiations permission was finally secured from the French government to hold the Congress, but the United States and the colonial powers refused to issue passports to those who wished to attend.[20]

Most of the delegates who attended were already in France in connection with the war effort. W. H. Jernagin finally was able to secure a passport as the official correspondent of the *Washington Bee*. William Monroe Trotter succeeded in getting to Paris by securing a job as a ship's cook and jumping ship when he reached Le Havre. Unlike Jernagin, he did not attend the Pan-African Congress, but instead issued his own protest to the Peace Conference and to representatives of the French and American press, condemning the failure of the Peace Treaty to contain a clause guaranteeing "life and liberty" to American Negroes.[21]

It was an NAACP financed Congress that opened in Paris on February 19, 1919.[22] Of the fifteen countries represented, nine were African with twelve

[19] Board Minutes, NAACP, February 10, 1919; Ovington to Du Bois, March 7, 1919, W. E. B. Du Bois Papers (now in the possession of Mrs. W. E. B. Du Bois, New York City). Grimke soon after announced his intention of retiring as branch president. Oswald Garrison Villard to Neval H. Thomas, May 7, 1919, Oswald Garrison Villard Papers (Houghton Library, Harvard University).

[20] Du Bois, "Memorandum of W. E. B. Du Bois to M. [Blaise] Diagne," January 1, 1919, in *Crisis*, XVII (March, 1919), 224–25; *New York Times*, February 16, 1919. According to this report, Acting Secretary of State Frank L. Polk "had been officially advised that no such conference would be held" and therefore no passports were issued to delegates. See also *Crisis*, XVII (March, 1919), 237; Du Bois, "Pan-Africanism: A Mission in My Life," p. 65; Du Bois, "The Pan-African Movement," p. 15. Among those who were at first refused passports either as delegates to the Congress or as newspaper correspondents were Monroe Trotter, Mrs. Ida Wells-Barnett, and W. H. Jernagin. *New York Call*, n.d. quoted in *Crisis*, XVII (March, 1919), 237.

[21] *Christian Science Monitor*, July 25, 1919; *Washington Bee*, August 2, 1919. See also William Monroe Trotter, "Protestation des Américans de Couleur et Pétition en Faveur de la Démocratie Mondiale: Adresse à la Conférence Mondiale de la Paix," Le Comité, William M. Trotter, Président, tenu les 18–20 December 1918, 12 pp., copy in Mary Church Terrell Papers (Manuscript Division, Library of Congress). For other activities of Trotter in France, especially his protest in behalf of Negro troops and against lynching in the United States, see *Christian Science Monitor*, July 25, 1919; and *Washington Bee*, August 2, 1919. For the efforts of Trotter and Jernagin to secure changes favorable to the American Negro in the League Convenant and the final Peace Treaty, see *New York Age*, August 30, 1919; *Washington Bee*, September 6, 1919; and *Christian Science Monitor*, July 25, 1919.

[22] Board Minutes, NAACP, March 10, 1919; April 14, 1919; *Crisis*, XVIII (May, 1919), 7–9. The NAACP paid the expenses of the Pan-African Congress ($750).

delegates out of the total of fifty-seven. Twenty-one representatives came from the West Indies, and sixteen from the United States.[23]

Blaise Diagne, a member of the Chamber of Deputies from Senegal, was elected president of the Congress. Du Bois was its secretary. NAACP members who attended were Du Bois, John Hope, and Mrs. W. A. Hunton. Joel Spingarn and two other Board members, Walling and Charles Edward Russell, were also present and addressed sessions of the Congress.[24]

Oswald Garrison Villard was in Europe but did not attend the Pan-African Congress. He had gone to Paris as the representative of *The Nation* to report the Peace Conference, and in Paris had secured permission from Colonel House to attend and report on the meeting of the Second Internationale at Berne, Switzerland, during the first week of February. From there he passed over the border into Bavaria, returning to France in March by way of Belgium. He was therefore out of France while the Pan-African Conference was held. There is no evidence that when he was in Paris either before or after his trip to Switzerland and Germany he came in contact with Spingarn, Walling, Russell, or Du Bois. Wartime tensions, added to years of sometimes frustrating service on the NAACP Board, had widened the gap between Villard and his old friends and fellow crusaders. Villard was a pacifist but no socialist. He was, in fact, extremely critical of what he called the "professed Socialists" Walling and Russell for their published criticism of the meeting at Berne, which he described as their "usual contemptible muddying of the stream of hope and progress for the people everywhere, and their constant attacks upon all real workers for peace."[25]

According to Du Bois, one of the chief fruits of the Pan-African Congress was the idea for the Mandates Commission of the League of Nations, which he claimed grew out of the Congress's request for an international organization for the administration and supervision of the former German colonies. Other resolutions adopted by the Congress dealt with such African problems as natural resources, concessions, investment of capital, labor, education, and the participation of the natives in government.[26]

[23] Du Bois, "Pan-Africanism: A Mission in My Life," p. 66; Du Bois, "The Pan-African Movement," p. 15; *Crisis*, XVII (April, 1919), 271–74.
[24] *Washington Bee*, March 29, 1919; John Hope Franklin, *From Slavery to Freedom: A History of American Negroes* (2d ed.; New York, 1965), p. 462; Board Minutes, NAACP, March 10, 1919; April 14, 1919; *Crisis*, XVII (April, 1919), 271–74.
[25] Villard, *Fighting Years: Memoirs of a Liberal Editor* (New York, 1939), pp. 384–441. Villard lived "for a time" at the Vouillement in Paris, together with "men more or less attached to the American delegation," among them Ray Stannard Baker, "the President's mouthpiece to the press." Sir Norman Angell, *After All: The Autobiography of Norman Angell* (London, 1951), p. 210.
[26] Du Bois, "Pan-Africanism: A Mission in My Life," p. 66; Du Bois, "The Pan-African Movement," p. 16.

The *New York Evening Globe* reported that the object of the Pan-African Congress was to draft an appeal to the Peace Conference to give the Negroes of Africa a chance to develop unhampered by other races. The Paris edition of the *New York Herald* reported that it was a reasonable program calling for the creation of a permanent bureau attached to the League of Nations to ensure observance of an international code of law, protecting Africans and thereby furthering their political and economic interests. It is likely that the stories in the *Herald* and the *Globe* came from the pen of Charles Edward Russell, who complained that the Congress failed to receive adequate publicity because of the lack of a press agent and that he himself had written special articles for Paris newspapers on the Congress.[27]

HAITI

Du Bois was frustrated in his plan to stop in Haiti on his return from Europe. On behalf of the NAACP, he had planned to investigate reports of intolerable conditions on the island which had been coming to the Association since 1915, when the United States had taken control of Haitian finances. This had been followed, in 1916, by military occupation of the country. The NAACP was concerned because Haiti, in Du Bois's words, was "a continuing symbol of Negro revolt against slavery and oppression, and [of] capacity for self-rule."[28]

Many of the civilian and military personnel sent to Haiti by the Wilson administration were known to the Association to be arrogant and prejudiced Southerners.[29] In 1915, Villard, on behalf of the NAACP, pressed for a commission to visit Haiti. In letters and private conversations with Joseph P. Tumulty, Secretary of State Robert Lansing, and other officials, he urged that the commission make a social and economic survey of the Republic,[30] so that the

---

[27] *New York Evening Globe*, February 22, 1919, quoted in Du Bois, "The Pan-African Movement," p. 15; *New York Herald*, Paris edition, February 24, 1919, quoted in Du Bois, "The Pan-African Movement," p. 17; Board Minutes, NAACP, March 10, 1919. Du Bois later reported that news of the Congress "appeared in the leading French papers and was sent out by several news agencies." Board Minutes, NAACP, April 14, 1919.

[28] Du Bois, *Dusk of Dawn: An Essay toward an Autobiography of a Race Concept* (New York, 1940), p. 239.

[29] Johnson complained that these officials were sent to the island, not because of their administrative capacity, but because of their supposed knowledge of "handling niggers." "Special Report of the Field Secretary on his visit to Haiti," appended to Board Minutes, NAACP, July 12, 1920. See Richard Hofstadter, *Social Darwinism in American Thought 1860–1915* (Philadelphia, 1944), pp. 154, 174–76, for racism as an outgrowth of Social Darwinism, and William E. Leuchtenburg, "Progressivism and Imperialism, The Progressive Movement and American Foreign Policy, 1898–1916," *Mississippi Valley Historical Review*, XXXIX (December, 1952), 483–504, for the relation of Darwinism to both movements.

[30] Villard to Joseph P. Tumulty, September 3, 1915; Villard to Robert Lansing, September 3, 1915, Villard Papers; Board Minutes, NAACP, September 13, 1915; Minutes, Annual Meeting, January 3, 1916, in Board Minutes, NAACP.

Haitian problem might be resolved not only from the standpoint of political and financial considerations, but also from that of social justice. Villard suggested John Hope and Robert Moton as members of the proposed commission, and recommended Colonel Charles Young as best qualified to serve as Commandant of the United States Constabulary in Haiti. Young was at that time in charge of the Liberian Constabulary, which he had organized.[31] Villard also urged that minor positions of the State Department should be reopened to Negroes and suggested capable candidates for such positions. This would reassure both Haitians and Negro voters in the United States who were uneasy about protectorates and who had been alienated by the Administration's policy of segregation in the departments in Washington.[32]

Lansing was cool to the proposal. He replied that he would keep Villard's suggestions in mind and would take them up for consideration as soon as pacification of the island was assured, an answer which Villard considered vague and indefinite. Tumulty, a better politician, wrote that Villard could rely on him in securing appointments for Negroes, because he considered it to be of political value as well as a matter of justice.[33]

Nothing was done by the Wilson Administration concerning the commission, however, and reports of bad conditions continued to leak out of the island republic in spite of tight government control. The news of these outrages, combined with news of the military expedition sent by Wilson to Mexico to put down Francisco Villa incensed both Storey and Villard, who were strongly anti-imperialist.[34]

[31] Villard to Lansing, September 3, 1915; Villard to Tumulty, September 3, 1915, Villard Papers. Villard had at first also suggested Booker T. Washington and Emmett Scott as capable candidates. *New York Evening Post*, quoted in *New York Age*, August 12, 1915.
[32] Villard's list of Negro candidates for office in the State Department was headed by James Weldon Johnson, to whom he attributed "unusual diplomatic experience," and Charles W. Anderson, whom he considered "the best Collector of Internal Revenue New York City ever had." Others he suggested were: Attorney George W. Ellis of Chicago, one-time secretary of the Legation in Liberia, and "author of excellent works on Africa"; L. M. Hershaw of the Land Office; Richard R. Wright, Jr., of Philadelphia; George J. Austin of St. Paul's Normal and Industrial School; Bishop John Hurst of the African Methodist Episcopal Church, a naturalized citizen who had been born in Haiti; and H. W. Furness, former United States minister to Haiti. Villard to Lansing, September 3, 1915, Villard Papers.
[33] Lansing to Villard, September 9, 1915; Tumulty to Villard, September 7, 1915, Villard Papers; Board Minutes, NAACP, September 13, 1915.
[34] Moorfield Storey to Villard, September 25, 1916; Villard to Storey, September 26, 1916, Villard Papers. When United States Marines landed in Vera Cruz on April 22, 1914, Villard persuaded the NAACP Board to wire Wilson, protesting the involvement of the United States "on any pretext whatever in war with Mexico which may result in complicating our unsolved race problem by incorporating 15,000,000 or more members of another alien race." Board Minutes, NAACP, special meeting, April 28, 1914.

Continued reports of mistreatment of the Haitians and suppression of self-rule came during the war years, and in 1918 the Board authorized James Weldon Johnson to make a trip to Haiti as soon as funds were available for an investigation. The Board prevented Du Bois from making the investigation, possibly because they thought Johnson's previous diplomatic experience in Latin America made him more qualified for the work. Johnson did not make the trip to Haiti until 1920. His revealing report led to strenuous efforts by the NAACP on behalf of the Haitians during the 1920's, efforts which were in large measure responsible for the evacuation of United States troops from Haiti and the end of American financial control.[35]

THE RED SCARE

In his *Crisis* articles about the treatment of Negro soldiers in France, Du Bois had lashed out at the United States government. Because the Justice Department had warned the NAACP the year before concerning the "tone" of its journal, Miss Ovington had given strict orders that Du Bois must submit his editorials to the *Crisis* committee before publication. In spite of these precautions, the attacks on the government continued, with the result that the Post Office Department held up the May, 1919, issue of *The Crisis* for a week without giving a reason.[36]

The cause of the action becomes apparent when we examine the May issue. In it were reproduced official documents showing prejudice and discrimination on the part of the army, including attempts to influence French attitudes and behavior toward American Negro troops. The same issue contained an inflammatory editorial, stating that members of the race were "cowards and jackasses" if they did not "marshal every ounce of brain and brawn to fight a sterner, longer, more unbending battle" in their own country.[37] The League of Nations, wrote Du Bois, was absolutely necessary to the salvation of the Negro race. Only an international organization could curb the anti-Negro policy of the United States and South Africa. Moreover, he held that unless such an agency should come into being, "we are doomed eventually to *fight* for our rights." Only such an organization could counteract the barbarism of the ruling classes in the South and their overwhelming political power. Peace for the Negro was not only peace from the wars of the past, but relief from the specter of a Great War of Races, which Du Bois held to be absolutely inevitable unless "the

[35] Board Minutes, NAACP, March 11, 1918; March 8, 1920; Report of the Secretary to Board of Directors, November 18, 1921, in Board Minutes, NAACP; Stenio Vincent, President of Haiti, to Roy Wilkins, quoted in *Crisis*, XLIV (October, 1934), 292.
[36] Ovington to Du Bois, April 11, 1919, Du Bois Papers; Board Minutes, NAACP, May 12, 1919.
[37] *Crisis*, XVIII (May, 1919), 13–14, 16–21; *Crisis*, XVIII (July, 1919), 63–87.

selfish nations of white civilization are curbed by a Great World Congress in which black and white and yellow sit and speak and act."[38]

Horrified at the violent tone of the editorial, Villard severely criticized Du Bois in *The Nation*, calling his opinions dangerous and mistaken, a counsel of madness that would lead "nowhere but to bloodshed without result."[39]

In the prevailing atmosphere of postwar reaction, it was not surprising that these utterances of Du Bois led Representative James F. Byrnes of South Carolina to hold the Negro press responsible for the wave of race riots that swept the nation in the summer of 1919. Byrnes called upon the Department of Justice to determine whether *The Crisis* had published material in violation of the Espionage Act and had incited Negroes to riot and mob violence. In the October *Crisis*, Du Bois replied that it was Byrnes and his kind—who had encouraged fifty years of lynching and had enforced ignorance on three million people and disfranchised half that number—who were primarily responsible for the riots.[40]

In August, the *Washington Bee* lent its pages to false charges of "Bolshevism," leveled against the NAACP by Joseph C. Manning, editor of *The Southern American*, and formerly a member of the Alabama Legislature and leader of the Populist-Republican Fusion Party in the South. Manning had been active in the fight against disfranchisement, organizing the Southern Ballot Rights League in 1895, but fear of Bolshevism led him to attack the Association. It was led by socialists, he claimed, and its program was one of converting Negroes to socialism.[41]

Trouble for the NAACP from within the race appeared when Dean L. B. Moore of Howard University made a statement to the effect that "a colored woman representing the National Association had advised colored men to go after what they wanted with a shotgun." This injudicious statement was given wide publicity by the National Security League. NAACP Board members feared that if the publicity were not checked it would inflame public opinion against the Negro in the North as well as in the South, since many whites believed that the Negro soldier's taste of equality in France during the war, intensified by postwar Russian propaganda, was behind the racial strife. The Association

---

[38] Du Bois, "The League of Nations," *Crisis*, XVIII (May, 1919), 10–11.
[39] "The Negro at Bay," editorial, *Nation*, CVIII (June 14, 1919), 931.
[40] *Congressional Record*, 66th Cong., 1st Sess., p. 4303; Du Bois, "Byrnes," editorial, *Crisis*, XVIII (October, 1919), 284–85.
[41] *Washington Bee*, May 31, 1919; Joseph C. Manning, "Bolshevism in New York," *Washington Bee*, August 2, 1919; December 20, 1919. In 1909, Manning addressed the National Negro Conference on "The Effect on Poor Whites of Discrimination Against Negroes," *Proceedings of the National Negro Conference 1909: New York, May 31 and June 1* (n.p., n.d.) pp. 207–10.

threatened to sue Dean Moore. This finally brought a letter of retraction in spite of Moore's previous denials that he had made the statement.[42]

The attitude of the NAACP and of most Negroes toward foreign ideologies was expressed in a letter to Judge Robert H. Terrell from George Wibecan, an NAACP founder, who was also chairman of the Frederick Douglass Community Center Forum of Brooklyn. Wibecan wrote:

I am opposed to Socialism and Bolshevism, fruitful parents of evil to the colored people. I am equally opposed to radicalism which takes us away from the American ideal. . . . Much of our troubles are [due] to the silence of the church and leading white men of the cities who seem to take no action on lynching and disfranchisement of the blacks. Perhaps the attack on Shillady and race riots may awaken them to their duty.[43]

Delegates to the annual conference of the NAACP in Cleveland in 1919, in an effort to impress upon the public the justice and seriousness of their demands for the Negro, prefaced their resolutions with a warning that Bolshevism offered an attractive program to the Negro.[44] The inference was clear that America could only counter this threat by extending full citizenship to the Negro and integrating him into American life.

William English Walling, a socialist, was sufficiently concerned by the persistent efforts to link the Negro with radicalism to alert the officers of the NAACP to what he called the pernicious campaign to tie the Negro to the Industrial Workers of the World. According to Walling, the Department of Justice, either through statements made on its behalf or made unofficially, spread the belief that the activities of the IWW were responsible for the general unrest among Negroes. Moorfield Storey brought the matter to the attention of the Department of Justice, but not before the rumors had reached Congress, and for a time there was a possibility there would be a congressional investigation of the activities of the IWW among Negroes.[45]

When Attorney General A. Mitchell Palmer's report on radical propaganda in the United States was published in November, 1919, James Weldon Johnson on behalf of the NAACP immediately took issue with the section entitled "Radicalism and Sedition Among Negroes as Reflected in Their Publications." Specifically, he challenged the statement that there was "a well-concerted move-

---

[42] Board Minutes, NAACP, September 9, 1919.
[43] George Wibecan to Robert H. Terrell, September 1, 1919, Terrell Family Papers (Manuscript Division, Library of Congress).
[44] *Crisis*, XVIII (August, 1919), 191–93.
[45] Minutes, Anti-Lynching Committee, Boston, November 14, 1919, in Board Minutes, NAACP; Board Minutes, NAACP, December 8, 1919.

ment" among certain Negro intellectual leaders to set themselves up as "a determined and persistent source of radical opposition to the Government, and to the established rule of law and order."[46]

Johnson held that the expression "well-concerted" was misleading. Likewise, "opposition to the Government" should have read "opposition to the Administration," a feeling held by many Americans and one that was not seditious. Furthermore the report was inaccurate in stating that Negro leaders were opposed to the established rule of law and order. In reality they were opposed to lynching, disfranchisement, Jim Crowism, and inequality in education and in industrial opportunities. The fight being made by the so-called radical Negro leaders was to establish and maintain law and order, and to interpret and enforce the laws and the Constitution impartially. Moreover, the Justice Department was well aware of this.[47]

Villard sprang to the defense of the NAACP in The Crisis, writing that Negroes, as taxpayers, were entitled to schooling and to protection by the courts and the police. He reminded his readers that the rallying cry of the American Revolution had been No Taxation without Representation. What the Negro now asked was merely good Americanism, not the doctrines of Bolshevists or anarchists, but that of the founders of the American Republic.[48]

The results of the "Red Scare" and the Attorney General's report were two bills introduced into Congress early in 1920, the Sterling Bill (S. 3317), and the Graham Bill (H.R. 11430), which denied postal privileges to all books, magazines, newspapers, and communications of any kind in which an appeal was made to racial prejudice with the intention of bringing about rioting and violence.[49]

This was correctly interpreted as an attempt to curb or possibly suppress The Crisis and other Negro publications. Any protest against lynching and mob violence could, if these bills passed Congress, be interpreted by the Southern-dominated administration as appealing to racial prejudice and inciting to riot.

[46] New York Times, November 16, 1919; James Weldon Johnson, editorial, New York Age, November 29, 1919. For the entire report see U.S. Department of Justice, "Radicalism and Sedition Among Negroes as Reflected in Their Publications," in Investigation Activities of Department of Justice, 66th Cong., 1st Sess., U.S. Senate Document No. 153, XII (1919), 161–87. This report (on p. 162) indirectly referred to The Crisis, stating that "in at least one instance men [Augustus G. Dill and Du Bois] holding degrees conferred by Harvard University" were the editors of one of the journals "always antagonistic to the white race and openly defiantly, assertive of its [the Negro race's] own equality and even superiority."
[47] New York Age, November 29, 1919.
[48] Villard, "Sword of the Spirit," editorial, Crisis, XVIII (August, 1919), 182–83.
[49] From Section 6 of Graham Bill (H. R. 11430), quoted in Crisis, XIX (February, 1920), 169.

Therefore the NAACP and the Negro press waged a vigorous and ultimately successful campaign of opposition against the passage of these bills.[50]

At the state level, Mississippi passed legislation forbidding the sale of publications "tending to disturb relations between the races," as a result of which a *Crisis* agent was arrested in April, 1920, badly beaten, heavily fined, and sentenced to six months imprisonment for selling the magazine. The lawyer retained by the Negro community to defend the agent was threatened by mob violence. When the NAACP wired Governor Lee M. Russell asking protection for the attorney, the lieutenant governor replied that, should the *Crisis* editors visit Mississippi, "We would make an example of them that would be a lasting benefit to the colored people of the South and would not soon be forgotten." The NAACP repeated the request for protection to the governor, who replied that he endorsed the sentiments of his lieutenant governor. (The governor later changed his mind and telegraphed that all persons would have the full protection of the law in securing their legal rights.)[51]

The North, too, was caught up in the postwar Red Scare. In the report of the so-called Lusk Committee, New York State, fearful and suspicious of the role of the Negro in revolutionary radicalism, listed some *Crisis* editorials as dangerous and attributed the NAACP's "decidedly radical stand" to certain Board members who were sympathetic to socialism, namely, John Haynes Holmes, Archibald Grimke, and Mary White Ovington. It was this report that inspired Joseph C. Manning to write his vitriolic criticism of the NAACP.[52]

The Crisis was at this time at the peak of its circulation. Increasing racial violence, attempts to silence or intimidate *The Crisis* by various state and federal agencies, the magazine's belligerent attacks on the government for failing to extend democracy to the Negro, together with Du Bois's arraignment of Moton and Scott as race leaders who had either failed in their duty or betrayed their trust, all helped to increase the circulation of *The Crisis* and to enhance the prestige of the NAACP.

---

[50] *Crisis*, XIX (February, 1920), 169.
[51] Board Minutes, NAACP, May 10, 1920; *Washington Bee*, May 1, 1920; May 8, 1920.
[52] New York Senate Document, "Propaganda Among Negroes," in *Revolutionary Radicalism*, Report of the Joint Legislative Committee of the State of New York Investigating Seditious Activities, 4 vols., filed April 24, 1920, in the Senate of the State of New York, Part I, Vol. II, 1318–21; 1476–1520; *Washington Bee*, August 2, 1919.

Conclusion

The objective of the NAACP in its formative period was to secure full citizenship and equal rights for the Negro through a militant but nonviolent course of action. The Association not only protested against injustice and abridgment of rights but actively sought to establish these rights in law and to tear away the legal basis of the sanctions responsible for second-class citizenship. In the pursuit of these objectives it was the policy of the NAACP to maintain a biracial organization which sought to identify the movement for the completion of emancipation with the old abolition movement and to reestablish the cause of the Negro in the general stream of the reform movement from which it had become separated.

The year 1919 marked a turning point in the history of the NAACP. By this time a number of the "old guard" had passed from the scene due to death or retirement. Their going marked the end of the emphasis upon abolitionist tradition within the Association. No longer was it referred to as the "new abolition movement."

The year 1919 also witnessed the beginning of the end of white leadership and control of the NAACP. From the beginning the Association had sought to secure Negroes of ability to serve on local and national levels. As early as 1915, suggestions were heard that the time was ripe for a Negro to become the executive head of the organization. By 1919, the branches had largely dispensed with the tutelage of advisory committees dominated by white liberals. Fewer whites were to be found as officers and members of the local branches. Only on the national Board did white leadership still predominate, but its influence was on the wane as more and more of the actual direction of the Association's affairs fell into the hands of the secretary and the executive committee, which was composed largely of Negroes. In 1920, James Weldon Johnson became the first

291

Negro secretary, succeeding John R. Shillady, who had effectively organized the national office.

The year 1919 saw *The Crisis* at the height of its circulation and influence. Du Bois's prediction of 100,000 Negro readers had been surpassed, although a decline was evident thereafter, owing to the development and maturing of the Negro press under a new generation of capable and militant leaders. Also in 1919, the NAACP at its annual conference under Shillady's leadership for the first time concerned itself with the problem of the Negro worker and the organized labor movement.

With the explosion of membership in 1918, the bulk of the support of the Association no longer came from a few wealthy members and friends, but from the membership at large. Income reached a peak in 1919, but the economic depression of the early twenties was felt severely by Negroes and caused a sharp drop in income of the NAACP.

By 1919, the Far West had been opened up to the Association and the branches there put on a firm basis through the organizing activities of James Weldon Johnson. Moreover, 1919 marked the first time that membership in the South outnumbered that in the North. As a result of this geographical shift the 1920 annual conference was held at Atlanta, Georgia, where NAACP objectives were openly proclaimed without incident.

As a result of the growth in membership and of pressure from the "grass roots," the structure of the NAACP was altered at the 1919 Cleveland conference to permit state and district organizations to cope more effectively with local and regional problems and activities.

The Cleveland conference was of great significance. It came at a time of crisis in Negro-white relationships throughout the country. New tendencies which had been observed at the 1917 conference came to maturity at the 1919 conference. Within the organization the distrust of white fellow workers by Negroes, a phenomenon that Mary White Ovington said was familiar in the early days, had disappeared. In addition, the rank and file Negro membership showed a growing confidence in their own ability and a maturing sense of their own dignity. As a result of the Amenia conference, the intellectual leaders of the race manifested a new solidarity and gained confidence in their ability as a group to make an impact on American society. And finally, acceleration of the economic advancement of the Negro during the war years gave him "a quick boost toward equality."[1]

The 1919 conference revealed a further development of militancy among Negroes, and an end of the former approach of philanthropically minded whites meeting to discuss what should be done for the Negro. Negro delegates had

[1] Mary White Ovington, "The Master of His Fate," *Crisis*, XIII (February, 1917), 164.

begun to take the direction of NAACP affairs into their own hands,[2] and for the first time the branches displayed an interest in electing successful local Negro leaders to the national Board.

Although the Association had from the first been considered militant and radical, after 1919 there was a clearly defined division between the militancy and biracialism of the NAACP and the extremism and geographical separatism of Marcus Garvey's Universal Negro Improvement Association, with its race chauvinism and Back-to-Africa movement. The NAACP continued to rely upon legal measures to achieve its aims by building up a body of judicial decisions to "fix beyond question the status of the American citizen of Negro descent."[3] Closely allied was the effort to secure the repeal and to prevent the passage of discriminatory legislation on local, state, and national levels and to promote and secure new civil rights legislation.

Two criteria determined whether or not the Association would enter a case. It must involve, first, discrimination based upon color and, second, some fundamental right of citizenship. Moorfield Storey had firmly impressed upon the NAACP that out-of-state counsel was at a serious disadvantage and that as far as possible local attorneys should handle local cases until they reached the federal courts. Storey himself would not argue any case before the United States Supreme Court which he felt he would not be able to maintain, and twice he refused to argue cases which he was convinced lacked the proper legal basis for making a successful appeal. The adoption of this policy had become well established by 1919 and accounts for the astounding number of victories in later years in the United States Supreme Court. By the early twenties three notable victories could be credited to the NAACP: "the grandfather clause" case of 1915, the Louisville segregation case of 1917, and the Arkansas peonage case begun in 1918 and brought to a successful conclusion in 1923. The Arkansas peonage case was notable in that it marked the emergence of capable Negro legal counsel on the local level, and the growing use of such counsel by the NAACP. Competent Negro lawyers had been almost nonexistent ten years earlier.

Another legal policy laid down was that of making local branches financially responsible so far as possible for litigation instituted by them with the advice and approval of the national legal committee. The Association tried to concern itself only with cases involving people with staying power, able to follow through and to take advantage of the rights won for them at law in spite of ostracism and other social pressures.

The end of the Association's first decade also witnessed its involvement in international affairs. The NAACP-sponsored Pan-African Congress held at Paris

[2] Ovington, *The Walls Came Tumbling Down* (New York, 1947), pp. 167–71.
[3] NAACP, "Sixth Annual Report 1915," in *Crisis*, XI (March, 1916), 245–46.

in 1919 and the Pan-African Conference at the 1919 annual meeting were protests on the international and national levels against continued imperialism and exploitation of Negroes in Africa. They proclaimed that the Association was concerned with the fate of the black man everywhere in the world. During the war attention was drawn to the subversion of the black Republic of Haiti. In 1920 an investigation of the occupation of the island by the armed forces of the United States was the beginning of prolonged agitation for the restoration of Haitian independence, which was finally achieved in 1934. NAACP action in regard to Haiti marked a transition from mere protest on the international level to successful action.

The war years and immediate postwar period saw the emergence of a number of Negro protest organizations in competition with the NAACP. By 1919, however, the Negro press was firmly behind the NAACP and even the Association's old enemy, the *New York Age*, complained of the propensity of Negroes to form a number of organizations in the area of race relations when there was already a well-established and competent organization functioning in that field. In a complete reversal of its earlier anti-NAACP editorial policy, the *Age*, in October, 1919, cited the NAACP as being "on the job all the time" and proposed that all efforts be unified under the NAACP in order to end confusion, duplication, and waste of money. In a similar vein the editor of the *Washington Bee* commended the NAACP as the only organization in its field doing effective work, and called upon all Negroes to support the Association.[4]

Thus at the end of the first decade of its existence, the organization, objectives, and methods of the National Association for the Advancement of Colored People in its battle for full citizenship for Negroes were firmly established and generally accepted in the Negro world. The Association was now in a position to press even more fully and effectively for the attainment of its ultimate goal— the complete abolition of the new slavery imposed by racism.

[4] *New York Age*, October 4, 1919; *Washington Bee*, December 27, 1919.

Illustrations

William English Walling

Mary White Ovington

Charles Edward Russell

Henry Moskowitz

Oswald Garrison Villard

Bishop Alexander Walters

The Reverend William Henry Brooks

William Edward Burghardt Du Bois

Mrs. Florence Kelley

Francis Jackson Garrison
(Courtesy Mrs. Wm. Lloyd Garrison)

Moorfield Storey

Mrs. Mary Dunlop Maclean

The Reverend John Haynes Holmes

A Reply to the Reverend Dr. Holmes from
Alabama—December, 1911

The Reverend Adam Clayton Powell, Sr.,
Pastor of the Abyssinian Baptist Church,
Harlem, New York City

Mrs. Mary Church Terrell   Mrs. Ida Wells-Barnett

Verina Morton-Jones, M.D.   Mrs. Frances R. Keyser

Booker T. Washington

Arthur B. Spingarn

Joel E. Spingarn

Archibald Grimke

Ernest E. Just, first Spingarn Medalist, 1915 "For Distinguished Research in Physiology and Biology"

The "Waco Horror" (1) Lynching of 19-year-old Jesse Washington
The Public Square—Waco, Texas, June, 1916
(2)—*preceding page*—The Mob

The First Amenia Conference—August, 1916

East St. Louis Race Riots—July 2, 1917
(1) Negro (*in front of car*) Attacked by
    Mob, Militia Standing By

(2) Search for the Bodies of Victims
    (6 were found)

An Answer to the East St. Louis Riots
Negro Silent Protest Parade
New York City—July 28, 1917

Major Charles Young, USA—Highest-ranking
Negro Officer, World War I
United States Military Academy,
Class of 1889

Negro Officers' Training Camp
Ft. Des Moines, Iowa—June 17, 1917

Court Martial of the 24th Infantry
August 23, 1917

Croix de Guerre Winners
396th Infantry, World War I

369th Infantry, 93rd Division—World War I

Occupation and Pacification of Haiti by the
United States Marines

The Pan-African Congress—February 19, 1919

Scipio A. Jones, Attorney-at-law

John R. Shillady

James Weldon Johnson
First Negro Secretary of the NAACP (1920)

The Chicago Race Riots (series of *three*   photographs) July 27-August 2, 1917

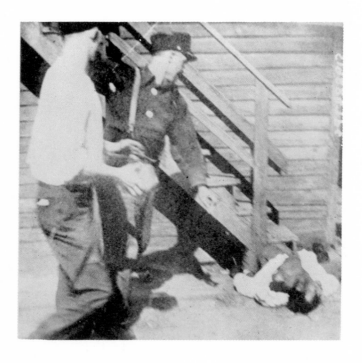

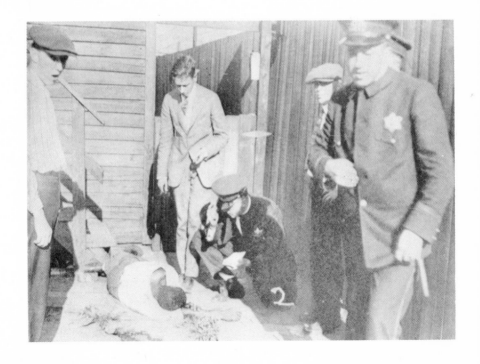

Negroes Leaving Wrecked Houses under Police
Protection

"After all there is but one race—humanity."
                                        George Moore

Appendixes

"The Call"[1]
A Lincoln Emancipation Conference

To Discuss Means for Securing Political and Civil Equality for the Negro

The celebration of the centennial of the birth of Abraham Lincoln widespread and grateful as it may be, will fail to justify itself if it takes no note and makes no recognition of the colored men and women to whom the great emancipator labored to assure freedom. Besides a day of rejoicing, Lincoln's birthday in 1909 should be one of taking stock of the nation's progress since 1865. How far has it lived up to the obligations imposed upon it by the Emancipation Proclamation? How far has it gone in assuring to each and every citizen, irrespective of color, the equality of opportunity and equality before the law, which underlie our American institutions and are guaranteed by the Constitution?

If Mr. Lincoln could revisit this country he would be disheartened by the nation's failure in this respect. He would learn that on January 1st, 1909, Georgia had rounded out a new oligarchy by disfranchising the negro after the manner of all the other Southern states. He would learn that the Supreme Court of the United States, designed to be a bulwark of American liberties, had failed to meet several opportunities to pass squarely upon this disfranchisement of millions by laws avowedly discriminatory and openly enforced in such manner that white men may vote and black men be without a vote in their government; he would discover, there, that taxation without representation is the lot of millions of wealth-producing American citizens, in whose hands rests the economic progress and welfare of an entire section of the country. He would learn that

[1] This copy of the "Call" is from the Oswald Garrison Villard Papers (Houghton Library, Harvard University).

297

the Supreme Court, according to the official statement of one of its own judges in the Berea College case, has laid down the principle that if an individual State chooses it may "make it a crime for white and colored persons to frequent the same market place at the same time, or appear in an assemblage of citizens convened to consider questions of a public or political nature in which all citizens, without regard to race, are equally interested." In many States Lincoln would find justice enforced, if at all, by judges elected by one element in a community to pass upon the liberties and lives of another. He would see the black men and women, for whose freedom a hundred thousand of soldiers gave their lives, set apart in trains, in which they pay first-class fares for third-class service, in railway stations and in places of entertainment, while State after State declines to do its elementary duty in preparing the negro through education for the best exercise of citizenship.

Added to this, the spread of lawless attacks upon the negro, North, South and West—even in the Springfield made famous by Lincoln—often accompanied by revolting brutalities, sparing neither sex, nor age nor youth, could not but shock the author of the sentiment that "government of the people, by the people, for the people shall not perish from the earth."

Silence under these conditions means tacit approval. The indifference of the North is already responsible for more than one assault upon democracy, and every such attack reacts as unfavorably upon whites as upon blacks. Discrimination once permitted cannot be bridled; recent history in the South shows that in forging chains for the negroes, the white voters are forging chains for themselves. "A house divided against itself cannot stand"; this government cannot exist half slave and half free any better to-day than it could in 1861. Hence we call upon all the believers in democracy to join in a national conference for the discussion of present evils, the voicing of protests, and the renewal of the struggle for civil and political liberty.

Miss Jane Addams, Chicago
Ray Stannard Baker, New York
Mrs. Ida Wells-Barnett, Chicago
Mrs. Harriet Stanton Blatch,
  New York
Mr. Samuel Bowles,
  (Springfield Republican)
Prof. W. L. Bulkley, New York
Miss Kate Claghorn, New York
E. H. Clement, Boston
Prof. John Dewey, New York
Miss Mary E. Dreier, Brooklyn

Prof. W. E. B. Du Bois, Atlanta
Dr. John L. Elliott, New York
Mr. William Lloyd Garrison, Boston
Rev. Francis J. Grimke,
  Washington, D.C.
Prof. Thomas C. Hall, New York
Rabbi Emil G. Hirsch, Chicago
Rev. John Haynes Holmes, New York
Hamilton Holt, New York
William Dean Howells, New York
Rev. Jenkin Lloyd Jones, Chicago
Mrs. Florence Kelley, New York

Rev. Walter Laidlaw, New York
Rev. Frederick Lynch, New York
Miss Helen Marot, New York
Miss Mary E. McDowell, Chicago
Prof. J. G. Merrill, Connecticut
Mr. John E. Milholland, New York
Dr. Henry Moskowitz, New York
Miss Leonora O'Reilly, New York
Miss Mary W. Ovington, New York
Rev. Charles H. Parkhurst, New York
Rev. John P. Peters, New York
J. G. Phelps-Stokes, New York
Louis F. Post, Chicago
Dr. Jane Robbins, New York
Charles Edward Russell, New York
William M. Salter, Chicago
Joseph Smith, Boston
Mrs. Anna Garlin Spencer, New York
Judge Wendell S. Stafford,
    Washington, D.C.
Lincoln Steffens, Boston
Miss Helen Stokes, New York

Mrs. Mary Church Terrell,
    Washington, D.C.
Prof. W. I. Thomas, Chicago
President Charles F. Thwing,
    Western Reserve University
Oswald Garrison Villard, New York
Mrs. Henry Villard, New York
Miss Lillian D. Wald, New York
Dr. J. Milton Waldron,
    Washington, D.C.
William English Walling, New York
Bishop Alexander Walters, New York
Dr. William H. Ward, New York
Mrs. Rodman Wharton, Philadelphia
Miss Susan P. Wharton, Philadelphia
Horace White, New York
Mayor Brand Whitlock, Toledo
Rabbi Stephen S. Wise, New York
President Mary E. Wooley,
    Mt. Holyoke College
Rev. M. St. Croix Wright, New York
Prof. Charles Zueblin, Boston

The Committee of Forty[1]

NATIONAL NEGRO COMMITTEE, 1909

William English Walling, Chairman, New York
Rev. William Henry Brooks, New York
Prof. John Dewey, New York
Paul Kennaday, New York
Jacob W. Mack, New York
Mrs. Mary Maclean, New York
Dr. Henry Moskowitz, New York
John E. Milholland, New York
Miss Leonora O'Reilly, New York
Charles Edward Russell, New York
Prof. Edwin R. A. Seligman, New York
Oswald Garrison Villard, New York
Miss Lillian D. Wald, New York
Bishop Alexander Walters, New York
Rabbi Stephen S. Wise, New York
Miss Mary White Ovington, Brooklyn, New York
Dr. Owen M. Waller, Brooklyn, New York
Rev. John Haynes Holmes, Yonkers, New York
Prof. W. L. Bulkley, Ridgefield Park, New Jersey

---

[1] Although provision was made for forty members, only thirty-eight names appear on this list. An additional name, the Reverend Joseph Silverman, New York, is included in Minutes, National Negro Committee, March, 1909, but is not included in *Proceedings of the National Negro Conference 1909: New York May 31 and June 1*, p. 225.

Miss Maria Baldwin, Boston, Massachusetts
Archibald H. Grimke, Boston, Massachusetts
Albert E. Pillsbury, Boston, Massachusetts
Moorfield Storey, Boston, Massachusetts
Pres. Charles F. Thwing, Cleveland, Ohio
Pres. W. S. Scarborough, Wilberforce, Ohio
Miss Jane Addams, Chicago, Illinois
Mrs. Ida Wells-Barnett, Chicago, Illinois
Dr. C. E. Bentley, Chicago, Illinois
Mrs. Celia Parker Woolley, Chicago, Illinois
Dr. William Sinclair, Philadelphia, Pennsylvania
Miss Susan Wharton, Philadelphia, Pennsylvania
R. R. Wright, Jr., Philadelphia, Pennsylvania
L. M. Hershaw, Washington, D.C.
Judge Wendell P. Stafford, Washington, D.C.
Mrs. Mary Church Terrell, Washington, D.C.
Rev. J. Milton Waldron, Washington, D.C.
Prof. W. E. B. Du Bois, Atlanta, Georgia
Leslie Pinckney Hill, Manassas, Virginia

Resolutions[1]

ADOPTED BY THE NATIONAL NEGRO COMMITTEE
June 1, 1909

We denounce the ever-growing oppression of our 10,000,000 colored fellow citizens as the greatest menace that threatens the country. Often plundered of their just share of the public funds, robbed of nearly all part in the government, segregated by common carriers, some murdered with impunity, and all treated with open contempt by officials, they are held in some States in practical slavery to the white community. The systematic persecution of law-abiding citizens and their disfranchisement on account of their race alone is a crime that will ultimately drag down to an infamous end any nation that allows it to be practised, and it bears most heavily on those poor white farmers and laborers whose economic position is most similar to that of the persecuted race.

The nearest hope lies in the immediate and patiently continued enlightenment of the people who have been inveigled into a campaign of oppression. The spoils of persecution should not go to enrich any class or classes of the population. Indeed persecution of organized workers, peonage, enslavement of prisoners, and even disfranchisement already threaten large bodies of whites in many Southern States.

We agree fully with the prevailing opinion that the transformation of the unskilled colored laborers in industry and agriculture into skilled workers is of vital importance to that race and to the nation, but we demand for the Negroes, as for all others, a free and complete education, whether by city, state, or nation, a grammar school and industrial training for all, and technical, professional, and academic education for the most gifted.

---

[1] The Resolutions are reported in this form in *Proceedings of the National Negro Conference 1909: New York May 31 and June 1*, pp. 222–25.

But the public schools assigned to the Negro of whatever kind or grade will never receive a fair and equal treatment until he is given equal treatment in the Legislature and before the law. Nor will the practically educated Negro, no matter how valuable to the community he may prove, be given a fair return for his labor or encouraged to put forth his best efforts or given the chance to develop that efficiency that comes only outside the school until he is respected in his legal rights as a man and a citizen.

We regard with grave concern the attempt manifest South and North to deny to black men the right to work and to enforce this demand by violence and bloodshed. Such a question is too fundamental and clear even to be submitted to arbitration. The late strike in Georgia is not simply a demand that Negroes be displaced, but that proven and efficient men be made to surrender their long followed means of livelihood to white competitors.

As first and immediate steps toward remedying these national wrongs, so full of peril for the whites as well as the blacks of all sections, we demand of Congress and the Executive:

(1) That the Constitution be strictly enforced and the civil rights guaranteed under the Fourteenth Amendment be secured impartially to all.

(2) That there be equal educational opportunities for all and in all the States, and that public school expenditure be the same for the Negro and white child.

(3) That in accordance with the Fifteenth Amendment the right of the Negro to the ballot on the same terms as other citizens be recognized in every part of the country.

The committee on permanent organization in its report proposed a resolution providing for "the incorporation of a national committee to be known as a Committee for the Advancement of the Negro Race, to aid their progress and make their citizenship a reality, with all the rights and privileges pertaining thereto." It presented also a resolution calling for a committee of forty charged with the organization of a national committee with power to call the convention in 1910.

We deplore any recognition of, or concession to, prejudice or color by the federal government in any officer or branch thereof, as well as the presidential declaration on the appointment of colored men to office in the South, contradicting as it does the President's just and admirable utterance against the proposed disfranchisement of the colored voters of Maryland.

NAACP Officers, Executive Committee, and General Committee[1] December, 1910

NATIONAL PRESIDENT
Moorfield Storey
CHAIRMAN OF THE EXECUTIVE COMMITTEE
William English Walling
TREASURER
John E. Milholland
DISBURSING TREASURER
Oswald Garrison Villard
DIRECTOR OF PUBLICITY AND RESEARCH
Dr. W. E. B. Du Bois
EXECUTIVE SECRETARY
Miss Frances Blascoer

EXECUTIVE COMMITTEE

Miss Gertrude Barnum
Rev. W. H. Brooks
Mr. Paul Kennaday
Mrs. F. R. Keyser
Mrs. M. D. Maclean
Rev. A. Clayton Powell
Mr. Charles Edward Russell
Rev. Joseph Silverman
Rev. John Haynes Holmes
Miss M. W. Ovington
Dr. O. M. Waller

Mr. W. L. Bulkley
Mr. Albert E. Pillsbury
Miss Jane Addams
Mrs. Ida B. Wells-Barnett
Dr. C. E. Bentley
Mrs. Celia Parker Woolley
Dr. N. F. Mossell
Dr. William A. Sinclair
Mrs. Mary Church Terrell
Rev. J. Milton Waldron

[1] From *Crisis*, I (November, 1910).

GENERAL COMMITTEE

Prof. John Dewey
Miss Maud R. Ingersoll
Mrs. Florence Kelley
Dr. Charles Lenz
Mr. Jacob W. Mack
Rev. Horace G. Miller
Mrs. Max Morgenthau
Mr. James F. Morton, Jr.
Dr. Henry Moskowitz
Miss Leonora O'Reilly
Mr. Jacob H. Schiff
Prof. E. R. A. Seligman
Mrs. Anna Garlin Spencer
Mrs. Henry Villard
Miss Lillian D. Wald
Bishop Alexander Walters
Dr. Stephen S. Wise
Rev. James E. Haynes
Miss M. R. Lyons
Mrs. M. H. Talbert
Hon. Thomas M. Osborne
Mr. George W. Crawford
Miss Maria Baldwin

Mr. Francis J. Garrison
Mr. Archibald H. Grimke
Mr. William Monroe Trotter
Dr. Horace Bumstead
Miss Elizabeth C. Carter
President Charles F. Thwing
Mr. Charles W. Chesnutt
President H. C. King
President W. S. Scarborough
Miss Sophonisba Breckinridge
Mr. Clarence Darrow
Miss Susan Wharton
Mr. R. R. Wright, Jr.
Mr. W. Justin Carter
Rev. Harvey Johnson
Hon. William S. Bennet
Mr. L. M. Hershaw
Prof. Kelly Miller
Prof. L. B. Moore
Justice W. P. Stafford
President John Hope
Mr. Leslie P. Hill

The First Board of Directors

Elected at the First "Annual Meeting of Members,"
Following Incorporation, January 4, 1912

Term Expiring 1913

George W. Crawford
Thomas Ewing, Jr.
Paul Kennaday
Joseph P. Loud
Royal F. Nash

Rev. A. Clayton Powell
Rev. Joseph Silverman
Dr. William A. Sinclair
Lillian D. Wald
Rev. Garnett R. Waller

Term Expiring 1914

Jane Addams
Dr. Charles E. Bentley
Rev. William H. Brooks
W. E. B. Du Bois
Mrs. Florence Kelley

Mrs. Frances R. Keyser
Dr. Nathan F. Mossell
Miss Mary White Ovington
Charles Edward Russell
Mrs. Mary Church Terrell

Term Expiring 1915

Rev. John Haynes Holmes
Mrs. Mary D. Maclean
John E. Milholland
Walter E. Sachs
Joel E. Spingarn

Moorfield Storey
Oswald Garrison Villard
Dr. Owen M. Waller
William English Walling
Bishop Alexander Walters

NAACP
Secretaries and Acting Secretaries
1909-20

FRANCES BLASCOER
February, 1910, to March 7, 1911
MARY WHITE OVINGTON
May 16, 1911, to June 4, 1912
MAY CHILDS NERNEY
June 1, 1912, to January 3, 1916
MARY WHITE OVINGTON
Acting Secretary
January 10, 1916, to February 15, 1916
ROYAL FREEMAN NASH
February 15, 1916, to September 1, 1917
JAMES WELDON JOHNSON
Acting Secretary
May 14, 1917, to January 1, 1918
JOHN R. SHILLADY
January 1, 1918, to May 10, 1920
JAMES WELDON JOHNSON
Acting Secretary
September 13, 1920, to December 13, 1920
Secretary
December 13, 1920, to January, 1931

NAACP
Board Chairmen and Acting Chairmen
1909-20

WILLIAM ENGLISH WALLING
Chairman of National Negro Committee
1909

CHARLES EDWARD RUSSELL
Acting Chairman of National Negro Committee

OSWALD GARRISON VILLARD
Temporary Chairman of National Negro Committee

WILLIAM ENGLISH WALLING
Chairman of Executive Committee, NAACP
May, 1910, to January, 1911

OSWALD GARRISON VILLARD
Chairman of Executive Committee, NAACP
January, 1911, to June 20, 1912

Chairman of Board of Directors, NAACP
June 20, 1912, to January, 1914

JOEL E. SPINGARN
Chairman of Board of Directors, NAACP
January, 1914, to January 6, 1919

MARY WHITE OVINGTON
Acting Chairman of Board of Directors, NAACP
May 14, 1917, to November 1, 1918

Chairman of Board of Directors, NAACP
January 6, 1919, to January 1, 1932

Bibliographical Notes

The most important sources for the study of the National Association for the Advancement of Colored People are the minutes of the Board of Directors, the reports of officers, annual reports, office files, and the official magazine, *The Crisis*. These are all available in the Library of Congress.

The personal papers of Oswald Garrison Villard at the Houghton Library at Harvard University are especially valuable as an almost day by day picture of events in the history of the NAACP until the death of Francis Jackson Garrison in 1916. The Woodrow Wilson Papers at the Library of Congress contain Villard's correspondence with Wilson concerning the presidential election of 1912, segregation in government departments, patronage for Negroes, and Villard's proposed Race Commission. A small amount of Villard's correspondence is in the office files of the NAACP.

Complementing the Villard manuscripts are the William Edward Burghardt Du Bois Papers, which are now in the possession of Mrs. Shirley Graham Du Bois, and closed to scholars.

The Booker T. Washington Collection in the Manuscript Division of the Library of Congress is important as a source for the Washington-Du Bois controversy and for Washington's opposition to the NAACP. A useful guide to this entire collection is *Booker T. Washington: A Register of His Papers* [Washington, D.C.: Library of Congress, 1958].

The Moorland Foundation at Howard University contains an important collection of the papers of Joel Elias Spingarn, although some of his letters are with the James Weldon Johnson Collection at Yale University, as are a few of the Du Bois Papers. Other J. E. Spingarn Papers were examined at "Troutbeck," Amenia, New York. These are now part of the Moorland Foundation at Howard University. Both the Spingarn Papers and the Villard Papers contain letters concerning issues which divided the NAACP Board on various occasions. Internal controversies are cautiously handled in the Arthur B. Spingarn correspondence and papers. The largest part of this collection, which concerns the period after 1920, is now in the Library of Congress, although some manuscripts have been deposited at Howard University.

A portion of the Moorfield Storey papers is in the Manuscript Division of the Library of Congress, but the greater part is in the possession of his son, Charles Storey of Boston.

The Mary Church Terrell Papers and the Terrell Family Papers at the Library of Congress deal with politics and Booker T. Washington, with some sidelights on the founding of the NAACP.

The Schomburg Collection of the New York Public Library contains letters of Booker T. Washington, Du Bois, and Francis Jackson Garrison. There are also a few relevant items in the John E. Bruce Papers.

A Documentary History of the Negro People in the United States, ed. Herbert Aptheker (2 vols.; New York: Citadel Press, 1951), is a valuable collection of documents taken principally from the Du Bois Papers. *Negro Protest Thought in the Twentieth Century,* ed. Francis L. Broderick and August Meier (New York: Bobbs-Merrill Co., Inc., 1965), has brought together documents illustrative of the chief movements of the period.

GOVERNMENT DOCUMENTS AND PUBLICATIONS

An analysis of the East St. Louis riots is given in: U.S., Congress, House, *East St. Louis Riots,* 65th Cong., 2d Sess. (1918), H.R. 1231. The role of Negro labor during World War I appears in a study under the direction of George E. Haynes, *The Negro at Work During the War and Reconstruction: Second Study on Negro Labor,* U.S. Dept. of Labor, Division of Negro Economics (Washington: U.S. Government Printing Office, 1921). The controversial work, *Negro Education: A Study of the Private and Higher Schools for Colored People in the United States,* under the direction of Thomas Jesse Jones, appears as a publication of the U.S. Dept. of the Interior, Bureau of Education, Bulletin Nos. 38-39 (1917). Of special interest is the attempt to secure a federal anti-lynching law during wartime, *To Protect Citizens Against Lynching,* the Brief of Captain George S. Hornblower, U.S. Congress, House, Hearing before the Committee on the Judiciary, 65th Cong., 2d Sess., H.R. 11279, Serial 66, Part II (July 12, 1918). Two reports concerning the Negro and radicalism are important: U.S. Congress, Senate, 66th Cong., 1st Sess., S. 153, "Radicalism and Sedition Among Negroes as Reflected in Publications," in *Investigation Activities of the Department of Justice* (1919), XII, and State of New York, Senate, "Propaganda Among

Negroes," in *Revolutionary Radicalism*, A Report of the Joint Legislative Committee Investigating Seditious Activities (Albany, N.Y., Vol. II, Part I, 1920).

ARTICLES AND PERIODICALS

An indispensable record of the Association's activities and philosophy, voiced chiefly by Du Bois, is to be found in the pages of *The Crisis* (New York, 1910–
). The *Branch Bulletin* (New York, 1917–1919), for a brief period supplemented *The Crisis* as a means of conveying the Association's program to the membership. The *Horizon: A Journal of the Color Line* (Alexandria and Washington, 1907–1908), official organ of Du Bois's Niagara movement, contains material of value relating to the Booker T. Washington-Du Bois controversy, and Du Bois's criticisms of Washington. For the earlier period, one should consult *The Voice of the Negro* (Atlanta, 1904–1907), which became *The Voice* (Chicago, 1907). *The Journal of Negro History* (Washington, 1916–   ), the *Journal of Negro Education* (Lancaster, Pennsylvania, 1932–   ), and the *Journal of Southern History* (Baton Rouge, La., 1935–   ), are helpful on a variety of aspects of the Negro problem. The *Nation* (New York, 1865–   ), *The Independent* (New York, Boston, 1848–1928), and *The Survey: A Journal of Constructive Philanthropy*[1] (New York, 1897–1952), were sympathetic to the objectives of the NAACP, and have a great deal of material of value concerning the race problem. Other liberal periodicals that were open to the cause of the Negro were *The Progressive* (Madison, Wisconsin, 1929–   ), *La Follette's Magazine* (Madison, Wisconsin, 1902–1929), which was superseded by the *Progressive*), and the *New Republic* (New York, 1914). Magazines with an interest in moderate reforms such as *Harper's Weekly: A Journal of Civilization* (New York, 1857–1916), *Century* (New York, 1870–1930), and *American Magazine*[1] (New York, 1875–1956), approached the Negro problem cautiously as did the more conservative and scholarly *Atlantic Monthly* (Boston, 1857–   ), *Harper's Magazine*[1] (New York, 1850–   ), and the *North American Review* (Boston, New York, 1815–1940). *Outlook*[1] (New York, 1870–1932), and *World's Work* (New York, 1900–1932) are valuable for numerous articles by Booker T. Washington and reflect his point of view. Of the Southern periodicals, the most useful for this study was the *South Atlantic Quarterly* (Durham, 1902–   ).

Newspapers that devote the most editorial and news space to the race issue are the *New York Evening Post* (1802–1919), and the *Boston Evening Transcript* (1830–1941). Material of value also appears in the *Boston Globe* (1872–   ), and the *Christian Science Monitor* (1908–   ). Other papers that were consulted with profit are the *New York Sun* (1883–1950), and the *New York Times*

[1] title varies

(1851–   ). Several Midwestern newspapers were used, the *Chicago Tribune* (1847–   ), the *Chicago Record-Herald*[1] (1881–1918), the *Chicago Inter-Ocean* (1872–1914), and the Emporia (Kans.) *Gazette* (1890–   ). Both the *Washington Post* (1877–   ), and the *Washington Evening Star* (1852–   ), contain reactions to the racial disturbances during the war. The most useful of the Negro newspapers were *The New York Age*[1] (1880–1960), and the *Washington Bee* (1882–1922).

BOOKS

Among the biographies of Negro leaders, Basil J. Mathews, *Booker T. Washington: Educator and Interracial Interpreter* (London: SCM Press, Ltd., 1949) has now been superseded by Samuel R. Spencer, Jr., *Booker T. Washington and the Negro's Place in American Life* (Boston: Little, Brown and Co., 1955). This should be supplemented by Hugh Hawkins, *Booker T. Washington and His Critics: The Problem of Negro Leadership* (Boston: D.C. Heath and Co., 1962). August Meier, "Toward a Reinterpretation of Booker T. Washington," *Journal of Southern History*, XXIII (May, 1957), 220–27, offers suggestions for a more comprehensive study of Washington's life and work. Washington's efforts to subvert the NAACP are discussed in Meier's article, "Booker T. Washington and the Rise of the NAACP" in *Crisis*, LXI (February, 1954), 69–76, 117–23.

An excellent biography of Du Bois is Francis L. Broderick, *W. E. B. Du Bois: Negro Leader in Time of Crisis* (Stanford, Calif.: Stanford University Press, 1959). Elliott M. Rudwick, *W. E. B. Du Bois: A Study in Minority Group Leadership* (Philadelphia: University of Pennsylvania Press, 1960) carries the Du Bois story to his break with the NAACP in 1934. W. E. B. Du Bois's own work, *Dusk of Dawn: An Essay Toward an Autobiography of a Race Concept* (New York: Harcourt, Brace and World, Inc., 1940), is of great value. Mary White Ovington, *Portraits in Color* (New York: The Viking Press, 1927), has good character sketches of Du Bois, James Weldon Johnson, and Walter White. Helen M. Chesnutt, *Charles Waddell Chesnutt: Pioneer of the Color Line* (Chapel Hill: University of North Carolina Press, 1952) contains a good deal of Chesnutt's correspondence. John Hope has been adequately treated in Frederic Ridgely Torrence, *The Story of John Hope* (New York: Macmillan Co., 1948).

Among the white leaders of the NAACP, Oswald Garrison Villard has no full length biography, but D. Joy Humes has written a valuable study, *Oswald Garrison Villard: Liberal of the 1920's* (Syracuse, New York: Syracuse University Press, 1960). Villard's autobiography, *Fighting Years: Memoirs of a Liberal Editor* (New York: Harcourt, Brace and World, Inc., 1939) is revealing of his

[1] title varies

character and temperament. Mark Antony De Wolfe Howe, *Moorfield Storey 1854–1929: Portrait of an Independent* (Boston: Houghton Mifflin Co., 1932) deals briefly with Storey's role in the NAACP. There is no adequate biography of Florence Kelley. Josephine Goldmark, *Impatient Crusader: Florence Kelley's Life Story* (Urbana, Illinois: University of Illinois Press, 1953) does not discuss her role in the NAACP, nor does either of the two biographies of Lillian Wald: Robert Luther Duffas, *Lillian Wald: Neighbor and Crusader* (New York: Macmillan and Co., 1938), or Beryl Williams Epstein, *Lillian Wald: Angel of Henry Street* (New York: Julian Messner, Inc., 1948).

Other useful biographies were Dewey W. Grantham, Jr., *Hoke Smith and the Politics of the New South* (Baton Rouge, La.: Louisiana State University, 1958); Henry F. Pringle, *The Life and Times of William Howard Taft* (2 vols.; New York: Farrar, Farrar and Rinehart, Inc., 1939); and Arthur S. Link, *Wilson: The Road to the White House* (Princeton, N.J.: Princeton University Press, 1947); *Wilson: The New Freedom* (Princeton, N.J.: Princeton University Press, 1956); and *Wilson: The Struggle for Neutrality* (Princeton, N.J.: Princeton University Press, 1960).

Autobiographies of varying merit by founders and officers of the NAACP include James Weldon Johnson, *Along This Way* (New York: The Viking Press, 1933); John Haynes Holmes, *I Speak for Myself: The Autobiography of John Haynes Holmes* (New York: Harper and Row Publishers Inc., 1959); Walter White, *A Man Called White: The Autobiography of Walter White* (New York: The Viking Press, 1948); and Alexander Walters, *My Life and Work* (Westwood, N.J.: Fleming H. Revell Co., 1917).

C. Vann Woodward's incisive study of the post-Reconstruction period, *Origins of the New South 1877–1913* (Baton Rouge, La.: Louisiana State University 1951) is important as is his *Strange Career of Jim Crow* (2d ed. rev.; New York: A Galaxy Book, Oxford University Press, 1957), which traces the development of segregation during the same period. Vincent P. De Santis in *Republicans Face the Southern Question: The New Departure Years, 1877–1897* (Baltimore: The Johns Hopkins University Press, 1959) and Stanley P. Hirshon's *Farewell to the Bloody Shirt: Northern Republicans and the Southern Negro, 1877–1893* (Bloomington, Ind.: Indiana University Press, 1962) are studies of the abandonment of the Negro by the Republican Party. An excellent general history is that of Francis Butler Simkins, *The South Old and New: A History 1820–1947* (New York: Alfred A. Knopf, Inc., 1947), while Wilbur J. Cash, *The Mind of the South* (New York: Alfred A. Knopf, Inc., 1941) is thought-provoking. Eric Goldman, *Rendezvous with Destiny: A History of Modern American Reform* (New York: Knopf, 1952) includes the rise of the NAACP in the general movement for reform. Richard Hofstadter, *The Age of Reform: From Bryan to F. D. R.* (New York: Knopf, 1955), and *Social Darwinism in American Thought 1860–1915* (Philadelphia: University of Pennsylvania Press, 1944) are essential for the period. Louis R. Harlan, *Separate and Unequal: Public School Campaigns and Racism in the Southern Seaboard States 1901–1915* (Chapel Hill, N. Carolina: University of North Carolina, 1958), is a study of discrimination in education. For a statistical analysis of Negro migration one should consult Henderson H. Donald, "The Urbanization of the American Negro," in G. P. Murdock (ed.), *Studies in the Science of Society* (New Haven, Conn.: Yale University Press, 1937). Still useful is Emmett J. Scott, *Negro Migration during the War* (New York: Oxford University Press, 1920). *The Negro Peasant Turns Cityward: Effects of Recent Migrations to Northern Centers* (New York: Columbia University Studies in History, Economics, and Public Law, No. 329, 1930) also deals with the period of the first World War. Two important studies of urban riots are Elliott M. Rudwick's, *Race Riot at East St. Louis, July 2, 1917* (Carbondale, Ill.: Southern Illinois University, 1964) and the report of the Chicago Commission on Race Relations, *The Negro in Chicago: A Study of Race Relations and a Race Riot* (Chicago, Ill.: University of Chicago Press, 1922). Also, Allen D. Grimshaw's "Three Major Cases of Colour Violence in the United States," in *Race: Journal of the Institute of Race Relations* (July, 1963), V, 76–87. For wartime hysteria, Ray H. Abrams, *Preachers Present Arms: A Study of Wartime Attitudes and Activities of the Church and Clergy in the United States 1914–1918* (Manhasset, N.Y.: Round Table Press, 1933), and Zechariah Chafee, Jr., *Free Speech in the United States* (Cambridge, Mass.: Harvard University Press, 1941) were consulted.

Gunnar Myrdal, *An American Dilemma: The Negro Problem and Modern Democracy* (2 vols.; New York: Harper and Row Publishers, Inc., 1944), is a comprehensive study of race relations. The unpublished memoranda for the Myrdal study is in the Schomburg Collection, New York Public Library. Especially useful was Ralph Bunche, "Memorandum on the Programs, Ideologies, Tactics, and Achievements of Negro Betterment and Interracial Organizations" (1940). The best history of the Negro in the United States is John Hope Franklin, *From Slavery to Freedom: A History of American Negroes* (2d rev. ed.; New York: Alfred A. Knopf, Inc., 1956). A standard sociological study is E. Franklin Frazier, *The Negro in the United States* (2d rev. ed.; New York: Macmillan and Co., 1957). Rayford W. Logan, *The Negro in American Life and Thought: The Nadir 1877–1901* (New York: Dial Press, Inc., 1954) is important for understanding the rise of the NAACP. August Meier, *Negro Thought in America 1880–1915: Racial Ideologies in the Age of Booker T. Washington* (Ann Arbor,

Mich.: University of Michigan Press, 1963) examines the ideas of prominent Negroes and institutional developments within the Negro world in relation to the intellectual climate of the period. The Negro in politics is discussed in Paul Lewinson, *Race, Class and Party: A History of Negro Suffrage and White Politics in the South* (New York: Russell and Russell, Inc., 1932) and in the more recent Vladimir O. Key, Jr., *Southern Politics in State and Nation* (New York: Alfred A. Knopf, Inc., 1950). Sterling D. Spero and Abram L. Harris, *The Black Worker: The Negro and the Labor Movement* (New York: Columbia University Press, 1931), Herbert R. Northrup, *Organized Labor and the Negro* (New York: Harper and Row Publishers, Inc., 1944), and Robert C. Weaver, *Negro Labor: A National Problem* (New York: Harcourt, Brace and World, Inc., 1946) are the chief works on the Negro and labor relations.

For Negro protest organizations prior to the founding of the NAACP, one should consult Emma Lou Thornbrough's article, "The National Afro-American League, 1887–1908," *Journal of Southern History*, XXVII (1961), 494–512, and Elliott M. Rudwick, "The Niagara Movement," *Journal of Negro History*, XLII (1957), 177–200. Several Works Progress Administration (WPA) Writers Project Studies on the Constitution League which are sketchy and not carefully documented can be found in the Schomburg Collection of the New York Public Library.

Two popular accounts of the history of the NAACP are Mary White Ovington's *The Walls Came Tumbling Down* (New York: Harcourt, Brace and World, Inc., 1947), which is valuable for the author's personal memories of the early days, although marred at times by inaccuracies, and Langston Hughes, *Fight for Freedom: The Story of the NAACP* (New York: W. W. Norton and Co., 1962). Robert L. Jack, *History of the National Association for the Advancement of Colored People* (Boston: Meador Publishing Co., 1943), as well as Warren D. St. James, *The National Association for the Advancement of Colored People: A Case Study in Pressure Groups* (New York: Exposition Press, 1958), are other worthy attempts to trace the development of the organization.

Personal interviews during 1956 and 1957 with Arthur B. Spingarn, attorney and President of the NAACP from 1940 until 1966; Richetta Randolph (Mrs. Frank Wallace), former secretary to Mary White Ovington, Officer Manager of the NAACP, and secretary to the Executive Secretary; Mrs. Charles Edward Russell; Mrs. James Weldon Johnson; Mrs. William English Walling; and Mrs. Joel E. Spingarn provided clarification and enlightenment on the early days of the Association.

Index

Johnson, Kathryn M., 131, 132n61
Johnson, Mordecai, 227
Johnson, Robert: lynched, 214
Jones, Jenkin Lloyd, 124, 125
Jones, Scipio Africanus, 243–45
Jones, Thomas Jesse, 86
Jones, Wesley L., 191
Just, Ernest Everett, 141

Kallen, Horace Meyer, 281n16
Kelley, Florence: invited to join founding group, 12–13; supports Villard against Du Bois, 101; as chairman of nominating committee, 105; proposes Shillady as secretary, 114; suggested for Commission on National Aid to Vocational Education, 190; first woman factory inspector, 191n28; works for federal aid to education, 192, 193–94; seeks help of Brandeis, 204; for woman's suffrage, 207; and anti-lynching drive, 217; seeks help for Colonel Young, 257
Kelley, George, 253
Kelley, Harry Eugene, 238n119
Kennaday, Paul: added to Committee of Forty, 37; at meeting, 48n7; on Finance Committee, 61n63; becomes assistant secretary, 92; supports Du Bois, 104; as assistant treasurer, 113; works on press committee, 145; seeks advertising for Crisis, 153; for federal aid to education, 193; and anti-lynching drive, 217
Kentucky Constitution: amended, 231
Keyser, Frances R., 47n1, 48n6 and n7, 61n63
Ku Klux Klan, 144, 235

Labor Movement: and the Negro, 34–35, 266–71
La Guardia, Fiorello, 264
Lake City, Florida: lynching, 211
Lansing, Robert, 177, 284, 285
Lathrop, Julia, 13
Lawson, Victor F., 238n119
League for Democracy, 265
League for Industrial Democracy, 35
League to Limit Armaments, 249
League of Nations, 281, 283, 286
League of Small and Subject Nationalities, 277
Leavell, R. H., 159, 160
Lee, Carrie, 195–96
Lee, Joseph H., 167n45
Lewis, William H., 73, 166n45, 199, 200
Lewisohn, Mrs. Walter, 118
Liberal Club, 11

Liberator, 5–6
Liberty Loan Committee, 265, 266
Life membership, 44n62
Lily-white party: in South, 155
Lima, Ohio, 219
Lincoln's Dream, 145
Lincoln Settlement, 104n61
Lindsay, Samuel McCune, 179
Lippmann, Walter, 257
Livermore, Kentucky: lynching, 210
Logan, Adella Hunt, 207
Longview, Texas, riot, 236
Loud, Joseph P.: fears collapse of NAACP, 108; for Negro control, 109; and Boston branch, 120n13; opposes segregated camp, 255; and Negro troops, 274
Loud, Mrs. Joseph P., 120n13
Louisville Courier-Journal, 231
Louisville, Kentucky: segregation case, 184, 185, 186–87
Lovejoy, Elijah P., 56
Lovejoy, Owen, 144
Low, Seth, 18n51, 56
Lowden, Frank O., 238
Lowell, C. R., 118
Lusk Committee Report, 290
Lynching: role of demagogues in, 4; causes membership expansion, 136; demand for federal legislation against, 137; publicity given, 148, 209–10; Seligmann investigates, 149; responsibility of the press for, 209; alleged crimes resulting in, 210; in Livermore, Kentucky, 210; in Lake City, Florida, 211; of women in Oklahoma, 212; in Coatesville, Pennsylvania, 212–14; of Robert Johnson, 214; of Anne Bostwick, 214; at Waco, Texas, 218; at Gainesville, Florida, 218–19; of Anthony Crawford, 219; definition of, 225; of Ell Persons, 226; at Estill Springs, Tennessee, 227, 228; of Mary Turner, 229; of Sandy Reeves, 229–30; witness intimidated, 229n82; Georgia press ignores, 230; in Texas, 230; in Wyoming, 231; at Shubata, Mississippi, 231; at Hillsboro, Texas, 233; of Eugene Green, 233; ignored by state officials, 231; anti-lynching bills introduced, 214, 231; campaign against, 148, 214, 216–21; 225; 232–35; after World War I, 237–38; in Omaha, Nebraska, 241
Lyons, Miss M. R., 48n6
Lyric Theatre, 123

designer:	Gerard A. Valerio
typesetter:	Baltimore Type and Composition Corp.
typefaces:	Bodoni Book and Ultra Bodoni display
printer:	Universal Lithographers
paper:	P & S, Olde Forge F
binder:	Maple Press
cover material:	Bancroft Kennett Black